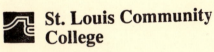

DOMESTIC VIOLENCE

Domestic Violence

The Changing Criminal Justice Response

EDITED BY
Eve S. Buzawa
&
Carl G. Buzawa

AUBURN HOUSE
WESTPORT, CONNECTICUT • LONDON

Library of Congress Cataloging-in-Publication Data

Domestic violence : the changing criminal justice response / edited by
   Eve S. Buzawa and Carl G. Buzawa.
        p.   cm.
   Includes bibliographical references and index.
   ISBN 0–86569–001–4
   1. Wife abuse—United States.   I. Buzawa, Eva Schlesinger.
II. Buzawa, Carl G.
   HV6626.D67   1992
   364.1'5553'0973—dc20   91–31937

British Library Cataloguing in Publication Data is available.

Library of Congress Catalog Card Number: 91–31937
ISBN: 0–86569–001–4

First published in 1992

Auburn House, 88 Post Road West, Westport, CT 06881
An imprint of Greenwood Publishing Group, Inc.

Printed in the United States of America

The paper used in this book complies with the
Permanent Paper Standard issued by the National
Information Standards Organization (Z39.48–1984).

10 9 8 7 6 5 4 3 2 1

Copyright Acknowledgment

The author and publisher gratefully acknowledge permission to use the following:

Demie Kurz, Social Science Perspectives on Wife Abuse: Current Debates and Future Directions,
Gender and Society 3(4): 489–505. Copyright © 1989 by Sage Publications, Inc. Reprinted by
permission of Sage Publications, Inc.

CONTENTS

Part III. Prosecutorial and Judicial Response

Part IV. Criminal Justice Intervention and Victims

INTRODUCTION

Eve S. Buzawa and Carl G. Buzawa

One of the most explosive issues facing the criminal justice system today is how to react to and control interpersonal violence. Until recently, primary attention was placed upon the control of violence committed by strangers. Such acts were properly seen not only as inflicting serious harm, if not fatalities, on their victims but also as challenging the essence of a public order committed to nonviolent resolution of disputes.

Within the last fifteen years, attention has also focussed on what is statistically the greater problem, violence within family structures. One 1986 statistical estimate by the U.S. Bureau of Justice was that over 50 percent of the violent attacks upon women and 33 percent of the attacks upon men were committed by family members or acquaintances. Because of the widespread nature of abuse, concerns that first arose over abused children enlarged to encompass other family members, as awareness grew of previously unreported incidents of brutal attacks upon intimates, even elderly relatives.

Headlines detailing vicious and sometimes fatal injuries inflicted on family members became the impetus for a spreading network of shelters designed to assist the victims of "wife abuse" or "wife battering." Advocates for these women came in time to realize that the police and courts extended, often deliberately, only the scantest attention to the needs of such victims. The minimal responses of these institutions to challenges to do more prompted the uncovering and publicizing of major attitudinal and structural impediments to performance.

The existence of a profoundly unresponsive criminal justice system in turn interacted with the growing consciousness that the "privacy" accorded to the traditional patriarchal family unit was one of the key structural barriers to the fulfillment of women's rights. Feminists began to discern a clear, if perhaps unconscious, pattern by which the criminal justice system ignored crimes committed against women. The response of the police and courts to allegations of rape and domestic violence became a recurrent theme in feminist literature.

As a reaction to such perceived shortcomings, pressure rapidly mounted from the late 1970s and through the 1980s to change and enhance the criminal justice system's interaction with crimes in the family. In these last fifteen years, successive movements have treated domestic violence as a crisis to be managed, a separate and distinct crime, a challenge to current concepts of prerequisites for police action, a justification of the use of arrest as a deterrent, and a justification for prosecution independent of ultimate conviction.

Today, the criminal justice system in this area may best be seen as poised at a crossroads. Responses are uneven and uncoordinated among jurisdictions, even within municipalities, among the police, the prosecutors, and the courts. As will be seen, some organizations have adopted an ideology concerning domestic violence directed toward the goal of proactively responding to instances of abuse, while others remain little changed. This anthology will explore a system in transition, both focussing on the procedures by which police, prosecutors, and the courts carry out their mission and exploring the scope and limitations of the innovative approaches that are being developed.

THE PROCESS OF CHANGE

Change in the provision of services by a public institution may be regarded as occurring in fairly predictable and in some ways essential stages. At first, a classic pattern is considered the best and indeed the only "practical" method of handling a given problem. This orthodoxy is considered by most to be grounded upon "commonsense" observations and rationalizations. At some point, perhaps in response to obvious shortcomings, the recognition arises that the classic pattern is inadequate. As bureaucracies tend to try to maintain their standard operating procedures and thereby resist change, the first efforts to change an organization's behavior usually occur "from the top down" as a response to dramatic performance failures, often by legislative fiat or administrative decree. Finally there often begins an incremental and, to observers, frustratingly slow process of changing behavior at the operational level.

The criminal justice system's response to domestic violence illustrates the slow process of achieving substantive change in the provision of services. As described in subsequent chapters, over an extended period the police, the prosecutors, and the courts have consistently failed to respond to domestic violence assaults, responsibility that should, because of their organizational mandates, be clearly within their cognizance. As awareness of this ineffectiveness grew, various explanations were advanced. At times, a failure to respond appropriately was considered to be inadvertent, perhaps a by-product of competing demands for limited service capabilities. At other times, seeming apathy resulted from "common knowledge" that such intervention had only a minimal substantive impact on the probability of subsequent assaults. Finally, the abject failure to address an area where the institution is uniquely qualified to intervene was considered by some indicative of an organizational ideology that tacitly tolerated or even encouraged the behavior that was expressly targeted for control.

The "classic" criminal justice response to domestic violence has been examined from all these perspectives. Police administrators and prosecutors, at least until recently, have long argued that they should not allocate scarce resources to the control of a "domestic" crime, no matter how severe the injuries. To do otherwise would expose officers to being unable to extricate themselves from the intervention. They would risk the obligation to pursue legal actions in cases where the victim often refused to charge the offender or to follow through with prosecution. Without the victim's commitment, common sense precluded involvement with the crime. In addition, this cavalier conduct was rationalized on the basis that the police were handicapped by numerous state constitutional restrictions that made warrantless arrests inappropriate in the case of misdemeanors, a category that included most domestic violence assaults.

As knowledge grew of the pain inflicted by domestic violence on its victims (and on society), other administrators, while sympathetic and often individually very knowledgeable, despaired of effectively influencing an offender's behavior. For example, Bannon (1974) stated that the reason police did not desire to intervene is that they did not know how to respond effectively. The National Association of District Attorneys stated that it was not worth prosecuting domestic violence assault cases if the victim didn't wish to press charges, as a prosecution that did not lead to a conviction could not help the victim and might even worsen her plight by infuriating the assailant.

Finally, the feminist movement has directly challenged the underlying ideology of the criminal justice establishment. They found it to be organized into male-dominated paramilitary command structures (Ferraro 1989; Stanko 1989), reporting further that a prime implicit tenet has been to reinforce the patriarchal hierarchy of Western society, even to the extent of tacitly condoning, by inaction, violence that effectively "puts women in their place."

The need for change was, not surprisingly, first recognized outside of the somewhat insular police and prosecutorial organizations. Women's rights and feminist groups questioned why the police and prosecutors aggressively pursued virtually all crimes other than crimes committed by men against women such as "spouse abuse," rape, and sexual assaults. The inference was not missed that these crimes were being ignored precisely because they involved women as victims (Ferraro 1988).

Feminist pressures on the political system have been coupled in the 1980s with an increasing orientation toward solving social problems through law enforcement. The amelioration of conditions that breed crime or attempted rehabilitation of offenders have become less-favored solutions, compared to more punitive perspectives that emphasize punishment for criminal acts and fear of such punishment as a deterrent. The result has been a society that at the present time imprisons over a million of its citizens, a higher proportion of its population than any other country in the world. For such reasons, the nation's prison population has doubled from 1980 to 1990 while the overall crime rate, at least by one measure, has declined by 3.5 percent (*New York Times*, 7 January 1991).

In such an atmosphere of strict enforcement of laws, the police and the criminal justice system rather than social welfare and community health agencies or the clergy have become, not unexpectedly, the primary focus of societal efforts to restrain domestic violence. The Binder and Meeker chapter in this anthology emphasizes how these political trends have developed, to criminalize the response not only to domestic violence but also to child abuse and drunk driving.

Researchers studying assaults among intimates also became prime agents of change. The failure of police to intervene effectively and their attempts to abdicate responsibility have been graphically portrayed for the last twenty years (see especially Parnas 1967, Loving 1980). Wilt and Bannon demonstrated with their 1977 study that the pattern of police behavior might itself effect the toll of domestic violence. From a study of the Kansas City and Detroit police departments, they reported that rates of domestic violence were strongly related overall to subsequent acts of homicide. They also showed that police had been repetitively called to the scenes of most domestic homicides. The inference was clear: Ineffective police responses to pre-homicidal assaults directly contribute to the high toll of such crimes. The Wilt and Bannon study suggested reforming the police response to train officers adequately for effective intervention.

After examining police capabilities and past practices, Bard (1973) developed the first systematic critique of the ad hoc treatment of domestic violence incidents. He advocated that each jurisdiction develop a highly trained and dedicated police family crisis intervention team. From his experience in New York City, he believed that such a policy would dramatically reduce or alleviate recidivism and reduce agency costs by minimizing officer injuries and necessitating fewer repeat calls.

Although one can argue with the particular remedies suggested, it is clear that the basic research and policy prescriptions of the 1970s effectively set the stage for a period of reform and experimentation in the 1980s in the criminal justice system's response to domestic violence.

CHANGE—THE FIRST WAVE

Pressure from politically aware action groups and early research first led to wholesale changes in state statutes dealing with domestic violence. By 1985, under the leadership of women's advocacy groups, legislators in over 50 percent of the states had passed statutes funding domestic violence shelters, providing training to police departments and prosecutors, and removing restrictions on warrantless arrests for misdemeanor domestic assaults. Further, such legislation developed clear policy guidelines that reflected the statutory intent to curb domestic violence by more vigorous application by criminal justice agencies of previously existing and newly enacted criminal statutes (see Buzawa and Buzawa 1985 for a summary of such legislation).

These early statutes may best be characterized as sending a somewhat ambiguous message: the criminal justice system should intervene in the traditionally off-limits area of violence in the family, but only if intervention is kept within strict limits. Severe restrictions on the very definition of domestic violence were found in many such statutes, limiting their scope to assaults among people who were married and excluding cohabitants. Restrictions on warrantless arrests were also usually lifted, but in many cases only if the violence had occurred within a short time prior to the police intervention, usually within several hours.

Clearly, the legislation passed in the late 1970s and early 1980s was a byproduct of extensive compromises among the defense bar concerned about unfettered police authority to make arrests and women's advocacy groups and battered women's supporters wanting a more proactive police response. Many police administrators were also eager to demonstrate their agency's relevance to an emerging social issue as well as to preserve or even enlarge their officers' discretionary powers to make arrests. To a surprising extent, the early statutes did manage to accommodate some degree of each of these groups' interests.

The goal of a more active criminal justice intervention was cited as the primary reason for statutory change in virtually all cases. However, the vehicle selected allowed increased discretion and thereby implicitly appealed to the good faith actions of criminal justice agencies. Accordingly, a high degree of statutory attention addressed the specific complaints and rationalizations of police departments for their poor performance. In contrast to the express removal of restrictions on police arrest powers, most statutes merely expressed "policy goals" for a more active police and prosecutorial involvement and did not establish mandatory standards for arrest or prosecutorial powers. Finally, the police departments or the statewide training councils heavily influenced by local police department administrators were given the funding to develop training programs in this area.

Implicit in this legislation was the faith that police and prosecutorial discretion, unfettered by antiquated restrictions and "guided" by statewide policy, would, by a more efficacious use of arrests and other proactive techniques, stop incidents from escalating into violence, punish actual assaults, and deter future violence in the family.

In addition to statutory changes and initiatives by police agencies, numerous prosecutorial agencies using federal and state grants developed multidisciplinary programs. These sought to refine the use of prosecutorial discretion in domestic violence cases and to further develop sophisticated sentencing schemes. As discussed in Naomi Cahn's chapter, many displayed insights from the behavioral sciences in furthering the goal of rehabilitating offenders and deterring future misconduct.

THE MOVE TO PUNITIVE ACTION

The Political and Legal Front

As might be expected, the consensus was very fragile for approaches that at their core relied upon the good faith of criminal justice organizations. As noted, many feminists and advocates of battered women profoundly mistrusted the motives as well as the actions of the police, the prosecutors, and the courts. Increasing the discretion and powers of these bureaucracies did not necessarily address feminist concerns. Many still believed that the criminal justice system was an uncoordinated group of organizations, many of which failed to give priority to or even were actively hostile to addressing the victimization of women.

Gradually, continuing reports of police and prosecutorial misfeasance throughout the early and mid-1980s demonstrated that in many cases the police, prosecutors, and courts had not changed their previous policy of benign neglect. A new strategy emerged for battered women's advocates, uniquely adapted to the more litigious era of the 1980s. As described in Marvin Zalman's chapter, lawsuits undertaken in a number of jurisdictions asserted that police (and occasionally the jurisdiction's prosecutors) failed to take reasonable actions to assist victims requesting protection from known offenders. This failure was deemed to be negligence that allowed the victim to sue for damages. The generic failure to protect women in spouse abuse cases was claimed to be sex-based discrimination, as most victims were female. This bias was asserted to be a violation of the equal protection clause of the Constitution applied to state action by the Fourteenth Amendment.

The key case featured a $2.3 million award granted in 1984 to Tracey Thurman in her suit against the city of Torrington, Connecticut, *Thurman et al. v. City of Torrington*, 595 F. Supp. 1521 (Conn. 1984). The plaintiff was a woman who was brutally assaulted and left paralyzed by her estranged husband after she had repeatedly called for police protection. The case, widely reported in the popular press and in professional and advocacy journals, stimulated individual lawsuits and class actions against other police departments throughout the country. Fear of legal liability, if not an actual change of heart, prompted many jurisdictions to tighten policies administratively and limit police discretion. The vehicle most often adopted was a policy that explicitly favored arrest as the preferred outcome, that is, "presumptive arrest," in police response to an actual domestic assault.

The Research Front

At virtually the same time as the *Thurman* lawsuit, Sherman and Berk (1984) published the results of a pilot study on domestic assault conducted in Minneapolis and funded by the National Institute of Justice. The study used an experimental design, randomly assigning the police response to domestic assaults to one of three possible dispositions—arrest, mediation, or mere separation—and tracking the subsequent recidivism of the offenders. The results showed that making an arrest had significantly greater effect in reducing future acts of violence by offenders than the other responses. Attempts to mediate were found to be markedly less effective. Least effective was the "classic" police response of merely separating the parties and restoring order. Although by their own admission this was a preliminary study, the authors recommended arrest as the preferred response, primarily because of its presumed ability to deter violence. As everyone "knew" that the police did not favor making arrests, it was natural to shift attention toward a mandatory arrest policy.

Despite its relatively modest scale, the study rapidly received widespread coverage in the public media and academic journals and among policy officials. As described in Binder and Meeker's chapter, this attention was partially due to the study's reinforcement of the pro-arrest policy then favored by women's rights groups and other policy elites. Further, the researchers made extraordinary efforts to publicize their study and to bring it to the attention of network news and the national print media.

After the Minneapolis study was published, federally supported studies exploring the criminal justice system's response to domestic violence were dominated by the assumption that arrests deterred domestic assaults. In such a climate, the subtleties of the Minneapolis study's conclusion and its inherent research limitations were ignored. A series of replications of this one experimental study were sponsored by the National Institute of Justice, to the virtual exclusion of other techniques.

Not surprisingly, virtually any approach not favoring mandatory arrest has been effectively labelled reactionary or challenged in the press, in legislatures, or in court. It is interesting but not yet relevant to policy that other studies have not consistently confirmed the advantages of a pro-arrest policy. For example, Dunford, Huizinga, and Elliott (1990) provided the first of the replication studies, in Omaha, Nebraska. They found that arrest, by itself, did not appear to have any greater impact on future acts of domestic assault than mediation or separation. Results from five additional replication sites are still pending. However, as the Omaha study has not received wide attention, it is unlikely that jurisdictions that have "solved" the domestic violence problem by mandating arrests will be affected by such research.

Similarly, as of December 1990, to the authors' best knowledge, no major empirical studies have been reported or even funded that seek to explore possible negative effects of arrests, including deterrence of future victim calls for assistance or costs to the agency of a pro-arrest policy, or the effect of reduced arrests and prosecutions for other crimes. To this extent, the new response that explicitly favors arrest has, in the unprecedented span of five or six years, achieved a new orthodoxy, at least among the federal government and policy elites.

STRUCTURE OF THIS VOLUME

Despite an apparent consensus among policy makers as to the proper role of arrests, there is enormous diversity in both the response of agencies and the range of scholarly research. As may be seen from the research reported in this volume, basic paradigms of desired organizational goals and implementation strategies are not necessarily shared. Not surprisingly, the authors of these chapters demonstrate this diversity. Articles range from Ferraro's critique of society's minimal reaction to in-group violence in general to an in-depth analysis of how specific elements of the criminal justice system have affected its outputs.

This volume deliberately provides a mix of original research projects and theoretical discussions that thoughtfully analyze how the system works in practice. This orientation is in sharp contrast to most works in the field of domestic violence, which, although well written, tend to limit their scope to a single perspective or orientation, which may be feminist, legalistic, or structural in nature. Other papers simply report one set of empirical data. The chapters in this anthology address varied issues including the evolving response of the criminal justice system to domestic violence (Binder and Meeker), a structural analysis of how and in what form intervention occurs (Manning, Pierce and Spaar, Buzawa et al.), feminist/societal perspectives (Chaudhuri and Daly, Ferraro and Boychuk, Stark), and an analysis of the key policy research in the field (Binder and Meeker).

The basic framework of this work is as follows. We seek to provide a detailed examination of how the police, prosecutorial staff, and courts, by their operational definitions of the crime, standard operating procedures, and technology, have determined their response to domestic violence. The impacts of recent innovations in the criminal justice response are explored; several chapters discuss how the victims' attitudes and actions interact with agency action.

A number of perspectives on the justice system's handling of domestic violence are explored in this volume. Several chapters review the societal context within which the criminal justice system operates. Binder and Meeker provide the historical context, showing how the criminal justice system's view of its role in handling domestic violence and similar crimes have affected performance. Ferraro and Boychuk pose the question of whether real limitations are imposed by the nature of our society's reaction to and acceptance of violence.

Several chapters examine how, often unintentionally, the interaction between an agency's standard operating procedures and the adoption of powerful new technology has shaped and altered reactions to incidents of abuse. For example, the chapters by Manning and by Pierce and Spaar demonstrate that the very essence of police response to a call has been shaped by the routinized adoption of 911 emergency response technology. Unintended consequences such as higher rates of rejection by call-screening of calls deemed unimportant, usually including the category of family fights, may arise because of such technological innovations and the concomitant demise of neighborhood patrols, once the police department's primary source of knowledge about violent situations.

It is probable that, with the arguable exception of the response to drunk driving, no other area of the criminal justice system has seen such massive changes in recent years, largely because of efforts to make the system more responsive to the needs of the victims and society. A number of chapters therefore cover the effects of new legal and operational definitions of domestic violence (Halsted), major police innovations including the adoption of centralized dispatch systems (Manning) and enhanced 911 (Pierce and Spaar), changes in how prosecutors dispose of their domestic violence caseloads (Ford and Regoli, Chaudhuri and Daly), and the increased sophistication shown in the sentencing of offenders (Cahn).

Finally, emphasis in many chapters is placed on how victims in domestic violence cases may affect and be affected by the lack of response by the criminal justice system. Such impact may occur in the form of helping to determine an officer's decision to arrest (Buzawa et al.) or the new wave of lawsuits against recalcitrant agencies (Zalman). Other chapters demonstrate that, despite this impact, the responsiveness of the criminal justice system as a system may be constrained by society's failure to treat all crimes of violence seriously (Ferraro), especially when the victim finds herself persecuted or prosecuted for taking direct action in self-defense (Stark).

POLICE INTERVENTION

The common opinion of the police response to domestic violence is that it has abjectly failed to meet the crisis of domestic violence. The police and local law enforcement agencies have historically assumed primary institutional responsibility for intervention in domestic violence. Such agencies usually have the initial contact with violence-prone families because they provide free services, are highly visible authoritative figures, maintain central dispatch, and are usually the only public agency in a position to provide rapid assistance around the clock. They initiate arrests, file reports justifying such action, and often are consulted about case disposition.

However, by the early 1970s it was widely noted that police practices had been of limited effectiveness. The police were accused not only of failing to try to alter the cycle of battering but also more specifically of being unwilling to arrest offenders or otherwise to protect victims as they would in other criminal cases. To the former charge, police disclaimed responsibility for a service task, stating that this was not part of their function of enforcing laws. To the latter charge, they offered the claim that their arrest powers were limited in cases of warrantless misdemeanor arrests as a reason for inaction.

Police intervention tended to be perfunctory, largely limited to separating the assailant briefly from the abused party and sternly warning both against "disturbances to the peace" (Dobash and Dobash 1979; Parnas 1967). Police officers usually were directed to avoid arrest except in cases of severe injury. In addition, numerous police departments limited their involvement in domestic violence through "call screening," a practice in which incoming calls are given priorities; calls with the lowest priority, usually including simple assaults, are not scheduled for immediate (or often any) dispatch of police units (Bannon 1974).

Despite the difficulty of obtaining estimates with any degree of accuracy, we do know that arrests were infrequent, with estimates ranging from 3 percent (Langley and Levy 1977) to 13.9 percent (Bayley 1986). In one recent study reported in this volume, Buzawa et al. discuss how only 16 percent of offenders were arrested even when the victim was injured. Even for the 33 percent of a sample that represented repeat service calls, there was no difference in the rate of arrest.

In this regard, most researchers have observed that traditionally the use of arrest powers in cases of misdemeanor violations is situationally determined, that is, the dynamics of the intervention greatly influence whether an arrest is made. The legal merits of making an arrest appear to be of secondary importance to the interpersonal relationship established in the encounter with the police. Specifically, arrests are reserved primarily for cases of disrespect or challenges to police authority (Berk et al. 1984; Black 1980; Ferraro 1988; Manning 1977).

Researchers have also found that officers were more inclined to arrest when they believed a subsequent disturbance would require another police response, rather than to base the decision to arrest on an overriding concern for the victim's welfare or the severity of the case (Ford 1987). Even the decision to arrest, normally considered to be an act committing the police to intervention, may merely represent a tactic to limit future organizational involvement in the problems of the family.

In most jurisdictions, prosecutors have an enormous degree of independent control over the criminal justice system. They typically are headed by an independently elected district attorney, possess the organizational mandate of reviewing the adequacy of police actions, decide whether to charge an offender with one or more crimes, and customarily are the key actors in sentencing decisions in the form of plea bargaining.

When faced with an overwhelming lack of resources in court bureaucracies, prosecutors often choose to exercise their discretion in domestic violence by refusing to bring or by later dismissing charges (Lerman 1981). They tend to use a number of extralegal variables, independent of the strength of the case, to differentially screen caseloads (Ellis 1984; Schmidt and Steury 1989; Stanko 1982).

Although overt screening of cases eliminates many cases, other methods are indirectly employed to "encourage" women to drop the cases. Procedural barriers may be imposed to screen out "undesirable" cases. Mandatory waiting periods, virtually unheard of outside domestic violence complaint processing, were used in one large county in Indiana (Ford 1983).

Therefore, the critical factors have been whether the injury could not be overlooked, as in a death or highly publicized attack or in a case where the victim has sufficient persistence and outside support or resources to demand action.

In making their decisions, prosecutors have consciously assumed that the motivation and commitment of victims is a legitimate case discriminator in deciding whether to prosecute an offender. The victim's commitment to prosecution reaffirms the prosecutor's organizationally centered goal of achieving a high conviction rate. This goal often assumes a greater significance than that of best serving victim needs. Further, there is the often-voiced opinion that victims who drop charges have "wasted" the time of the criminal justice system and are viewed as failures. The victim may, of course, have accomplished her goal of stopping the violence or have initiated divorce proceedings. The possibility that the victim may have accomplished her interim goals is not relevant in an organizational context. Thus, there is no shared agreement on what constitutes a successful outcome.

Schmidt and Steury (1989) observed a number of victim and offender characteristics that affect the decision to prosecute. A victim's continued relationship with the offender decreased the likelihood of charges. In contrast, the use of drugs and/or alcohol, contrary to many other types of offenses, increased the likelihood of case processing. They did not find a history of prior abuse to be predictive of charging decisions (Buzawa and Buzawa 1990).

Organizational dictates beyond the victim's control also affect the continued case prosecution. Police-initiated arrests are generally treated more seriously than complaints filed by victims (Cole 1984; Jacoby 1980; Schmidt and Steury 1989), because of the natural synergy betwen prosecutors and the police. Prosecutors legitimize officer arrests in exchange for receiving necessary evidence for convictions from the police (Buzawa and Buzawa 1990).

Clearly a complex interaction occurs between the domestic violence victim and the prosecutor's office. Each profoundly misunderstands or is incapable of responding to the other's individual and organizational motives and needs. Victims assume the criminal justice processing to be a predictable, straightforward process. They have little support for their continued involvement, nor are they prepared for the protection the offender receives for his constitutional rights. A general dissatisfaction with the criminal justice system is typical of many victims. When exacerbated by the domestic violence victims' often ambiguous or conflicting motives for prosecution and the unresponsiveness of the system they expected to assist them, it is not surprising that attrition rates are so high. The simultaneous failure to comprehend why victims refuse to leave abusive partners and/or express ambivalence about prosecution affects their behavior in a manner that reinforces these misperceptions. Consequently, even greater numbers of women fail to cooperate because of the apparent indifference or lack of support from court personnel. Low prosecution and conviction rates then serve to justify continued police reluctance to arrest in domestic assault cases. Thus, the inevitable cycle continues.

Although empirical research attempting to explain judicial behavior is lacking, judges appear to have shared the operational behavior of prosecutors that most domestic violence cases could not readily be helped by full prosecution of an offender (Dobash and Dobash 1979; Field and Field 1973). Given organizational and financial restraints like those of the prosecutors, it is not surprising that judges tried to minimize domestic violence cases by disproportionately dismissing them at early stages (Parnas 1970, 1973).

The sentencing of convicted domestic violence offenders is an area where the judge has primary authority. Sentences imposed upon the small minority of assailants convicted of an abuse-related charge has traditionally been very lenient, partly because sentencing options are limited. In addition, the reasons for judicial reluctance to apply strict punishments such as jail were multifaceted. Most judges believed that the traditional jail term might adversely affect the financial situation of the victim and her children, who may be dependent on the assailant's income. Further, victims often did not request a sentence involving jail. Some were fearful of reprisals, thus indirectly increasing judicial reluctance to impose a jail sentence. Alternately such sentences may have reflected societal judgments that violence committed within the family (and against women in particular) was less disruptive to the social order than violence against strangers.

REFERENCES

Bandy, C., D. R. Buchanan, and C. Pinto. 1986. Police Performance in Resolving Family Disputes—What Makes the Difference? *Psychological Reports* 58(3):743–56.

Bannon, J. 1974. *Social Conflict Assaults: Detroit, Michigan.* Unpublished report for the Deport Police Department and the Police Foundation.

Bard, M. 1973. *Training Police in Family Crisis Intervention.* Washington, D.C.: U.S. Government Printing Office.

Bard, M., and J. Zacker. 1974. Assaultiveness and Alcohol Use in Family Disputes. *Criminology* 12: 281–92.

Bayley, D. H. 1986. The Tactical Choices of Police Patrol Officers. *Journal of Criminal Justice* 14: 329–48.

Bell, D. 1984. The Police Responses to Domestic Violence: A Replication Study. *Police Studies* 7: 136–43.

Berk, R. A., S. F. Berk, P. J. Newton, and D. R. Loseke. 1984. Cops On Call: Summoning the Police to the Scene of Spousal Violence. *Law and Society Review* 18(3): 479–98.

Berk, S. F., and D. R. Loseke. 1980–81. "Handling" Family Violence: Situational Determinants of Police Arrests in Domestic Disturbances. *Law and Society Review* 15(2): 317–46.

Binder, A., and J. Meeker. 1988. Experiments as Reforms. *Journal of Criminal Justice* 16: 347–58.

Black, D. 1976. *The Behavior of Law.* New York: Academic Press.

———. 1980. *The Manners and Customs of the Police.* New York: Academic Press.

Brosan, G., L. Edwards, E. Whiteman, R. J. Spangler, J. Vespa, E. Mercer, B. Shapiro, and D. Scherer. 1987. *Maryland Battered Spouse Report, 1986*. Maryland State Police Criminal Records Repository, Pickesville, MD 21208.

Buzawa, E. 1976. Unpublished survey.

Buzawa, E., and C. Buzawa. 1985. Legislative Trends in the Criminal Justice Response to Domestic Violence. In A. J. Lincoln and M. A. Straus, eds., *Crime and the Family*, pp. 134–47. Springfield, Ill.: Charles C. Thomas.

———. 1990. *Domestic Violence: The Criminal Justice Response*. Newbury Park, Calif.: Sage Publications.

Cohn, E., and L. Sherman. 1987. *Police Policy on Domestic Violence, 1986: A National Survey*. Crime Control Institute, Washington, D.C.

———. 1990. Effects of Research on Legal Policy in the Minneapolis Domestic Violence Experiment. In Douglas Besharov, ed., *Family Violence: Research and Public Policy Issues*, pp. 205–07. Lanham, Md.: University Press of America.

Cole, G. 1984. The Decision to Prosecute. In George Cole, ed., *Criminal Justice: Law and Politics*. 5th ed. Monterey, Calif.: Brooks/Cole.

Coleman, D. H., and M. A. Straus. 1986. Marital Power, Conflict and Violence in a Nationally Representative Sample of American Couples. *Violence and Victims* 1: 141–57.

Connecticut State Police. 1990. *Family Violence Reporting Program: Law Enforcement Semiannual Report, January 1, 1990 to June 30, 1990*. Meriden, Conn.: Connecticut State Police.

Dobash, R., and R. Dobash. 1979. *Violence Against Wives: A Case Against the Patriarehy*. New York: Free Press.

Dolan, R., J. Hendricks, and M. Meagher. 1986. Police Practices and Attitudes Toward Domestic Violence. *Journal of Police Science and Administration* 14(3): 187–92.

Dunford, F., D. Huizinga, and D. S. Elliott. 1990. Role of Arrest in Domestic Assault: The Omaha Police Experiment. *Criminology* 28, no. 2(May): 183–206.

Dutton, D. 1987. Criminal Justice Response to Wife Assault. *Law and Human Behavior* 11(3): 167–264.

———. 1988. *The Domestic Assault of Women: Psychological and Criminal Justice Perspectives*. Boston: Allyn & Bacon.

Elliott, D. 1989. Criminal Justice Procedures in Family Violence Crimes. In L. Ohlin and M. Tonry, eds., *Crime and Justice: A Review of Research*, pp. 427–80. Chicago: University of Chicago Press.

———. 1991. Cited in R. Gelles, *Constraints Against Family Violence: How Well Do They Work?* Paper presented to the American Society of Criminology, San Francisco, November.

Ellis, D. 1987. Policing Wife Abuse: The Contribution Made by 'Domestic Disturbances' to Deaths and Injuries Among Police Officers. *Journal of Family Violence* 2(4): 319–33.

Ellis, J. W. 1984. Prosecutorial Discretion to Charge in Cases of Spousal Assault: A Dialogue. *Journal of Criminal Law and Criminology* (Spring):56–102.

FBI Law Enforcement Bulletin. 1991. Domestic Violence: When Do Police Have a Constitutional Duty to Protect? *FBI Law Enforcement Bulletin* 60(1): 27–32.

Ferraro, K. 1988. The Legal Response to Woman Battering in the United States. In J. Hanmer, J. Radford and E. Stanko, eds., *Women, Policing, and Male Violence*, pp. 155–84. London: Routledge & Keegan Paul.

Field, M., and H. Field. 1973. Marital Violence and the Criminal Process: Neither Justice nor Peace. *Social Science Review* 47(2): 221–40.

Ford, D. 1983. Wife Battery and Criminal Justice: A Study of Victim Decision Making. *Family Relations* 32: 463–75.

———. 1987. *The Impact of Police Officers' Attitudes Toward Victims on the Disinclination to Arrest Wife Batterers*. Paper presented at the Third International Conference for Family Violence Researchers, Durham, N.H.

Garner, J., and E. Clemmer. 1986. Danger to Police in Domestic Violence Disturbances: A New Look. In *National Institute of Justice: Research in Brief*. Washington, D.C.: U.S. Department of Justice.

Jacoby, J. 1980. *The American Prosecutor: A Search for Identity*. Lexington, Mass.: Lexington Books.

Kantor, G. K., and M. A. Straus, 1987. The "Drunken Bum" Theory of Wife Beating. *Social Problems* 34(3): 213–30.

Langan, P., and C. Innes. 1986. *Preventing Domestic Violence Against Women*. Bureau of Justice Statistics. Washington, D.C.: U.S. Department of Justice.

Langley, R., and R. Levy. 1977. *Wife Beating: The Silent Crisis*. New York: Dutton.

Lerman, L. 1981. *Prosecution of Spouse Abuse Innovations in Criminal Justice Response*. Washington, D.C.: Center for Women Policy Studies.

———. 1984. Mediation of Wife Abuse Cases: The Adverse Impact of Informal Dispute Resolution of Women. *Harvard Women's Law Journal* 7: 65–67.

Liebman, D., and J. Schwartz. 1973. Police Programs in Domestic Crisis Intervention: A Review. In J. R. Snibbe and H. M. Snibbe, eds., *The Urban Policeman in Transition*. Springfield, Ill.: Charles C. Thomas.

Loving, Nancy. 1980. *Responding to Spouse Abuse and Wife Beating: A Guide for Police*. Washington, D.C.: Police Executive Research Forum.

Loving, N., and M. Quirk. 1982. Spouse Abuse: The Need for New Law Enforcement Responses. *FBI Law Enforcement Bulletin* 51(12): 10–16.

Manning, P. 1977. *Police Work: The Sociological Organization of Policing*. Cambridge, Mass.: MIT Press.

———. 1988. *Symbolic Communication: Signifying Calls and the Police Response*. Cambridge, Mass.: MIT Press.

———. 1991. *Technological and Material Resource Issues Endemic to Policing*. Paper presented at the Seminar Series on Executive Issues, Law Enforcement Management Institute, Lubbock, Texas, July.

Martin, M. 1991, November. *Dual Arrest: Arresting Women Victims of Domestic Violence*. Paper presented to the American Society of Criminology, San Francisco.

Meeker, J., and A. Binder. 1990. Experiments as Reforms: The Impact of the 'Minneapolis Experiment' on Police Policy. *Journal of Police Science and Administration* 17(2): 147–53.

National Organization of Black Law Enforcement Executives. 1990. *Law Enforcement Family Violence Training and Technical Assistance Project, October 1988–July 1990, Final Report*. U.S. Department of Justice, Washington, D.C.

Parnas, R. 1967. The Police Response to the Domestic Disturbance. *Wisconsin Law Review* 2: 914–60.

———. 1970. Judicial Response to Intra-Family Violence. *Minnesota Law Review* 54: 585–644.

————. 1973. Prosecutorial and Judicial Handling of Family Violence. *Criminal Law Bulletin* 9: 733–69.

Pennsylvania Task Force. 1989. *Domestic Violence: A Model Protocol for Police Response*. Pennsylvania Attorney General's Family Violence Task Force.

Pierce, G., and S. Deutsch. Forthcoming. Do Police Actions and Responses to Domestic Violence Calls Make a Difference? A Quasi Experimental Analysis. *Journal of Quantitative Criminology*.

Pleck, E. 1989. Criminal Approaches to Family Violence 1640–1980. In L. Ohlin and M. Tonry, eds., *Crime and Justice: A Review of Research, Vol. 11*, pp. 19–58. Chicago: University of Chicago Press.

Punch, M. 1985. *Conduct Unbecoming*. London: Macmillan.

Radford, J. 1989. Women and Policing: Contradictions Old and New. In J. Hanmer, J. Radford, and E. Stanko, eds., *Women, Policing and Male Violence*, pp. 13–45. London: Routledge and Keegan Paul.

Reiss, A. J. 1971. *The Police and the Public*. New Haven, Conn.: Yale University Press.

Saunders, D., and P. Size. 1986. Attitudes About Women Abuse Among Police Officers, Victims and Victim Advocates. *Journal of Interpersonal Violence* 1: 24–42.

Scargzi, J. 1991. *Attitudes of New Police Recruits Concerning Domestic Violence*: A *Pre and Post Test Design*. Paper presented to the American Society of Criminology, San Francisco, November.

Schmidt, J., and E. Steury. 1989. Prosecutorial Discretion in Filing Charges in Domestic Violence Cases. *Criminology* 27 (3): 587–10.

Sherman, L., and R. Berk. 1984. The Specific Deterrent Effects of Arrest for Domestic Assault. *American Sociological Review* 49: 261–72.

Sherman, L., and E. Cohn. 1989. The Impact of Research on Legal Policy: The Minneapolis Domestic Violence Experiment. *Law and Society Review* 23(1): 117–44.

Stanko, E. 1982. Would You Believe This Woman? In N. H. Rafter and E. Stanko, eds., *Judge, Lawyer, Victim, Thief: Women, Gender Roles and Criminal Justice*. Boston: Northeastern University Press.

————. 1989. Missing the Mark? Policing Battering. In J. Hanmer, J. Radford, and E. Stanko, eds., *Women, Policing and Male Violence*, pp. 46–49. London: Routledge and Keegan Paul.

Stith, S. 1987. *Individual and Family Factors Which Predict Police Response to Spouse Abuse*. Paper presented to the Third National Family Violence Research Conference, Durham, N.H., July.

Van Maanen, J. 1974. Working the Street: A Developmental View of Police Behavior. In H. Jacob, ed., *The Potential for Reform of Criminal Justice*, pp. 83–130. Beverly Hills, Calif.: Sage.

————. 1978. Observations on the Making of Policemen. In P. Manning and J. Van Maanen, eds., *Policing: A View from the Street*. Santa Monica, Calif.: Goodyear Publishing.

Victim Services Agency. 1988. *The Law Enforcement Response to Family Violence: A State by State Guide to Family Violence Legislation*. New York: Victim Services Agency.

————. 1989. *The Law Enforcement Response to Family Violence: The Training Challenge*. U.S. Department of Justice, Washington, D.C.

Walker, L. 1979. *Battered Women*. New York: Harper and Row.

Westley, W. 1970. *Violence and the Police: A Sociological Study of Law, Custom and Morality*. Cambridge, Mass.: MIT Press.

Wilt, M., and J. Bannon. 1977. *Domestic Violence and the Police: Studies in Detroit and Kansas City*. Washington, D.C.: The Police Foundation.

Worden, R., and A. Pollitz. 1984. Police Arrests in Domestic Disturbances: A Further Look. *Law and Society Review* 18: 105–19.

I

HISTORY OF THE RESPONSE TO DOMESTIC VIOLENCE

THE DEVELOPMENT OF SOCIAL ATTITUDES TOWARD SPOUSAL ABUSE

Arnold Binder and James Meeker

The following chapter by Arnold Binder and James Meeker places the evolving societal response to domestic violence in the context of an overall change in societal attitudes toward offenses that had not been acknowledged in the past. Specifically, significant attitudinal changes have occurred in society's treatment of abused children and more recently in its response to drunken driving.

The authors illustrate how the historical context of attitudes toward the family has influenced attitudes toward violence in the family. Not surprisingly, they found that, when the family was regarded as the ultimate source of civilization, wide latitude was given to the male to control the family. The male was the patriarch, often legally responsible for the acts of other family members. Women and children were viewed as mentally and even morally inferior. The common-law English statutes cited in the chapter vividly illustrate the disparity between men and women and the right of the former to exercise control over the latter.

Binder and Meeker trace the change in societal attitudes to the initial recognition of the costs of spousal abuse in the 1970s. They review attempts to treat such violence as a "family problem" and the efforts to resolve such violence as a matter belonging to a "family in conflict." Finally, the chapter shows how in the 1980s society's response changed from treating domestic violence as a crime of less import than violence among strangers to considering the more severe societal sanctions that have been proposed and often adopted.

When key political and societal elites view a problem such as family violence as of paramount importance and as neglected in practice, the agencies responsible for control are subject to attack and lower their resolve to handle problems in older, established ways. Not surprisingly, the response of many agencies is to demonstrate changes, even before these changes are

subjected to careful empirical analysis. Such an organizational need to demonstrate rapid change can be seen as the key trend that has led to the service
innovations discussed in the following chapters.

OVERVIEW

The degree of tolerance shown for a given type of abusive or potentially
abusive behavior may vary considerably over the developmental progress of a
culture. For example, de Mause (1975) and Watson (1970) have pointed to the
socially accepted brutality shown toward children in the ancient era of Western
society, including the wide use of exposure of unwanted children, in which
infants were left out unattended until they died. Contrast that with the protective
attitude toward children in modern society. We have child protective agencies;
requirements that such professionals as physicians, teachers, and counselors
report any evidence, even a minor wound, indicative of child abuse; and an array
of educational and counseling programs aimed at making children aware of their
rights and the support services available to protect them.

That change in society reflects a transition over hundreds of years, starting
with a gradual lessening of brutality toward children during the Middle Ages
under the influence of Christianity. Then, in the early modern era of the sixteenth
and seventeenth centuries, there was an increasing awareness of the "special
nature" of the child that was accompanied by an increase in expression of
tenderness and decrease in hostility (see Ariès 1962 and Muncie 1984). Further
progress in the development of protectiveness toward children continued through
the family orientation of the Puritans in colonial times (Demos 1970) and the
spirit of loving acceptance that became most evident in the nineteenth century
(Bushnell 1947), up to the modern era, when American society can properly be
described as child-centered.

Another example of a marked change in society's tolerance of abusive or
potentially abusive behavior is in the realm of automobile driving by a person
with elevated blood alcohol. As little as a generation ago, most states in the
United States had loose behavioral tests for drunkenness while driving, with
only scattered enforcement of relevant control laws. Under the influence of
organizations like Mothers Against Drunk Driving (MADD) and various advances in knowledge and technology, American society today shows little tolerance for drunk drivers because of the well-documented rate of injury and death
resulting from their behaviors. In terms of controlling statute, by way of illustration, California in under a dozen years moved from a broad statute making
it unlawful to drive while "under the influence of intoxicating liquor" to specifying, in 1982, that it is unlawful to drive with 0.10 percent or more blood
alcohol to specifying, in 1989, that the unlawful level is 0.08 percent (see *Statutes
of California*, 1978, Ch. 790; 1980, Ch. 1004; 1982, Ch. 53; 1989, Ch. 479).
Over that period of time, too, punishments became more severe and more difficult
to avoid. Moreover, there is currently the widely used (and constitutionally valid,

according to the U.S. Supreme Court—*Michigan Department of State Police v. Sitz*, No. 88–1897, decided June 14, 1990) approach in which police stop cars at sobriety checkpoints to look for signs of excessive drinking in the form of blood-alcohol level (using a breathalyzer or otherwise).

As society shifts to lower levels of tolerance in that manner, an increasing tendency to regard the abuser as a pariah leads to less care in protecting the abuser's civil rights and diminished concern about harsh or inappropriate punishment. Illustrating that process is the attitude of a young lady with whom one of us worked, a gentle, kind humanitarian who participated in advocacy groups for reducing the use of imprisonment and eliminating capital punishment. Yet she had so much antipathy toward rapists, for whom societal tolerance is now quite low, that, when asked what punishment she favored for such offenders, she replied strongly and with sincerity, "Castration."

This book deals in substantial detail with another type of abusive behavior for which society has recently reached a very low level of tolerance. That is the abuse, mostly physical but also psychological, by a man of his wife or female cohabitant. Such terms as wife battering and wife abuse have been used to designate the process, but "spousal abuse" is a virtually equivalent term because of the general assumption of gender based on preponderant frequency and the directional concerns of society, as motivated by factors discussed in this chapter. The low tolerance and accompanying considerable antipathy toward offenders have been fueled principally by two social movements: that for women's rights and that for crime victims' rights. This chapter will briefly review social attitudes toward women and wife abuse over history and emphasize the stark changes in those attitudes as a result, primarily, of the consciousness-raising efforts of those movements.[1] That will provide the context for understanding the phenomenon discussed in the next chapter—the glowing acceptance of a weak, unconvincing study and the widespread adoption of recommendations based on its results.

DEVELOPMENT OF CURRENT ATTITUDES TOWARD SPOUSAL ABUSE

The Family as a "Precious Emotional Unit"

Gough (1971) has estimated that the nuclear family originated at least 100,000 and possibly as long as 2,000,000 years ago, and evidence collected by anthropologists has convinced many (see for example, Murdock 1949) that the family occurs as a clear functional unit over all societies. By and through the Middle Ages in Europe, however, the structure of governmental control and the modes of economic survival were such that the extended family predominated. Then, as urbanization and industrialization proceeded and the control of production and other activities of daily living passed to employers and governments, there was a decline in the role of kin outside the nuclear grouping (see Zimmerman 1947, Shorter 1975, Stone 1975, and Redfield 1947). Three overlapping phases of development for the English family, illustrating that process, have been described by Stone (1975) over the years from 1500 to 1750: (1) "the kin-oriented family of the Middle Ages, in which the conjugal unit of husband, wife, and unmarried children was of relatively lesser importance than the wider kinship affiliations of the cousinhood" (1975:14); (2) "the more nuclear family of the sixteenth century in which loyalty became increasingly focussed inward on the conjugal core" (1975:14); and (3) "the compassionate nuclear family of the eighteenth century, in which affective relationships were becoming as important as economic functions" (1975:14).

According to Shorter (1975), relationships within the family became more intimate and emotionally intense over subsequent years, while ties to the general community became looser and of diminished importance. (See also Pleck 1979, for discussion of the importance of religion, with the home considered a center of worship in evolving Protestantism, as a factor in the shift to the notion of the home as a very private institution.) The following elaboration by Stone (1975:205) is helpful in understanding that process:

What really distinguishes the nuclear family—mother, father, and children . . . is a special sense of solidarity that separates the domestic unit from the surrounding community. Its members feel that they have much more in common with one another than they do with anyone else on the outside—that they enjoy a privileged emotional climate that they must protect from outside intrusion, through privacy and isolation.

The privacy and isolation of the family as the institution developed in Great Britain and the United States, moreover, were often reinforced by law (see Pagelow 1984). Given that array of factors, the following statement by Margaret Mead in 1953 surprised no one (1953:4): "It [the family] is, in fact, the institution to which we owe our humanity."

But efforts to maintain the family as a solid emotional unit, protected from outside interference, were challenged when convincing data showing the extent and degree of criminal violence within families became available. The earliest such data were presented by Kempe and his associates in 1962, demonstrating the medical characteristics of battered children. Supportive evidence came later in abundance, beginning in the late 1960s. To illustrate the extent of the problem brought to national attention, the 1975 National Family Violence Survey estimated that of the "nearly 46 million children between the ages of 3 and 17 years . . . who lived with both parents, . . . between 3.1 and 4.0 million have been kicked, bitten, or punched by parents at some time in their lives, while between 1.0 and 1.9 million were kicked, bitten or punched in 1975 [alone]" (Gelles 1979:82; see also Gelles 1978, 1987). Other estimates placed the number of deaths of children from abuse by their parents between several hundred and several thousand each year (Gelles 1979). Finally, investigators like Carlson (1977), Rounsaville (1978), and Dobash and Dobash (1977–78) studied women who had been victims of domestic violence and found patterns of battering over years, with severe physical and emotional consequences.

Women as Inferior People

Although not often dealt with as a social problem, wife abuse has probably been a commonly occurring phenomenon throughout history (see Goode 1971 and Dobash and Dobash 1979), occurring at a rate and intensity concordant with the rate and intensity of general violence in a given culture (see Masumura 1979). To illustrate, Pleck (1987) reported on three periods of reform in the area of domestic violence in American history: from 1640 to 1680, when the Puritans enacted laws against wife beating; from 1874 to 1890, when societies for the prevention of cruelty to children were founded and directed some effort to reduce wife abuse; and beginning in the 1970s to the present. But between those reform periods, that is, from 1680 to 1874 and from 1890 to 1970, there was almost complete inattention to the problem. In particular, Pleck (1979:182) commented, "There was virtually no public discussion of wife beating from the turn of the century until the mid-1970s." The array of factors that contributed to that lack of concern during those periods of American history, and of earlier English history, included the notion of the preciousness of the family and the sanctity of the home; but important too was the inferior status of women, especially married women, in legal codes that reflected general cultural practices.

That inferior status is evident in the earliest codes of the Anglo-American legal heritage, that is, in the laws of Anglo-Saxon kings, where women are often referred to as possessions and sexual objects. For example, decree 82 of the Laws of Ethelbert (dating from about 602 A.D.) states, "If anyone carries off a maiden by force, [he is to pay] to the owner 50 shillings, and afterwards buy from the owner his consent [to the marriage] (Whitelock 1979:393). Similarly, decree 31 of the Laws of Ine (about 690 A.D.) states, "If one buys a wife, and the marriage does not take place, the money is to be paid back, and as much again, and the surety is to receive compensation, as much as the breach of his surety costs" (Whitelock 1979:402). And finally, we have the following contrasting methods of dealing with adultery in the Laws of Cnut (about 1020 A.D.):

50. If anyone commits adultery, he is to pay compensation for it in proportion to the deed.

50.1 It is wicked adultery that a married man should commit fornication with a single woman, and much worse if with another's wife or with a woman consecrated [to God] (Whitelock 1979:462).

53. If a woman during her husband's lifetime commits adultery with another man, and it becomes known, let her afterwards become herself a public disgrace and her lawful husband is to have all that she owns, and she is to lose her nose and ears (Whitelock 1979:463).

In the thirteenth century, according to Pollock and Maitland (1909), in public law, that is, the law governing the relationship between the individual and the state, unmarried women had neither rights nor duties; while in private law, dealing with relationships among individuals, women were almost equal to men. Married women were in a different position (Pollock and Maitland 1909:485): "The main idea which governs the law of husband and wife is not that of an 'unity of person,' but that of the guardianship, the *mund*, the profitable guardianship, which the husband has over the wife and over her property."

On the other hand, Blackstone (1884) does refer to a "unity of person" in the laws of England, when he wrote, in the latter half of the eighteenth century. The unity he describes continues a picture of inferiority (1884:Bk.II, 433):

A sixth method of acquiring property in goods and chattels is by *marriage*; whereby those chattels, which belonged formerly to the wife, are by act of law vested in the husband with the same degree of property and with the same powers, as the wife, when sole, had over them.

This depends entirely on the notion an unity of person between the husband and wife; it being held that they are one person in law, so that the very being and existence of the woman is suspended during the coverture, or entirely merged or incorporated in that of the husband.

According to Perkin (1989:2), "Male privilege and domination [in England] began to be eroded in the nineteenth century. It was the Victorians who pioneered the emancipation of women." However, she makes it clear that the changed laws and cultural values had little effect for the great majority of women, that is, those women not in the upper classes; they remained subordinate to men, most especially to their husbands.

Similar subordination has been reported for Great Britain and the United States in the twentieth century as noted in Dobash and Dobash (1979), Stetson (1982), Pleck (1979, 1987, 1989), and Buzawa and Buzawa (1990).

The relationship between having power over other people, as in the case of men over women, and the tendency to behave aggressively toward the underdogs has been firmly established (see Berlyne 1967; McClelland 1985; and House and Singh 1987). That relationship is hardly surprising to observers of the inferiority assigned in the history of our culture to racial and ethnic minorities, to children, and to animals and the frequent use of physical violence against members of those groups; seemingly, indeed, the greater the perceived inferiority, the more the violence in terms of frequency and intensity. Consequently, it is safe to assume that even during eras of British and American history for which there is little or no direct evidence of the physical abuse of women, the power differential between men and women made it likely that such abuse did occur.[2]

In the words of feminist writers like Dobash and Dobash (1979:24), "men who assault their wives are actually living up to cultural prescriptions that are cherished in Western society—aggressiveness, male dominance and female subordination. . . . " Similarly, Martin (1978:195) commented, "But the basic problem . . . is the institution of marriage itself and the way in which women and men are socialized to act out dominant-submissive roles that in and of themselves invite abuse." These feminists, of course, are aiming to explain more than just the historical past in their comments.

Recognition of Spousal Abuse as a Major Problem

In 1971, a group of feminists on the outskirts of London formed the first shelter for women who found it necessary to flee from abusive men; the shelter movement arrived in the United States about four years later (see NiCarthy, Merriam, and Coffman 1984). Interviews with residents of these shelters provided shocking revelations about the extent, repetitiveness, and severity of spousal beatings (see for example, the reports of Gayford 1975, 1976, 1979; Carlson 1977; and Pagelow 1981).

Early information regarding wife abuse came, in addition, from various types of court action and agency statistics. Thus, in 1971, O'Brien reported that 15 percent of the women interviewed in divorce actions spontaneously mentioned that marital violence was an important contributing factor. (Incidentally, O'Brien highlighted the earlier lack of concern about wife beating in his revelation that between 1939 and 1969 there was no reference to such violence in the indices of the *Journal of Marriage and the Family*.) Whitehurst (1971) studied over a hundred court cases that involved marital violence and found it a common reaction by husbands against wives who could not be controlled, particularly in the realm of extramarital sexual activity. Finally, Fields (1977) reported that 57.4 percent of 500 female clients seen at a legal services agency in divorce actions admitted marital beatings and that the women had been assaulted on average about four years before seeking a divorce.

Scores of studies since those earlier ones have all supported the importance of elevating wife abuse to the status of national social problem, as urged separately by victims' rights advocates and feminists. Discussions of these studies and their implications may be seen in such sources as Bowker (1983), Gelles and Cornell (1985), Okun (1986), Gelles and Straus (1988), and Buzawa and Buzawa (1990). Other studies have tried to estimate the extent and manifestation of spousal abuse in the general population. Gelles (1979, 1987), Straus (1978), and Straus, Gelles and Steinmetz (1980) reported the results of a national survey of the extent of family violence and of factors that precipitated the violence. About "16% of those surveyed reported some kind of physical violence between spouses during the year of the survey, while 28% of those interviewed reported marital violence at some point in the marriage" (Gelles 1987:37). As a consequence, over a marital career, the probability of serious violent encounter between mates was estimated to be .28. Gaquin (1977–78) analyzed data relevant to spousal abuse from the National Crime Survey. She found that, for women who were married or previously married, abuse of the wife or former wife constituted one-fourth of all assaults upon them. Moreover, wife abuse or former wife abuse constituted 27.9 percent of all assaults on divorced women and 54.6 percent of all assaults on separated women. Finally, attacks by spouses or ex-spouses were

more serious than nonspousal attacks in producing physical injury and hospitalization or other medical care.

THE NATIONAL PROBLEM: ATTEMPTS AT SOLUTION
AND THE EFFECTS OF CONSCIOUSNESS-RAISING

Initial Attempts

With the recognition that spousal abuse was indeed a problem of national
importance, there arose the question of how best to deal with it. In formulating
attempts at solution, moreover, it was recognized that the issue was predominantly one of wife abuse; indeed, that recognition led, as mentioned earlier, to
the use of the terms "spousal abuse" and "wife abuse" as virtually inter-
changeable in popular discourse and in professional publications. As a result,
there has been growth in the numbers of shelters for women, the emergence of
groups for abused women, an increased availability of marriage counseling and
crisis intervention by mental health professionals for abused women, and ex-
panded social services that help in obtaining temporary restraining orders for the
generally weaker sex. A woman who is being abused can take several courses
of action: (1) call the police in response to a given incident; (2) seek support
and counsel from a friend, relative, clergyman, or professional counselor; (3)
persuade her husband to accept mutual marital counseling; (4) leave home and
move in with relatives or enter a shelter—possibly seeking a divorce simultaneously (see Gelles 1976, for comments on why this is not done regularly); (5)
join a mutual-help group for battered women, where legal advice and agency
information as well as counseling and support may be obtained [NiCarthy, Merriam, and Coffman (1984:9) advocated a "feminist, all-women, women-led,
mutual-help, drop-in model" for such groups]; (6) or some combination of these.[3]

The first response, calling the police, has not been a favored choice among
women for many reasons, including unproductive disinterest on the part of the
police. As an early illustration, Pleck (1979) has shown that, while wife beating
was illegal in most states by 1870, the criminal justice system was more likely
activated by (1979:67) "the victims themselves and the prosecuting attorneys"
than by actions of the police. She hypothesized, on the basis of data from the
city of Baltimore in the late nineteenth century, that severe state criminal statutes
for dealing with abuses may actually have deterred officers from arresting wife
abusers (Maryland law authorized whipping and a year in jail at the time). The
era in question was one of reform against domestic violence (that is, the second
reform period of 1874 to 1890). Wife abuse was considered morally reprehen-
sible, which produced social reactions on the part of intervenors who were not
associated with the justice system. These ranged from moral condemnation by
clergymen to severe beatings and the uses of tar and feathers by such vigilante
groups as the Ku Klux Klan.

A picture of the handling of wife abuse in modern policing has been provided
by Black (1980). His analysis was based on systematic observation of police

behavior in three major cities supplemented by more restricted observation in a fourth city. The general attitude of police officers for those settings is reflected in the following statement (Black 1980: 117): "Often the police intentionally dally in route to 'family trouble' calls, hoping that the conflict will be resolved—at least superficially—by the time they arrive."

Despite the fact that disputes between married couples are likely to be the most violent type of disturbance call, the police were more likely to be conciliatory than coercive and legalistic in that context. Black concludes (1980: 164), "when the parties are intimately related, in most cases neither the police nor the complainant wants the alleged offender to be arrested. . . . The police . . . tend to be neutral, and to do little or nothing to settle the dispute." A similar pattern of response by the police to situations of domestic violence was reported by Parnas (1967), Truninger (1971), Field and Field (1973), Langley and Levy (1978), Paterson (1979), and others, without, however, the solid empirical basis of the data used by Black (1980, see particularly pp. 69–70 and 111–113). See also Berk and Loseke (1981) and Worden and Pollitz (1984) for the results of studies aimed at evaluating the effects of situational characteristics on police arrest practices in domestic disturbances and Ferraro (1988) for discussion of the continuing role of police discretion when a presumptive arrest policy is implemented.

In accordance with the high expectations in the 1960s and early 1970s that the social sciences would contribute to the solution of the ongoing problems of society, a significant effort was made to enhance the social service aspect of police response.[4] An early effort in that direction was Bard's project (1969, 1970, 1971) in which officers of the New York Police Department were trained in family crisis intervention (see also Bard and Zacker 1971, 1976, and Bard and Connolly 1978). Training included lectures, workshops, and role-playing in simulated crisis situations. During a twenty-one-month trial period, the Family Crisis Intervention Unit (as the group of officers was called) participated in 1,375 interventions with 962 families. Bard described the success of the unit in general terms, but others (see for example Liebman and Schwartz 1973; Driscoll, Meyer, and Schanie 1973; Sherman and Berk 1984) have expressed doubts about the degree of success on the basis of details in his final project report. Nevertheless, Bard's approach was repeated in places like Louisville, Kentucky, using essentially the same model, and in northern California with important modifications (see Driscoll, Meyer, and Schanie 1973; Liebman and Schwartz 1973). Other counseling and helping approaches to police crisis intervention that became significant nationally were the use of police–social worker teams in Illinois and Rhode Island and the availability to the police of specially trained volunteer-citizens in Arizona (see Michaels and Treger 1973; Treger 1975; Burnett, Carr, Sinapi, and Taylor 1976; Carr 1979, 1982).

Consciousness-Raising and Changes in Direction

Efforts to enhance the operation of the criminal justice system by policy implementation derived from social theory, including special police training and police–social service teams, may be characterized as soft approaches. As the 1970s advanced, many began to object to soft approaches in the criminal justice system in general and its use in spousal (wife) abuse specifically. Both the women's and the victims' rights movements were particularly vocal in their support of a more punitive approach by the system. Their perspective is summarized in statements that the police put "too much emphasis on the social work aspect [of wife abuse] and not enough on the criminal" (Langley and Levy 1977:218) and "Through arrest, deterrence of the violent man is immediate" (Stanko 1989). The emotional context in which those developments and that emphasis occurred is reflected in the following comments about marital relationships from books on wife abuse written by feminists: "The modern marriage contract still obliges the husband to render to his wife the basic necessities of food, clothing, and shelter, just as slave owners had to provide those necessities to their slaves under the southern slave codes! The wife is still required to render unpaid labor and sexual services, much as slaves were required to do" (Fleming 1979:1). "The married woman's loss of identity begins with the loss of name" (Martin 1976:37). "The bride who was catered to before marriage becomes the caterer after marriage" (Martin 1976:39). It is hardly surprising to find that writers with attitudes of that sort were not warm and sympathetic in their recommendations for dealing with males who abuse wives even beyond the normal abuse expected in master-slave relationships.

Discussions of the victims' rights movement; its lobbying efforts to increase the severity of penalties against offenders, including mandatory arrest and mandatory prison sentences; and some of the results of that lobbying may be found in Carrington (1977a, b), Galaway and Hudson (1981), and Karmen (1984).

As a result of the diverse array of consciousness-raising efforts with such themes, wife abusers joined the ranks of child molesters in terms of popular hatred, and there emerged the need for vengeance that generally goes with that feeling. Interestingly, many who continued to advocate softer approaches to criminals in general made dramatic exceptions in the case of wife abusers, as is often (too often) the case when hatred and the need for vengeance become uppermost.

The raised consciousness that resulted from the vigorous advocacy led to lawsuits against the New York (see *Bruno v. Codd*, 90 Misc 2d 1047, 1976, for decisions regarding special issues in the litigation) and Oakland police departments for failing to arrest and to further the prosecution of wife abusers. Similar suits were filed in other states, including *Thurman et al. v. City of Torrington*, 595 F. Supp. 1521 (Conn. 1984), which resulted in the award of $2.3 million to a woman denied police protection from disabling assaults by her husband. See Eppler (1986), Woods (1986), and Buzawa and Buzawa (1990) for discussions of such suits, their legal justifications, and their impacts on policing.

The same vigor was used in changing state laws to facilitate arrest, prosecution, and punishment. The California legislature, for example, created a separate section of the state's Penal Code in 1977 devoted to abuse of a cohabiting partner (West's Annotated California Penal Code § 273.5). Prior to that enactment, spousal abuse and child abuse were components of the same section of the code (§ 273d). That new section, with amendments in 1980 and 1985, made it a felony, punishable for up to four years in the state prison, to inflict upon a cohabiting person a "corporal injury resulting in a traumatic condition." A "traumatic condition" was defined in the code as "a condition of the body, such as a wound or external or internal injury, whether of a minor or serious nature, caused by a physical force." Some police departments, incidentally, including the one in San Francisco, have interpreted "traumatic condition" to include "extreme mental anguish," making behavior leading to that psychological condition a felony. As another example of changes in law furthering criminalization, in 1986 the state of Connecticut (in which the city of Torrington is located) enacted the following [West's Connecticut General Statutes Annotated § 46b–38b (a)]:

Whenever a peace officer determines upon speedy information that a family violence crime [including "physical harm" and "an act of threatened violence that constitutes fear of imminent physical harm"] has been committed within his jurisdiction, he shall arrest the person or persons suspected of its commission and charge such person or persons with an appropriate crime. The decision to arrest and charge shall not (1) be dependent on the specific consent of the victim, (2) consider the relationship of the parties, or (3) be based solely on a request by the victim.

To emphasize the spirit of the era reflecting the desire to treat spousal abusers harshly, consider the contrast between the law of Connecticut and the following recommendation thirteen years earlier from the *Standards Relating to the Urban Police Function* of the American Bar Association (1973:12). The police should "engage in the resolution of conflict such as that which occurs so frequently between husband and wife . . . in the highly-populated sections of the large city, without reliance upon criminal assault or disorderly conduct statutes."

It is perhaps of passing interest to emphasize, in concluding, that an important component of the early advocacy of harsher treatment for wife abusers was the argument that they should be treated by the criminal justice system exactly as it treats equally violent offenders against strangers. That is no more than one would expect on Constitutional grounds. When the balance shifted in the other direction, as in the laws of California and Connecticut and in judicial decisions, making assaultive behavior within domestic circumstances a special category subject to more vigorous control and sanctioning, those arguments no longer appeared. In short, the arguments of such advocates for equality of treatment in all cases of assault, whether occurring in the home or on the streets, stopped abruptly when the system called for treating wife abusers more harshly than assaulters in stranger violence. The following illustrates the type of reasoning used to justify differential treatment (*People v. Gutierrez*, 171 Cal. App. 3d at 952, 1985):

Some other offenses do require higher degrees of harm to be inflicted before the crime denounced by them is committed: felony battery, section 243, subdivision (d), requires "serious bodily injury" and felony assault, section 245, subdivision (a), requires "force likely to produce great bodily injury." But, the Legislature has clothed persons of the opposite sex in intimate relationships with greater protection by requiring less harm to be inflicted before the offense is committed. Those special relationships form a rational distinction which has a substantial relation to the purpose of the statute.

NOTES

1. Though emphasizing two forces for consciousness-raising in this chapter, we recognize that social changes result from a complex interplay of many factors. In the Introduction to this book and in Buzawa and Buzawa (1985), for example, there are descriptions of the disparate forces such as the defense bar, the police, and women's advocacy groups that produced the compromise legislation aimed at controlling spousal abuse in the late 1970s and early 1980s. The directed emphasis in this chapter (and the following chapter), however, is consistent with the position of Pleck (1987:4), in her discussion of the three reform movements against family violence in American history, that "Reform against family violence has mainly occurred as a response to social and political conditions, or social movements. . . . " Moreover, it has been our goal to highlight the emotional component of the social movement in order to provide a context for understanding the almost blind acceptance of the inadequate research discussed in the next chapter.

2. An interesting discussion of the relationship between power and abuse within families of the ancient world may be found in Pleck (1987). She points out that the husband and father in that era was the head of household, with authority to force obedience from his wife and children that included a "right of correction." Moreover (1987:9), "A mother whose power to punish was delegated by her husband, could also use force in disciplining her children." That led to the connection between power and abuse in the following way (1987:9): "Although abuse has always been separate from correction, the right of discipline has served as a justification for virtually all forms of assault by parents and husbands short of those that cause permanent injury."

3. Pleck (1987), like several other humanists and feminists, argues that the programs available in support of those courses of action have not been and cannot be effective in eliminating or even significantly reducing family violence, except perhaps in mild cases. She advocates, instead, the strengthening of "alternatives to the traditional family." Her position (1987:203)

demands social services on a scale far larger than the public appears willing to support. A Swedish-style welfare state, though perhaps needed, is impractical, at least for the present conservative moment. . . . Nonetheless, these remedies are far more important than 24-hour hot lines and public awareness campaigns. Many more resources should go into strengthening alternatives to the family and many fewer into "prevention" programs of dubious utility.

4. Those high expectations led to such other grand efforts during that era as pretrial intervention and diversion for even serious offenders. See, for example, Rovner-Pieczenik 1974 and Lemert 1971.

REFERENCES

American Bar Association Project on Standards for Criminal Justice, Approved Draft. 1973. *Standards Relating to the Urban Police Function.* New York: Institute of Judicial Administration.

Ariès, Philippe. 1962. *Centuries of Childhood: A Social History of Family Life,* trans. by Robert Baldick. New York: Vintage.

Bard, Morton. 1969. Family Intervention Police Teams as a Community Mental Health Resource. *Journal of Criminal Law, Criminology, and Police Science* 60(2):247–50.

———. 1970. *Training Police as Specialists in Family Crisis Intervention.* National Institute of Law Enforcement; and Criminal Justice, Department of Justice. Washington, D.C.: U.S. Government Printing Office.

———. 1971. The Role of Law Enforcement in the Helping System. *Community Mental Health Journal* 7:151–60.

Bard, Morton, and Harriet Connolly. 1978. The Police and Family Violence: Police and Practice. In *Battered Women: Issues of Public Policy.* Washington, D.C.: U.S. Commission on Civil Rights.

Bard, Morton, and Joseph Zacker. 1971. The Prevention of Family Violence: Dilemmas of Community Intervention. *Journal of Marriage and the Family* 33:677–82.

———. 1976. *The Police and Interpersonal Conflict: Third-party Intervention Approaches.* Washington, D.C.: The Police Foundation.

Berk, Sarah F., and Donileen R. Loseke. 1981. Handling Family Violence: Situational Determinants of Police Arrest in Domestic Disturbances. *Law and Society Review* 15:315–46.

Berlyne, D. E. 1967. Arousal and Reinforcement. In D. Levine, ed., *Nebraska Symposium on Motivation: 1967.* Lincoln: University of Nebraska Press.

Black, Donald J. 1980. *The Manners and Customs of the Police.* New York: Academic Press.

Blackstone, Sir William. 1884. *Commentaries on the Laws of England,* vol. 1, 3d ed., revised. Chicago: Callaghan and Company.

Bowker, Lee H. 1983. *Beating Wife-Beating.* Lexington, Mass.: Lexington Books.

Burnett, Bruce B., John J. Carr, John Sinapi, and Roy Taylor. 1976. Police and Social Workers in a Community Outreach Program. *Social Casework* 57:41–49.

Bushnell, Horace. 1947. *Christian Nature.* New Haven, Conn.: Yale University Press.

Buzawa, Eve S., and Carl G. Buzawa. 1985. Legislative Trends in the Criminal Justice Response to Domestic Violence. In Alan J. Lincoln and Murray A. Straus, eds., *Crime and the Family.* Springfield, Ill.: Charles Thomas.

———. 1990. *Domestic Violence: The Criminal Justice Response.* Newbury Park, Calif.: Sage.

Calvert, Robert. 1974. Criminal and Civil Liability in Husband-Wife Assaults. In Suzanne K. Steinmetz and Murray A. Straus, eds., *Violence in the Family*. New York: Dodd, Mead.

Carlson, Bonnie E. 1977. Battered Women and Their Assailants. *Social Work* 22:455–60.

Carr, John J. 1979. An Administrative Retrospective on Police Crisis Teams. *Social Casework* 60:416–22.

———. 1982. Treating Family Abuse Using a Police Crisis Team Approach. In Maria Roy, ed., *The Abusive Partner: An Analysis of Domestic Battering*. New York: Van Nostrand Reinhold.

Carrington, Frank. 1977a. Victims' Rights Litigation: A Wave of the Future? *University of Richmond Law Review* 11:447–70.

———. 1977b. *The Victims*. New Rochelle, N.Y.: Arlington House.

de Mause, Lloyd. 1975. The Evolution of Childhood. In Lloyd de Mause, ed., *The History of Childhood*. New York: Harper Torchbooks.

Demos, John. 1970. *A Little Commonwealth: Family Life in Plymouth Colony*. New York: Oxford University Press.

Dobash, R. Emerson, and Russell P. Dobash. 1977–78. Wives: The "Appropriate" Victims of Marital Violence. *Victimology* 2:426–42.

———. 1979. *Violence Against Wives: A Case Against the Patriarchy*. New York: Free Press.

Driscoll, James M., Robert G. Meyer, and Charles F. Schanie. 1973. Training Police in Family Crisis Intervention. *Journal of Applied Behavioral Science* 9:62–82.

Ehrlich, J. W. 1959. *Ehrlich's Blackstone*. San Carlos, Calif.: Nourse Publishing.

Eppler, Amy. 1986. Battered Women and the Equal Protection Clause: Will the Constitution Help Them When the Police Won't? *Yale Law Journal* 95:788–809.

Ferraro, Kathleen J. 1988. The Legal Response to Woman Battering in the United States. In Jalna Hanmer, Jill Radford, and Elizabeth A. Stanko, eds., *Women, Policing, and Male Violence: International Perspectives*. London: Routledge.

Field, Martha H., and Henry F. Field. 1973. Marital Violence and the Criminal Process: Neither Justice nor Peace. *Social Service Review* 47:221–40.

Fields, Marjory D. 1977. Wife-Beating: Facts and Figures. *Victimology* 2:643–47.

Fleming, Jennifer B. 1979. *Stopping Wife Abuse: A Guide to the Emotional, Psychological, and Legal Implications for the Abused Woman and Those Helping Her*. Garden City, N.Y.: Anchor Press/Doubleday.

Galaway, Burt, and Joe Hudson, eds. 1981. *Perspectives on Crime Victims*. St Louis: CV Mosby.

Gaquin, Deidre A. 1977–78. Spouse Abuse: Data from the National Crime Survey. *Victimology* 2:632–43.

Gayford, Jasper J. 1975. Wife Battering: A Preliminary Survey of 100 Cases. *British Medical Journal* 1:194–97.

———. 1976. Ten Types of Battered Wives. *Welfare Officer* 25(1):5–9.

———. 1979. The Aetiology of Repeated Serious Assaults by Husbands on Wives (Wife Beating). *Medicine, Science and the Law* 19:19–24.

Gelles, Richard J. 1976. Abused Wives: Why Do They Stay? *Journal of Marriage and the Family* 38:659–68.

———. 1978. Violence toward Children in the United States. *American Journal of Orthopsychiatry* 48:580–92.

————. 1979. *Family Violence*. Beverly Hills, Calif.: Sage.

————. 1987. *Family Violence*, 2d ed. Newbury Park, Calif.: Sage.

Gelles, Richard J., and Claire P. Cornell. 1985. *Intimate Violence*. Beverly Hills, Calif.: Sage.

Gelles, Richard J., and Murray A. Straus. 1988. *Intimate Violence*. New York: Simon and Schuster.

Goode, William J. 1971. Force and Violence in the Family. *Journal of Marriage and the Family* 33:624–36.

Gough, Kathleen. 1971. The Origin of the Family. *Journal of Marriage and the Family* 33:760–70.

House, Robert J., and Jitendra Singh. 1987. Organizational Behavior: Some New Directions for I/O Psychology. In Mark R. Rosenzweig and Lyman W. Porter, eds., *Annual Review of Psychology*. Palo Alto, Calif.: Annual Reviews, Inc.

Karmen, Andrew. 1984. *Crime Victims: An Introduction to Victimology*. Pacific Grove, Calif.: Brooks/Cole.

Kempe, Henry, Frederick Silverman, Brandt Steele, William Droegemueller, and Henry Silver. 1962. The Battered Child Syndrome. *Journal of the American Medical Association* 181(1):17–24.

Langley, Roger, and Richard C. Levy. 1977. *Wife Beating: The Silent Crisis*. New York: E. P. Dutton.

————. 1978. Wife Abuse and the Police Response. *FBI Law Enforcement Bulletin* 47(5):4–9.

Lemert, Edwin. 1971. *Instead of Court: Diversion in Juvenile Justice*. Washington, D.C.: U.S. Government Printing Office.

Liebman, Donald A., and Jeffrey A. Schwartz. 1973. Police Programs in Domestic Crisis Intervention: A Review. In John R. Snibbe and Homa M. Snibbe, eds., *The Urban Policeman in Transition*. Springfield, Ill.: Charles C. Thomas.

Martin, Del. 1976. *Battered Wives*. San Francisco: Glide Publications.

————. 1978. In *Battered Women: Issues of Public Policy*. U.S. Commission on Civil Rights. Washington, D.C.: U.S. Government Printing Office.

Masumura, Wilfred T. 1979. Wife Abuse and Other Forms of Aggression. *Victimology* 4:46–59.

McClelland, David C. 1985. *Human Motivation*. Glenview, Ill.: Scott, Foresman.

Mead, Margaret. 1953. The Impact of Cultural Changes on the Family. In *The Family in the Urban Community*. Detroit, Mich.: The Merrill-Palmer School.

Michaels, Rhoda A., and Harvey Treger. 1973. Social Work in Police Departments. *Social Work* 18:67–75.

Muncie, John. 1984. *"The Trouble with Kids Today": Youth and Crime in Post-War Britain*. London: Hutchinson.

Murdock, George P. 1949. *Social Structure*. New York: Macmillan.

NiCarthy, Ginny, Karen Merriam, and Sandra Coffman. 1984. *Talking It Out: A Guide to Groups for Abused Women*. Seattle, Wash.: The Seal Press.

O'Brien, John E. 1971. Violence in Divorce Prone Families. *Journal of Marriage and the Family* 33:692–98.

Okun, Lewis. 1986. *Woman Abuse: Facts Replacing Myths*. Albany, N.Y.: State University of New York Press.

Pagelow, Mildred D. 1981. *Woman-Battering: Victims and Their Experiences*. Beverly Hills, Calif.: Sage.

————. 1984. *Family Violence*. New York: Praeger.

Parnas, Raymond I. 1967. The Police Response to the Domestic Disturbance. *Wisconsin Law Review* (Fall):914–60.

Paterson, Eva J. 1979. How the Legal System Responds to Battered Women. In Donna M. Moore, ed., *Battered Women*. Beverly Hills, Calif.: Sage.

Perkin, Joan. 1989. *Women and Marriage in Nineteenth Century England*. London: Routledge.

Pleck, Elizabeth. 1979. Wife Beating in Nineteenth Century America. *Victimology* 4:60–74.

————. 1987. *Domestic Tyranny: The Making of Social Policy Against Family Violence from Colonial Times to the Present*. New York: Oxford.

————. 1989. Criminal Approaches to Family Violence 1640–1980. In Lloyd Ohlin and M. Tonry, eds., *Crime and Justice: A Review of Research*, vol 11. Chicago: University of Chicago Press.

Pollock, Sir Frederick, and Frederic W. Maitland. 1909. *The History of English Law*, vol. 1. *Before the Time of Edward I*, 2d ed. Cambridge: The University Press.

Redfield, Robert. 1947. The Folk Society. *American Journal of Sociology* 52:293–308.

Rounsaville, Bruce J. 1978. Theories in Marital Violence: Evidence from a Study of Battered Women. *Victimology* 3:11–31.

Rovner-Pieczenik, R. 1974. *Pretrial Intervention Strategies: An Evaluation of Policy-Related Research and Policymaker Perceptions*. Washington, D.C.. National Pretrial Intervention Service Center, American Bar Association, Commission on Correctional Facilities.

Sherman, Lawrence W., and Richard A. Berk. 1984. *The Minneapolis Domestic Violence Experiment: Police Foundation Reports*, 1. Washington, D.C.: Police Foundation.

Shorter, Edward. 1975. *The Making of the Modern Family*. New York: Basic Books.

Stanko, Elizabeth A. 1989. Missing the Mark? Policing Battering. In Jalna Hanmer, Jill Radford, and Elizabeth A. Stanko (eds.), *Women, Policing, and Male Violence: International Perspectives*. London: Routledge.

Star, Barbara. 1978. Comparing Battered and Nonbattered Women. *Victimology* 3:32–42.

Stetson, Dorothy M. 1982. *A Woman's Issue: The Politics of Family Law Reform in England*. Westport, Conn.: Greenwood Press.

Stone, Lawrence. 1975. The Rise of the Nuclear Family in Early Modern England: The Patriarchal Stage. In Charles E. Rosenberg, ed., *The Family in History*. Philadelphia: University of Pennsylvania Press.

Straus, Murray A. 1978. Wife-Abuse: How Common and Why? *Victimology* 2:499–509.

Straus, Murray A., Richard J. Gelles, and Suzanne R. Steinmetz. 1980. *Behind Closed Doors: Violence in the American Family*. Garden City, N.Y.: Anchor Press/Doubleday.

Treger, Harvey. 1975. *The Police-Social Work Team: A New Model for Interprofessional Cooperation*. Springfield, Ill.: Thomas.

Truninger, Elizabeth. 1971. Marital Violence: The Legal Solutions. *Hastings Law Journal* 23:259–76.

Watson, Alan. 1970. *The Law of the Ancient Romans*. Dallas, Tex.: Southern Methodist University Press.

Whitehurst, Robert M. 1971. Violence Potential in Extramarital Sexual Responses. *Journal of Marriage and the Family* 33:683–91.

Whitelock, Dorothy. 1979. *English Historical Documents. c. 500–1042*, 2d ed. London: Eyre Methuen.

Woods, Laurie. 1986. *Resource List: Battered Women: Litigation*. New York: National Center on Women and Family Law.

Worden, Robert E., and Alissa A. Pollitz. 1984. Police Arrests in Domestic Disturbances: A Further Look. *Law and Society Review* 18:105–19.

Zimmerman, Carle C. 1947. *Family and Civilization*. New York: Harper and Row.

LEGAL CASES

Bruno v. Codd, 90 Misc 2d 1047, 1979.

Michigan Department of State Police v. Sitz, 110 S. Ct. 2481, 1990.

People v. Gutierrez, 171 Cal. App. 3d 944, 1985.

Thurman v. City of Torrington, 595 F. Supp. 1521, 1984.

2

BATTERING AND THE CRIMINAL JUSTICE SYSTEM: A FEMINIST VIEW

Demie Kurz

Demie Kurz acknowledges that since 1970 there have been major attempts to reform the reaction of the criminal justice system to violence among intimates. Legislation has extended police powers and increased available penalties for violence in a family setting. Similarly, administrative policies such as presumptive arrest have been widely adopted.

Despite such good-faith efforts, Kurz finds that many of these efforts are flawed. At their core, they implicitly rely on a gender-neutral "family violence" approach. Kurz finds that this attention to "spouse abuse," while well developed in the literature, masks the continuing reality of the inequality between males and females. Failure to realize that most serious family violence occurs against women denies its systematic, predictable nature. This omission in turn inappropriately focusses research attention and administrative action upon the individual and social pathology of the offenders and often of the victims. As a result, the systematic denial of the victimization of women as a class continues, and efforts to "reform" the system will predictably fail.

Kurz's analysis of the actual implementation of a "presumptive arrest" policy in Phoenix as developed in a study undertaken by Kathleen Ferraro illustrates what she believes is likely to happen when a nominally proactive gender-neutral policy conflicts with organizational expectations, inertia, and the patriarchal policies of many police departments. Finally, Kurz provides a valuable contrast in reporting how police and court reforms sponsored by the battered women's movement and the police led to implementation of serious reforms.

In reviewing such policies, we need further research to see whether the key variables are the department's attitudes toward the "service function" of policing leadership's enforcement of such innovations or the unusual interactions between the police and the battered women's movement.

In the 1970s, the battered women's movement brought to public attention the fact that an estimated 1.5 million wives are injured each year by husbands (Straus et al. 1980) and 1.5 million single, separated, and divorced women are injured by male intimates (Rosenberg et al. 1985). Since that time, supporters from within the criminal justice system have helped to bring about a variety of reforms, including legislation increasing police powers and criminal penalties against abusers (Attorney General's Task Force 1984; Buzawa and Buzawa 1990; Schecter 1982; Tierney 1982). These reformers argue that, because the criminal justice system has broader powers than any other institution to enforce laws and take action against batterers, it is a strategic place for change.

The subject of this chapter is, Will these reforms be effective? Will they be successfully implemented? Will they reduce the amount of battering? These are obviously complex questions. Many things are necessary for successful criminal justice intervention on behalf of battered women. In this chapter I argue that, along with whatever else is necessary to implement an effective response to battering, the criminal justice system needs to adopt reforms that incorporate a feminist perspective on battering. A feminist view of battering is one based on an understanding of battering as a structural problem in which it is women, primarily, who are abused by men. I believe that such a view must be adopted throughout the criminal justice system in order to bring about effective interventions. I argue that at present the criminal justice system does not have a feminist view of battering, but rather operates with a view that I call a "family violence" view.

In the first section of this chapter I compare a feminist view of what I call "battering" with a family violence view. I demonstrate why I think a feminist view of battering is more accurate than a family violence view, which is because it accurately locates the origins of the problem in male-female relationships and in norms about men's right to control women. I argue that the family violence perspective errs in viewing battering as similar to other types of violence in the family. This perspective also directs attention away from women as the victims of domestic violence and encourages "family solutions" to problems.

In the second section of this chapter I analyze a case study of an important new reform, a presumptive arrest policy. This case study, conducted by Ferraro (1989), presents data showing that the reform did not achieve its goal of significantly increasing arrests. I present this case as an example of how, in the absence of a consistently applied, strongly enforced feminist view of battering, reforms will have difficulty responding to battering or aiding its victims. In the final section of the chapter, I suggest what types of reforms in the criminal justice system would promote a feminist response to battering, that is, one consistent with the analysis of battering as a problem of men's control of women.

SOCIAL SCIENCE PERSPECTIVES ON WIFE ABUSE

In this section I examine two major social science perspectives on the study of physical abuse of husbands and wives. One perspective will be referred to here as the family violence approach, after the name used by proponents. Those who take this perspective view violence between husbands and wives, which they call "spouse abuse," as part of a pattern of violence occurring among all family members (Gelles 1974, 1979, 1983, 1985; Gelles and Straus 1988; Straus 1980a, 1980b, 1980c; Straus et al. 1980). The other perspective is called here a feminist approach. Feminists place male-female relations at the center of their analysis and view inequality between men and women as a key factor in violence (Bowker 1986; Dobash and Dobash 1979; Pagelow 1987; Russell 1982; Stanko 1985; Stark, Flitcraft, and Frazier 1979; Yllo 1988).

I will compare the basic premises, methodology, and conclusions of these two perspectives with respect to their views of women and gender. I argue that each perspective treats women differently and therefore each has consequences for our understanding of physical abuse of women by male intimates. While both perspectives emphasize the importance of women's subordinate position in creating violence, family violence researchers believe it is only one of several contributing factors. For feminist writers, women's subordination is central in their analyses of violence. After comparing the two perspectives, I argue that the feminist perspective portrays the realities of battering more accurately.

The Family Violence Perspective

Straus, Gelles, and Steinmetz have published the largest body of social science research on domestic violence (see Gelles 1974, 1979, 1983, 1985; Gelles and Straus 1988; Steinmetz 1977, 1977–78; Straus 1973, 1976, 1979, 1980a, 1980b, 1980c; Straus and Gelles 1986; Straus et al. 1980). They began to research in this area soon after the battered women's movement brought the issue to public attention, and they have been substantially funded by the U.S. National Institutes of Mental Health. They have trained many researchers, and their methodology has been used by researchers in different parts of the United States (Straus and Gelles 1986:470).

Both the theoretical approach of these researchers and their data lead them to name the problem family violence. They believe that all family members carry out and are victims of violence. They base their claims on data showing an equivalent amount of violence committed by both husbands and wives toward each other, physical violence of parents toward children and children toward elders, and sibling abuse (Straus 1979, 1980c, 1983). As will be described, they believe family violence originates in wider social norms condoning violence and in the structure of the contemporary family.

Straus, Gelles, and Steinmetz have written extensively on the topic of violence between male and female intimates, which they call "spouse abuse." Their research findings and conclusions about spouse abuse are based on data they have collected with the Conflict Tactics Scales (CTS), an instrument that asks one member of a couple, drawn from a random sample of married people composed of an equal number of men and women, to fill out a form indicating whether and how many times he or she performed specific actions during the previous 12 months (Straus 1979). This survey instrument asks about conflicts between husbands and wives in the previous year and measures conflict resolution on a continuum from nonviolent tactics (calm discussion) to the most violent tactics (use of a knife or gun).

Using this scale, Straus et al. (1980:36) obtain the following results: 12.8 percent of the husbands direct acts of violence toward their wives, and 11.7 percent of the wives direct acts of violence toward their husbands. According to Straus et al. (1980:36), whereas "traditionally men have been considered more aggressive and violent than women," looking at the couples in which the husband was the only one to use violence and those in which both used violence, "the most common situation was that in which both used violence." Of those couples reporting any violence, 49 percent were in situations in which both were violent. For the year previous to the study, a comparison of the number of couples in which only the wife was violent shows the figures to be very close: 27 percent of the husbands committed violent acts compared with 24 percent of the wives (1980:37).

On the basis of this study, a member of the research team concluded that there was a battered husband syndrome, which had not previously been recognized and which deserved attention (Steinmetz 1977–78). Feminist researchers (Berk et al. 1983; Dobash and Dobash 1979; Pleck et al. 1977–78; Russell 1982) criticized this syndrome for its failure to measure how much of women's violence was in self-defense or who was injured by the violence. These criticisms will be described in more detail in the next section. However, ten years later, Straus and Gelles (1986) repeated the survey with almost no change in the methodology. This time they found an increase in violence on the part of wives. They again conclude, "The violence rates . . . reveal an important and distressing finding about violence in American families—that in marked contrast to the behavior of women outside the family, women are about as violent within the family as men" (1986:470).

Straus et al. conclude that violence is an all-pervasive feature of family life. Their analysis, as well as their use of the terms family violence and spouse abuse, rather than battering or wife abuse, indicate that it is the family, not the relationship between women and men, which is their central unit of analysis (Gelles 1985; Gelles and Straus 1988).

A fundamental solution to the problem of wife-beating has to go beyond a concern with how to control assaulting husbands. It seems as if violence is built into the very structure of the society and family system itself. . . . It (wife-beating) is only one aspect of the general pattern of family violence, which includes parent-child violence, child-to-child violence, and wife-to-husband violence. (1980:44)

Straus et al. (1980), Gelles (1985), and Gelles and Straus (1988) isolate three causes of violence in the contemporary American family. First is the structure of the family. They believe that the contemporary American family is subject to serious stresses from difficult working conditions, unemployment, financial insecurity, and health problems, which cause family members to be violent to one another. This structural proclivity to violence is exacerbated by the large amount of privacy accorded the contemporary American family, privacy that allows family violence to go unchecked by outside scrutiny or control (Gelles 1985; Gelles and Straus 1988).

Second, these authors believe that the family, borrowing from the society at large, accepts violence as a means of solving conflict. They see evidence of the cultural acceptance of violence in television programming, folklore, and fairy tales (Straus 1980b) and in surveys showing widespread public acceptance of violence. In their own survey, one of four wives and one of three husbands thought that "a couple slapping one another was at least somewhat necessary, normal, and good" (Gelles and Straus 1988:27).

Straus et al. also frequently cite sexism as a factor in family violence and believe that there are some differences in the violent behavior and experiences of women and men. They state that despite the high rate of violence by wives, "It would be a great mistake if that fact distracted us from giving first attention to wives as victims as the focus of social policy" (1980:43). The reasons they give are the following: (1) Husbands have higher rates of the most dangerous and injurious forms of violence. (2) Because men are physically stronger, women may be more seriously injured than men. (3) Husbands repeat their violent acts more than wives do. (4) Some of the women's acts of violence may be in self-defense. (5) There are many acts of violence toward pregnant women, and thus the fetus or unborn child is in danger also. (6) For economic and social reasons women have fewer alternatives to staying in a violent situation than do men. In other words, women are as responsible as men for causing violence; but because women are more victimized by violence, they deserve some special consideration.

Straus et al. also state that the sexist organization of society and its family system is one of the fundamental factors in the high level of wife beating, and they cite the power of men over women, at the societal level and in the family, as a cause of violence. They claim that "violence is used by the most powerful family member as a means of legitimizing his or her dominant position" (1980:193). After dividing families into those that are "wife dominant," those that are "husband dominant," and those that are "democratic," Straus et al. conclude that wives are more likely to be beaten in homes in which power is concentrated in the hands of the husbands and that similarly, husbands are more likely to be beaten by their wives in wife-dominant homes. They claim that the least amount of battering occurs in democratic households. They conclude, "It seems that violence is used by the most powerful family member as a means of legitimizing his or her dominant position. Even less powerful members of the family tend to rely on violence as a reaction to their own lack of participation in the family decision-making process" (1980:193). Thus, while Straus et al.

raise the issue of the use of power by husbands and wives, they assume that power can be held equally by a wife or a husband.

The policy recommendations of Straus et al. follow from their perspective. To reduce violence in the home, they recommend changing norms that legitimize and glorify violence in society and in the family. They suggest public-awareness campaigns, gun control, abolition of the death penalty and corporal punishment, and the reduction of violence in the media. They also recommend reducing violence-provoking stresses created by society, such as unemployment, underemployment, and poverty. They advocate integrating families into a network of kin and community and the provision of adequate health and dental care. Finally, in keeping with their view of marital inequality as a factor in family violence, they recommend changing the sexist character of society and the family (Straus et al. 1980; see also Gelles and Straus 1988).

The Feminist Perspective

Some work by feminist researchers on violence, such as the Dobash and Dobash book *Violence against Wives* (1979), has become influential and well-known; and feminist social scientists are frequently cited in scholarly and popular sources. Feminist social scientists focus on a variety of substantive issues and themes; however, they make certain common assumptions that challenge the family violence perspective (Bowker 1986; Pagelow 1981; Russell 1982; Stanko 1985; Stark, Flitcraft, and Frazier 1979).

First, for acts of violence in heterosexual couples, feminist researchers argue against the claim that men and women engage in equal amounts of violence. They argue that data proving such an equivalence of violence, particularly data based on the CTS, are flawed. The scale does not ask what acts were done in self-defense, who initiated the violence, or who was injured. In their view, the validity of the scale is undermined because the continuum of violence in the scale is so broad that it fails to discriminate among very different kinds of violence (Dobash and Dobash 1979; Stark and Flitcraft 1985). If these questions were asked, the picture would be clear: Overwhelmingly, men abuse women (Breines and Gordon 1983; Brush 1990; Dobash and Dobash 1979; Gubman and Newton 1983; Pleck et al. 1977–78; Russell 1982; Saunders 1988). These researchers believe that when women engage in acts of violence, they do it primarily in self-defense. Other criticisms of the CTS include its failure to question the validity of data based on self-reporting and male-female differences in self-reporting; men are more likely to underreport the extent of their violent acts than women are.

Feminist researchers support their point of view with official crime statistics and data from the criminal justice system and hospitals. The National Crime Survey of 1982 reported that 91 percent of all violent crimes between spouses were directed at women by husbands or ex-husbands, while only 5 percent were directed at husbands by wives or ex-wives (cited in Browne 1987:7). Analyzing police records from Scotland, Dobash and Dobash (1979) found that, when gender was known, women were targets in 94 percent and offenders in 3 percent of cases. Also examining police records, Berk et al. (1983) found that in 94 to 95 percent of cases, it is the woman who gets injured and that, even when both partners are injured, the woman's injuries are nearly three times as severe as the man's. Data from hospitals (Kurz 1987; McLeer and Anwar 1989; Stark, Flitcraft, and Frazier 1979) show women to be overwhelmingly the injured party. These data challenge the existence of the battered husband syndrome (Pagelow 1985; Pleck et al. 1977–78).

Feminist researchers believe that men use violence as a way to control female partners, citing interview data from men and women that demonstrate that battering incidents occur when husbands try to make their wives comply with their wishes. Using data from interviews with 109 battered women, Dobash and Dobash (1979) demonstrate how, over the course of their marriages, batterers increasingly control wives through intimidation and isolation, findings confirmed by other interview studies (Pagelow 1981; Walker 1984). Violence, therefore, is just one of a variety of controls that men try to exercise over female partners; others are anger and psychological abuse (Adams 1988; Dobash and Dobash 1979; Mederos 1987). Interviews with batterers (Adams 1988; Dobash and Dobash 1979; Ptacek 1988) show that men believe they are justified in their use of violence by their wives' behavior or by what they feel are acceptable norms.

Second, feminist researchers point out that both historically and in the present, major institutions have permitted and condoned the use of physical abuse by husbands to control wives. In the United States, in the early nineteenth century, some state laws specifically approved wife beating. The first law in the United States to recognize a husband's right to control his wife with physical force was an 1824 ruling by the Supreme Court of Mississippi permitting the husband "to exercise the right of moderate chastisement in cases of great emergency" (quoted in Browne 1987:166). This and similar rulings that followed in court in Maryland and Massachusetts were based on English common law, which gave a husband the right of "correction" of his wife, although he was supposed to use it in moderation.

In 1871 wife beating was made illegal in Alabama. The court stated, "The privilege, ancient though it be, to beat her with a stick, to pull her hair, choke her, spit in her face or kick her about the floor, or to inflict upon her like indignities, is not now acknowledged by our law. . . . (T)he wife is entitled to the same protection of the law that the husband can invoke for himself" (quoted in Browne 1987:167).

A North Carolina court made a similar decision in 1874 but limited the kinds of cases in which the court should intervene: "If no permanent injury has been inflicted, nor malice, cruelty nor dangerous violence shown by the husband, it is better to draw the curtain, shut out the public gaze, and leave the parties to forget and forgive" (quoted in Browne 1987:167).

Until recent legal reforms were enacted, the "curtain rule" was widely used by the legal system to justify its nonintervention in wife-abuse cases. While the law and the nature of marriage have changed dramatically since the early twentieth century, feminists argue that important social and legal norms still support the use of violence against women as a means of control in marriage.

Despite the American ideology of spousal equality in contemporary marriage, feminists claim that marriage still institutionalizes the control of wives by husbands through the structure of husband-wife roles. As long as women are responsible for domestic work, child care, and emotional and psychological support and men's primary identity is that of provider and revolves around work, the husband has the more important status and also controls the majority of issues and decisions in the family. It is through such a system, coupled with the acceptance of physical force as a means of control, that, in the words of the Dobashes (1979), the wife becomes an "appropriate victim" of physical and psychological abuse. Feminists argue further that the use of violence for control in marriage is perpetuated not only through norms about a man's rights in marriage but through women's continued economic dependence on their husbands, which makes it difficult to leave a violent relationship. This dependence is increased by the lack of adequate child care and job training, which would enable women to get jobs with which they could support themselves.

Feminist policy recommendations are to make women more economically independent in order to give them alternatives to violent marriages (Dobash and Dobash 1979; Pagelow 1987; Stark, Flitcraft, and Frazier 1979). Feminists also favor reforms to make institutions more responsive to battered women and public education campaigns to arouse support for those reforms. Finally, feminists favor much stricter arrest and prosecution policies in the criminal justice system.

Some might argue that the two perspectives are relatively similar and have only minor differences of emphasis. For example, they could point to the fact that the family violence perspective focusses not only on stresses in the family and norms of violence in American culture, but on sexism as well. However, from a feminist perspective, the critical question of whether sexism is "a" factor or "the" factor at the root of violence reveals basic differences in assumptions about gender. One such difference is that family violence researchers use the family as their primary unit of analysis, while feminists place male-female relations at the center of their analysis. Family violence researchers make the assumption that, while not completely equal, American men and women have a fair amount of equality in marriage (Straus and Gelles 1986), while feminists believe that, in general, American women have fewer resources and less power than men. Finally, for family violence researchers, violence is the primary problem to be explained, while for feminists an equally important question is why women are overwhelmingly the targets of violence.

Feminists view the two approaches as significantly different because they believe that male dominance must be a central aspect of an analysis of violence in the family. When male dominance is not a central feature of the analysis, as in the family violence perspective, feminists believe that women come to be seen as one of several groups of victims, not particularly different from other victims of family violence. Feminists believe that comparing wife abuse to child abuse, elder abuse, and sibling abuse—as family violence researchers do—deflects attention from women. Some feminists (Russell 1982; Stanko 1985; Wardell, Gillespie, and Leffler 1983) argue that battering should be compared with related types of violence against women, such as rape, marital rape, sexual harassment, and incest, not just with other types of family violence. They argue that these acts of violence against women share common characteristics as products of male dominance.

Feminists believe that the decontextualized family violence perspective denies a central element of women's experience by deflecting attention from one of the key places where women's oppression occurs, in the family (Dobash and Dobash 1979; Breines and Gordon 1983; Russell 1988; Saunders 1988; Stark, Flitcraft, and Frazier 1979). As a result, feminists believe that the family violence perspective encourages individualistic explanations of the behavior of targets and aggressors. Similarly, while family violence researchers emphasize the social origins of the stress that they say is related to violence—stress resulting from unemployment, bad working conditions, and inadequate income and health care—the emphasis on coping with stress further suggests individual and family pathology. They also believe that research that identifies the problem of wife battering as one of family violence and spouse abuse contributes to society's denial of male violence against women (Breines and Gordon 1983; Dobash and Dobash 1979; Russell 1988).

The framework one chooses for investigating different types of violence in the family has serious implications for policy. Feminist scholars fear the family violence perspective contributes to the adoption of social policies that fail to address the inequality between women and men. They fear, for example, that practitioners will increasingly counsel battered women in an individualistic framework, advising them to solve their personal problems without taking into account the context of power in the family (Adams 1988; Stark, Flitcraft, and Frazier 1979). They fear that a family violence perspective encourages the criminal justice system to view this as a problem caused by both couples, by "family fights"; makes it easier for battering victims to be ignored in the criminal justice system; and increases the likelihood that couple counseling will take precedence over the prosecution of batterers.

THE CRIMINAL JUSTICE RESPONSE TO BATTERING

As noted, historically the legal view of battering was that it was a family problem and that the criminal justice system was to avoid becoming involved in this issue. Recently many reforms have been enacted which mandate the involvement of the criminal justice system in battering cases, including the widespread implementation of expedited arrest procedures, police training programs, protection orders, and victim support and advocacy programs. These reforms reflect some radical departures from past policies and some positive changes on behalf of women, changes that acknowledge women's need for legal protection from their partners. The question is, will these reforms be successful?

This section examines Ferraro's (1989) case study of a recent reform, favored by feminists, that was implemented in one city. There were a variety of obstacles to the successful implementation of this policy. Examining these obstacles and analyzing their causes demonstrates how the lack of a strong feminist perspective was a major factor in the failure of this reform effort to bring about a significant increase in arrests. This case illustrates why reforms must embody a feminist perspective.

In the last decade many states have adopted tougher arrest policies and procedures, and some jurisdictions have adopted mandatory arrest policies (Buzawa and Buzawa 1990). Such policies are the centerpiece of efforts to stop battering. Although laws can be passed that make battering illegal, they must be enforced by the police to have any impact. Thus it is particularly important to know whether these policies are successfully implemented. Observers have long noted that police officers have been reluctant to make arrests in battering cases and have been concerned that the police will not comply with new arrest policies (Bell 1985; Berk and Loseke 1981; Black 1980; Davis 1983; Smith and Klein 1984; Waaland and Keeley 1985). However, only recently do we have some data about the effectiveness of these new policies.

Ferraro (1989) studied the implementation of a presumptive arrest policy in Phoenix, Arizona. The policy stated that police officers should arrest offenders whether or not the victims desired prosecution and that, when there was probable cause, an arrest should be made, even if the offense did not occur in the officer's presence. The presumptive arrest policy was supported by the police chief, and all officers received training in how to implement the policy. The officers were to treat domestic violence as a crime and to arrest batterers regardless of other characteristics of the situation. The policy change was directed toward the police only and was not coordinated with any changes in other parts of the criminal justice system.

Although arrest rates did increase for a short time after the introduction of the presumptive arrest policy, in the majority of cases arrests were not made. Ferraro found many obstacles to the implementation of the policy, including police views that battering cases are "family fights" and are therefore low priority; police judgments of battered women based on their demeanor; and sexist views of women, including a lack of police understanding of women's vulnerability in a battering situation.

First, according to Ferraro, police officers viewed these situations as "family fights." The police see their mandate as maintaining public peace and order. If they determined that a "family fight" was impinging on public peace and order, they viewed it as legitimately within their jurisdiction; otherwise they did not. Further, police disliked responding to what they label "domestic" calls. They perceived them as no-win situations and believed there was nothing they could do about them; frequently they viewed responding to "domestic" calls as a kind of social work. Police officers also frequently viewed battered women as "inconsistent complainants"; they believed that, although a woman called the police, there was no guarantee that she would pursue the case. Then the officer felt that he had wasted his time.

Similarly, Stanko (1989) claims that police officers most value extraordinary events such as the ability to save a life, even at the risk of putting oneself in danger. These events are also the ones that bring the police organizational and professional recognition, whereas there is no such recognition for handling battering cases. Stanko also claims that police officers find battering cases frustrating, particularly if they have to return to the same address or if they put effort into a case and then the woman drops the charges and the couple become reconciled.

Second, Ferraro found that police reactions varied according to how they assessed a woman's demeanor. If a woman was from a subculture the police viewed as "deviant"—from a family where someone wasn't working, where someone was nonwhite, spoke a foreign language, lived in a run-down home, or was drunk—police were likely to perceive battering as a "family fight" of little concern to them, and they usually did not make an arrest. On the other hand, if offenders were drunk and/or belligerent in the presence of the officer, an arrest was more likely. Others have also noted that police respond to the demeanor of the assailant toward the police. Ford (1983) and Pepinsky (1976) found police more sympathetic to those victims who were rational, deferential, and nondemanding towards police. Black (1980) notes that police believe that, for some victims, violence is "a normal way of life"; and Smith and Klein (1984) found that police tended to disregard a woman's request for an arrest if she lived in a poorer neighborhood.

Third, Ferraro found that police attitudes towards women affected their responses. Like many in the population at large, police officers believed that women could easily leave a battering situation if they wanted to. They felt that battered women had voluntarily selected a violent partner and were choosing to remain in an abusive situation. Because they assume that these adult women choose to live in violent relationships, police believe their own response should be limited to situations where public peace and order are disturbed, that is, when the neighbors are complaining. Stanko (1989) also asserts that police attitudes towards battering are affected by cultural assumptions about violence in intimate relationships and that the police assume that in a "domestic case" women are as at fault as men.

To conclude, there was strikingly little change in the police response to battered women after the introduction of a presumptive arrest policy. The police did not make a feminist response to battering, that is, a response based on an understanding of women as victims of male violence; in fact, they rarely "saw" battering. Instead, their response was strongly influenced by their view of the problem as one of family violence and their view of women. These responses were reinforced by the occupational self-conceptions of the police and by their organizational priorities. Each of these factors by itself would constitute a strong obstacle to changing the police response to battering. Together, they make the prospects for change seem even more difficult.

One could ask, however, whether this reform might have had a more successful outcome. Perhaps if the new policy had been supported at all levels of the criminal justice system, the police would have made more arrests. In Ferraro's case study, the creation of a presumptive arrest policy in the police department was not accompanied by changes in any other part of the criminal justice system. However, one could also argue that, because the "family violence" view is so pervasive in the criminal justice system, the commitment of personnel at higher levels and in other parts of the criminal justice system to arresting male abusers would be as low as that of the police.

One could also ask whether longer or more intense training in a feminist view of battering would have made for a more positive outcome in this reform. It is possible that a good training program could lead the police to "see" battering more clearly, to discard their old labels of battered women in favor of more favorable, feminist ones. But one wonders whether the effects of training would remain over time, given the strength of the factors just cited. Finally, perhaps if more care had been taken to monitor the enforcement of this presumptive arrest policy, the outcome would have been different. One could certainly design an appropriate monitoring system for such a policy. On the other hand, one could argue that unless organizational priorities are changed, enforcement of such a policy would not create a more successful outcome.

Given the goal incorporating a feminist view of battering into the criminal justice system and the obstacles just discussed, what kinds of reforms should be introduced? As it is so easy for those in the criminal justice system to redefine battering in terms of their own needs and interests, I believe that selected outside groups with knowledge of battered women should have input into the development of reforms in the criminal justice system and should have a role advocating for battered women's interests within the system. The groups that have such knowledge of and concern for battered women are battered women's organizations. Such a suggestion may initially sound farfetched. What interest would the police or other groups in the criminal justice system have in cooperative efforts with the battered women's movement? One would assume that, like most other institutions and professions, the criminal justice system would like to retain ultimate control of its operations and would not be eager to cooperate with outside groups. One could imagine a police department allowing a battered women's group to participate in police training. However, would any more substantial cooperation be possible? The final section argues that more cooperative efforts are possible.

NEW DIRECTIONS FOR A FEMINIST CRIMINAL JUSTICE RESPONSE TO BATTERING

This section reports on three programs that involve cooperative efforts between the criminal justice system and battered women's groups. There are many more such programs (Schneider 1990), and I believe they offer the best hope for a feminist response to battered women in the criminal justice system. These programs also promote systemwide change, another element necessary to create significant reforms. Although these programs are in cities that may have certain unique characteristics and although they may not last indefinitely, they provide productive models for change in the criminal justice system.

The Domestic Abuse Intervention Project, Duluth, Minnesota

As reported by Pence and Shepard (1988), the Domestic Abuse Intervention Project (DAIP) grew out of the Minnesota battered women's movement. The first program, developed in Duluth, was replicated in over twenty Minnesota communities. One of DAIP's first activities was to use police reports to make contact with victims of battering. Minnesota state law requires that police write reports on all domestic violence cases. DAIP helped develop an innovative policy that allows advocates at the shelter for battered women to review all police reports three times a week, from which to provide follow-up advocacy to women in situations in which arrests were not made. The key to this project is that the city attorney's office, which discourages the dismissal of charges, links battered women with advocates at the beginning of the criminal process, a significant change for women. Also, women who participate in the program are not required to prosecute.

DAIP staff also do victim advocacy work in the case of arrest. Duluth has a mandatory arrest policy that requires arrest when the police determine that a protection order has been violated. Where an arrest has been made and the assailant has been imprisoned, the police contact the shelter and provide advocates with the victim's name, address, and phone number. The shelter then sends an advocate to meet with the woman and inform her about court procedures and community resources. Conviction rates increased from 20 percent in 1980 to 87 percent in 1983.

Where battering is established by a reasonable preponderance of the evidence by the court, the batterer is typically ordered to limit or cease contact with the victim and to participate in a DAIP counseling and educational program for batterers, and in some cases to limit or cease contact with the children. First-time misdemeanor offenders are sentenced to six months of education or counseling groups. Second offenses carry sentences of twenty to ninety days, in addition to counseling and treatment. The courts have agreed to obtain input from DAIP project staff and probationary officials on the safety needs of victims during the probationary period to see if they need restricted or limited contact with the assailant. The courts also agreed to enforce their orders vigorously and to support the monitoring by DAIP staff of court orders and assailants' compliance with probation agreements.

Another recent change in this system, promoted by DAIP, is a policy that civil protection orders can be issued for cases where the batterer and the battered woman are living together and want to continue to live together. If the woman so requests, once the batterer has begun the counseling or education program, the court permits the batterer to return to the home after a hearing has determined what safety precautions are necessary.

The Family Violence Project, San Francisco

According to Schneider (1990), the Family Violence Project (FVP) of San Francisco, like the DAIP, has brought feminist personnel and ideas into the criminal justice system and has also helped to create change at various points in the criminal justice system. The FVP was started by community activists and attorneys who received national funding to create a demonstration program. In 1980, the police in San Francisco, at the urging of a coalition of attorneys and community and women's rights groups, adopted a presumptive arrest policy. The police also agreed to institute data collection and tracking systems to identify domestic violence cases. Shortly after the adoption of the presumptive arrest policy, the Family Violence Project developed a domestic violence training curriculum for the police. After the first year of these reforms, police reports on domestic violence increased by 100 percent, and arrests increased by 60 percent.

In 1982, the Family Violence Project and the Coalition for Justice for Battered Women convinced the San Francisco District Attorney's office to establish a special prosecution program for domestic violence cases. The District Attorney's office established formal policies for misdemeanor and felony domestic violence cases. The policies have two particularly important characteristics from the point of view of feminist reforms. First, the San Francisco DA's office agreed to refer all battered women to the Family Violence Project's Victim Advocacy Unit for follow-up. Second, the advocates were then given permission to advise the assistant district attorneys on how to proceed with each case. At the end of the first year of this program, according to Schneider, "positive dispositions in domestic violence cases increased by 171 percent . . . and felony domestic violence cases booked on 'corporal injury to spouse' increased by 272 percent."

Finally, in 1988, the Family Violence Project developed a training program on domestic violence for the judiciary of criminal courts in California, under the auspices of the State Justice Institute. The project also developed a curriculum and reference guide for the judiciary entitled *Domestic Violence: A Bench Guide for the Criminal Courts.* Recently the State Justice Institute has awarded the Family Violence Project a grant to conduct training for the judiciary nationwide.

Project Safeguard, Denver

According to Schneider (1990), Project Safeguard developed out of the Colorado Coalition for Justice for Abused Women (JAWS), founded in 1982 by feminist attorneys, therapists, and social workers. After a successful suit against the police, JAWS helped write police policies on domestic violence and a domestic violence manual, which provides a comprehensive guide to procedures and guidelines for all persons who deal with domestic violence cases within the criminal justice system. Project Safeguard also conducts education and outreach activities; does training for the police, criminal court, and civil court; and works closely with the City and District Attorneys' offices. In addition to counseling battered women, Project Safeguard provides victim advocacy on many levels.

Finally, Project Safeguard coordinates and monitors the civil and criminal justice systems' response to domestic violence. In civil court, Project Safeguard offers women assistance in obtaining restraining orders *pro se*. In criminal court an advocate helps women negotiate the criminal system and supports them in testifying against their abusers. Advocates also work with judges to have the victims' wishes considered prior to sentencing. Finally, similar to the Family Violence Project in San Francisco, Project Safeguard has collected and analyzed data to monitor the activity of appropriate departments within the criminal justice system.

CONCLUSION

In order to make an effective response to battering, the criminal justice system must develop reforms based on a feminist perspective on battering. The analysis presented here has shown that the basic cause of battering is male dominance of women. However, it will be difficult for the criminal justice system to change its perspective from a "family violence" view to a feminist view. I describe the fate of a recent reform introducing a presumptive arrest policy in one city as an example of the difficulty of introducing a feminist perspective in the criminal justice system. Without a strong feminist perspective, police and others in the criminal justice system will continue to judge women by their family status and their demeanor, and not see or understand their victimization as women. Police organizational priorities and occupational self-conceptions will continue to reinforce the police view of battering as a "family violence" problem.

As shown by the foregoing examples, programs that incorporate a feminist view of battering, initiated by battered women's groups, are cooperative efforts with the criminal justice system that provide productive models for change in that system.

REFERENCES

Adams, D. 1988. Treatment Models of Men Who Batter. In K. Yllo & M. Bograd, eds., *Feminist Perspectives on Wife Abuse*. Newbury Park, Calif.: Sage.

Attorney General's Task Force on Family Violence. 1984. Washington, D.C.: Department of Justice.

Bell, Daniel J. 1985. A Multiyear Study of Ohio Urban, Suburban, and Rural Policy Dispositions of Domestic Disputes. *Victimology* 10:301–10.

Berk, R., S. F. Berk, D. Loseke, and D. Rauma. 1983. Mutual Combat and Other Family Violence Myths. In D. Finkelhor et al., eds., *The Dark Side of Families: Current Family Violence Research*. Beverly Hills, Calif.: Sage.

Berk, S.F., and D.R. Loseke. 1981. "Handling" Family Violence: Situational Determinants of Police Arrest in Domestic Disturbances. *Law and Society Review* 15:317–46.

Black, D. 1980. *The Manners and Customs of the Police*. New York: Academic Press.

Bowker, L. 1986. *Ending the Violence*. Holmes Beach, Fla.: Learning Publications.

Breines, W., and L. Gordon. 1983. The New Scholarship on Family Violence. *Signs* 8:490–531.

Browne, A. 1987. *When Battered Women Kill*. New York: Free Press.

Brush, L. D. 1990. Violent Acts and Injurious Outcomes in Married Couples: Methodological Issues in the National Survey of Families and Households. *Gender and Society* 4, no. 1 (March): 56–67.

Buzawa, E.S., and C.G. Buzawa. 1990. *Domestic Violence: The Criminal Justice Response*. Newbury Park, Calif.: Sage.

Davis, P.W. 1983. Restoring the Semblance of Order: Police Strategies in the Domestic Disturbance. *Symbolic Interaction* 6:216–74.

Dobash, R.E., and R. Dobash. 1979. *Violence against Wives*. New York: Free Press.

Ferraro, K. 1989. Policing Woman Battering. *Social Problems* 36:61–74.

Ford, D.A. 1983. Wife Battery and Criminal Justice: A Study of Victim Decision-making. *Family Relations* 32:463–75.

Gelles, R. 1974. *The Violent Home: A Study of Physical Aggression between Husbands and Wives*. Beverly Hills, Calif.: Sage.

———. 1979. *Family Violence*. Beverly Hills, Calif.: Sage.

———. 1983. An Exchange/Social Control Theory. In D. Finkelhor et al., eds., *The Dark Side of Families: Current Family Violence Research*. Beverly Hills, Calif.: Sage.

———. 1985. *Intimate Violence in Families*. Beverly Hills, Calif.: Sage.

Gelles, R., and M. Straus. 1988. *Intimate Violence*. New York: Simon & Schuster.

Gubman, G., and P. Newton. 1983. "When Two Are Too Many: The Configuration of a Battering Incident." Paper presented at the American Sociological Association Meetings, Detroit, Michigan.

Kurz, D. 1987. Responses to Battered Women: Resistance to Medicalization. *Social Problems* 34:501–13.

———. 1989. Social Science Perspectives on Wife Abuse: Current Debates and Future Directions. *Gender and Society* 3, no. 4 (December): 489–505.

McLeer, S., and R. Anwar. 1989. A Study of Battered Women Presenting in an Emergency Department. *American Journal of Public Health* 79:65–66.

Mederos, F. 1987. Theorizing Continuities and Discontinuities between "Normal" Men and Abusive Men: Work in Progress. Paper presented at the Third National Family Violence Research Conference, University of New Hampshire, Durham.

Pagelow, M. 1981. *Woman-Battering: Victims and Their Experiences*. Beverly Hills, Calif.: Sage.

―――. 1985. The "Battered Husband Syndrome": Social Problem or Much Ado about Little? In N. Johnson, ed., *Marital Violence*. London: Routledge and Kegan Paul.

―――. 1987. *Application of Research to Policy in Partner Abuse*. Paper presented at the Family Violence Research Conference for Practitioners and Policymakers, University of New Hampshire, Durham.

Pence, E., and M. Shepard. 1988. Integrating Feminist Theory and Practice: The Challenge of the Battered Women's Movement. In K. Yllo & M. Bograd, *Feminist Perspectives on Wife Abuse*. Newbury Park, Calif.: Sage.

Pepinsky, H.E. 1976. Police Patrolman's Offense-reporting Behavior. *Journal of Research in Crime and Delinquency* 13:1, 33–47.

Pleck, E., J. H. Pleck, M. Grossman, and P. Bart. 1977–78. The Battered Data Syndrome: A Comment on Steinmetz' Article. *Victimology* 2:680–84.

Ptacek, J. 1988. Why Do Men Batter Their Wives? In K. Yllo and M. Bograd, eds., *Feminist Perspectives on Wife Abuse*. Newbury Park, Calif.: Sage.

Rosenberg, M. L., E. Stark, and M. A. Zahn. 1985. Interpersonal Violence: Homicide and Spouse Abuse. In J. Last, ed., *Public Health and Preventive Medicine*. 12th ed. East Norwalk, Conn.: Appleton Century Crofts.

Russell, D. 1982. *Rape in Marriage*. New York: Macmillan.

―――. 1988. Foreword. In K. Yllo and M. Bograd, eds., *Feminist Perspectives on Wife Abuse*. Newbury Park, Calif.: Sage.

Saunders, D. 1988. Wife Abuse, Husband Abuse, or Mutual Combat? In K. Yllo and M. Bograd, eds., *Feminist Perspectives on Wife Abuse*. Newbury Park, Calif.: Sage.

Schecter, Susan. 1982. *Women and Male Violence*. Boston: South End Press.

Schneider, Elizabeth M. 1990. Legal Reform Efforts to Assist Battered Women: Past, Present, and Future. Report to the Ford Foundation. Brooklyn Law School, July.

Smith, D.A., and J. R. Klein. 1984. Police Control of Interpersonal Disputes. *Social Problems* 31:466–81.

Stanko, E. 1985. *Intimate Intrusions*. London: Routledge and Kegan Paul.

―――. 1989. Missing the Mark? Policing Battering. In J. Hanmer, J. Radford, and E. Stanko, eds., *Women, Policing, and Male Violence*. London: Routledge and Kegan Paul.

Stark, E., and A. Flitcraft. 1985. Woman Battering, Child Abuse and Social Heredity: What Is the Relationship? In N. Johnson, ed., *Marital Violence*. London: Routledge and Kegan Paul.

Stark, E., A. Flitcraft, and W. Frazier. 1979. Medicine and Patriarchal Violence: The Social Construction of a "Private" Event. *International Journal of Health Services* 98:461–91.

Steinmetz, S. 1977. *The Cycle of Violence: Assertive, Aggressive, and Abusive Family Interaction*. New York: Praeger.

―――. 1977–78. The Battered Husband Syndrome. *Victimology* 2:499–509.

Straus, M. 1973. A General Systems Theory Approach to a Theory of Violence between Family Members. *Social Science Information* 12:105–25.

————. 1976. Sexual Inequality, Cultural Norms, and Wife-beating. *Victimology* 1:54–76.

————. 1979. Measuring Intrafamily Conflict and Violence: The Conflict Tactics (CT) Scales. *Journal of Marriage and the Family* 41:75–88.

————. 1980a. The Marriage License as a Hitting License: Evidence from Popular Culture, Law, and Social Science. In M. Straus and G. Hotaling, eds., *The Social Causes of Husband-Wife Violence*. Minneapolis: University of Minnesota Press.

————. 1980b. A Sociological Perspective on the Prevention of Wife Beating. In M. Straus and G. Hotaling, eds., *The Social Causes of Husband-Wife Violence*. Minneapolis: University of Minnesota Press.

————. 1980c. Victims and Aggressors in Marital Violence. *American Behavioral Scientist* 23:681–704.

————. 1983. Ordinary Violence, Child Abuse, and Wife Beating: What Do They Have in Common? In D. Finkelhor et al., eds., *The Dark Side of Families: Current Family Violence Research*. Beverly Hills, Calif.: Sage.

Straus, M., and R. Gelles. 1986. Societal Change and Change in Family Violence from 1975 to 1985 as Revealed by Two National Surveys. *Journal of Marriage and the Family* 48:465–79.

Straus, M., R. Gelles, and S. Steinmetz. 1980. *Behind Closed Doors: Violence in the American Family*. Garden City, N.Y.: Doubleday.

Tierney, K. 1982. The Battered Women's Movement and the Creation of the Wife Beating Problem. *Social Problems* 29:207–20.

Waaland, P., and S. Keeley. 1985. Police Decision Making in Wife Abuse: The Impact of Legal and Extralegal Factors. *Law and Human Behavior* 9:355–66.

Walker, L. 1984. *The Battered Woman Syndrome*. New York: Springer.

Wardell, L., C. Gillespie, and A. Leffler. 1983. Science and Violence against Women. In D. Finkelhor et al., eds., *The Dark Side of Families: Current Family Violence Research*. Beverly Hills, Calif.: Sage.

Yllo, K. 1988. Political and Methodological Debates in Wife Abuse Research. In K. Yllo and M. Bograd, eds., *Feminist Perspectives on Wife Abuse*. Newbury Park, Calif.: Sage.

II
POLICE
INTERVENTION

3

SCREENING CALLS
Peter K. Manning

Peter Manning has written extensively on the subject of communication within organizations. In this chapter, he addresses how an organization's standard operating procedures effect and condition its actions. He asserts that "messages" to organizations are shaped by the organization to fit in with the organization's format and to conform to the organization's desired outcome. Consequently, the organization's response to a given pattern such as a domestic violence case is determined by a series of classification processes as the message moves through the organizational network.

In adopting this perspective on the police handling of domestic violence calls, Manning finds "call screening" a natural response. Call screening is the widely employed practice whereby police departments selectively sift out "frivolous," "inappropriate," or "undesired" calls, assign priorities to those remaining, and delineate specific responses (if any). Manning observes that domestic violence has historically been typologized as a low-priority call, a misdemeanor deserving little police interest.

Manning's article also demonstrates the ambiguity of many domestic violence messages received by a police agency. A seemingly mundane function of the police department, call processing, significantly mediates the final outcome. His explanation of how calls are typologized clarifies why domestic violence cases are often discounted by police officers even before they reach the dispute site.

The 911 number and Computer-Aided Dispatch have merely served to increase the likelihood that calls will be screened out of the system. Further, by increasing the pressure to produce, tangible measures effectively increase pressure on officers to adhere to a "production schedule," that is, to utilize less time per call and less emphasis on solving domestic violence problems. Not surprisingly, Manning finds less attention given to the highly individual needs and desires of victims and offenders as technological control increases.

However, the organizational goals of efficiency as measured by arrest or nonarrest are enhanced.

Finally, Manning's chapter provides an excellent counterpoint to the standard analysis of an organization's actions. He demonstrates how tensions between the organizational goals of managing demand and reducing workload and of maintaining control may overwhelm, or at least greatly modify, the impact of the raw information received by the agency.

Does computer-based data processing technology, first adapted in the 1970s by modern urban American police departments, increase departmental capacity to diagnose, respond to, and more subtly and creatively manage events termed "domestic violence"? If so, how and why does this occur? If the quality of police management of incidents is not enhanced, why is this the case? What can be done to improve the policing of such incidents?

This problem-definition raises the vexing difficulty of how to gather, format, and collate data drawn from talk, such as telephone calls to the police, in order to insure appropriate, context-sensitive processing and organizational response. It is well known that messages, regardless of their content, are shaped by complex organizations and lodged in conventionalized formats. Specific content, however, may produce differences in processing and responses. Thus, a sociological analysis of police screening of calls about domestic violence must explicate the organizational structure and the information technology that enable message processing, as well as the sociolinguistic tools that facilitate understanding interactions between content and meaning. Let us begin with the sociolinguistic issues and then proceed to organizational matters.

Sociolinguistics provides fundamental concepts for the analysis of the context-based nature of the interpretation of calls to the police (de Saussure 1966; Cicourel 1985; Manning 1986, 1988). What does a context-based analysis of calls require? Several points should be made initially. What is called information is the result of transformation of data or facts into socially acceptable and credible knowledge through interpretation. Talk is made sensible not only by the invisible work of syntax, grammar, and phonemics but also through active interpretive work. Perhaps such work is accessible in organizational context, as shared meanings are an essential precondition for sustained collective action. An important aspect of interpretive work is the context, or what the listener brings to the materials he or she hears. Interpretive work is particularly important when everyday talk is being rapidly transformed by means of interviews into organizational files, forms, or records.

All conversations with a purpose, such as interviews, dramatize the complexity of sense-making between strangers. These are exaggerated, it should be emphasized, when the idiosyncratic particulars of individual communicants are suppressed as a result of channel-specific communication such as telephone interactions. Two processes play central roles over the course of an interview: on the one hand the idiosyncratic or context-dependent particulars of individual speech and on the other such features of formal logical declarative systems as the format of the medical interview or a preestablished algorithm for questioning. Everyday or folk knowledge is context-dependent (Cicourel 1986:251). Speaker-hearers combine rules of inference and general rules of speech that are based on some learned schemata for understanding, chunking, and coding talk with their everyday knowledge about the understanding of lexical items, phrases, or sentences and the narrative-like context-dependent structure of everyday knowledge (Cicourel 1986:261). Formal systems are constituted by general decision rules independent of any given set of facts, setting, or participants. Thus, the analytic problem is one of how to "map" everyday talk onto formal schemes such as police classification systems.

Clearly, the ways in which these sociolinguistic features of talk are integrated with organizational routines and goals is not well understood. What is viewed as the relevant range and types of police work is rather broad, of course, but because in fact all service organizations are overloaded and overworked, relatively permeable boundaries must be maintained, priorities established, and formal and informal rules used to screen potentially overwhelming demand (Lipsky 1980). The organizational context within which talk is heard and screened, the "institutional bias" (Douglas 1985) of the organization, how it functions to favor and reward certain kinds of interpretations and action choices, is critical in determining culturally sanctioned organizational output. Organizations interact with environments, encoding, decoding, and producing output; but they also enact, or reproduce, their own ideologies, moral codes and preferences, and modes of maintaining patterns of horizontal and vertical differentiation in the social world.

Before exploring message processing and the analysis of individual message content, let us consider some features of the police communication system (PCS) of large urban departments.

THE ROLE OF TECHNOLOGY IN THE POLICE COMMUNICATIONS SYSTEM

The primary source of police work is telephone calls from the public that are screened and passed on to officers (Reiss 1971). "Call screening" here refers to selectively sorting and classifying calls in advance of police decisions to attend the scene or serve the caller. It is clear, for example, that ex post facto reclassification of calls using data gathered from the scene (Davis 1983; Dunford, Huizinga, and Elliott 1990), according to sociological standards of validity and reliability, produces quite a different distribution of types of calls than using the organizational records (see Percy and Scott 1985). The ethnographic fieldwork reported here, including observation of call screening in action, is an attempt to explicate the phenomenological grounds employed by organizational members to constitute calls as instances of categories for practical purposes (Garfinkel and Bittner, in Garfinkel 1967).

To understand the role of call screening in the police response to domestic violence, the firmly held "technological conceit" that has shaped policing must be appreciated. The assumption is that, by enhancing the technological capacity of police, one can better manage and control demand and rationalize the distribution or rationing of police services (see Lipsky 1980).

Police departments until very recently used rather simple means of collecting and processing information from calls. Typically, they used a telephone-based system that required an operator, usually a sworn officer, to scribe handwritten notes on a card or sheet of paper detailing in an often informal format the address, nature of the call, and caller. Some systems mandated forwarding the call to a dispatcher to assign the call to an officer, while others combined the operator and dispatcher roles (compare the descriptions in Manning 1988, chapter 3, with those in Percy and Scott 1985).

Most large urban American police departments now collect and queue calls from the public by means of one or more computers and some form of computer-assisted dispatch (CAD).[1] This system of recording and processing calls, supported and financed by LEAA, began about twenty years ago. By 1973, a few large departments (New York, Detroit, and Chicago among them) had adopted CAD systems. They vary from highly automated and expensive (about $21 million) installations like those found in Boston and Detroit to "electronic conveyor belts" that simply reduce pass-through time (Larson 1989:28). Most automatically assign an accepted call received on dedicated 911 lines as an incident to an area dispatcher who, in time, will send out the message via radio to officers as an assignment. This processed message, subject to both formal and informal screening at every point from the citizen's decision to call to the officer's decision to attend the scene, if accepted by the officer, becomes a job.

Around 1980, some departments, among them Tampa-St. Petersburg, Florida, and Wichita, Kansas, adopted what Larson (1989) calls an "enhanced 911 system" with the capacity to display on a screen the address of the phone from which a call was made. This allows checks of address and simplified data-gathering from sometimes distressed, confused, or anxious callers. As of 1989, 89 of the 125 largest American cities use an enhanced 911 system, and some 36 states now have or plan to pass laws requiring a 911 system (Larson 1989).

Several CAD functions are relevant to the screening of violence. CAD serves managerial and recordkeeping functions. It possesses the capacity to store in retrievable format(s) information about the *caller* (often nothing is noted about the person), the *call* (time of day, day of the week, and so on), the *operator* (I.D. number, time spent processing the incident), the *incident* (once accepted by the operator), and its *organizational transformation* (routing, assignment, and disposal). It serves to record and allocate screened calls as jobs automatically to dispatchers responsible for a given area of the city, to record the assignments and current workload of officers, and to facilitate retrieval of operational data (computer records permit a brief storage of records on the mainframe, a few weeks at most, and storage in paper form for longer periods of time). CAD assists in screening and assigning work to officers and assists in maintaining a more refined monitoring and supervision of work "on-line." CAD can produce data for longer-term planning and reallocation of resources, given a pattern of events; and it permits officers and commanding officers to respond more quickly and sensitively to large-scale disorders and disasters.

The installation of CAD stimulated a series of experiments in police management that were, in the end, rather disappointing. More speedy pass-through and response time did not reduce crime or increase arrests. The notion that more precise rendering of the content of the call would result in improved classification and control of incidents and reduce pass-through effects was not confirmed by a series of funded research projects. Emphasis then switched to refining police priorities and altering citizens' expectations of the nature and timing of police response. It was assumed that careful and systematic call screening coupled with differential police response (DPR) would free police resources for reallocation. Differential response schemes are slowly being adopted, but the corollary reallocation of patrol duties is not. Recent research, in part technologically driven, has focused on the relationship between the spatial location of calls, the patterning of repeat calls, and attempts to reduce calls by proactive or preventive police work (see below, and Sherman, forthcoming). Minicomputers and terminals in cars have also been advanced as means to better call management.

Unfortunately, after some twenty-five years of experimentation, it has been concluded that these modifications in management little alter the quality of police response to reported incidents or order problems (Goldstein 1990). CAD does not increase crime control effectiveness nor alter routine nonpatrol functions; it may in time produce subtle changes in typical management style or command and control procedures (see Manning, forthcoming). Advances in information technology, even when linked with policy changes, seem to operate on the margins of policing. To what degree could one expect CAD to alter the range of police responses to a specific category of calls, those reporting "domestic violence"?

A SIMPLE MESSAGE

A woman calls the Midwestern Police Department (MPD):

PD: Police, where is the problem?

Caller: He's going to beat me.

PD: Police, where is the problem?

Caller: I live at 1330 Beaubein, Midwest City.

PD: What sort of place is that—apartment, house. . . .

Caller: An apartment.

PD: Is he using a weapon?

Caller: I don't know; he has one.

PD: You think he's going to harm you?

Caller: Yes, that's why I called!

PD: O.K., a unit has been requested.

Processing the Message

Let us walk through the call processing as it is done in the MPD.[2] It should be recalled that there are wide variations in these systems (Manning 1982). It should further be understood that this process conflates temporarily three analytically distinct items: the sender, the message, and the receiver.

The operator first must decide whether she or he trusts the caller, then whether to refer or terminate the call. About 10 percent of all calls are terminated at source by the operator (see Percy and Scott 1985:67). Emergency medical services (EMS) and fire calls are screened by police operators and transferred. If accepted, the call is coded—given a five-digit incident classification number from a list of 245 categories—and entered into the computer. The items in the message must be entered into the preestablished computer file format and all items must be completed. The operator may add "remarks" such as "weapon present" before she or he sends on a hard copy to the dispatcher, including the address, nature of the dwelling or location, description of the event, and a classification. The computer adds the date, time, operator's terminal and number, and the incident number. About 50 percent of the calls are not forwarded by the operators (Percy and Scott 1985:67–78; Bercal 1970).

As he or she receives incidents, the dispatcher screens them and puts some incidents out on the air, requesting that units respond and consider further action in connection with the assignment. Once an incident is assigned, the dispatcher first places the card in a slot for the unit, and then clears the slot when the unit reports availability to return to service. The data on these cards are entered into the computer the next day. About 25 percent of the calls forwarded by the operators are actually attended to by officers.

Some distinctions made during the course of screening are rather subtle. For example, the call used as an example could have been classified by the operator in at least 55 of the 245 categories in the MPD incident list. Think of these possibilities: the category 32 or "sex" has sixteen subcategories; 34 or "assault" has sixteen subcategories; 39 or "family trouble" has fifteen subcategories; and two subcategories under 82 or "disturbance" are relevant. In addition, categories 50 and 51 (EMS codes that include "accidental cutting" and "injured") could conceivably be used. Very refined distinctions are made between "in progress," "just happened," and "happened" (the latter is implied by calling an incident 1–3900, "F.T. [family trouble] homicide"). Distinctions among these categories and subcategories are made on an ad hoc basis by operators, often with informal consultation among themselves.[3]

The operator treats calls as if they were reports of events without relevant history, almost random in their appearance and mentally sorts and classifies them, on the basis of a constructed gloss of the content of the call, into associative contexts, or types of calls. Of these types, crime makes up about 10 percent of the workload and noncrime internal communications makes up about 33 percent to 58 percent of the workload of the communications center (Percy and Scott 1985:78); other calls are classified as information given, information received.

The computer directs the incident to the appropriate dispatcher according to the address given by the caller and entered by the operator. A small card printed at the dispatcher's desk is used to sort and prioritize incidents. The dispatcher locates a unit in that precinct by radio to accept the assignment as a job.

The dispatcher responds to calls in serial order, mentally sorting them into types, as the operator did. In the MPD, the dispatcher typically radios the officers brief verbal descriptors such as "family trouble at 1330 Beaubein," rather than numbers or official categories. Sometimes "any unit nearby" will be asked to respond; sometimes a specific unit will be called. Units responding to the dispatcher give the vehicle number. The disembodied voices of officers who volunteer to take a job can often be heard: "10–71; I'll take that call . . . ." Outcomes of accepted calls are rarely given to the dispatcher and are never forwarded to the operator in the MPD. Outcomes are not entered into the computer; it records only the description of the incident, the address and unit number, and the time at which the unit returned to service. Neither officers nor dispatchers reclassify a job after they have attended it (or not) in the MPD. Other departments require reclassification and keep records that include these changes (Pierce, Spaar, and Briggs 1984).

SENSE-MAKING AND AMBIGUOUS CALLS

Most calls are either referred, terminated, or coded without great difficulty, in part because the operators believe they should act quickly; they are more concerned with processing calls—either refusing, referring, or forwarding the call as an incident—than with producing a valid, reliable, or even accurate label. They act in good faith, believing that the ultimate decision as to nature of the call and its disposition must rest with the officers and, secondarily, with the dispatchers who, unlike the operators, are in direct contact via radio with the officers.

However, once accepted by the operator as valid, some calls remain ambiguous with respect to their classification. Practical rules of thumb operate to reduce these calls to organizationally shaped units.[4] These rules facilitate rapid forwarding of calls and reduce the operators' anxiety and concern about delaying and being "out of service" too long while handling a single call.

Rules for Processing Ambiguous Calls in the Message Stream

Incoming calls are considered on one level merely as a stream or series of emergent events. As such, all will be processed in some fashion, regardless of their content. To do this quickly and expeditiously, at least seven rules are used. These enable operators to order and classify ambiguous calls in the message stream:

The *rule of social reality* obtains: All calls are assumed to be made by callers about events taking place in the immediate here and now. It should be noted that any call/message, in theory as in everyday life, can be framed as or have very diverse epistemological status as a dream, a fantasy, a wish or hope, a delusion or hallucination, or a lie or intentional systematic distortion. The incident the caller is referring to can be occurring in the present, have occurred in the near or distant past, or be expected to occur in the near future (a fear that an event may occur) or the very distant future.

The *rule of tacit knowledge* applies: Common sense is used to understand the true nature of the call. This means drawing on one's own experience with "things like this" and penetrating beneath the surface of mere words to extract the core or sense of the problem. Tacit knowledge seems particularly valuable and important when callers report threats and fears and/or make predictions about future behavior. Organizational rules and regulations, notebooks, and laws are useless in the immediate period (a minute or less) in which the decisions must be made.

The *rule of a coherent yet invisible order* holds: Calls are indices of an invisible, underlying, and ongoing social order, a commonsense reality itself unexamined (Garfinkel 1967). Any call is an instanciation of this tissue of social rules, practices, behaviors, and discourse. Spouse beating, for example, is assumed to be a normal feature of some life-styles.

The *rule of analogy* is operative: Ambiguous calls are to be treated as similar to previous calls. The precise nature of the relationships between similarly classified calls or across categories or types of calls remains unexplored. Operators make no attempt to pin down the pattern of frequent calls, to allocate resources to them, or to conceptualize their relevance in advance.

The *temporality rule* is relevant to interpretation: Calls are given meaning by their arrival time. The timing of the call gives it a background. Calls on Friday from wives about drunken and abusive husbands are seen as "typical wife calling about a drunken husband on payday" calls, but such calls may be taken more seriously at other times of the day or week. Calls from children after school, even those reporting crimes, are discredited as "bored kids playing on the telephone." The level of work experienced by all members of the system affects the salience of certain elements in the calls, which means that routine service calls are dropped to the bottom of the list by dispatchers and officers.

The *rule of "pragmatic interactional primacy"* (Leaf 1972:236) applies: The call is defined and classified according to unstated definitions of events and the pragmatic aims of the operator, using the format, classification, and technology available. Many kinds of communications from callers are omitted, dispreferred, or ignored, especially if the caller is distrusted. Operators use this rule to talk people out of their wish to have an officer dispatched, to terminate calls, and to refuse to accept others.[5]

The *rule referential reality* is operative. This means that the operator assumes that the caller is describing an event that is currently happening in the real world, and that the caller is telling the truth. If the operator concludes that the caller is dreaming, hallucinating, or is drunk or on drugs, for example, the operator may conclude that this rule is to be suspended for this call (see *rule of social reality*).

These working rules enable operators to narrow the focus of concern when listening to the calls, to omit as irrelevant many diverse features of the calls, to seize on a selected set of reported facts, and to rationalize their interpretations. Many socially operative matters central to active encoding are a function not of the content of the calls, but of the rules used to interpret them.

Thus far, we have not discussed the particulars of the analysis of message content once messages have been isolated from the message stream.

INTERNAL MESSAGE ANALYSIS

Orientation and Isolation of the Message

Batch processing and internal message analysis are done mentally simultaneously, although a shift from batch processing to attending to the content of the given message requires a reflective pause. In order to attend to the content of a message, two fundamental mental processes must take place: isolating the message as a unit and orienting oneself to the message.

The first action required is to isolate the message as a phenomenological unit (Manning 1988:250–257). The mental operation of isolating the message includes separating the call from socially defined noise, divorcing the call from the field of activity occurring around the listener, and placing the message in an ordering frame or metaphoric context. The first two processes are not discussed here, but the last, providing the ordering frame, involves typification and grouping calls into "crime," "noncrime," and "other" calls (see Manning 1988:117–128).

The second action required is orienting to the message. Messages are heard always within a social context, what is brought to the message by the hearer and the speaker. In an organization, the context is in part rationally constructed, rewarded, and sustained by close supervision; the constraints on orientation are greater than in everyday life. Any message that arrives in a police organization from the "external world" comes into a preconstituted culturally partitioned context and is processed using preestablished social routines by people carrying out organizationally sanctioned roles and tasks, within organizational segments (e.g., operators, dispatchers, and officers). Each segment has distinctive information-processing technology.

The orientation process can be understood by employing Guiraud's (1975) modification of Jakobson's (1960) model of the functions of the sign or speech act. A listener can be oriented in one of five ways to the message: (1) to the communication itself as a ritual act or as a way of checking on the existence of a shared channel (the phatic function); (2) to the objects to which the signs in the message refer (what might be called the commonsensical referential rule, or the referential function); (3) to the sender's relationship to the message emitted (the emotive function); (4) to the receiver-message connection (the cognitive function); or (5) to the aesthetics of the message, the message's relationship to itself. This last orientation is important in poetry or the arts, in which the form, for example, the shape of the words and letters (the type face or iconic symbolism), and the arrangement of words on the page communicate as well as the content.

Organizations provide a metalinguistic or framing (Goffman 1974) activity that reduces the difficulty of transforming the message into actionable communication units. Some framing work is done in computer formatting and in writing, for example, by the use of quotation marks, "domestic disturbance," or of *italics*. Other framing is accomplished by the rules previously listed, which serve to reduce ambiguity by answering questions about the underlying code itself, into which calls are to be encoded and from which they can best be decoded. Some questions of orientation are answered by organizational fiat. Orientation to the referential function or the content of the message, the cognitive connection between the message and the hearer (the operator in this case), is assumed by the operators, dispatchers, and officers. This orientation, however, varies empirically from call to call and from caller to caller. What is assumed is a matter of perspective and framing and cannot be suppressed easily by organizational rules and regulations.

Internal Message Analysis: Units, Salience, and Surround

Once a message is isolated for attention and an orientation is accomplished, several further steps can be observed.

The communicational units are further broken down. Content-based decisions depend on internal message analysis. Organization members divide the message into units and then establish the salience of the units arrayed. To some degree, aspects of the caller's talk, the social event described in the call, and the perspective of the operators and dispatchers on the nature of the work of the officers are conflated.

The units or syntagms used in the incident classification scheme of the MPD, for example, are: location of the incident, character of the location (house, bar, intersection), description of the problem ("domestic"), actions involved in the reported incident (hitting, threats, etc.), to whom or what (spouse/partner), incident number, and potential for development. This last dimension is built into the classification scheme and is attached to the name given the incident by the operator. If the operator codes the call as "person screaming" it is listed as 1–3951, or first priority (1-), family trouble (39), screaming (5), of the first type (1). If she codes it as spouse abuse-law-injunction/peace bond, it is listed as 3–3989: third priority (3), family trouble (39), legal action (89) (see Manning 1988:165, table 5.1).

The bases for such coding are exceedingly complex. The bases for assigning an incident to one or another category could be related to the operator's orientation to the caller—stress in the voice, dialect, register or speed—or "key words" such as those describing weapons or physical hitting. Before hearing key words the operator has mentally typified the call or imagined it. The operators imagine the meaning of such an event as told by this caller at this time and place and include their own tacit or background assumptions about the nature of the danger, its potential and imminence. Even the presence of key words, when they do not conform to the operator's preestablished image of the event described by the caller, will not lead the operator to "upgrade" the call to a more serious category (see Manning 1988:80ff).

The salience of the units must be established. In the operators' subsystem, the salience of the units within the format is based on their anticipation of the processing activities of the dispatchers and the actions of the officers. Because operators are constrained by format to "fill in all the boxes," the presence and salience of any item are less important for operators' decisions than for dispatchers and officers (see Manning 1988:178–179, 188). The rank of an item makes no difference in whether operators send it on; it bears only on their initial decision about how to encode it.

The surround, the background and foreground of calls, is noted. The actions of operators and dispatchers, especially their preliminary classifications of calls, shape the expectations of officers who receive the call-incident-message-assignment as a job (Pepinsky 1976). Let us assume that a job has been labelled a "domestic" and accepted by an officer. At this point, as at each stage in the call-processing activity, the question arises of the widely varying *background* or surround against which the call is heard. Ethnographic work suggests that the area of a city, past calls to such an area, the nature of assumptions about the kinds of people who live in this area, on this street, or in this building and how they live (Bittner 1970; Rubinstein 1973), matters Ferraro (1989:67–69) terms "ideological," are features of a somewhat stable background knowledge surrounding a call.

Social forces and events can modify background knowledge, converting it into foreground. Background factors that can be abruptly converted to foreground appear to be crisis events such as riots, demonstrations, natural disasters, severe weather, and changes in the political environment of an area or in a city (Manning, forthcoming a). Some changes are more subtle and unfold over time. There is evidence recently of changes in background. The emergent moral ambience of a "war on drugs" gives license to officers to act more violently and with impunity toward "crack dealers" or users or those found in "crack houses." Changes in the law and police policy in the last five or six years have altered officers' responsibilities in domestic violence cases.

There are real consequences of changes in the surround, albeit marginal ones (Ferraro 1989). Since the introduction of state laws requiring officers to arrest on felony charges in domestic disputes if the facts justify it or to provide service or assistance to the battered spouse or partner, there is a greater awareness of the political potential of a mishandled battering case. Policy changes that require arrest in a job involving a "domestic" will be seen and defined by officers as more likely to be reviewed by supervisors, to reach public attention, and have a potential to become news. As a result, greater care is taken in constructing the evidence on the scene, writing the report, and providing feedback to police dispatchers. Policy changes, if well implemented, could mean that a "domestic," "family trouble," or "family fight" job will be in seen in a different set of *surrounding understandings* than other calls and not as "domestics" have been seen previously (see Dunford, Huizinga, and Elliott 1990).

PRACTICAL INFERENCES

Several summary points derived from ethnographic work can highlight misconceptions implicit in advocating technological solutions to the ambiguities of call processing.

The role of information in determining the results of call processing is exaggerated. The assumption that information shapes police classification and drives the nature and quality of the police response is true for a small set of calls. Aside from calls whose arrival is linked to a nonproblematic response, such as alarm calls and internal management calls such as "call the station" from the precinct captain to an officer in the field, those named by operators as "serious" are defined by a few key informational elements in the call. These are, other things being equal, elements that connote danger, a possible arrest for the officer on the scene, crimes in progress, or threats to property or public order.

The role of referential orientation in information-based processing is also exaggerated. It assumes incorrectly that the content of messages, files, cases, reports, and records is limited in meaning to its declarative, logical informational functions. Informational aspects of messages encoded by operators on computers for citizen demand processing are a small but significant determinant of patterns of message processing. Allocation and intervention decisions made by urban police with high-technology computer dispatching systems are governed primarily by conventional practices and interpretations, the roles and tasks of organizational members, the classification system into which messages are cast, and other noninformational aspects of the message itself (see Cicourel 1986; Manning 1982).

An information-based conception of call-processing denies the important role of ignorance and error and of unanticipated, emergent consequences of decisions. Systems are never fully cybernetic, closed, and error- or glitch-free. Rather, the interactive features of informational systems and actors produce sociotechnical beliefs that define and shape "error."

The initial classification is reified in much police research. Each formal classification is affected by organizational matters of technology, roles and tasks, interpretative work, and the nature of the classification and coding scheme. Furthermore, for each message, taken as a content-unit, an internal message analysis must be carried out. "Noninformational features of messages" shape the definition of messages and the associated resultant actions. Virtually all calls screened in or trusted will result in a unit's being "requested," unless there is a departmental policy about the use of "call-in" techniques or delayed response to certain calls. The police response to a call, sending a unit if the call is trusted and screened in (accepted and not terminated or referred), depends little on the initial classification and coding work of the operators, because the basic working rule of the operators and dispatchers is to send everything on and let the officers on the scene determine the appropriate character of the event. The stream of messages is treated as a series of sequential strings, one at a time, while calls are also clustered as associated types of messages regardless of their precise content. This means that at each stage in call processing, messages are typified and given a rough priority on a scale of immediate, soon, and maybe.

Metalinguistic signals that serve to frame calls are overlooked as sources of meaning. Recall that the orientation of the hearer to the call need not be to its referential content, but to the emotional tone of the caller, the garbled message form, or the receiver's response to the message. A series of steps establishes the meaning of a given message, once it is sorted out for attention. The message is partitioned into organizationally mandated units, based in part on the format of the message; the units are given rank and salience and typified as to type of call in each of the three subsystems.

The PCS is not a closed system with mere pass-through effects in which information is neither gained nor lost, nor is it governed by systematic feedback. It is an open system, changes in which are sent forward but not back. The movement of messages through the PCS (the three subsystems of operators, dispatchers, and officers on the ground) alters and transforms their meaning. Each subsystem has its own context-specific connotative responses that spin off from the denotative signs found within the message (Manning 1985). For example, any call that connotes an arrest on the scene, regardless of the factual content of the call, will be given importance by officers because it connotes "crime" and "good police work."

The unit, a message, is not the basic term for the analysis of police calls. The message is rather an *interpretant*, or something from which something else can be read (Eco 1976:68–72). Classifications within the system are not of equal power and importance; connotative coding has increasing significance as the message moves through the PCS. The semiotician Eco terms this connotative process *undercoding*, as a call is taken to mean more than is revealed in the communication itself.

The role of the social organization and social control of police work is underemphasized in technologically based research. Police officers have an active role in using, shaping, and subjectively constructing technology to maintain a dialectic between objective constraints and individual choices and between the conservative and controlling forces of the organization and their own autonomy. For example, police officers, like other industrial workers, control their output. Assignments handled come under the workers' control of output, as does any industrial production process, and are shaped very powerfully by shared and sanctioned peer practices governing number of calls handled, speed of response, and reporting return to service. These matters of workload control are facets of police microculture and can be expected to vary from department to department.

Practical matters count as well. The level of demand affects the pattern of response to a given message (Manning 1988). The wish to maintain discretion and autonomy and the production and amplification of uncertainty suffuse organizational relationships in the police and pattern the response of organization members to calls for service. Under high workload conditions, calls grouped as "crime calls" are given priority, order calls are pushed down the list regardless of their time of arrival, and "dirty work" or service of a general sort may not be done.

COMMENT

This chapter describes technologically shaped responses to calls concerning domestic violence by operators in one large police department. This account probably captures the outlines of the process in any large CAD-based operation. Probably, CAD or other formalized modes of managing calls will increase in time, standard practice in this country will be based on CAD modalities of service delivery (Manning, forthcoming). All domestic calls processed by CAD systems and sent through to officers will be subject to very powerful organizational constraints as well as ideological, practical, legal, and political constraints that pattern responses to reports of domestic violence (Ferraro 1989).

This chapter has addressed the screening process from the organization's perspective, rather than that of the caller. Reports ex post facto of the mishandling of calls should recognize that the sense-making activities of operators are guided by context-bound understandings rather than by the perceptions of callers. The distressed caller's perspective has been overemphasized in journalistic reports in which the trauma is viewed with the acuity of retrospective vision. Reproduction of long interactions between speakers and hearers in 911 interactions, as in newspaper reports, are misleading. It is mistakenly assumed that the orientation is mutual: that the cognitive and emotive orientations are shared by speaker-hearer dyads, and the referential reality of the signs or words used is identical. The metalinguistic aspects of framing the call are not explored.

In any case, it is not possible to determine orientation nor metalinguistic functions of the signs or words from typed transcripts. These transcripts are edited by journalists; they omit any indication of changes in voice speed, register, dialect, pauses, and hesitations, external noise and activities in the room, and the field of other events.

The police maintain their control over events by controlling the channels through which information flows and the codes used to transform everyday talk into organizational materials. They both sustain and amplify drama, the selective use of symbols to convey a social message, through four features of message processing. One essential source of police drama in the PCS lay in suppressing emotive and symbolic self-referential aspects of the message from the callers' perspective and officially denying their relevance. Another is encoding human misery in binary categories and denying callers feedback on organizational decisions. By converting information into ritual, the police mandate their symbolic control over social order (Manning 1982).

Managing domestic violence calls in a sensitive and humane way would appear to be in tension, on the one hand, with organizational goals of reducing workload, managing demand, and maintaining police control over events and, on the other hand, with sustaining the drama of police work, which is based on two rather contrary goals: to stand ready to serve, protect, and surveill a population and to react rapidly to actual and potentially life-threatening and property-damaging events. It is in the interest of the latter goal that the former service is rationed.

What can be said about the potential of changes in call screening as a means of mitigating the effects of domestic violence? There are three levels at which policy changes can be made: alterations of strategies such as the use of community policing and specialized units, changes in the technology, and modifications of current practices.

Community policing may lead to alterations in the balance of effort devoted to reactive strategies. Such matters as assisting those locked out of a car or taking insurance reports or reports on "cold burglaries" (more than a day old) may be refused by operators, be referred to towing companies or locksmiths to be handled privately, or be referred back to the caller to handle by private conversations with a neighbor. Community policing may increase average response time because tasks not driven by responses to calls for service are given more time and attention, while it may free cars to respond more rapidly to the three to five percent of calls about events that are potentially life-threatening. Community policing may mean that some problematic calls, such as calls reporting domestic violence, will be given low priority.[6]

Action can be taken to provide specialized forms of response to domestic violence calls. In the 1970s, police crisis units were developed and trained to better manage family violence (Bard 1972). This useful innovation seems to have been abandoned. It would seem logical to have specialized domestic violence units in large police departments. All domestic violence calls would be referred to them, while they would stand outside the normal rotation for service calls and be assigned other duties at "slack times."

Opportunities are also inherent in the enhanced 911 system. The operator in receipt of a call can pull up data on the screen for previous calls to the ten-block area from which the current call came, features of those calls, and what if any police response was made or is being made to the problem. This technique is very useful, for example, in identifying repeat calls about an event that affects an entire area, such as a flood, traffic accident, or neighborhood-wide dispute. It can reduce the ahistorical character of police response. Recent research by Sherman and others (1989, forthcoming) in Minneapolis is based on the premise that, by locating and characterizing high-use areas of the city (defined as address from which a high rate of phone calls issue), one can attempt to intervene or change the pattern of calls. They argue that by targeting areas of the city in an attempt to reduce calls from those locales one can (a) reduce the workload of operators, dispatchers, and officers; (b) focus officers' efforts on "serious calls"; (c) save time not spent on trivial calls; and (d) focus officers' attention on "hot spots" of crime. Such approaches are suggested also by Pierce (this volume). Sherman's research, however, shows that serious violence, as opposed to recalls to the same address or building about fights, is very rare and unpredictable. Changes in operators' habits would have to be mandated and supervision be altered to produce awareness of patterns of domestic assault, if operators were to be expected to alert officers.

Action can be taken to modify other current practices. Operators can be told to code any call in which the threat of violence is treated as a key word that elevates the call to first priority; departments will have to accept that if this is done, callers will learn to use these "magic words" to ensure that a car is sent. This means, in effect, encouraging greater trust in the caller, rather than rationing and restricting service for these kinds of events. As Chaudhuri and Daly's (this volume) research based on interviews with battered women suggests, legal restraining orders can be effective if taken seriously by operators. If operators inquire about whether the caller has an order, more consistent police responses can be made to women who already have been beaten and known to be vulnerable.

Changes can be made in officers' practices only with difficulty. Police workloads can be expected to increase, as a result of computer-assisted dispatching, and crime levels to rise in large cities. Will police be willing to devote the required personnel and imagination to respond more sensitively to domestic violence reports? Such calls constitute one of the most time-consuming, frustrating, and occasionally dangerous of calls. Criminalizing an event that indexes broad life-style and coping mechanisms and resources by arresting one party is a severely limited option (Sherman and Berk 1984). Policies that mandate arrest under experimental conditions do not seem to produce the claimed reduction in rearrests in any case (Dunford, Huizinga, and Elliott 1990). Other strategies, targeted at various points in the message stream, must be considered to reduce the very considerable damage of domestic violence.

NOTES

1. Police have long been fascinated with technology and science; CAD is only one version of the technological conceit. For a review of police use of technology see Manning 1980, 1988, and forthcoming.

2. For details of the MPD and the ethnographic bases for my analytic scheme, see

Symbolic Communication (1988). The Midwestern Police Department is one of the ten largest cities in America with a very large black population and a police force of around 6,000 officers.

3. Methodologically, it is important to note that slicing into the PCS at any point in time will produce a different set of records labelled "domestic assault," "family problems," or the like. Consider the MPD list of "incident codes" on p. 72, Fig. 3.6, in Manning 1988. See also Davis 1983, Percy and Scott 1985, pp. 60–62ff.

4. The basic rules employed by operators and dispatchers for making sense of these messages are summarized in *Symbolic Communication* (1988).

5. The nature of the screening may have to do with the degree of formalization and computer automation of the system. If police officers work as dispatchers or operators, they may reduce workload by more restrictive definitions of events requiring police assistance in advance. In my research, operators rarely spoke to callers outside the formatted sequence unless they threatened suicide. Mistakes and errors are rife, but it is perhaps impossible to provide human services without a level of routine errors. The question is whether and to what degree operators should be made scapegoats for carrying out organizationally sanctioned procedures for rationing service.

6. I am grateful to Bob Trojanowicz for enlightening me on these points in conversation.

REFERENCES

Bard, M. 1972. *Police Family Crisis Intervention and Conflict Management: An Action Research Analysis*. Washington, D.C.: LEAA.

Bercal, T. 1970. Calls for Police Assistance. *American Behavioral Scientist* 13:681–91.

Bittner, E. 1970. *The Functions of the Police in Modern Society*. Bethesda: National Institute of Mental Health (NIMH).

Cicourel, A. 1985. Text and Discourse. *Annual Review of Anthropology* 14:159–85.

———. 1986. Social Measurement as the Creation of Expert Systems. In D. Fiske and R.A. Schweder, eds., *Metatheory in Social Science*. Chicago: University of Chicago Press.

Davis, P. 1983. Restoring the Semblance of Order: Police Strategies in the Domestic Dispute. *Symbolic Interaction* 6(2):261–78.

Douglas, M. 1985. *Risk Assessment According to the Social Sciences*. New York: Russell Sage.

Dunford, F., D. Huizinga, and D. S. Elliott. 1990. The Role of Arrest in Domestic Assault: The Omaha Police Experiment. *Criminology* 28, no.2 (May): 183–206.

Eco, U. 1976. *A Theory of Semiotics*. Bloomington: University of Indiana Press (paper edition, 1979).

Ferraro, K. 1989. Policing Woman Battering. *Social Problems* 36:61–74.

Garfinkel, H., ed. 1967. *Studies in Ethnomethodology*. Englewood Cliffs, N.J.: Prentice-Hall.

Garfinkel, H., and E. Bittner. 1967. Good Organizational Reasons for "Bad" Clinic Records. In H. Garfinkel, ed., *Studies in Ethnomethodology*, pp. 186–207. Englewood Cliffs, N.J.: Prentice-Hall.

Goffman, E. 1974. *Frame Analysis*. Cambridge, Mass.: Harvard University Press.

Goldstein, H. 1990. *Problem-Oriented Policing*. New York: McGraw-Hill.

Guiraud, P. 1975. *Semiology*. London: Routledge and Kegan Paul.

Jakobson, R. 1960. Closing Statement. In T. Sebeok, ed., *The Uses of Language*. Cambridge, Mass.: MIT Press.

Larson, R. 1989. The New Crime Stoppers. *Technology Review* 10:28–31.

Leaf, Murray. 1972. *Information and Behavior in a Sikh Village*. Berkeley: University of California Press.

Lipsky, M. 1980. *Street-Level Bureaucracies*. New York: Russell Sage.

Manning, P. K. 1980. Crime and Technology: The Role of Scientific Research and Technology in Crime Control. In vol. 2. *Five Year Outlook for Science and Technology in the United States*. Washington, D.C.: National Science Foundation.

———. 1982. Producing Drama: Symbolic Communication and the Police. *Symbolic Interaction* 5(Fall):223–41.

———. 1985. Limits upon the Semiotic Structuralist Perspective on Organizational Analysis. In N. Denzin, ed., *Studies in Symbolic Interaction*, vol. 6. Greenwich, Conn.: JAI Press.

———. 1986. Signwork. *Human Relations* 39:283–308.

———. 1988. *Symbolic Communication*. Cambridge, Mass.: MIT Press.

———. Forthcoming. Technologies and the Police: The Police and Technologies. In N. Morris and M. Tonry, eds., *Crime and Justice Annuals*. Chicago: University of Chicago Press.

———. Forthcoming a. Big Bang Decisions. . . . In K. Hawkins, ed., *Discretion*. Oxford: Oxford University Press.

Markus, Lynne. 1984. *Systems in Organizations*. Boston: Pitman.

Pepinsky, H. 1976. Police Patrolmen's Offense-Reporting Behavior. *Journal of Research in Crime and Delinquency* 13:33–47.

Percy, S., and E. J. Scott. 1985. *Demand Processing and Performance in Public Service Agencies*. University, Ala.: University of Alabama Press.

Pierce, G., S. Spaar, and L. Briggs. 1984. The Character of Police Work. Unpublished paper, Center for Applied Social Research, Boston University.

Reiss, A. J., Jr. 1971. *The Police and the Public*. New Haven: Yale University Press.

Rubinstein, J. 1973. *City Police*. New York: Farrar, Straus and Giroux.

de Saussure, F. 1966. *Course in General Linguistics*, edited by C. Bally and A. Sechehaye and translated by W. Baskin. New York: McGraw-Hill (originally published in 1915).

Sherman, L. W., and R. Berk. 1984. The Specific Deterrent Effects of Arrest for Domestic Assault. *American Sociological Review* 49:261–72.

Sherman, L. W., P. Gartin, and M. E. Buegner. 1989. Hot Spots of Predatory Crime: Routine Activities and the Criminology of Place. *Criminology* 27: 27–55.

———. Forthcoming. Police and Crime Control. In N. Morris and M. Tonry, eds., *Crime and Justice Annuals*. Chicago: University of Chicago Press.

4

IDENTIFYING HOUSEHOLDS AT RISK OF DOMESTIC VIOLENCE

Glenn L. Pierce and Susan Spaar

Glenn Pierce and Susan Spaar's chapter addresses how technology impacts upon organizational performance. They deal with the implications of the emerging possibility that households at risk of domestic violence may be identified and singled out for differential responses. After years of analysis of an elaborate Boston data base consisting of all calls for service between 1977 and 1982, they conclude that domestic violence is both highly repetitive and predictable. Individuals using police emergency services in response to incidents of domestic violence are also more likely to avail themselves of other emergency services. Through identification of such repeat households, they show how it is possible to better address a broad range of related problems, including medical emergencies, drug abuse, unspecified disturbances, and assaults among other family members.

Pierce and Spaar deal with the potential benefits of new technology. No police department to date systematically uses this technology to develop a comprehensive data base, let alone bases its policies thereon. However, the potential to identify individuals and families at risk may perhaps inevitably lead to this practice as an ultimate outcome. This information could also improve and enhance not only the responses of police but those of other social agencies as well. In an era where policing emphasizes a problem-oriented approach (Goldstein 1990) and a proactive rather than reactive response, this area is clearly a fruitful one for research and policy development.

The implications of such a data base may be enormous. For example, should families prone to domestic violence be differentially treated by police and other agencies? For instance, a jurisdiction might select a progressively more punitive approach for recidivists. Similarly, policy analysts should test whether preventive intervention would be cost effective. Such a family might benefit from a response by a police/social work team free to deal with an incipient problem in a less punitive manner than is needed after a serious incident has occurred. Intervention strategies may also be based on an analysis of the frequency and severity of injuries incurred at the household level. In the present approach, frequency and severity of prior incidents do not significantly affect the likelihood of arrest or the intervention style chosen by the police.

Domestic violence is a widespread reality in American society. A national survey of more than two thousand families in 1975 (Straus, Gelles, and Steinmetz 1980) found that over 10 percent of all respondents surveyed reported at least one incident of husband to wife abuse or injury during the previous year, and the researchers estimated that over two million women had been severely beaten by their spouse. Ten years later, a replication of the 1975 study found fairly similar rates of domestic violence against women (Straus and Gelles 1986). Even more disturbing, research on long-term exposure to domestic violence suggests that almost 30 percent of all women will experience physical abuse and injury by a male partner sometime during their lives (Straus, Gelles, and Steinmetz 1980; Teske and Parker 1983). Finally, research also indicates that domestic violence is rarely an isolated event; once a woman is victimized, she faces a high risk of being victimized again (Langan and Innes 1986).

Over the fifteen years, there has been a growing societal response to domestic violence (Hotaling and Sugarman 1986). For example, between 1975 and 1980, forty-four states passed legislation on domestic violence. Unfortunately, despite growing national concern, there is still no national surveillance system to monitor domestic violence (Bowen and Sedlak 1985). Even more important, there are very few, and only rudimentary, state and local surveillance systems designed to monitor this problem (Bowen and Sedlak 1985).

The failure to develop client and community level surveillance systems to monitor domestic violence probably relates to a complex set of cultural, organizational, and technical issues. The organizational and cultural issues concern how police and other service providers perceive and are organized to respond to domestic violence; how service providers and victims interact and cooperate; and finally how different service providers cooperate and coordinate their responses to victims. The technical issues concern how information is collected and managed.

In the case of police departments, research indicates that, at least in the past, many police officers have viewed domestic violence calls as a nuisance, not as real police work (Loving 1980). Studies (cf. Nan Oppenlander 1982 for a review of the literature) have shown that a consistent downgrading of the priority given police response to domestic disturbance calls results in slower response time than for other calls of the same order of seriousness (Dobash and Dobash 1979). In addition, research indicates that police are sometimes reluctant to arrest suspects in domestic violence cases because of the hardship arrest would impose on the family (possible loss of wages) and its futility, given the courts' attitude toward processing domestic assault cases (Black 1971). Finally, another reason sometimes cited for police reluctance to deal with such calls is that they do not feel qualified to handle them effectively (Barocas 1973).

Although police receive a great many requests for assistance, incidents of family violence or disturbances often are not systematically recorded by police departments, even when an incident results in the conviction of an offender (Hammond 1977; Reed et al. 1983). Under these circumstances, instances of repetitive spouse abuse may be perceived as isolated unrelated occurrences, not justifying serious consideration by police personnel. The research of Barancik et al. (1983) suggests that individuals with intentionally caused injuries seek medical services even if no "formal" police reports are filed. This research suggests there may be serious interagency disjunctions (between police and emergency medical services) when violence in a family situation escalates to more serious levels.

In reviewing research on individuals served by a variety of agencies, Gamache, Edelson, and Schock reported that "there has been no serious discussion that we know of concerning a data gathering organization which could effectively gather police, social agency and survey data in some coherent fashion so that the resulting data could be used to make estimates of the incidence and the consequences of crimes on a national level" (U.S. Department of Justice 1984).

Fortunately, developing a comprehensive domestic violence surveillance system is well within the capacity of most municipal and county governments in the United States today. Such systems can be based on the interlocking public safety and medical services provided by police departments, emergency medical ambulance services (EMS), and hospital emergency rooms (ERs).

Police, EMS, and ER systems undoubtedly represent the primary municipal government resources available for most victims of domestic violence. The doors of each of these services are open twenty-four hours a day, and they meet the most pressing needs of many victims of domestic violence, that is protection from violence and medical attention.

Importantly, in many American communities, police and emergency medical services are linked together via 911 emergency response communication systems (Gruber, Meckling, and Pierce 1991). Typically, modern 911 communications systems, when integrated with computer aided dispatching (CAD) systems, collect enormous amounts of information on the public safety and emergency medical problems facing citizens. Moreover, their service personnel (e.g., police officers, emergency medical personnel, nurses) also collect additional significant amounts of information concerning the crime and health-related problems facing citizens (Pierce et al. 1988).

Currently, however, much of this information is often unavailable for monitoring victims of domestic violence or any other type of intentional injury. It may be stored in relatively unmanageable forms (such as paper reports or magnetic tapes) or may not be accurately or fully recorded by the service providers (see Gruber, Meckling, and Pierce 1991). Not surprisingly, few if any efforts are being made by public administrators to utilize the information routinely collected by police and emergency medical response systems to identify individuals at risk of domestic violence or to monitor its scope in the community. Information from these systems can provide a major part of the infrastructure for a community-wide domestic violence surveillance system.

In the following analysis, we first examine the information retrieval and management characteristics of the Boston Police Department's (BPD) 911/CAD system. Boston's system is a conventional first-generation 911/CAD that is fairly typical of systems still in use in larger American cities.

Next, we examine the character of information collected from Boston's 911/CAD system and also from police crime reports on requests for assistance related to domestic disturbance and on households generating such requests. Finally, we examine how 911/CAD information can be used to identify households at risk of domestic violence.

CHARACTERISTICS OF CONVENTIONAL 911 COMPUTER AIDED DISPATCHING (CAD) SYSTEMS

The Flow of Information in a Conventional 911/CAD System

Boston's current CAD system became operational in the late 1970s. The system was designed to be an integral part of the overall Command, Control, and Communication system of the police department. The department's preexisting 911 complaint-reporting system was linked directly to the CAD system (via CRT terminals), and the CAD system itself essentially operated as an on-line inventory system to keep track of both citizen calls for police assistance and available patrol units for police dispatch.

A schematic representation of the flow of information through Boston's CAD system is presented in Figure 4.1. The numbers in Figure 4.1 correspond to each of the steps we are about to examine. This diagram and these steps are not intended to specify all the possible sources and channels of information in Computer Aided Dispatching/911 communications systems.

Step 1: Requests for police assistance to the CAD system generally originate from citizens via the 911 phone system. Other potential sources of requests for assistance include (1) citizens via station house calls, (2) police officers providing on-site services, (3) hotlines, and (4) ADT alarms.

Step 2: The call is answered by a 911 call-taker, who enters the information concerning the nature of the call into the computer. Each call-taker's video display terminal (VDT) is linked directly to the CAD system. The basic data required by the CAD to process a call are (1) the nature of the call, (2) street address (and apartment number if necessary), (3) the priority of the call, and (4) the service response. The nature code is a six-character (or shorter) description of the type of call. For example, FAMTRB stands for family trouble and SCKPSN is a sick person. When the 911 call-taker inputs the address given by the caller,

Figure 4.1
The Flow of Information in the Boston Police Department

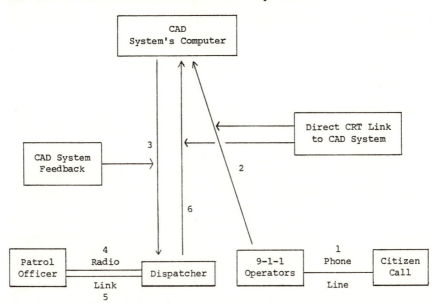

a Geographic Base File (GBF) is activated to verify the location. The GBF uniquely identifies most street addresses in the city. After verifying the address, the CAD system assigns a unique identifier to the particular request. The CAD system records this information and also transmits it to a dispatcher's VDT.

Step 3: Once the dispatcher receives the information on a request for assistance, he or she then examines information on patrol car availability.

Step 4: The dispatcher assigns a police unit via radio. The dispatcher enters both the dispatch time and the officer's arrival time. The dispatch time is recorded as soon as a response unit is notified of the call.

Step 5: After servicing the call, the officer contacts the dispatcher via radio and reports on the clearance time and also on the type of problem encountered. If the problem generating the request is not considered a crime, it must be cleared with a "miscellaneous disposition" code. If a call is reported as a crime, an incident report must be filled out by the police officer.

Step 6: The dispatcher enters the patrol unit's clearance time, information on the type of service rendered, and information on the type of problem serviced into the CAD system computer via the CRT terminal. This information is recorded and stored along with the other information on the call for assistance on the CAD hard disk, mass-storage devices.

In summary, the CAD system collects and stores the following information on all calls for service: (1) street address, including apartment number; (2) type of location (e.g., park, school, street intersection); (3) original categorization of the request for assistance entered by the 911 call-taker or, in the case of on-site intervention, by the police dispatcher (nature code); (4) classification of the request for service upon clearance by the police officer (miscellaneous); and (5) date of the request.

Classification of Requests for Assistance at the Call-Taking and Police Response Points

Although most researchers agree that the majority of police work is not directly crime-related, less agreement is found on the relative distribution of noncrime problems in police work for at least two reasons. First, as Scott (1980) points out, inconsistency in the classification schemes used by police departments to categorize requests for assistance makes cross-study comparisons impossible. Second, studies comparing the demand for police services across departments often rely on different information from different points in the reporting and classification process when they examine the substantive character of requests for police services. Research indicates frequent differences between how citizens perceive problems needing police assistance and how police ultimately define and classify the problems upon clearance (see Black 1971, Pierce et al. 1988).

Table 4.1 examines the distribution of the demand for police services in Boston as initially defined by 911 call-takers or police dispatchers. The 911 call-takers are generally the first actors to receive citizen requests for police services, and police dispatchers are typically the first to be notified about police-initiated activities (e.g., an investigation, an on-site intervention). These actors provide important information on how requests or incidents are originally characterized by citizens or by police officers. The initial characterization or categorization of a request was measured using the six-character description of it that these actors generally provide.

"Crimes in progress" is the first category of requests for police services presented in Table 4.1. These requests represented only 2.2 percent of the police workload during the period under study. The next four categories of requests can be characterized as "crimes against the person" (assault and battery, fights, assaults or threats, and weapons). Together these categories represent 189,021 requests or 5.8 percent of the total police workload. In addition, 71,962 calls initially were characterized as "domestic disturbance," representing 2.2 percent of the total. Requests characterized as "property crime" accounted for 10.8 percent of all the calls (i.e., robbery, 1.5 percent; burglary, 5.3 percent; and larceny, 4.0 percent).

Noncrime-related requests for services, as shown in Table 4.1, fall into a broad variety of areas, including motor vehicle-related problems, order main-tenance problems, and medical emergencies. "Motor vehicle-related problems" including car accidents, abandoned cars, or cars blocking passageway accounted for 8.7 percent of the total police workload. Requests initially characterized as "order maintenance problems" included drunks, minor disturbances, gang-

Table 4.1
Requests for Police Assistance as Initially Classified by 911 Call-Takers in Boston, 1977–1982

INITIAL CLASSIFICATION BY 9-1-1 CALL-TAKERS	NUMBER	PERCENT
CRIME EMERGENCY	70,674	2.2
VIOLENT CRIME (e.g., murder, rape)	3,355	0.1
ASSAULT AND BATTERY	62,292	1.9
FIGHT	68,630	2.1
ASSAULT THREAT	28,658	0.9
WEAPONS	26,146	0.8
ARGUMENT	12,357	0.4
DOMESTIC DISTURBANCE	71,962	2.2
ROBBERY	48,062	1.5
BURGLARY	170,632	5.3
LARCENY	128,516	4.0
DRUNKS	57,882	1.8
DISTURBANCE	205,456	6.4
GANGS OF YOUTHS	206,101	6.4
VANDALISM	96,692	3.0
LOUD PARTIES/MUSIC	39,604	1.2
CAR HIT RUN	24,253	0.8
CAR ACCIDENT	78,111	2.4
MEDICAL SERVICE	91,352	2.8
DEPENDENT PERSON	41,025	1.3
INVESTIGATE	340,091	10.6
ALARM (Burglar, etc.)	211,995	6.6
PUBLIC NUISANCE	45,380	1.4
CAR ABANDONED	80,166	2.5
CAR BLOCKING	80,413	2.5
MOTOR VEHICLE	117,603	3.7
ASSISTANCE	125,849	3.9
INTERNAL SERVICE	266,318	8.3
OTHER	413,106	12.9
TOTAL CALLS	3,212,681	100.0

related disturbances, vandalism, and loud parties or music; these accounted for 18.8 percent of the total demand for all police services.

Finally, requests characterized as medical emergencies accounted for 2.8 percent of the total demand for police service. However, a majority of such requests are referred directly to emergency medical services and not counted as part of the police department's workload. Nevertheless, requests sent to emergency medical services contain potentially important data for issues related to public safety (e.g., domestic violence).

Table 4.2 examines the distribution of requests for police services as finally classified either by the responding police officer(s) upon clearance of an incident or by the BPD's records-review department upon submission of a 1.1 crime report by the responding police officer(s). As noted, police officers may either use a miscellaneous code to clear a request for services or fill out an incident 1.1 crime report to characterize the nature of an incident or problem they or the police dispatcher identifies as a potentially crime-related problem.

What is immediately obvious in examining the demand for police services as

Table 4.2
Requests for Assistance as Finally Classified by the Responding Police Officer(s) in Boston, 1977–1982

FINAL CLASSIFICATION BY RESPONDING OFFICER(S)	NUMBER	PERCENT
MURDER	500	0.0
RAPE	2,662	0.1
A AND B ASSAULT	17,771	0.6
AGGRAV ASSAULT	5,622	0.2
SIMPLE ASSAULT	25,820	0.8
DOMESTIC DISTURBANCE	90,680	2.8
ROBBERY	41,793	1.3
LARCENY	139,712	4.3
BURGLARY	91,568	2.9
AUTO THEFT	122,633	3.8
OTHER PART II	45,344	1.4
MEDICAL EMERGENCY	34,885	1.1
CAR ACCIDENTS L.S.	34,070	1.1
CAR ACCIDENT	32,482	1.0
LANDLORD TENANT	8,916	0.3
NOISY PARTY	43,046	1.3
VANDALISM	72,176	2.2
DRUNK DISORDERLY	10,316	0.3
GANG DISTURBANCE	278,135	8.7
MINOR DISTURBANCE	138,078	4.3
FALSE ALARM	214,644	6.7
INVESTIGATION	680,422	21.2
SERVICE RENDERED	949,789	29.6
OTHER	131,617	4.1
TOTAL	3,212,681	100.0

defined at this end point of the reporting classification process is that approximately 50 percent of all requests fall into two highly ambiguous clearance categories—services rendered (29.6 percent) and investigations of persons or premises (21.2 percent). Both of these are "Miscel" codes used by police officers when they respond to some presumably noncriminal incident and/or some incident that has resolved itself without police assistance (e.g., a gang of youths have left a street corner before police arrive to "broom" them off the corners). In practice, responding police officers may use these codes to classify incidents that appear relatively unimportant and/or where evidence of a problem or crime is ambiguous. Thus it appears that a good deal of information is often either not recorded or not available at the time a request for assistance is cleared by a patrol officer.

Another notable feature indicated by Table 4.2 is that generally more requests for police assistance are identified as serious crimes at the initial point in the reporting classification process than at the final point in this process. For example, 5.8 percent of the total police workload was identified as a crime against the person (murder, rape, and assault) by 911 call-takers; only 1.7 percent was classified as a crime against the person by responding police officers at the final point in the process. Similarly, 5.3 percent of all requests for police assistance were initially identified as a burglary by 911 call-takers, but only 2.9 percent were finally classified as a burglary by responding police officers. This pattern of results provides support for Reiss's finding that citizens report events as serious crimes more often than the clearance would indicate (Reiss 1971). Somewhat in contrast to this pattern, however, Table 4.2 also shows that more incidents were finally cleared as domestic disturbances than were originally classified as such by 911 operators. This may occur because some calls that originate as criminal or assaultive incidents are subsequently cleared by responding police officers as domestic disturbances when the police find that the problem is between family members or because a family member will not press criminal charges.

With regard to order maintenance problems, Table 4.2 shows that 278,135 calls (or 8.7 percent of the workload) were finally cleared as gang disturbances. Minor disturbances account for 4.3 percent of the workload, vandalism for 2.2 percent, and noisy parties for 1.3 percent.

Police as a Resource of First Resort for Victims of Domestic Violence

Police departments are one of the few public agencies that keep their door open twenty-four hours a day, seven days a week. Only 15 percent of all requests for assistance formally classified as a domestic disturbance were received by the Boston Police Department between 8 A.M. and 5 P.M. on a weekday. Thus, 85 percent of domestic disturbance calls are received by the police during times when very few other public agencies are open.

The only organizations available to victims of domestic violence during the times when such violence is most likely are the police, battered women's hotlines, hospitals, and emergency medical services. In addition, the police department's 911 phone number may be more universally known to the public than the phone numbers of other agencies and services. Victims of domestic violence, when first seeking assistance, may be less aware of nonpolice resources to help them.

In addition, some research (Barancik et al. 1983) suggests that police departments may sometimes be the primary service providers for less serious forms of family-related disturbances and assaultive behavior. In contrast, medical personnel and especially emergency medical personnel may become the more important service providers when family violence-related injuries become more serious. (At the most severe level of assaultive injury, both police and medical authorities probably become involved.) Thus, although individuals at risk of family violence-related injuries may contact both public safety and emergency medical systems, there is virtually no continuity in services and very little continuity in recording and evaluating such citizen requests for service.

REQUESTS FOR POLICE ASSISTANCE FROM DOMESTIC VIOLENCE HOUSEHOLDS

A major problem in monitoring domestic disturbance cases reported to the police is that many are not classified as such once the police have provided service to the household in question. Fortunately, using data from Boston's 911 system, we can examine the occurrence of both formally classified incidents of domestic trouble (measured via a miscellaneous service response code used by BPD police officers) and also incidents initially identified as domestic disturbance by 911 operators (measured via a nature code recorded by 911 operators) that are sometimes subsequently defined upon disposition as something else. The "something else" usually tends to be an ambiguous catchall category such as "services rendered" or "person investigated."

As previously noted, approximately 50 percent of all 3.2 million calls for police assistance between 1977 and 1982 were defined upon completion by police as an investigation or a service rendered. If the officer feels a crime has been committed, an official crime report is filled out; no computerized record of whether the crime involved domestic violence is retained. Thus, for a more accurate picture of police work regarding domestic disturbances, it is necessary to draw on information available from 911 operators.

Over the time period under study (1977 to 1982), the Boston Police Department received over 71,000 requests to 911 operators identifiable as a domestic violence-related problem. Over this same period, police officers formally classified some 90,680 requests for police assistance (2.8 percent of all requests) as a family disturbance. These figures do not include the potentially large numbers of victim requests that may not be recorded as related to a domestic violence situation. For example, police officers may file an aggravated assault report and not indicate that the offender was the spouse of the victim. Perhaps more commonly, however, police officers may use ambiguous service codes such as "persons investigated" or "services rendered" to classify requests related to domestic disturbance.

In order to gain a better understanding of the dimensions of domestic violence-related requests for police service, the following analysis compares households having one or more domestic disturbance calls to those households having only non-domestic service calls. Domestic disturbance households are defined as apartment units (a street address with an accompanying apartment number) that generated either a domestic disturbance-related request for assistance to a 911 operator in the previous year or had a request for assistance classified as a domestic disturbance by a police officer within the last year. Non–domestic disturbance households are defined as apartment units that had no domestic disturbance-related requests for police assistance in the previous year.

Comparison of character and incidence of requests for police assistance from domestic disturbance and non–domestic disturbance households provides some information on whether the former experience a higher rate and broader range of problems than households with no recorded past domestic violence. Significantly, a higher rate of problems such as assault or medical emergencies in domestic violence households may signal that police departments are not accurately identifying the underlying cause of these events. As a result, victims of domestic violence may fail to receive adequate protection from recurring problems.

The Character and Incidence of Requests for Police Assistance from Domestic Disturbance and Non–Domestic Disturbance Households

Part A of Table 4.3 displays the rate of occurrence for selected types of requests for police services as originally classified by 911 operators for domestic and non–domestic disturbance households. Comparison of the two types of households reveals dramatic differences. First, domestic disturbance households show nearly twice the rate of requests as non–domestic disturbance households (341.8 versus 179.0 calls per 100 households). More important, however, are the differences in the substantive character of requests generated from these two types of households. Domestic disturbance households show nearly four times as many assault reports to 911 call-takers (55.3 versus 14.2), almost twice as many reports of unspecified minor disturbances, and higher levels of medical emergency reports. These latter reports include only medical emergencies for which police officers accompanied emergency medical personnel to locations generating the request. Non–domestic disturbance households, on the other hand, show higher rates of reports to 911 call-takers concerning property crimes and loud parties.

Part B of Table 4.3 sets forth the rate of requests for police assistance, as classified by police officers, for domestic and non–domestic disturbance households. The incidence of selected types of requests for assistance, in both absolute and relative terms, is significantly altered when police classifications of requests are examined instead of 911 call-taker's classifications. First, the incidents of assaults are dramatically lower in both types of households, but domestic disturbance households show a greater decline in assaults. Similarly, for most types of requests for police assistance (e.g., minor disturbances, property crimes, and medical emergencies), domestic disturbance households have greater declines in incidence of problems when classified by police than when classified by 911 operators. Interestingly, medical emergencies show the greatest discrepancy. As classified by 911 operators, domestic disturbance households reported an annual rate of 15.5 medical emergencies per 100 households while non–domestic disturbance households reported 12.9 per 100. In contrast, when classified by police officers, domestic disturbance households reported an annual rate of only 3.8 medical emergencies per 100 households, while non–domestic disturbance households reported a higher rate of 6.3 per 100.

Of course, there are other, more questionable reasons that police officers may use substantively meaningless codes to classify requests for assistance. Research cited previously suggests that police officers may not treat domestic violence incidents as seriously as other types of assaults. Finally, other research (Maxfield

Table 4.3
Annual Rate of Occurrence of Selected Types of Requests for Police Assistance as Originally Classified by 911 Call-Takers for Domestic Disturbance and Non-Domestic Disturbance Households, 1978–1982

	Annual Rate Per 100 Households	
A. Requests as Classified by 9-1-1 Call-Takers	Domestic Disturbance Households[1]	Non-Domestic Disturbance Households[2]
Crime Emergency	3.1	2.2
Assault	55.3	14.2
Property Crimes	26.5	53.2
Family Disturbances	124.4	–
Other Disturbances	34.2	18.6
Vandalism	5.4	10.8
Loud Party	4.6	7.9
Medical Emergency	15.5	12.9
Investigation	25.6	18.3
B. Requests as Classified by Responding Police		
Murder/Rape	.3	.3
Assault	7.1	3.3
Property Crimes	9.2	37.5
Family Disturbance	150.0	–
Other Disturbance	18.1	6.6
Vandalism	3.6	7.9
Loud Party	4.7	8.9
Medical Emergency	3.8	6.3
Investigation/ Services Rendered	129.8	89.9
C. Total Requests	341.8	179.0
Total Number of Households	30,474	132,753

[1] A household is classified as a domestic disturbance household if the location (as identified by street address and apartment number) produced either a formally or informally classified domestic disturbance related request for police assistance within the year prior to the request.

[2] A household is classified as a non-domestic disturbance household if the location (as identified by street address and apartment number) did not produce either a formally or informally classified domestic disturbance related request for police assistance within the year prior to the request.

et al. 1980) suggests that, as the total demand for police services increases, it becomes more likely that requests for service regarding property or non-index crimes will be downgraded to unverified offenses. The next section compares the propensity to downgrade or reclassify requests for police assistance in do-mestic disturbance and non–domestic disturbance households.

Table 4.4
**Probability that the Final Police Classification of a Request for Assistance Is
Consistent with the Original Classification by the 911 Call-Taker for Domestic
Disturbance and Non-Domestic Disturbance Households, 1978–1987**

Request as Originally Classified by 9-1-1 Call-Taker	Percent Consistent with Original 9-1-1 Classification	
	Domestic Disturbance Households[1]	Non-Domestic Disturbance Households[2]
Assault	5.7 (16,865)	13.5 (18,810)
Family Trouble	60.1 (37,920)	--
Property Crime	27.0 (8,072)	59.0 (70,491)
Disturbance	9.9 (10,397)	14.0 (24,734)
Vandalism	30.0 (1,649)	42.7 (14,391)
Loud Party	52.7 (1,387)	58.9 (10,512)
Medical Emergency	13.8 (4,709)	29.5 (17,086)
Investigation	39.1 (7,807)	64.6 (24,267)

[1]See Footnote 1, Table 4.3.
[2]See Footnote 2, Table 4.3.

Reclassification of Requests for Police Assistance in Domestic Violence and Non-Domestic Violence Households

Table 4.4 examines the probability that police officers will classify requests for assistance in a manner substantively consistent with the classifications made by 911 call-takers for domestic violence and non–domestic violence households. From the information on the probability of consistent classification, it becomes apparent that, for every type of request for police assistance examined (i.e., assaults, property crimes, minor unspecified disturbances, vandalism, medical emergencies, and investigations), domestic violence households show a significantly lower percentage of requests classified by the police into the categories originally identified by 911 call-takers. For example, among requests for service originally identified by 911 call-takers as assaults, 13.5 percent of these cases in non–domestic disturbance households (with no prior requests for assistance) are subsequently classified by police officers as assaults, whereas only 5.7 percent of comparable cases in domestic violence households were so classified. Similarly, only 27 percent of the requests from domestic violence households orig- inally identified as a property crime by 911 call-takers were subsequently so classified by responding police officers, a contrast to the 59 percent so labeled in non–domestic violence households. As Table 4.4 indicates, similar discrep- ancies between domestic violence and non–domestic violence households are the rule for other types of requests.

The generally lower levels of substantively consistent classifications by police officers in domestic violence households are largely attributable to officers' classifying cases as family disturbance incidents. This practice may arise because police officers are less willing to charge individuals with burglary or assault if the incident involves a domestic problem. It may also arise because victims of domestic violence sometimes use other categories of requests for police assistance (such as a burglary in progress) to help ensure that police will respond expe- ditiously. Finally, discrepancies between domestic violence and non–domestic violence households may also in part be attributable to the tendency of responding police officers to use ambiguous clearance codes such as "services rendered" or "persons investigated," instead of the original designation assigned by a 911 call-taker, when they find that a potential offender has left or that a problem has dissipated.

IDENTIFYING HOUSEHOLDS AT RISK OF DOMESTIC VIOLENCE

Identifying households at risk of domestic violence is often complicated by a variety of factors. Perhaps one of the greatest problems in identifying victims of domestic violence is that the definition of an act of violence is particularly dependent on its context and also on the perspective of the parties who describe the incident. The problem of identifying households at risk of violence further complicates the picture. Here we are concerned with perhaps many acts of violence. If different police officers and various other service providers such as emergency medical personnel respond to separate incidents of violence from the same household, a chronic problem is unlikely to be discovered. These problems are compounded by the fact that information from the various actors who respond to such domestic violence incidents is typically collected and analyzed after the particular event that produced a request for assistance.

Boston's 911/CAD system provides an illustrative opportunity to examine how information obtained from different service delivery personnel (police officers and 911 call-takers) and information collected on possibly domestic disturbance- related incidents from the same household over time can be analyzed to identify households at risk of violence. Part A of Table 4.5 presents information on the probability of a request for police assistance for a domestic disturbance from households with a prior request for assistance classified by the responding police officer as a domestic disturbance. Part B of Table 4.5, presents information on a more expansive definition of domestic disturbances (i.e., the probability of a

Table 4.5

Probability of a Request for Police Assistance from Households with a Prior Request Regarding a Domestic Disturbance

A. The Probability of Recurrence[1] from Households with a Prior Request that was Classified by Responding Police Officer(s) as a Domestic Disturbance

| | Time to a Subsequent Request | | | |
	3 Mos.	6 Mos.	12 Mos.	Number of Requests
Probability	.230	.301	.392	45,725

B. The Probability of Recurrence[2] from Households with a Prior Request that was either Classified by a Responding Officer(s) or was Identified by a 9-1-1 Call-Taker as a Domestic Disturbance

| | Time to a Subsequent Request | | | |
	3 Mos.	6 Mos.	12 Mos.	Number of Requests
Probability	.239	.321	.407	60,580

[1] This is the probability of a subsequent request that is classified by a responding police officer(s) as a domestic disturbance.

[2] This is the probability of a subsequent request that is either classified by a responding police officer(s) or identified by a 9-1-1 call-taker as a domestic disturbance.

request for police assistance from households with a prior request that was classified either by the responding police officer(s) or by the 911 call-taker as a domestic disturbance). Note that, with the more expansive definition, we identified 60,580 requests as potential domestic disturbances whereas, when relying only on the police officers' classifications, we identified 45,725 requests as potential domestic disturbances. Interestingly, for both methods of identification, the probability of a subsequent request for assistance is about the same (approximately $p = .40$).

Table 4.6 presents evidence that information on the number of prior requests for assistance from a household is a strong predictor of the risk of future domestic disturbances in that household. For both the more restrictive (based only on responding police officers' classifications) and the more expansive definitions of a domestic disturbance, the probability of a subsequent request for assistance regarding domestic disturbance is strongly related to the number of prior requests from a household.

IMPLICATIONS FOR THE DELIVERY OF SERVICES

The preceding analysis indicates that households associated with domestic disturbance-related requests for police services experience a broad range of other, possibly related problems. In contrast with non–domestic disturbance households, those that have requested assistance for domestic problems also report far

Table 4.6

Probability of a Subsequent Domestic Disturbance-Related Request for Assistance within 12 Months from Domestic Violence Households, Controlling for the Number of Prior Domestic Disturbance-Related Requests

A. The Probability of Recurrence[1] from Households with One or More Prior Requests that were Classified by Responding Police Officer(s) as a Domestic Disturbance

Number of Prior Requests		Probability of Recurrence	Number of Requests
1.	One	.247	27,845
2.	Two	.472	8,167
3.	Three	.607	3,645
4.	Four or more	.815	6,068
All Requests		.392	45,725

B. The Probability of Recurrence[2] from Households with One or More Prior Requests that were either Classified by a Responding Police Officer(s) or Identified by a 9-1-1 Call-Taker as a Domestic Disturbance

Number of Prior Requests		Probability of Recurrence	Number of Requests
1.	One	.222	34,720
2.	Two	.464	10,721
3.	Three	.597	5,150
4.	Four or more	.816	9,989
All Requests		.530	60,580

---

[1] This is the probability of a subsequent request that is classified by a responding police officer(s) as a domestic disturbance.

[2] This is the probability of a subsequent request that is either classified by a responding police officer(s) or identified by a 9-1-1 call-taker as a domestic disturbance.

more assaults, medical emergencies, and unspecified disturbances. Moreover, domestic disturbance households produce approximately twice the level of requests for police services as their non–domestic disturbance counterparts.

The analysis also indicates that domestic violence may be a highly repetitive and in some instances predictable phenomenon. For example, the analysis indicates that if a household generates two requests for police assistance regarding domestic problems, there is a 60 percent probability of a third such request within twelve months.

Finally, our analysis suggests that information received regarding domestic violence-related households can be very complex. Importantly, the analysis suggests that information from multiple points in the reporting, classification, and servicing of domestic problems should be retained and analyzed. This is particularly important because domestic violence problems often persist over a long period of time. Thus, information from 911 operators, police officers, or other parties may prove to be important not only in the response to specific domestic violence-related requests for police assistance but equally in the potential prevention of the recurrence of similar problems in the future. As Lerman and Livingston note, "Lack of adequate data on the nature and scope of family violence has hindered improvement of law enforcement response to the problem" (1983).

If comprehensive data is collected on a timely basis on households at risk of domestic violence, proactive approaches to domestic violence become possible. Today, however, very few police departments have the capability to routinely track repeated requests for service from specific households. The inability to utilize "repeat call" information to identify at-risk households probably prevents domestic violence programs from employing proactive strategies to reduce further violence. Typically, current domestic violence approaches rely on receiving citizen requests to activate police assistance.

The preceding analysis, however, indicates that the likelihood of future domestic disturbances is directly related to the number of prior requests for police assistance regarding the problem. Most important, the probability of a subsequent request within the next year nearly doubles after one prior request regarding a domestic disturbance (see Table 4.5). This pattern suggests that police not only can use information on prior requests to evaluate a current problem but also can use such information to activate police assistance before domestic violence recurs.

A proactive domestic violence intervention strategy would have to place heavy emphasis on diagnosing the potential for further domestic violence within a household. For households where victims indicated the need for further assistance, police could provide a variety of services ranging from referral to social service agencies to the provision of police protection and/or the arrest of the offender, where legally permitted. The assistance provided would be based on the police officer's informed diagnosis of the problem and would be designed to prevent further violence.

A proactive strategy utilizing "repeat call" information would also have an advantage over purely reactive strategies in that it would use both current and prior data. The use of multiple sources of information might allow a more accurate identification of households at risk for violence. Importantly, police departments with advanced 911 and computer-aided communication systems are in a strong position to develop the comprehensive data collection systems necessary to identify households at risk of domestic violence.

REFERENCES

Aitkin, M., and D. Clayton. 1980. The Fitting of Exponential, Weibull and Extreme Value Distributions to Complex Censored Survival Data Using GLIM. *Applied Statistics* 29:156–63.

Allison, Paul D. 1984. Event History Analysis. Regression for Longitudinal Event Data. Beverly Hills, Calif.: Sage.

Attorney General's Task Force on Family Violence. 1984. *Final Report*, September.

Barancik, J. I., B. F. Chatterjee, Y. C. Greene, E. M. Michenzi, and D. Fife. 1983. Northeastern Ohio Trauma Study. I. Magnitude of the Problem. *American Journal of Public Health* 73:746–51.

Barocas, H. A. 1973. Iatrogenic and Preventive Intervention in Police-Family Crisis Situation. *International Journal of Social Psychiatry* 20(1–2): 113–21.

Black, D. J. 1971. Production of Crime Rates. In *American Sociological Review* 35:733–48.

Bowen, Gary L., and Andrea J. Sedlak. 1985. Toward a Domestic Violence Surveillance System: Issues and Prospects. In *Response* (Summer).

Committee on Trauma Research. 1985. *Injury in America*. Washington, D.C.: National Academy Press.

Cox, D. R. 1972. Regression Models and Life Tables. *Journal of the Royal Statistical Society*, Series B34:187–202.

Dobash, R. E., and R. P. Dobash. 1979. *Violence against Wives: A Case against the Patriarchy*. New York: Free Press.

Field, Martha M., and M. F. Field. 1973. Marital Violence and the Criminal Process: Neither Justice nor Peace. *Social Science Review* 47(2): 221–40.

Fleming, Jennifer B. 1979. *Stopping Wife Abuse*. Garden City, N.Y. Anchor/Doubleday.

Goldstein, H. 1990. *Problem-Oriented Policing*. New York: McGraw- Hill.

Gruber, C., J. Meckling, and G. Pierce. 1991. Information and Law Enforcement. In *Local Government and Police Management*, ed. W. Gellen. Washington, D.C.: ICMA.

Hammond, N. 1977. *Domestic Assault: A Report on Family Violence in Michigan*. State of Michigan.

Hotaling, Gerald T., and David B. Sugarman. 1986. "An Analysis of Risk Markers in Husband to Wife Violence: The Current State of Knowledge." *Violence and Victims* 1(2): 101–24.

Langan, Patrick A., and Christopher A. Innes. 1986. "Preventing Domestic Violence Against Women." *Criminal Justice Automated Information Network* (Fall): 1–3.

Lerman, Lisa, and Franci Livingston. 1983. State Legislation on Domestic Violence. *Response* (Sept./Oct.).

Loving, Nancy. 1980. *Responding to Spouse Abuse and Wife Beating: A Guide for Police*. Washington, D.C.: Police Executive Research Forum.

Maltz, M. *Recidivism*. 1985. New York: Academic Press.

Martin, Del. 1976. *Battered Wives*. New York: Pocket Books.

Maxfield, Michael G., Dan A. Lewis, and Ron Szoc. 1980. Producing Official Crimes: Crime Reports as Measures of Police Output. *Social Science Quarterly* (September).

Oppenlander, Nan. 1982. Coping or Copping Out: Police Service Delivery in Domestic Violence Disputes. *Criminology* 20:449–65.

Parnas, R. 1967. The Police Response to the Domestic Disturbance. *Wisconsin Law Review* 2: 914–46.

Pierce, Glenn, Susan Spaar, and LeBaron Briggs. 1988. *The Character of Police Work: Strategic and Tactical Implications*. Report to the National Institute of Justice, November.

Pierce, Glenn, Susan Spaar, LeBaron Briggs, and R. Hyatt. 1984. The Police and Domestic Violence: The Need to Coodinate Community Resources. Paper presented at the Governor's Anti-Crime Council, Boston.

Reed, David, Sonia Fischer, Glenda Kantor, and Kevin Karales. 1983. *All They Can Do: Police Response to Battered Women's Complaints.* Report by the Chicago Law Enforcement Study Group: Chicago.

Reiss, A. J. 1971. *The Police and the Public.* New Haven, Conn.: Yale University Press.

———. 1980. Victim Proneness in Repeat Victimization by Type of Crime. In S. Fienberg and A. Reiss, eds., *Indicators of Crime and Criminal Justice: Quantitative Studies.* U.S. Department of Justice, Bureau of Justice Statistics, Washington, D.C.

Scott, E. J. 1980. *Calls for Service: Citizen Demand and Initial Police Response.* Washington, D.C.: National Institute of Justice.

Sherman, L., and Richard Berk. 1984. The Specific Deterrent Effects of Arrest for Domestic Assault. *American Sociological Review* 49(2):261–72.

Sodlak, A. 1986. Existing Surveillance: Aids and Obstacles in Selected Community. In *Domestic Violence Surveillance*, September, *Feasibility Study: Phase II Report*, Westat, Inc., Rockville, Md.

Straus, M. A., and R. J. Gelles. 1986. Societal Change and Change in Family Violence from 1975 to 1985 as Revealed by Two National Surveys. Paper presented at the annual meeting of the American Society of Criminology, San Diego, California.

Straus, M. A., R. J. Gelles, and S. K. Steinmetz. 1980. *Behind Closed Doors: Violence in the American Family.* New York: Anchor/Doubleday.

Teske, R. H. C., and M. L. Parker. 1983. Spouse Abuse in Texas: A Study of Women's Attitudes and Their Experiences. Huntsville, Tex.: Criminal Justice Center, Sam Houston State University.

U.S. Department of Justice, Bureau of Justice Statistics. 1984. *Family Violence: Special Report.* Washington, D.C.

5

THE COURTS' RESPONSE TO POLICE INTERVENTION IN DOMESTIC VIOLENCE

Marvin Zalman

Marvin Zalman writes about the legal impetus forcing changes in police practices. He reviews how factors that include the new statutes emerging in the 1970s, the feminist movement, and new social research and advocacy papers converged to favor an interventionist role for the police. Despite this, the initial police response was to retain their existing practices of limited intervention. Not surprisingly, the failure of police to adapt to the emerging consensus toward rigorous law enforcement has not been unchallenged. The initial lawsuits described in this chapter centered upon egregious cases in which the police clearly abdicated their responsibility to protect victims of domestic violence.

Constitutional challenges were mounted, and courts found that police practices often did violate protections guaranteed by the due process and equal protection clauses of the Fourteenth Amendment of the Constitution. Similarly, tort actions demonstrating negligent dereliction of a duty owed to known victims of domestic violence have successfully been mounted. Zalman observes that such legal challenges are likely to increase in the future. The advent of new domestic violence statutes has both clarified state policies and in effect set a legal standard for police intervention.

The tendency to litigate such issues is somewhat troubling. As Zalman notes, litigation is not the preferred method of effecting organizational change; it is far preferable to have such policies receive voluntary compliance. However, it is likely that litigation shall remain one of the primary methods of enforcing the legislative will as long as many police departments, or at least their operational units, do not agree with the current mandate for an active police response and consequently decide to resist such policies.

This chapter examines the response of American federal and state courts to police reaction to violence between spouses and intimate partners, with a special focus on the issue of mandatory arrest policies. My goal is to transcend a narrow description of cases and legal doctrines in order to explain the courts' reactions in their political and social contexts and to point out limitations of courts as policy-making agencies.

THE COGNIZANCE OF SPOUSE ABUSE: FROM PRIVACY TO CRIME

The virtual absence of wife battering as a prominent topic in medical, legal, and criminal justice literature before 1970 and the rapid proliferation of interest in the topic thereafter in the popular (Martin 1981) and scholarly (Gelles and Straus 1988:40–41) literature indicate a relationship between the social definition of wife beating and the new feminism that emerged after 1970 (Harris 1987:76–97; Dobash and Dobash 1979:1–4). In the past, spousal violence was so countenanced by custom and social thinking that, in the minds of many, wife beating was not considered a crime. A 1970 survey found that 25 percent of the male respondents and 17 percent of the female sample approved of a husband's slapping his wife under certain circumstances (Frieze and Browne 1989:165). Feminist consciousness, justly outraged as much by the condonation of wife beating as by the acts themselves, sought to change public consciousness to view wife beating as a crime. To a significant degree this campaign has succeeded.

The social redefinition of spouse abuse from a matter generally within the sphere of marital privacy (Zimring 1989) to a "normal crime" (Sudnow 1965) generated a wave of legislation designed to make the courts, police, and social agencies more responsive to the problem. Within a decade forty-nine states and the District of Columbia enacted new laws to provide legal remedies to the victims of domestic violence. The legislation went beyond enhanced arrest power to include judicial protection orders, shelters for battered women, and diversion programs for offenders subjected to prosecution (Lerman 1984), indicating an intention to provide new or enhanced options to police, courts, and social agencies and not simply to create redundant rights designed to magnify the symbolic value of labeling spouse abuse as a crime (Zalman 1975:914).

The rapid acceptance of the criminal designation of spouse abuse is seen by the change of the International Association of Chiefs of Police (IACP) training manuals between 1967 and 1976. The earlier manual recommended that police officers separate couples in a domestic fight and leave without making an arrest. The revised manual stated, "Today, the manual recommends dealing with domestic assault in the same manner that all assaults are dealt with" (IACP 1967, in Gelles and Straus 1988:114). The early policy reflected the then-popular view that the bitter conflict between police and inner-city residents, which sparked violent outbreaks in the 1960s, could be alleviated if police acted more like "social workers" by adopting peacekeeping rather than law enforcement methods. The 1976 manual stated:

A policy of arrest, when the elements of the offense are present, promotes the well-being of the victim. Many battered wives who tolerate the situation undoubtedly do so because they feel they are alone in coping with the problem. The officer who starts legal action may give the wife the courage she needs to realistically face and correct her situation. (IACP 1976)

This rapid shift indicates several things: that the police regained some confidence in their law enforcement role, that an independent law enforcement expertise does not really exist in social aspects of policing that require interaction with people, and that to a significant degree agencies that exercise the state's monopoly of force in a democracy are responsive to public opinion. The predominance of the crime/law enforcement approach to wife beating was confirmed by the publication of the *Final Report* of the U.S. Attorney General's Task Force on Family Violence, recommending a control and criminal justice approach: "Family violence should be recognized and responded to as a criminal activity" (U.S. Attorney General 1984:10). Shortly thereafter, several city police departments established mandatory arrest policies in domestic violence cases (Gelles and Straus 1988:166). These positions and actions ratified the feminist perspective. Whether the changes in public perception and official pronouncements modified police behavior in domestic calls or reduced violence between intimates is a matter for empirical investigation. Nevertheless, such a massive change in public opinion virtually demanded a change in the perspective of the judiciary.

THE SOCIAL CONTEXT OF LAW AND DOMESTIC VIOLENCE REFORM

Domestic Violence, Feminism, and the Courts

Undoubtedly, "[v]iolence between spouses and intimates existed before history was written" (Zimring 1989:548). Viewing family violence as a criminal and as therefore a public matter has been traced back to colonial times (Pleck 1989). Yet, as noted, in mid–twentieth century America, wife beating was a low-visibility issue, rarely involving full enforcement of the criminal law (Goldstein 1960). This selective blindness to spouse abuse has been partially lifted in the last two decades, and the legal reaction to claims that rights have been violated because police failed to protect injured wives must be understood in its broader social context.

Even the most technical analysis of statutes, legal cases, and constitutional provisions occurs within cultural, social, and political contexts that inform the silent assumptions of the judge penning an opinion, the attorney drafting a brief, or the scholar writing an article. Assumptions are appropriate where the social context is stable and widely accepted. But when the subject under consideration is an arena of ideological conflict and shifting norms, we must explicate the extralegal considerations that influence the outcome of legal disputes. Additionally, when the law is used as a means of social change, reformers should be aware of the limits as well as the advantages of litigation as a means of reform (Horowitz 1977). Thus, for legal scholarship to be more than a chronicle of legal ephemera, an appreciation of the values, principles, and institutions that give life and meaning to legal rules and doctrines is necessary. Moreover, if legal doctrines are to support lasting social change, they must be based on a sound empirical basis and an adequate appreciation of the capacity of agencies designated to carry out policy. It is therefore critical to assess the underlying sources of judicial opinions.

The prime reason for recent interest in spouse abuse and arrest as a deterrent strategy, as suggested, has been the rise of the new feminist movement, gathering force from about 1970 and affecting virtually every aspect of American life and thought, including the law. Although changed material circumstances may be the source of the new feminism (Harris 1987), the ideological basis of the new feminism, in general, has been gender equality in most spheres of life. As a legal and political phenomenon, feminism has without doubt "empowered" women. As an empowered group, women forced society at large to shake off the selective social vision that formerly took little notice of the physical abuse of spouses. In a sense, women constituted themselves into an interest group after 1970, and as an interest group they developed sufficient organizational cohesion to bring pressure to bear on public policy decision makers to pass legislation and develop policies that benefitted their needs and demands. The feminist movement, concerned as it is with the direct experience of half the population and the relations of this half of the population with the other half, has the potential to thoroughly rearrange social concepts of acceptable behavior and appropriate thought. But, as with every radical movement, feminism has generated a spectrum of opinion on a variety of issues ranging from equal pay to pornography. In a period of revolutionary ferment we should expect a spectrum of thought from the "fighting faith" of proponents to the reactionary resistance of diehards. Many, perhaps most, men and women accept numerous feminist premises while spurning extreme proposals or categorical rejection of gender equality. With no monolithic feminist position on all issues, a range of opinion is likely, at least as to means if not as to goals. Difficult issues of implementation and conflicting values arise, for example, regarding comparable worth as a means of fostering pay equality, or censorship as the answer to pornography, or mandatory arrest as the best method of dealing with domestic violence.

Courts are being expected to shape society's response to domestic assault at a time when general agreement has been achieved concerning its seriousness but when there is no unanimity over many remaining details. Court decisions are necessarily political, create winners and losers, and, in a new and fluid area of law, tend to create or consolidate social policy. Where public opinion is not settled, the courts do not have the luxury of drawing on a consensus to support the perceived rationality and the legitimacy of their opinions. Unpopular or unworkable opinions can generate public hostility, undermining the usual respect in which courts are held, diminishing their political salience (Graham 1970:1–3). Courts, therefore, strive to decide cases in accord with due process procedures at the trial level and with well-reasoned appellate opinions in order to increase their legitimacy. Appellate courts must also be sensitive to the mood and direction of public policy to achieve a general congruence with the "felt necessities of the times" (Holmes 1963:1; de Tocqueville 1969:150). Court-made policies based on flawed facts may prove unworkable, creating a need to continuously revise a doctrine and generating discontent and undermining the popular base of judicial authority. In the face of these considerations courts may decide to risk leading public opinion or may lag considerably behind, but in doing either they face a set of legal and political considerations involving the potential for enhanced or diminished public respect and authority. Thus, it is to be expected that the judiciary, as a body, will approach new areas of legal concern cautiously, attempting novel approaches in a few cases, while remaining alert to possible negative popular reactions or new evidence to confirm or disapprove new directions.

Domestic Violence, Police, and Social Science

The "first wave" of reform legislation for battered wives encouraged arrest as a law enforcement option. A common thread in the complaints of women was the unresponsiveness of police officers to battered wives. Thus, Dobash and Dobash, in a restrained, reform-oriented review of scholarship, wrote in 1979, "Research relating to the use of discretion among police officers has revealed that officers are *very unlikely* to make an arrest when the offender has used violence against his wife. In other violent situations, officers typically arrest the attacker regardless of the characteristics of the victim and offender or the circumstances surrounding the crime" (Dobash and Dobash 1979:207, emphasis in original). This perspective became the received truth, was repeated in law journal articles (e.g., Beck 1987:1001; Hathaway 1986:672; Lerman 1984:127), and has been the basis of testimony to legislatures, which was enhanced by chilling instances of police insensitivity to abused women (Gundle 1986:260).

The concern that police were underenforcing the criminal law when the victims were battered wives coincided with a belief, apparently confirmed by research, that arrest was a likely deterrent to spouse abuse. This belief was the basis of the 1976 IACP statement that arrest "promotes the well-being of the victim . . . [and] may give the wife courage she needs to realistically face and correct her situation" (IACP 1976, quoted in Gundle 1986:260). By 1982 a mandatory arrest proponent could argue that a mandatory arrest policy was superior to legislation that merely encouraged arrest (e.g., by dropping the common-law rule that a misdemeanor warrantless arrest was permissible only when the crime was committed in the presence of the arresting officer) (Lerman 1982:67–68).

The ground was ripe, so to speak, when the results of the Minneapolis Domestic Violence Experiment were released in 1984, showing that a policy of arrest in misdemeanor assault cases, compared to separation of the parties or mediation, produced lower recidivism rates (Sherman and Berk 1984). The study was not simply published in a narrowly circulated research journal but was also made available to the public through the Police Foundation and through the news media by one of the researchers (Sherman and Cohn 1989). The wide dissemination of these results were rapidly absorbed and generated greater enthusiasm for mandatory arrest, led several police departments to adopt mandatory arrest policies, and were generally given credence by legal writers. As many professionals in domestic violence had been calling for stricter arrest policies since the mid-1970s, the Minneapolis study fed into an existing ideological framework of activist feminism on this issue. Legitimate resentment at the shabby treatment of women by an insensitive criminal justice system led many to accept the Minneapolis experiment findings as established scientific truth, without close examination of the caveats even of the researchers themselves. This phenomenon gave rise to some concern within the research community (Lempert 1984, 1989), and the last word on the question has not yet been heard. Space does not permit a full discussion of this fascinating, and yet unfinished, chapter in the impact of research on policy formation. It is raised here to show how public perceptions of research findings had an impact on legal policy in this area. Because these results form the basis for concluding whether or not discrimination exists, and discrimination is the touchstone of equal-protection violations, accurate assessments of empirical findings will have a significant impact on the further development of legal doctrines regarding spouse abuse.

The relation between social science research and law reform is not new. Empirical studies of social phenomena have been intertwined with court-generated legal change in this century, ranging from the use of health data in the original Brandeis brief in *Muller v. Oregon* in 1908 (Baker 1984:3–17) to Kenneth Clark's experiments with children's reactions to different-colored dolls that had such a telling impact in *Brown v. Board of Education* in 1954 and beyond (Kluger 1977:315–21, 353–56). Social analysis of all disciplines is brought to bear on many questions that lead to legislation. Although studies are often ignored, in our scientific and technological society the work of social scientists has tremendous policy impact. Social scientific findings usually have an impact on policy making and court decisions by generating new information about human behavior and social relations, although they may also influence law and policy by confirming widespread societal beliefs. In either case a problem with the acceptance of social research by legal scholars and practitioners is that the findings are accepted secondhand. There is no mechanism within the world of legal scholarship to test the reliability and validity of research findings. The courtroom method of testing facts by cross-examination may be suitable to ascertain the truth of a concrete event or the general acceptability of a scientific finding, but it is not inherently suited to replicate research findings.

These concerns prompted the National Institute of Justice to authorize replications of the Minneapolis experiment and has led not only friendly critics but also one of the authors of the Minneapolis experiment to express concern that social policy not be based on a single experiment (Lempert 1989; Sherman and Cohn 1989). Indeed the first published replication experiment, conducted in Omaha, has failed to replicate the results of the first Minneapolis experiment (Dunford et al. 1989). An exhaustive review of the research literature on criminal justice responses to domestic violence has raised serious questions about the received wisdom about the police response to wife beating (Elliott 1989). The body of research does not confirm many of the stereotypes about police response that have been accepted in much of the legal literature. Thus, it appears that about one-third of all family disturbance calls involve violence, a fact that is rarely mentioned in the legal or policy literature (Elliott 1989:434). Furthermore, the general belief that police are more lenient in domestic assault than other assaults is neither confirmed nor contradicted by the little research that focuses on the question (Elliott 1989:438–441). "[T]he existing evidence is insufficient to support the claim that police respond differently to violence on the part of family members as compared to persons who are not related" (Elliott 1989:446). Thus, according to the most complete review of scientific research on these points, no conclusion can be drawn as to whether police respond differently to domestic assaults than to other assaults.

Scientific findings are important inputs into legislative and judicial policies. Legislatures have been fairly quick to respond to the results of the Minneapolis experiment, which offered a basis for action regarding the safety of battered women. Courts tend to be somewhat more conservative in accepting scientific findings, perhaps because it is more difficult to overturn precedents than to modify legislation. In any case, accepted beliefs in scientific findings about the police response to spouse abuse has influenced legal scholarship, and legal scholarship influences judicial policy. In the legal cases discussed hereafter, constitutional or common-law doctrines act as a brake on judicial innovation. On the other hand, where the legislature firmly sets policy, the courts act to support the policy if it is deemed constitutional. In states without strong legislative policy and in federal courts hearing cases from the states, this judicial conservatism is frustrating to activists who favor a strong mandatory arrest policy. Yet, as courts are governing institutions, they must be prudent in the speed with which they adopt proposed reforms. A failure to adopt reforms long after the social need for change is abundantly clear, harms society and undermines respect for the courts; too quick an adoption of reform can lead to the blunder of adopting an unworkable or unwise policy, creating unwanted side effects and likewise undermining respect for the courts. The current confusion of research results in domestic violence tends to confirm this observation.

Legal Rights and Remedies

To introduce several federal and state cases that address the issue of police officer and state liability for failure to protect victims of domestic violence, a few words on legal rights and remedies and the difficulty of translating rights into action are in order. Legal rights are established by "the people," the legislature, and appellate courts through constitutions, statutes, and appellate cases. Courts play a pivotal role in establishing the contours of rights because, in America, they generally have the last word in interpreting constitutional and statutory provisions (Levi 1949; de Tocqueville 1969). Statements of these legal rights can be found by diligent research in the law library, in statutory codifications, and in case reporters. It is the stuff of standard legal research to analyze a large number of cases to precisely delineate the contours of rights under a variety of factual circumstances, and many law review articles and treatises provide sophisticated studies of every important legal issue.

This kind of research is important and has its place. However, a radically different kind of inquiry is found in the broad field of law and society studies. The question for sociolegal researchers is not to determine the precise nature of the "law in the books" but to ascertain the configuration of the "law in action." While this chapter primarily explores the "law in the books," we should remain alert to the fact that there is normally some divergence between stated rights and how those rights are claimed and enforced in the "real world" (Zalman 1982). I make this conventional observation in order to stress its importance to the subject of wife beating. The recent rediscovery of spouse abuse has coincided with a period in American history of judicial activism and the expansion of rights (Pleck 1989). Social movements are quick to use the legislative and judicial arenas to win political and legal victories for their interests. Yet, it cannot be emphasized too strongly that the complete achievement of social policies is far from simple in the United States and that even legislative victories are often the starting point for attaining policy goals (Jones 1984). This is not unique to the issue of domestic violence but, given the human tragedies involved, failures of policy in this complex area carry a heavy burden in human suffering.

The awareness of partial success in social legislation was noted by Ruth Gundle (1986) in describing the strategy pursued by the Oregon Coalition against Domestic and Sexual Violence. The Coalition was successful in creating a legislative package resulting in the Oregon Abuse Prevention Act in 1977 that included a mandatory arrest provision for domestic violence. However, within four years amendments were necessary. For example, an exception to mandatory arrest, the objection of victims, was dropped because it was misused by police to put the burden of deciding whether to arrest on the woman (Gundle 1986:262). Indeed, updates of initial domestic violence legislation appears to be common (Brady 1988). Despite the legislative revision, the Oregon law was far from a complete success. A 1979 study by the Governor's Commission for Women found that one-third of all law enforcement agencies in the state had not changed their policies despite the existence of a statute. "By 1980, frustration over the lack of compliance with the mandatory arrest laws was high. Nearly three years had passed and the new laws had made no discernable change in police practice" (Gundle 1986:262). Rather than turning to the "time-consuming task of working with law enforcement agencies around the state on a one-to-one basis,'' which ''was not going to result in statewide compliance,'' the Coalition decided to find a test case to seek damages on behalf of an individual on the theory of tort, that is a wrong leading to injury not based on contract. The Coalition reasoned that a successful tort action, leading to a large money judgment against police officers and a city, ''would get the serious attention of every law enforcement agency in the state'' (Gundle 1986:262).

No practicing lawyer would be surprised at Ms. Gundle's frustration at attempting social reform through legislation and ultimately turning to the lawsuit as a means to force compliance. Even where specialized agencies are set up to enforce legislation, interested parties often have to sue to notify officers and municipalities that in an era of generous jury awards, often in the hundreds of thousands or even millions of dollars, compliance with the wishes of the legislature is prudent. Thus, the law cases reviewed in this chapter are mostly suits by injured spouses and intimate partners against police officers and municipalities. They allege that the officers either did not respond to calls for help or responded in a deficient manner. In these cases the courts have to look to constitutional rights, general common law principles of liability, and special statutory rights, many of which were enacted within the past decade. In deciding these appeals the courts have to make decisions within a principled framework and thus, at times, reject a claim where there is no larger legal framework allowing or requiring a decision in favor of an injured spouse.

FEDERAL COURT RESPONSES

The Impact of Federal Courts

For two generations federal courts have stimulated and participated in several social revolutions that have transformed political and social behavior in America. The desegregation rulings hastened the civil rights revolution, spelling an end to legal apartheid, American style. Court rulings gave shape and content to civil rights legislation of the 1960s. Legislative apportionment cases broke the back of rural domination of state legislatures. Criminal procedure cases brought the Bill of Rights to bear on state and local police. Prisoners' rights litigation resulted in direct federal court intervention in the administration of prisons to prevent cruel and unusual conditions. Traditionally powerless groups such as welfare recipients and students won procedural due process rights that limited the officiousness with which welfare agencies and schools could treat them. Women won significant gender equality lawsuits, striking down arbitrary exclusions of women from economic and social positions of authority (see, generally, Gunther 1985).

Throughout this remarkable period of judicial activism both the legitimacy and the competence of the federal courts to effect these sweeping changes have been challenged. In no area of federal court intervention has the underlying social problem that gave rise to the litigation been entirely solved. To a large degree the races still live apart, and economic inequalities between black and white gnaw at the promise of legal equality (Jaynes and Williams 1989:88–91). Crime rates remain high, and prison overcrowding has made a mockery of attempts to insure basic decency in prison living conditions. Poverty is widespread, and women do not generally enjoy equal pay for equal work. These failings suggest the limits of legal action to root out persistent social problems. Yet, it is hard to deny that American constitutional ideals, especially those of equality (Pole 1978) and fair treatment, are more a reality today. Although the tenor of the Supreme Court and the lower federal judiciary has become more conservative than before as a result of appointments by presidents Nixon and Reagan (Goldman 1989), federal courts continue to maintain an activist role within the confines of the process of legal reasoning (Levi 1949). To the extent that legislation and prior cases create precedent, this judicial activism often has a decided ''reformist'' cast.

It is understandable that battered wives and feminist organizations set on challenging spouse abuse would turn to the federal courts for relief. Federal courts have traditionally been a more salient avenue of reform because their attachment to the national government has produced a more universal and less parochial perspective. Although drawn from among local practitioners and sharing many local values and prejudices, federal judges are usually the most eminent local attorneys who are best endowed to rise above the tug of parochialism in politically salient cases. Lifetime tenure, the fellowship of a relatively small national peer group (575 federal district court judges and 168 court of appeals judges in 1984), a working appreciation of national standards, a caseload replete with constitutional issues and direct political loyalty to the national government has produced a bench capable of placing constitutional ideals above local interests. It is small wonder, then, that litigants challenging the status quo turn to the federal courts, especially when the basis of the complaint is a lack of equality. Feminists pinpoint a cultural matrix of gender inequality as the basis of various practices and laws that discriminate against women. The Fourteenth Amendment, which guarantees to all persons the equal protection of the laws against state action, is an attractive basis for litigation, as women's legal victories based on equal protection confirm their analysis of gender inequality. Also, favorable doctrines achieved in the federal courts have a broader base of applicability. However, I point out in the next section some serious impediments to using constitutional avenues in the federal courts as the best way to secure legal rights calculated to secure the safety of spouses against abusive partners.

Spouse Abuse Cases in the Federal Courts

Since the 1984 district court decision in *Thurman v. City of Torrington*, the first reported federal case to find that police failure to arrest an abusive husband amounted to a constitutional violation (Hathaway 1986:669), several federal courts have found that failure to arrest constitutes a violation of either the due process or the equal protection clause of the Fourteenth Amendment. However, it seems to me that in the future federal courts will not be hospitable to claims by women injured in domestic violence. Although in some cases it may be possible for battered spouses to win claims in federal court, the obstacles will generally be higher than in state courts under evolving legislation. In order to explain this conclusion, I examine federal cases separately under the doctrines of due process and equal protection of the Fourteenth Amendment:

All persons born or nationalized in the United States and subject to the jurisdiction thereof, are citizens of the United States and of the State wherein they reside. No State shall make or enforce any law which shall abridge the privileges or immunities of citizens of the United States; nor shall any State deprive any person of life, liberty, or property without due process of law; nor deny to any person within its jurisdiction the equal protection of the laws. (*U.S. Constitution*, Amendment XIV, Section 1 [1868])

The Fourteenth Amendment, ratified in 1868, fundamentally changed the authority structure in American government. By making explicit the "dual citizenship" of Americans, it made the federal government, for the first time, the guarantor of basic rights of Americans against encroachment by state governments, thus consolidating the Union victory in the Civil War. The amendment has been the vehicle for an enormous body of litigation that has enlarged the role of the federal courts in the social, economic, and political affairs of the nation.

Most lawsuits against municipalities or state or local officials that claim that laws, rules, written or unwritten policies, or "customs" violate the Fourteenth Amendment are brought under the Civil Rights Act of 1871. It was originally designed to protect newly freed southern blacks from attack by the Ku Klux Klan, during which local government had stood by, doing nothing, giving tacit approval to KKK crimes and outrages. Since 1961 the statute (codified as 42 UNITED STATES CODE, section 1983) has been the vehicle for hundreds of thousands of lawsuits inquiring into every facet of state and local policy. Section 1983 authorizes a person to bring any kind of civil action ("an action of law, suit in equity, or other proper proceedings for redress") where an actor "under color of any statute, ordinance, regulation, custom, or usage of any State or Territory" causes the person to suffer a violation of federal statutory or constitutional rights. The wording of section 1983 allows a suit where the local government actor is doing things that are illegal, as long as the actor reasonably is acting in a governmental role.

At first blush, the combination of the Fourteenth Amendment and section 1983 seems to create a federal court juggernaut allowing federal court intervention into virtually every facet of local government. Despite the enormous growth of section 1983 litigation, the concern for federalism and respect for the autonomy of state and local government has generated an important limiting doctrine.

Federal courts find jurisdiction under section 1983 when the government's acts are egregious, grossly negligent, deliberate, or evoke a deliberate indifference to the rights of the plaintiff. They will not find jurisdiction where the acts of the government officers are merely negligent. In other words, a constitutional violation must be seen as an especially serious governmental intrusion on the plaintiff's rights. In legalese, the federal courts do not wish to turn section 1983 and the Fourteenth Amendment into a "national Tort Claims Act." Under section 1983, individuals acting "under color of" state law and a municipal government may be sued for affirmative acts in violation of a plaintiff's rights. State governments, however, are not subject to this kind of lawsuit because the Framers of the Fourteenth Amendment intended to preserve the "sovereign immunity" of the states (see Gunther 1985:922–23; *Monnell v. DSS* [1978]).

A Special Relationship: Due Process Cases

The facts in *Balistreri v. Pacifica Police Department* (1988, Ninth Circuit), repeat a sad pattern found in many of the egregious domestic abuse cases. In February 1982 Jena Balistreri was severely beaten by her husband, requiring medical treatment for injuries to her nose, mouth, eyes, teeth, and abdomen. Despite this, police officers refused to arrest the husband, did not offer Mrs. Balistreri medical assistance and were, according to her complaint, rude and insulting, even stating that she deserved the beating. After the incident, police officers pressured her not to press charges against her husband. Mrs. Balistreri obtained a divorce in 1982, but vandalism and harassing telephone calls from her former spouse continued and she complained to the police about them. In November 1982 she obtained a restraining order prohibiting her former husband from "harassing, annoying or having any contact with her." After the order was served, Balistreri crashed his car into his former wife's garage. Although the police were summoned immediately, they refused to arrest him. In 1983 a firebomb was thrown through a window of her house, but the police determined that her former husband was not responsible. Telephone harassment continued from 1983 to 1985, traceable to her former husband, but he was never arrested. Mrs. Balistreri alleged that the acts caused her to suffer a bleeding ulcer and emotional distress.

In this case the court of appeals found that police inaction violated the plaintiff's due process rights. It is vital to note, however, the general rule that the due process clause does not insure safety to the public or guarantee any recovery because one is victimized by a crime committed by a private party.

[N]othing in the language of the Due Process Clause itself requires the State to protect the life, liberty, and property of its citizens against invasion by private actors. The Clause is phrased as a limitation on the State's power to act, not as a guarantee of certain minimum levels of safety. . . . Its purpose was to protect the people from the State, not to ensure that the State protected them from each other. The Framers were content to leave the extent of obligation in the latter area to the democratic political process. (*DeShaney v. Winnebago County Department of Social Services*, 1989)

Despite this well-understood limitation, since the Supreme Court's 1980 decision of *Martinez v. California*, the lower federal courts have created an exception to the general rule that the due process clause does not create a legal duty on the part of the state (or municipality) to protect individuals from crime. The exception allows a finding of liability by the police if a "special relationship" exists between the police and the particular injured party:

> To determine whether a "special relationship" exists, a court may look to a number of factors, which include (1) whether the state created or assumed a custodial relationship toward the plaintiff; (2) whether the state was aware of a specific risk of harm to the plaintiff; (3) whether the state affirmatively placed the plaintiff in a position of danger; or (4) whether the state affirmatively committed itself to the protection of the plaintiff. (*Balistreri*, p. 1425).

Relying on the fact that other federal circuits have found a special relationship outside a custodial situation, the Ninth Circuit concluded that a special relationship existed between Mrs. Balistreri and the Pacifica Police Department based on the restraining order and her repeated calls for help, a relationship that created a duty on the part of the department to take reasonable steps to protect her.

In *Bailey v. County of York* (1985, Third Circuit), a special relationship was found to exist between an abused child and a county department of social services that had been informed of the danger to the child by her mother's live-in boy-friend. The *Balistreri* ruling was similar, yet in both cases dissenting judges argued that the *Martinez* case, which found that a parole board was not liable for a murder committed by a parolee, required that agency failure to act must *cause* the harm to the victim before a special relationship could be established. In *Bailey* the dissenting judge found the relationship between the failure to act and the injuries too remote, because five weeks elapsed between the agency's control of the child and her death. The dissenting judge in *Balistreri* felt that the existence of the restraining order was too slim a reed to support a special relationship. He also questioned whether the decision in that case gave police firm guidelines as to when such a relationship existed.

Contrary to the *Balistreri* holding, several district courts found that the majority's due process reasoning did not create special relationships. In *Dudosh v. City of Allentown* (1987, E.D. Pa.) the trial court's analysis of precedents led it to conclude that police knowledge of a spouse's previous beatings does not create a special relationship. Here, police escorted the battered woman back to the apartment where her sometime boyfriend, who had threatened to kill her, was known to be. The officers allowed her to open the door and enter the house first, whereupon the boyfriend shot and killed Kathleen Dudosh. Finding that the officers neither ordered Kathleen to stay outside or to accompany them, the court concluded that she "willingly and of her own volition escorted the police officers to her apartment" (p. 386). Thus, while the officers may have been negligent under state law, mere negligence does not rise to a constitutional wrong and the causation requirement of *Martinez* was not met.

A similar conclusion was reached in *Turner v. City of North Charleston* (1987, D.S.C.) where, after a series of domestic assaults, notifications to the police, and a restraining order, the court could not find that the municipality "placed the plaintiffs in a position of danger, nor did it single out the plaintiffs and place them in its care," when an estranged husband shot his wife and shot at her child (p. 319). The court pointed out that a state statute, the Protection from Domestic Abuse Act, did not create a duty of protection by the police but only required police to take several protective steps when notified of abuse. In any event, "a state statute, by itself, cannot create a substantive constitutional right" enforceable in federal courts (p. 319).

The positions of the dissenters in *Balistreri* and *Bailey* and of the courts in *Dudosh* and *Turner* were confirmed by the Supreme Court in 1989. Chief Justice Rehnquist, writing for a six-justice majority in *DeShaney* (1989), threw cold water on the special relationship doctrine. The victim in *DeShaney* was a child beaten and permanently injured by his father after the Department of Social Services had reason to believe that he was abused. The DSS failed to remove him from the home. The Court flatly rejected the special relationship argument except when the state places the injured party in custody (e.g., jail, prison, mental institution). A special relationship, with an affirmative duty to care for a person, does not arise from knowledge of danger or expressions of an intent to care, but from the fact that persons in involuntary custody are deprived of all means to care for themselves and are wholly dependent on the state to provide for basic human needs. Even Justice Brennan's inventive and closely woven dissent would probably be of no avail to women abused by their spouses, because it relied on the unusually comprehensive authority and intrusiveness of Wisconsin's child-protection program as the basis for his finding a special relationship.

The *DeShaney* case may not have entirely ended the special relationship doctrine where there is no custody. If the state places a person in danger from private persons "as if it had thrown him into a snake pit" (*Bowers v. DeVito*, 1982, p. 618), it may be possible for a court to find a duty on the part of the police to protect a person. For example, the Seventh Circuit found that the Chicago police created a special relationship where they arrested an uncle who was drag racing on the Chicago skyway and against his pleas refused to take his young nephews to the police station or a phone booth to call their mother. The children, left alone in the abandoned car on a cold night, finally left the car, crossed eight lanes of the freeway, and wandered along it until reaching a telephone. The Chicago police, called by the mother who had no car, again refused to bring the children home. The court found a sufficient duty to allow the case to go to trial for alleged mental anguish and hospitalization of one of the children for an asthma attack. It would appear that such an egregious situation of placing minors in the risk of danger may survive the *DeShaney* rule, but it seems unlikely that the typical spouse abuse scenario will be found to be a due process violation by federal courts hereafter.

Gender Bias: Equal Protection Cases

The equal protection clause seems to be a stronger basis for legal protection of abused women. Three federal courts of appeal have found equal protection violations based on police unresponsiveness to spouse abuse, and there is no Supreme Court case that directly undermines their doctrinal basis. Yet, as equal protection violations are based on findings of discrimination, their factual predicate may be undermined either by changed police policies that are gender neutral but not protective of women or by empirical findings that do not support the contention that failure to respond or arrest in domestic violence cases is based on gender bias.

In order to make sense of the equal protection clause, the Supreme Court has created "a morass of doctrines" (Gunther 1985:586). To oversimplify, because nearly all legislation classifies, the equal protection of the laws cannot require that laws level all social and economic distinctions. Generally, a tripartite classification scheme has evolved by which the Court is less or more likely to declare legislation or governmental policy void and in conflict with the equal protection clause. At one end of the spectrum, the courts find legislative classifications dealing with ordinary social or economic policies constitutional if the classification bears a reasonable relationship to the legitimate goals of the legislation. At the other end, the Warren Court developed the doctrine of strict scrutiny: where a fundamental right (e.g., freedom of speech) or a "suspect classification" (especially race) is the subject of a legislative classification, the classification will not be upheld unless the state meets a heavy burden of showing that the classification meets an overriding state objective independent of the racial or other classification (*Loving v. Virginia* [1967]). While the Burger Court generally did not extend the strict scrutiny standard to encompass a variety of social and economic conditions, it added an intermediate standard of review.

The Court's rulings on gender-based classifications are the clearest examples of "intermediate scrutiny." Where the state makes gender-based classifications, the law or custom is invalidated unless it serves important governmental objectives that are substantially related to the achievement of those objectives (*Craig v. Boren* [1976]). Applying these standards, the Court has found unconstitutional a law that prohibits the sale of 3.2 beer to males under the age of 21 but only to females under 18, a legislative preference for males as executors of estates, a requirement that men but not women must pay alimony upon divorce, a law that automatically allotted dependent's benefits to wives of military servicemen but required proof of dependency before the husband of a servicewoman could collect, a law that paid survivor's benefits to widows based on a deceased husband's earnings but to widowers only if they received one-half of their support from their wives, and a law restricting enrollment to a university nursing program to women. On the other hand, where legislation classified according to sex in cases where males and females were not objectively similarly situated, the Court has upheld them, finding no equal protection violation. This was the case with a state law punishing males but not females for statutory rape where the female was under 18 years of age. Also, laws that are gender neutral on their face but have a disproportionate adverse impact on women will be upheld if their purpose was not to discriminate. Under this standard, the Court upheld veterans' preferences for civil service jobs even though most veterans are male (see, generally, Hathaway 1986:679–87).

The underlying rationales for invalidating gender-based classifications are relevant to cases of domestic violence. The Court has stated on several occasions that classifications based on archaic and overbroad classifications were insufficient bases for discriminating between women and men, as were "increasingly outdated misconceptions concerning the role of females in the home rather than in the 'marketplace and world of ideas.' " These notions were "loose-fitting characterizations incapable of supporting state statutory schemes that were premised upon their accuracy" (*Craig v. Boren*, 1976). Thus, challenges to police inactivity in spouse abuse cases must show that the police acted on policies generated by these criteria.

Following *Thurman* in 1984, several lower federal courts have found invidious discrimination and equal protection violations in spouse abuse cases where police inaction resulted from policies based either on the gender of the victim or on the nature of the call (i.e., a domestic dispute). Thus far, except for the *Thurman* case in which an award of almost $2 million was made (Hathaway 1986:668–69), these issues have been resolved on motions for summary judgment or appeals from denials of qualified immunity to defendant police officers. In these procedural cases, the courts have found only that the plaintiffs claiming sex bias have raised sufficient facts to send the cases on to trial.

In *Hynson v. City of Chester* (1988, Third Circuit), for example, it was not clear whether a valid protection order was in effect, although Ms. Hynson's killer, her former boyfriend and father of her children, had earlier in the evening broken into her apartment to frighten a babysitter and the children. After the police watched Ms. Hynson depart with her children to her mother's house, they failed to search for or arrest the assailant, who, a day later, killed her at her place of employment. On the one hand, *Hynson* refused to apply the public duty–private duty dichotomy to this case. The rule that the police owe only a general duty to the public to enforce law and preserve order and not a specific duty to an injured party that may result in liability, barring a special relationship (Shapiro, n.d., 41 ALR3d), had been applied under the due process clause, as we saw in the previous section, with the Supreme Court narrowing the application of the special relationship exception to a small group of cases. But other legal doctrines are available. The *Hynson* court framed this issue as one of qualified immunity under the Supreme Court doctrine in *Harlow v. Fitzgerald* (1982).

The *Harlow* rule states that a police officer is protected by a qualified immunity where it was not *clearly apparent* that his action was illegal. While the *Hynson* result may be gratifying to partisans, the court of appeal's reasoning appears to rest more on assumptions about the liberal direction of the cases toward granting awards to battered women than on a solid factual foundation, which clearly established a gender-based classification. Thus, *Hynson* twice referred to a growing trend of reliance on section 1983 to sue police on the grounds that policies in domestic abuse cases violate the equal protection of women victims. But reference to five cases as a growing trend and a quote from a student's law review article does not affirmatively establish such a policy. Thus, the value of *Hynson* as a basis for an equal protection rule favoring recovery by battered women is limited.

Nevertheless, cases such as *Hynson, Thurman, Balistreri,* and *Dudosh* (in *Dudosh*, an equal protection claim succeeded although the due process claim failed), which found that plaintiffs pleaded sufficient facts regarding a discriminatory policy so that it would be premature to dismiss the claims, show that some federal judges desire to find within the equal protection doctrine a means of upholding the claims of battered wives. Their policy goal is to modify police policies that leave women at the mercy of attacks by their cohabitants.

[The equal protection] clause applies to the activity of police agencies, and protects persons from irrational discrimination in either acts of commission or omission. . . . Police officers and agencies who are under an affirmative duty to protect persons within their area of authority must fulfill this duty without intentionally discriminating against such persons on an irrational basis. . . . [A] section 1983 plaintiff must allege and establish that the defendant failed to fulfill an affirmative duty to enforce the laws equally and fairly. (*Bartalone v. County of Berrien* (1986, W.D. Mich.), pp. 576–77)

As I noted, it appears as of this writing that only *Thurman v. City of Torrington* (among the reported cases) has resulted in a judgment that "[i]f officials have notice of the possibility of attacks on women in domestic relationships or other persons, they are under an affirmative duty to take reasonable measures to protect the personal safety of such persons in the community" (p. 1527). It seems premature to hope that the *Thurman* ruling will be the springboard for police policies of mandatory arrest. The reason for this cautious conclusion lies not in the constitutional theory of equal protection. Indeed, equal protection violations should and will be sustained if it can be shown that police practices of not answering domestic calls or failing to arrest abusive husbands in domestic assault cases are founded on "archaic, stereotypic notions of the inferior legal or social status of women" and that "such classifications, even if facially neutral with regard to gender, may be characterized as gender based and may be shown to disproportionately favor men and disfavor women, reflecting covert or invidious gender based discrimination" (Hathaway 1986:691).

The problem is proof. A more penetrating inquiry into claims of discriminatory policies may be more difficult to sustain where no such written policy exists, where a state has adopted legislation either mandating arrest or making arrest a more likely option (e.g., by eliminating the common-law arrest rule requiring a misdemeanor to occur in the officer's presence), and where police training and manuals reflect a positive stance toward arrest. In such cases there is no gender-based policy based on archaic stereotypes, and failures to arrest can often be covered by a police assertion that probable cause did not exist. Additionally, assumptions made in several law journal articles, that discriminatory policies or practices are the norm, is not universally sustained by more careful empirical inquiries (Elliott 1989).

In the 1989 case of *McKee v. City of Rockwall* (Fifth Circuit) Gayla McKee summoned police to an apartment she shared with Harry Streetman, claiming he assaulted her. Police arrived, made no arrests, but drove McKee to another location. Streetman, however, soon after found McKee and slashed her leg with a knife. She claimed that the officers acted pursuant to a discriminatory policy against making arrests in domestic assault cases and cited two pieces of evidence to support her claim: (1) a statement by the police chief to McKee's mother to the effect "that his officers did not like to make arrests in domestic assault cases since the women involved either wouldn't file charges or would drop them prior to trial," and (2) summary statistics of the number of arrests in "cleared assault" cases compared to "domestic violence calls" from 1982 to 1986, showing 36 percent of assault cases resulted in arrest compared to 21 percent in domestic violence for those years. The court noted that the plaintiff's evidence inflated the assault arrest figures by including assault arrests for 1985 but no baseline figure for that year. Eliminating 1985 statistics for both assault and domestic violence calls produced a difference of 7 percent (30 percent for assaults vs. 23 percent for domestic calls) rather than the 15 percent difference claimed.

The court concluded that McKee presented no evidence of a discriminatory policy and dismissed the case against the police officers on a summary judgment appeal. The court concluded, first, that "[a] dislike is not a policy." Turning to the statistics proffered as evidence of the policy, the court criticized the inclusion of the 1985 denominator for assault cases without including the numerator (arrests) and pointed out that in two of the five years arrest rates were higher in domestic cases than assault calls. More importantly, the court raised several reasons why the bare complaint and arrest numbers leave out too much information to draw conclusions about the city's policy:

[T]he statistics do not correct for the wide variety of factors which might influence the likelihood that police would make an arrest: whether the assault was in progress when police arrived; whether a gun or knife had been used; whether the victim refused to press charges when the police arrived. . . . [T]he statistics do nothing to suggest gender-based discrimination. The statistics do not indicate how many of the victims in the cleared assault cases were women, or how many of the victims in the domestic violence cases were men. (*McKee v. City of Rockwall*, p. 415)

Also, since McKee had requested to be driven to her mother's house, the court noted that if the police followed her wishes, the statistics would have recorded a domestic violence with no arrest, thus generating a purportedly discriminatory statistic.

The *McKee* court has raised cogent questions regarding the use of raw statistics to infer a policy hostile to the interests of women. Even the point regarding the number of male victims of spouse abuse, admittedly a small proportion of domestic violence cases, as noted in *Thurman*, must be taken into account if an accurate and meaningful statistical presentation is to be made.

McKee was decided after the Supreme Court's *DeShaney* case was handed down. Noting that *DeShaney* was a due process case and not directly applicable, Court of Appeals Judge Higginbotham nevertheless could not miss the implication of the Supreme Court's ruling:

DeShaney is nonetheless relevant to our analysis in this case. The Court's opinion in *DeShaney* endorses the general principle that choices about the "extent of governmental obligation" to protect private parties from one another have been left "to the democratic political processes." . . . There is no constitutional violation when the "most that can be said of . . . state functionaries . . . is that they stood by and did nothing when suspicious circumstances dictated a more active role." (*McKee v. City of Rockwall*, p. 413)

The upshot of these cases, it seems to me, is that the equal protection clause is not as promising a prospect on which to base liability as appeared in *Thurman* in 1984. The Supreme Court and many lower federal judges clearly do not want the federal courts to turn municipalities and officers into insurers for battered wives. The message to spouse abuse victim advocates is that federal courts need clear evidence of unconstitutional policies before they conclude that a particular police failure to arrest a spouse, who later injures his partner, is conclusive evidence of a policy. This avoidance by federal courts is not necessarily cruel, for the states have been forthcoming in modifying laws and policies in favor of facilitating arrest. Additionally, in light of the current confusion about the deterrent effect of automatic arrest policies, there is good reason for caution in adopting judicial doctrines that make mandatory arrest policies the only way to avoid liability (Elliott 1989; Dunford et al. 1989).

Cases such as *McKee* and *DeShaney* do not mean that it will be impossible to prove that some cities maintain domestic violence policies that are indeed based on archaic stereotypes of women's social place or other invalid reasons. Two instructive cases found sufficient facts to infer discriminatory policies where the battering males were police officers. In *Watson v. Kansas City* (1988 Tenth Circuit), a woman twice married to and abused by a police officer (Watson) filed a formal complaint against her husband, informing the department's Internal Affairs Unit that he had beaten her severely. In one episode he placed a gun to her head and threatened to kill both her and himself. In none of these cases was Watson ever arrested. In the last violent episode, Watson followed his wife and children as they were shopping. She drove to a police station and asked a sergeant who knew of the Internal Affairs investigation to detain him. The sergeant promised to do so, but when Nancy Watson returned home her husband was there. He locked the children in a room and then raped, beat, and stabbed Nancy. She jumped through a picture window onto the front lawn to escape. Watson drove off and committed suicide. A police lieutenant told a local newspaper that Watson "was like a time bomb waiting to go off."

The court in *Watson* specifically found that the plaintiff could not sustain an equal protection complaint on the ground of a gender-based policy to deny police protection to women. On the other hand, the court said: "We doubt whether evidence of deliberate indifference in the plaintiff's case alone would be sufficient evidence of *different* treatment. We do find, however, that taken with other evidence plaintiff has proffered, a pattern such as the one alleged by plaintiff in this case constitutes some evidence of custom or policy" (*Watson v. Kansas City*, p. 696). The *Watson* opinion did not precisely spell out all the elements that led it to infer a policy. Various factors included the egregious facts of the case, an apparent pattern of deliberate indifference on the part of the police department to Nancy Watson's continued complaints against serious assaults, statistical evidence of lower arrest rates in domestic violence cases, and evidence that police training in Kansas City encouraged police to "defuse" the situation and arrest only as a last resort and that the wife beater was a police officer. If each element must be made out for later cases to rely on *Watson*, its precedental value will be quite limited. If not read so narrowly, *Watson* could provide a basis for finding discriminatory policies when the victims are not the wives or ex-wives of police officers.

The basis of liability was more clearly stated in *Sherrell v. City of Longview* (1987, E.D.Tex.), where the district court found a basis on the claim that "a departmental policy provid[ed] favored treatment to police officers accused of domestic violence" (p. 1112). The plaintiff must prove that there is an official policy or custom, and a custom can be established by using the facts of the plaintiff's case alone, that is, that over a long period of time the police refused to arrest a fellow officer despite complaints of abuse (p. 1114). Next, the court found that the custom was the "moving force" or cause of the injury: "[b]y repeatedly shielding [the officer] from arrest and, presumably, from full investigation of his abusive behavior, the plaintiff contends that the custom or policy in fact permitted or encouraged [him] to continue his child abuse" (p. 1115). Finally, an equal protection violation must rest on intentional discrimination, that is, on more than mere negligence. The Court in *Sherrell* found that by knowingly tolerating a pattern of abuse the department's acts were purposeful and intentional.

Finally in *Dudosh v. City of Allentown* (1987, E.D.Pa. 1987), the case where the threatened woman entered the door to her apartment first and was killed by her boyfriend and no due process violation was found, the court nevertheless did find a discriminatory policy based on testimony by high police officials that if the case were a burglary or other "unknown assailant," the police would not have allowed the homeowner to enter the premises first and would likely have approached the door with guns drawn in the expectation of violence. This is the kind of direct evidence of a policy that can sustain equal protection claims.

STATE COURT RESPONSES

Liability under the Common Law: The Public Duty Doctrine

The common-law rule regarding police protection in domestic violence as well as in general law enforcement is similar to federal due process rules and does not offer significant protection to the interests of battered spouses. In *Morgan v. District of Columbia* (D.C.Ct.App. 1983), for example, a husband who was a police officer beat and threatened his wife over a considerable period of time, and she called on his superior officers to restrain him on several occasions. Officer Morgan eventually shot and killed his wife. Pointing out that Mrs. Morgan never filed an official complaint or requested that her husband be disarmed and thus suspended, the court said that Morgan's superiors were left with the discretion to decide whether to suspend him or to counsel him. The simple request for help did not establish a special relationship between the wife and the police department. The general rule that "law enforcement officials and, consequently, state governments generally may not be held liable for failure to protect individual citizens from harm caused by criminal conduct" (p. 1310) goes back at least 125 years to the United States Supreme Court case of *South v. Maryland* (1856) and is based on several policies. It has been argued that juries and courts are ill-equipped to second-guess legislative and executive decisions regarding the allocation of resources; that if every crime led to a successful lawsuit, essentially insuring the public against criminal losses, the public treasury would be depleated; that police act in situations "fraught with uncertainty" and jury verdicts from the position of hindsight would lead police to act more to avoid liability than to exercise their discretion fearlessly; that allowing a call for help to establish a special relationship would make the individual the determiner of police priorities; that the system could be unfair or unworkable if police could not prioritize calls for assistance (*Morgan*, pp. 1310–13, citing many cases). In these cases the legal formula used to deny liability is that the police owe a duty to the public rather than to a private individual injured by crime. If the public feels that police allocation of priorities are wrong, it can seek to modify them through political pressure designed to change police administrative and operational decisions.

An exception to the public duty doctrine is recognized where a special relationship between police and the individual develops that creates a special duty owed by the police to the individual to protect her from a specific type of criminal harm. Generally speaking, a special relationship is not created when a person requests police protection, even when police promise to send assistance, for this "adds nothing to the obligation law enforcement officers have already assumed as members of a police force guided exclusively by the public interest'' (*Morgan*, p. 1313). The typical situations where a court finds a special relationship, and hence a predicate for liability if the police fail to protect, involves informers, persons who assist the police in their duties, and witnesses (*Morgan*, p. 1312). A special relationship has been found where the police ''affirmatively act to protect a specific individual or a specific group of individuals from harm, in such a way as to engender particularized and justifiable reliance'' (*Morgan*, pp. 1313–14). Liability was established where a parent relied on the regular presence of school crossing guards, backed up by police who would fill in when a guard was absent, and her child was injured on a day when there was no crossing guard or back-up police officer present (*Florence v. Goldberg* [N.Y. 1978]). In *Ashford v. County of Suffolk* (N.Y.App.Div. 1986) the court found a special duty to protect where a chiropractor, assaulted by a client, informed the police of the assault. The police failed to execute an arrest warrant against the assaulter and a prosecutor called the chiropractor with the news that the charges against the assaultive client would be dropped, telling the chiropractor that he ''had no reason to further fear'' the assaulter. But the client later shot and killed the chiropractor and committed suicide. The court determined that ''false assurances of safety given to the [chiropractor] by Assistant District Attorney . . . constitutes positive involvement of Suffolk County's law enforcement officials'' (*Ashford*, p. 200).

The difficulty of establishing a special relationship is seen in the reasoning of *Sorichetti v. City of New York* (N.Y. 1985). A father (Sorichetti) with known violent tendencies and a long history of assaulting his wife was nevertheless given visitation with his six-year-old daughter, despite the fact that his estranged wife had obtained a protection order from the family court. Sorichetti picked up his daughter from a police precinct house on Saturday and was to return the girl to her mother the next day. The mother throughout this period feared that Sorichetti would harm his daughter and conveyed her fears to the police but they refused to arrest him. On Sunday, an hour after he was to return his daughter, Sorichetti was found by his sister, unconscious, in his apartment. His daughter was lying next to him, in a coma, severly wounded from a stabbing he inflicted. She was hospitalized for forty days and suffered brain damage from loss of blood and permanent scarring and disability. The court did find liability based on a special duty. However, the special duty was not predicated on the order of protection, which only applied to Mrs. Sorichetti, but to a special and fact-specific set of circumstances: the protection order, Sorichetti's known propensity for violence, Mrs. Sorichetti's continuous pleas for assistance during the weekend, and the fact that officers told the wife that they would send a car to investigate if Sorichetti did not return with the child within a reasonable time. Such a ruling may show that the New York Court of Appeals was willing to stretch the boundary of the special relationship exception in an egregious case; it does not indicate that the common-law rules provide a regular avenue for the protection of abused spouses and family members.

As with federal cases, common-law liability may be a useful avenue to pursue where official action is grossly deficient. In some states, however, lawsuits will be barred or limited by sovereign immunity, the doctrine that would have barred the suit in *Sorichetti* were a special duty not found (Anderson 1985). In a few states, the courts have acted to reduce this barrier and to place the state on a similar footing as any organization in facing liability suits for negligent or other legally improper acts. Arizona has apparently taken this route in cases finding the police liable to injured citizens when informed of the likelihood of serious violence and the police (1) violate their telephone handling procedures, (2) fail to attempt to inform potential victims of serious threats, or (3) fail to act reasonably where it was in their power to do so to prevent injury (*Austin v. City of Scottsdale* [Ariz. 1984]). This sort of a rule can be the basis for liability in domestic violence cases, but few state supreme courts have taken such a bold step in law reform.

Liability and Police Authority under Domestic Violence Legislation

It seems, given the limits built into constitutional and common-law litigation, that the best opportunity for using the law as a vehicle for social reform in domestic violence requires a combination of a sound legislative framework and enforcement lawsuits intended to define the extent of statutes. As noted above, legislation is not self-enforcing; and if a statute breaks new ground, resistance can be expected, perhaps from inertia and perhaps because the legislation encounters negative public opinion.

It is beyond the scope of this chapter to review the legislation passed in every state in the past fifteen years to respond to domestic violence. As an example, we briefly review the *Illinois Domestic Violence Act* (IDVA) passed in 1982 and revised in 1986 (Brady 1988). It begins by declaring that the Act "shall be liberally construed and applied to promote its underlying purposes." The purposes include a recognition that domestic violence is a serious crime against the individual and society that "promotes a pattern of escalating violence which frequently culminates in intra-family homicide . . . ." The effect of a liberal interpretation is reflected in the few Illinois cases thus far decided under the IDVA. The statute's constitutionality was upheld in a case where a couple, Donald and Virginia Hagaman, married for over ten years, were in divorce litigation but residing in the same house (*In re Marriage of Hagaman* [Ill.App. 1984]) with Virginia's nineteen-year-old daughter by a previous marriage. One December night Donald came home after drinking and got into an argument with Virginia over nonpayment of the mortgage; the argument escalated into a scene with Donald entering the teenager's room, asking her to tell Virginia to leave him alone, and Donald (5 foot 9 inches tall, 190 pounds) dragging the teenage girl (5 foot tall, 98 pounds) by her feet into the living room, attempting to throw her out of the house in her pajamas, and knocking her head against a wall.

Donald had not beaten the girl previously. The trial court found that the events had not been extremely violent and did not cause great bodily harm but did constitute abuse under the IDVA, entered a protective order, and required Donald to leave the residence, a finding that was upheld on appeal.

The purpose of the [IDVA] is to expand the civil and criminal remedies for victims of domestic violence including, if necessary, the physical separation of the parties to prevent further abuse. . . . [D]omestic violence and family disharmony often involve a pattern of escalating violence. The Act provides a statutory framework for effecting a brake on that escalation and, as such, is to be liberally construed. (*In re Marriage of Hagaman*, pp. 1279–80)

In *People v. Blackwood* (Ill.App. 1985) an ex-husband under an order of protection to refrain from "striking, threatening, harassing or interfering with" his ex-wife's "personal liberty in any fashion" was found guilty of violating the order by yelling at his ex-wife "that she was a 'f____ing whore,' a dead bitch, and that he had a plot waiting for her, and . . . that 'it's not over and he would get his chance.' " The appeals court found that there was no unconstitutionality in failing to specifically mention a mental element of the crime where "it cannot be seriously argued that the defendant was not informed that he was charged with a knowing violation of the order of protection. The defendant was charged with threatening and harassing his ex-wife. Even in day-to-day usage, these terms imply that the protagonist knowingly causes his victim to suffer undue distress."

The Domestic Violence Act contemplates the protection of a potential victim from the universe of physical and psychological abuses which only someone as close as a relative can inflict. A statute which has its [sic] objective a safety net against such interferences cannot be expected to address every conceivable form of abuse. Thus, a certain measure of generality must be tolerated to give effect to the intended scope of the Act. (*People v. Blackwood*, p. 745)

Finally, in *People v. Whitfield* (Ill.App. 1986) harassment was found when an ex-husband under an order of protection looked at his ex-wife, in an angry manner, from a distance, at five o'clock in the afternoon as she left work with a girl friend and followed their car in his truck. Both the friend and the ex-wife testified that they felt intimidated by his acts. The appellate court upheld the ex-husband's conviction and his sentence of two days' imprisonment, sixteen hours of public service work, and twelve months probation.

[T]he word "harass" as used in the Domestic Violence Act takes color from the words "striking," "threatening," and "interfering with the personal liberty of." Harassment results from intentional acts which cause someone to be worried, anxious, or uncomfortable. Harassment does not necessarily require an overt act of violence. . . .

Based upon the intent of the legislature and the meaning of the surrounding terminology, harassment occurs when protagonist knowingly causes his victim to suffer undue distress. ... The protagonist must act with knowledge of the protective order for there to be a violation. As the defendant knew of the protective order, and intentionally caused his exwife to suffer undue distress there is no error. (*People v. Whitfield*, pp. 265–66)

These cases demonstrate a willingness on the part of the courts to uphold the intent of strong legislation designed to suppress domestic violence, intruding into domestic privacy and covering acts which hitherto would probably have been overlooked as private matters. In the cases where women took legal action by obtaining protection orders, the police seemed more likely to respond positively, and the prosecutors and judges clearly enforced the law to the hilt. It is too soon to say whether such laws can suppress the overall level of serious domestic violence, and one cannot be sure from the reported cases whether the Illinois Act is uniformly enforced. Yet, it is intuitively obvious that this expansive law has the potential to bring home to violent husbands, boyfriends, and exspouses that the relationship between the parties cannot include physical violence or harassment.

Thus far no Illinois cases have been reported regarding police failure to respond. The IDVA both expands police powers and limits police liability, two provisions designed to make the police more intrusive into the realm of domestic privacy in such cases. Thus, the Act allows a law enforcement officer to make an arrest without a warrant on probable cause of a crime, "including but not limited to violation of an order of protection . . . even if the crime was not committed in the presence of the officer" (*Smith-Hurd Ill. Ann. Stat.* sec. 2313–1). This provision abrogates the common-law rule not allowing a warrantless arrest for a misdemeanor unless committed in the officer's presence. This law does not go as far as mandatory legislation, but it does expand the police officers' options. In addition, the IDVA provides that "any act of omission or comission by any law enforcement officer acting in good faith in rendering emergency assistance or otherwise enforcing the Act shall not impose civil liability upon the law enforcement officer or his or her supervisor or employer, unless the act is a result of wilful or wanton misconduct" (*Smith-Hurd Ill. Ann. Stat.* sec. 2313–5). This provision is obviously designed to allay the police officer's concern that the vigorous enforcement of this statute should not generate liability.

An instructive Oregon case on the liability of police for failure to arrest under a domestic abuse law is *Nearing v. Weaver* (Ore. 1983). After her estranged husband entered her house without permission and struck her, Henrietta Nearing obtained an order of protection. A month later Robert Nearing again entered the premises, caused property damage, and attempted to remove their two children, aged three and four. Henrietta asked the police to arrest Robert, but they refused to do so because they did not see the husband on the premises. This pattern of events reoccurred at least three times. The court found that the police did not owe Henrietta a common-law duty "of due care to avoid predictable harm." Rather, they owed "a specific duty imposed by statute for the benefit of individuals previously identified by a judicial order'' (*Nearing v. Weaver*, p. 140). The very purpose of the statute was to eliminate ad hoc, discretionary police decisions; and the evaluation of facts to determine whether a report is true and fits within the statute is not the sort of discretion that gives the officer responsibility to make value judgments and policy choices. The courts also held that the Oregon statutes did not preclude a defense that the police acted in good faith.

In summary, Illinois provides an example of how a strong domestic violence law can direct the policy of prosecutors and courts towards treating domestic harassment and violence as matters for the public authorities. The Oregon case of *Nearing v. Weaver* provides an example of how legislation can help to modify police practices by requiring arrest and how litigation may be necessary for the act to be vigorously enforced.

CONCLUSION

This chapter has reviewed the current state of the law on the question of the courts' responses to police intervention in domestic violence cases. I have attempted to examine every published federal case on point decided as of January 1990, but only a few state cases. Several federal courts have found police officers and departments to be liable under 42 *U.S.C.* sec. 1983 for violations of the due process or equal protection clauses where police have failed to respond to calls for help from domestic abuse. I believe that these cases will play a small role in the movement by women to use the courts as a vehicle for reform. The Supreme Court's 1989 *DeShaney* decision has effectively foreclosed due process as a reform vehicle because of its disapproval of the special relationship doctrine. I also believe that as the equivocal findings of current research on police response to domestic violence become common knowledge, it will be more difficult to prove that level of discrimination which is necessary for a finding that a victim's equal protection rights have been violated, absent flagrant circumstances.

It seems to me, therefore, that the best avenue for effective action to deal with domestic violence—to heighten awareness, to gain the attention of police agencies and courts, to insure that wise action is taken to reduce the overall incidence of domestic violence—is through a variety of state actions. As I have shown, lawsuits under common-law liability doctrines are not likely to produce significant victories for battered women. On the other hand, clear legislation designed to place the authority of the courts and law enforcement agencies behind a strong policy to reduce domestic violence can be the basis of actions that are not limited by considerations of federalism or constrained by common-law rules designed to prevent lawsuits from undermining municipalities. By authorizing the police to interfere with domestic privacy under conditions that the legislature considers wise, guided by court-issued protection orders, state statutes are potentially an important vehicle to reduce domestic violence.

Appropriate legislation, therefore, is critically important, for it establishes the framework for action. In the area of the police response to domestic violence, legislation is necessary to establish the boundaries of appropriate police behavior, to modify common-law rules that hamper appropriate police action, and if deemed necessary to reduce the liability of officers who act reasonably under legislative mandates. Furthermore, legislation designed to resolve a social problem will be interpreted by the courts. In this way, understanding the legal issues helps us appreciate domestic violence policy, for every policy is eventually subjected to a court test. The direction and extent of the courts' interpretations will determine in large part whether the legislation will have a strong or weak effect. The Illinois legislation and cases reviewed in this chapter are examples both of legislation designed to promote stricter control of abusive spouses and of case law that has interpreted the legislature's intent broadly. In a sense the courts thus validate the legislation by reassuring society, for example, that the statute does not violate important due process interests of defendants.

However, even in states like Illinois, with strong domestic violence legislation bolstered by vigorous court implementation, many empirical questions remain unanswered. The existence of legislation and decided appellate cases are not necessarily indicators that the underlying problem is being dealt with adequately or is being resolved. Unfortunately, in legal circles, getting desired legislation and winning cases are victories that can blind advocates to the fact that legal victories may not be having the desired effect of alleviating the social problem at hand. It seems plausible to guess that liability suits would make police more apt to train and respond to domestic violence, but we really do not know this without good surveys of police work. Legislated reforms and even the nightstick of the tort suit may lack effectiveness where budget squeezes, low staffing, internal police inefficiencies or corruption, and other critical priorities divert police attention from domestic abuse cases. It is my belief that too heavy a reliance on legislation and litigation as a measure of policy success can be risky. Battered spouse advocacy groups or appropriate agencies must closely monitor available data on the incidence of domestic violence in order to have the baseline data necessary to measure significant changes of behavior. Alternative means of problem resolution—domestic abuse shelters, counseling programs for abusive partners, hotlines, personal relations training, family support programs—must also be available for the more effective handling of domestic violence situations either to protect victims who are leaving a battering situation or to prevent recurrences where the parties remain together. Within police agencies, legislation that expands the discretion of officers to arrest in domestic cases and limits liability is also just a beginning. Leadership on the issue from command officers, training, and feedback systems that inform higher officials how successful are their policies are also necessary if the laws are to be effective. Again, research into this facet of policing is necessary if police officials, governmental leaders, and the public at large are to see that the legislature's policies really work. Unfortunately, as is typically the case in criminal justice and social problem areas, data bases are grossly inadequate. Yet, effective and wise policy cannot arise without good information; funding for improved information systems and an ethic that makes information gathering and use a high police priority are imperative.

It is also important not to confuse legality with wisdom. Legislation and judicial decisions cannot be removed from the influences of their time, whether right or wrong. As suggested in the section on "domestic violence, police, and social science," some of the state statutes and police department policies that mandated arrest in domestic violence cases were using an inadequate foundation of scientific knowledge on which to base this policy. This chapter is not the right place to review the wisdom of mandatory arrest in its entirety. However, whether the policy is wise or not, the pell-mell manner in which it was adopted indicates that conclusions were being made by lawyers, police chiefs, legislators, and policy advocates about a scientific finding (deterrence) based more upon a desired outcome than on a careful analysis of the Minneapolis Domestic Violence Experiment. This raises serious questions about the relationship between social knowledge, research findings, and legal action. There is little opposition to the use of properly executed social-scientific research in policy formation. But, while there are canons of what constitutes good research, there are no canons for the reception of findings by nonscientists. Thus, the interpretation of research by lay policymakers, including judges and legislators, by policy advocates, and by lawyers (including legal scholars) will probably be filtered through all kinds of mental "lenses" mediated by the outcomes desired by these individuals. The driving force behind the domestic violence legislation and policy changes has been a change in social consciousness that, whatever its material basis (Harris 1987), has rightly tied spouse abuse to broader issues of gender equality. Ideological motivation is a powerful and necessary engine of social change, for it is hardly to be expected that entrenched interests and established patterns will yield without forceful and even emotional demands for change. Ideological motivation, however, works on an intellectual as well as on an emotional level. A risk in all advocacy movements is that specific programs and positions tend to be tinged with some of the emotional force of the movement's overarching aspirations; this at times leads to specific policy positions that are generated more by support for the "big goals" of the movement than the best solution to the specific problem. What this suggests (without making any conclusion on the substantive point) is that some of the advocacy for mandatory arrest policies by legal writers and by advocates was such an ideologically attractive stance that it led many to downplay several difficult questions regarding the wisdom of such a fixed policy. It is also becoming clear that the leap to accept the results of the Minneapolis experiment as received truth by the lay community was generated by similar motives.

In this area as in others, litigation is not the best first alternative; the law works best as a threat to lax police departments or recalcitrant husbands that their failures to act in accordance with legal norms can prove costly. But reliance simply on legislation and the threat of suits cannot alone resolve the underlying problems.

Even in this day of substantial sociolegal research, there is a wide gap between the worlds of law and social science. It is too much to expect, as a general matter, for legal practitioners to become social scientists or for social scientists to develop a deep appreciation of substantive law. In areas of social life where legal issues are prominent, however, there is value in attempts to bring relevant ideas of these diverse fields to practitioners who may have to rely on one another to act wisely and effectively. In this chapter I have attempted to demonstrate that advocates for battered women who are not legally trained should pay close attention to the reasoning, trends, and internal dynamics of the appellate decisions in domestic violence cases, because a few early and scattered victories may not be indicative of the direction of the case law. It is also important for them to appreciate the significant limitations of constitutional law or of common law standing alone in this area, as opposed to judicial doctrines developed in support of legislation. I have also attempted to demonstrate that lawyers and legal scholars ought to be careful in appreciating the limits of social scientific research. One study rarely establishes an irrefutable body of knowledge that is a solid basis for public policy. Although there does come a point when action must be taken in the face of inevitable gaps in the available scientific knowledge base regarding some issue, it is another matter to make legal arguments on the basis of simplified assumptions of what the research shows. Thus, it behooves legal scholars to be more careful in their handling of such data and to carefully distinguish the basis of their policy conclusions: ethical arguments, expediency, ideological presuppositions, and "the data." Social scientists must understand the broader social contexts of their research and should thus also be aware of the legal dynamics of the issues they study. Given the robust debate in criminological circles that has surrounded the issue of the policy implications of domestic arrest experiments, this level of self-scrutiny stands as a good model for the community of legal scholarship to emulate.

NOTE

I wish to thank Ms. Brenda Taylor for her research assistance.

REFERENCES

Anderson, Greg. 1985. *Sorichetti v. City of New York* Tells the Police that Liability Looms for Failure to Respond to Domestic Violence Situations. *University of Miami Law Review* (student comment) 40:333–58.

Baker, Leonard. 1984. *Brandeis and Frankfurter: A Dual Biography*. New York: Harper and Row.

Beck, Lisa R. 1987. Protecting Battered Women: A Proposal for Comprehensive Domestic Violence Legislation in New York. *Fordham Urban Law Journal* (student comment) 15:999–1048.

Brady, Terrence J. 1988. The Illinois Domestic Violence Act of 1986: A Selective Critique. *Loyola University Law Journal* 19:797–808.

de Tocqueville, Alexis. 1969. *Democracy in America*, ed. by J. P. Mayer. Garden City, N.Y.: Anchor Books.

Dobash, R. Emerson, and Russell Dobash. 1979. *Violence against Wives: A Case against the Patriarchy*. New York: Free Press.

Dunford, Franklyn W., David Huizinga, and Delbert Elliott. 1989. *The Omaha Domestic Violence Police Experiment: Final Report*. National Institute of Justice and City of Omaha.

Elliott, Delbert S. 1989. Criminal Justice Procedures in Family Violence Cases. In L. Ohlin and M. Tonry, eds., *Family Violence*, pp. 427–80. Chicago: University of Chicago Press.

Frieze, Irene H., and Angela Browne. 1989. Violence in Marriage. In L. Ohlin and M. Tonry, eds., *Family Violence*. Chicago: University of Chicago Press.

Gelles, Richard J., and Murray A. Straus. 1988. *Intimate Violence*. New York: Touchstone.

Goldman, Sheldon. 1989. Reagan's Judicial Legacy: Completing the Puzzle and Summing Up. *Judicature* 72(6):318–30.

Goldstein, Joseph. 1960. Police Discretion Not to Invoke the Criminal Process: Low-Visibility Decisions in the Administration of Justice. *Yale Law Journal* 69:543–94.

Graham, Fred P. 1970. *The Due Process Revolution: The Warren Court's Impact on Criminal Law*. New York: Hayden.

Gundle, Ruth. 1986. Civil Liability for Police Failure to Arrest: *Nearing v. Weaver*. *Women's Rights Law Reporter* 9:259–65.

Gunther, Gerald. 1985. *Constitutional Law*, 11th ed. Mineola, N.Y.: Foundation Press.

Harris, Marvin. 1987. *Why Nothing Works: The Anthropology of Daily Life*. New York: Touchstone Books.

Hathaway, Carolyn R. 1986. Case Comment: Gender Based Discrimination in Police Reluctance to Respond to Domestic Assault Complaints. *Georgetown Law Journal* (student comment) 75:667–91.

Holmes, Oliver Wendell, Jr. 1963. *The Common Law*, ed. by Mark DeWolfe Howe. Boston: Little, Brown.

Horowitz, Donald L. 1977. *The Courts and Public Policy*. Washington, D.C.: Brookings Institute.

International Association of Chiefs of Police. 1967. *Training Key 16: Handling Disturbance Calls*. Gaithersburg, Md. In R. Gelles and M. Straus, *Intimate Violence*. New York: Touchstone.

———. 1976. *Training Key 245: Wife Beating*. Gaithersburg, Md.

Jaynes, Gerald David, and Robin M. Williams, Jr. 1989. *A Common Destiny: Blacks and American Society*. Washington, D.C.: National Academy Press.

Jones, Charles O. 1984. *An Introduction to the Study of Public Policy*, 3d ed. Monterey, Calif.: Brooks/Cole.

Kluger, Richard. 1977. *Simple Justice*. London: Andre Duetsch.

Langan, Patrick A., and Christopher A. Innes. 1986. *Bureau of Justice Statistics Special Report: Preventing Domestic Violence Against Women*. Washington, D.C.: U.S. Department of Justice.

Lempert, Richard. 1984. From the Editor. *Law & Society Review* 18:505.

———. 1989. Humility Is a Virtue: On the Publicization of Policy-Relevant Research. *Law & Society Review* 23(1):145–61.

Lerman, Lisa G. 1982. Expansion of Arrest Power: A Key to Effective Intervention. *Vermont Law Review* 7:59–70.

———. 1984. Statute: A Model State Act: Remedies for Domestic Abuse. *Harvard Journal on Legislation* 21:61–143.

Levi, Edward. 1949. *An Introduction to Legal Reasoning.* Chicago: Phoenix.

Martin, Del. 1981. *Battered Wives*, rev. ed. San Francisco: Volcano Press.

Ohlin, Lloyd, and Michael Tonry. 1989. Family Violence in Perspective. In L. Ohlin and M. Tonry, eds., *Family Violence.* Chicago: University of Chicago Press.

Pleck, Elizabeth. 1989. Criminal Approaches to Family Violence: 1640–1980. In L. Ohlin and M. Tonry, eds., *Family Violence.* Chicago: University of Chicago Press.

Pole, J. R. 1978. *The Pursuit of Equality in American History.* Berkeley, Calif.: University of California Press.

Shapiro, Robert A. n.d. Annotation: Personal Liability of Policeman, Sheriff, or Similar Peace Officer or His Bond, for Injury Suffered as a Result of Failure to Enforce Law or Arrest Lawbreaker. ALR3d, 41:700–11.

Sherman, Lawrence C., and Richard A. Berk. 1984. The Specific Deterrent Effects of Arrest for Domestic Assault. *American Sociological Review* 49:261–72.

Sherman, Lawrence C., and Ellen G. Cohn. 1989. The Impact of Research on Legal Policy: The Minneapolis Domestic Violence Experiment. *Law & Society Review* 23(1):117–44.

Sudnow, David. 1965. Normal Crimes: Sociological Features of the Penal Code in a Public Defender's Office. *Social Problems* 12:255–76.

U.S. Attorney General's Task Force on Family Violence. 1984. *Final Report.* Washington, D.C.: U.S. Attorney General.

Zalman, Marvin. 1975. The Federal Anti-Riot Act and Political Crime: The Need for Criminal Law Theory. *Villanova Law Review* 20:897–937.

———. 1982. Mandatory Sentencing Legislation: Myths and Reality. In M. Morash, ed., *Implementing Criminal Justice Policies.* Beverly Hills, Calif.: Sage.

Zimring, Franklin E. 1989. Toward a Jurisprudence of Family Violence. In L. Ohlin and M. Tonry, eds., *Family Violence.* Chicago: University of Chicago Press.

LEGAL CASES

Ashford v. County of Suffolk, 123 A.D.2D 733, 507 N.Y.Supp.2d 204 (1986)

Austin v. City of Scottsdale, 140 Ariz. 579, 684 P.2d 151 (1984)

Bailey v. County of York, 768 F.2d 503 (3rd Cir. 1985)

Balistreri v. Pacifica Police Dept., 855 F.2d 1421 (9th Cir. 1988)

Bartalone v. County of Berrien, 643 F.Supp. 574 (W.D. Mich. 1986).

Bowers v. DeVito, 686 F.2d 616 (7th Cir. 1982)

Craig v. Boren, 429 U.S. 190, 97 S.Ct. 451, 50 L.Ed.2d 397 (1976)

DeShaney v. Winnebago County Department of Social Services, 489 U.S. 189, 109 S.Ct. 998, 103 L.Ed.2d 249 (1989)

Dudosh v. City of Allentown, 665 F.Supp. 381 (E.D. Pa. 1987)

Florence v. Goldberg, 44 N.Y.2d 189, 375 N.E.2d 763, 404 N.Y.S.2d 583 (1978)

Harlow v. Fitzgerald, 457 U.S. 800,102 S.Ct. 2727, 73 L.Ed.2d 396 (1982)

Hynson v. City of Chester Legal Dept., 864 F.2d 1026 (3rd Cir. 1988)

In re Marriage of Hagaman, 123 Ill.App.3d 549, 78 Ill.Dec. 922, 462 N.E.2d 1276 (1984)

Loving v. Virginia, 388 U.S. 1, 87 S.Ct. 1817, 18 L.Ed.2d 1010 (1967)

Martinez v. California, 444 U.S. 277, 100 S.Ct. 553, 62 L.Ed.2d 481 (1980)

McKee v. City of Rockwall, Texas, 877 F.2d 409 (5th Cir. 1989)

Monnell v. Department of Social Services, 436 U.S. 658 (1978)

Morgan v. District of Columbia, 468 A.2d 1306 (D.C. Ct. App. 1983) (en banc)

Nearing v. Weaver, 295 Or. 702, 670 P.2d 137 (1983)

People v. Blackwood, 131 Ill.App.3d 1018, 476 N.E.2d 742 (1985)

People v. Whitfield, 147 Ill.App.3d 675, 498 N.E.2d 262 (1986)

Sherrell v. City of Longview, 683 F.Supp. 1108 (E.D. Tex. 1987)

Sorichetti v. City of New York, 65 N.Y.2d 461, 482 N.E.2d 70, 492 N.Y.Supp.2d 591 (1985)

South v. Maryland, 59 U.S. (18 How.) 396, 15 L.Ed. 433 (1856)

Thurman v. City of Torrington, 595 F.Supp. 1521 (D. Conn. 1984)

Turner v. City of North Charleston, 675 F.Supp. 314 (D.S.Car. 1987)

Watson v. Kansas City, Kan., 857 F.2d 690 (10th Cir. 1988)

6

ARREST AND THE REDUCTION OF REPEAT WIFE ASSAULT

Donald G. Dutton, Stephen D. Hart, Les W. Kennedy, and Kirk R. Williams

Donald Dutton, Stephen Hart, Les Kennedy, and Kirk Williams review both long-term and short-term effects of arrest upon the future behavior of offenders. Currently, there is significant controversy in the literature concerning both types of impacts, for several reasons. Questions have been raised over the methodology and findings of past research on the deterrent effects of arrest, particularly with the Sherman and Berk pilot study in Minneapolis (as more fully described in Binder and Meeker's following chapter). There has also been a failure to adequately explain the mechanism by which deterrence might occur. Without such an understanding, it will be problematic whether any intervention strategy will be used appropriately.

This chapter first analyzes the reasons for recidivism, focussing on how acts of aggression may become a habit, although not necessarily. In earlier research, Dutton addressed the question of whether the effect of arrest is dependent upon the treatment. In an attempt to answer that question, this research examines whether arrest itself (without treatment) might serve a deterrent function. It is theorized that, by changing and increasing the social costs of continued violence or by changing the power dynamics within a couple, future acts of assault would be less likely to occur. Using survey research, the authors show that the experience of arrest and subsequent prosecution appears to heighten perceived risks of legal and social sanctions, and especially the risk of possibly "losing" a spouse. The wife gains more power in the marriage, as both the victim and the offender tell others about the problem of violence. Increased visibility in turn may be correlated with future legal and social sanctions.

This chapter presents a substantial analysis of how arrest may reduce recidivism. Deterrence is shown not to be the only method of altering the probability of future violence. For example, the indirect change in the power dynamics of the couple and the encouragement of social disclosure may make a "private" event public. Public breaking of the peace, as more fully set forth in Chaudhuri and Daly's chapter in Part III, may be met by a greater commitment of police and prosecutorial effort, because such incidents may disrupt the "social order." Hence, this chapter raises important questions as to the relative importance of deterrence through fear of formal sanctions and deterrence by covarying informal sanctions. The editors suggest that if visibility and informal sanctions give arrest much of its deterrent value, the same effect might be accomplished by means other than arrest, such as notification to social agencies for follow-ups or other methods.

Policy-makers have increasingly looked to legal intervention as a strategy for reducing husband-to-wife violence (Sherman and Cohn 1989). Yet despite the highly publicized findings of the Minneapolis Domestic Violence Experiment (Sherman and Berk 1984), little is known about the potential deterrence process mobilized by such intervention. Moreover, this lack of knowledge results from more than methodological problems with previous research (Binder and Meeker 1988) and thus questions about its evidential basis for policy (Lempert 1989). Rather, investigators have failed to specify how legal intervention might achieve deterrence (see Carmody and Williams 1987; Williams and Hawkins 1989a, 1989b, for exceptions), meaning in this context the reduction of wife assault because male perpetrators fear the legal (e.g., conviction, jail time) and social costs (subsequent life disruptions such as loss of partner, social disapproval) resulting from arrest (see Gibbs 1986; Williams and Hawkins 1986, for a more general discussion).

The present analysis is an exploratory attempt to begin specifying the potential deterrence process generated by arrest. We say "potential" because the data analyzed do not allow the direct estimation of deterrence effects. Instead, we draw from three independent studies—two surveys of separate general populations (a U.S. national survey and an Alberta, Canada, provincial survey) and a survey of arrested wife assaulters in Vancouver, Canada—to compare nonarrested and arrested repeat wife assaulters concerning their perceptions of the consequences associated with this form of male aggression. Specifically, deterrence theory asserts that norm violations (in this case, wife assault) can be reduced by an increase in the perceived likelihood and severity of sanctions for such violations. Accordingly, we address the following empirical question: Does an arrest experience increase such perception, thus enhancing the potential for deterrence? Before describing the data and findings bearing on this question, a brief review of literature bearing on the incentives and incidence of repeat wife assault, along with the few studies of legal intervention, is in order.

REPEAT WIFE ASSAULT

There are several reasons why men who physically assault their wives might repeat this act: aggression serves an expressive and cathartic function (Bandura 1979; Novaco 1976) and, accordingly, is self-rewarding (see also Zimbardo

1969; Dutton, Fehr, and McEwen 1982; Dutton 1988). Furthermore, the violence frequently is used as a power tactic in spousal conflict. To the extent it succeeds in "resolving" the conflict in a manner favorable to the male, it is further rewarding and hence, tends to be repeated. Bandura (1979) describes aggression as a response to "aversive stimuli" (real or perceived). The removal of the stimulus provides negative reinforcement for the habit of aggression, increasing the probability of repeat aggression.

Once committed, the aggression tends to be minimized and rationalized through a process Bandura (1979) calls "neutralization of self-punishment," whereby ordinary self-punishment processes are suspended or diminished. Through this process, males who are aggressive toward intimate female partners may minimize or deny the effects thereof or may alter their perceptions of who initiated the aggression. Dutton (1986b) described this process by differentiating wife assaulters in terms of their perception of the causes of their violence or "rationalization patterns." Extreme minimizers tended to discount the severity and frequency of their violence as well as the severity of the consequences. From the perspective of Bandura's social learning theory, such cognitive tendencies should serve to maintain an aggressive habit, increasing the likelihood of repeat assault through denial of the man's own responsibility for the aggression and minimizing the effects of the aggression.

Retrospective studies of family violence have supported the notion of wife assault as a repeated habit. Straus (1977) reported the average frequency of wife beating to be eight times per year for the 3.8 percent of respondents in the 1975 U.S. national survey who reported serious wife assault on the Conflict Tactics Scale. This finding, moreover, has been replicated in the 1985 Family Violence Re-survey (Straus and Gelles 1989). Wilt and Bannon's (1977) investigation of spousal homicides and aggravated assaults in Detroit and Kansas City found that police had been called to the address of the offender and victim for at least one "domestic disturbance" in 90 percent of all cases and five or more times in 50 percent of all cases. Jaffe and Burris (1982) found that women who charged their husbands with assault had been previously assaulted by them an average of thirty-five times. The problem with retrospective studies, however, is that they work backward from a population which, by definition, represents repeat occurrences of the problem behavior. This raises the question of whether such repetition might occur in couples who have been contacted after one assault.

Data from the U.S. National Crime Survey indicate that of all women who report spousal assault, 25 percent report repeat or "series" assaults (Schwartz 1987). The Canadian Urban Victimization Survey reported that 16 percent of women who reported any spousal assault reported series assaults within the year of the survey (Solicitor General of Canada 1985). Survey data using the Conflict Tactics Scale (Straus 1977; Schulman 1979) suggest that, for one-third of couples reporting assault, the violence appears to end "spontaneously" (i.e., without police intervention) after one incidident, at least within a one-year time frame. As only about 14.6 percent of serious wife assaults are reported to police (Dutton

1987), police intervention could not account for this reduction in frequency of violence in these 33 percent of one-time wife assaulters.

We do not know the circumstances surrounding this cessation or reduction in use of repeat violence (e.g., Feld and Straus 1989). It could occur because the male follows the violence with threats of repeat violence to maintain a power advantage over his spouse, thus generating sufficient control that further violence is not required as a control technique. Or it could occur because the woman threatens to leave the relationship or call the police if the violence is repeated. What is known is that, at least within the one-year period covered by the survey report, 33 percent of respondents indicate that assaultive behavior occurred one time only and 67 percent reported repeat violence.

Given the unsettling problem of repeat wife assault, it is important to begin exploring the possible effects of various intervention strategies. This chapter focusses exclusively on one strategy that has been increasingly adopted: police intervention through arrest.

POLICE INTERVENTION AND RECIDIVISM REDUCTION

Several studies have been recently conducted on the reduction of recidivism in identified populations of wife assaulters when police intervention has occurred. Jaffe, Wolfe, Telford, and Austin (1986) monitored pre-arrest and post-arrest assaultive behavior of males through both interviews with their wives and examination of police files. Jaffe et al. found substantial post-arrest reductions in violence directed toward wives regardless of whether the police records or wives' self-reports were used as the dependent measure.

Sherman and Berk (1984) randomly assigned domestic disturbance calls to three treatment conditions: arrest, separation, and mediation. They found that within six months of police intervention, arrested men had recidivism rates of 13 percent by police records and 19 percent by wives' reports. Corresponding rates for separation were 26 percent and 28 percent. Mediation produced rates of 18 percent and 37 percent. This finding was quite impressive, given that 80 percent of this sample had committed prior assaults on the victim in the six months preceding police intervention. Sherman and Berk attributed this between-treatment difference in recidivism to ''specific deterrence.'' Such an explanation assumes that the main cause of recidivism reduction is fear of criminal justice reprisal itself (e.g., conviction and fine or jail time as a result of arrest) for future illegal actions. However, the design of the Sherman and Berk study did not assess alternative explanations of how arrest might reduce recidivism.

As fear of criminal justice sanctions is a subjective state, inference of its presence based only on behavioral patterns is problematic. For example, arrest may serve a ''didactic'' function, conveying to the man that his violence is wrong. This message, apart from fear of subsequent legal sanctioning, may produce recidivism reduction. Alternatively, arrest may change the constellation of informal social costs for the couple. The man's violence may become public by virtue of arrest, bringing greater public disclosure of the aggressive action, with informal social pressures from friends and/or family resulting. These issues cannot be explored unless the meaning of arrest (i.e., the subjective states of repeat wife assaulters; see Williams and Hawkins 1989a) is explored.

Additionally, the power dynamic within the relationship may alter as a consequence of arrest. As couples with extreme power imbalances are most violent (Coleman and Straus 1986), power equalization due to arrest may also produce recidivism reduction.

Fagan (1988) has also argued that power equalization may contribute to "desistance" from wife assault. Citing data from Fagan, Friedman, Wexler, and Lewis (1984) and from Bowker (1983), Fagan points out that the most frequently mentioned factors that contributed to desistance from battering by the male aggressor was fear of relationship loss. In this case, the wife-victim has the power to end the relationship (or to remove something valued by the aggressor). Fear of legal sanction was mentioned third most frequently by this sample. Wives in these studies had sought external support either through shelter house or criminal justice system intervention. These women may have attained equalization of power differentials through this third-party intervention, but it is not known whether this mechanism also occurred for the 33 percent "desisting" couples in the surveys previously described, because it is not known whether third-party intervention occurred for these women. At best, we can speak only to the issue of what factors seemed to have reduced repeat assault in couples who have come to the attention of outside agencies. This information is important in its own right, however, as it could help shape social policy to effectively reduce recidivist wife assault.

Dutton (1986a) examined recidivism in a population that had both been arrested and undergone court-mandated treatment for assaultive behavior. Over a two-and-a-half-year period following arrest, members of the untreated group were rearrested for assault 40 percent of the time, but members of the treated group only 4 percent. By comparing his sample population with that of Jaffe et al., both in terms of demographics and Conflict Tactics Scale scores filled out by their wives, Dutton was able to demonstrate a greater decrease in recidivism when treatment was appended to arrest. Whereas the results found by Jaffe et al. demonstrated decreases in violence toward wives of about 66 percent of the pre-arrest total, Dutton showed that this post-arrest total could be further reduced by at least another 50 percent through psychological treatment. By extending the follow-up assessment period, Dutton (1986a) was also able to provide a new perspective to the Sherman and Berk (1984) study. Sherman and Berk's police data for repeat wife assault indicated a 13 percent recidivism rate for arrested men within six months of arrest. Dutton's arrested (but untreated) control group demonstrated a similar 16 percent recidivism rate for this initial six-month period. However, within the two years following this initial six-month period (which at the time of the data collection was the period of probation), the recidivism rate increased from 16 percent to 40 percent, suggesting that the recidivism reduction produced by arrest may occur through short-term deterrence that loses its impact after the probation period expires and the salience of criminal justice system sanctions is diminished.

Deterrence notions suggest that heightened awareness of the likelihood of negative criminal justice sanctions is the key variable in reducing recidivism. Deterrence is commonly conceived of as involving a "rational" decision-making process in which an individual weighs the costs and rewards of illegal versus legal behavioral alternatives. The behavior committed presumably provides the greatest net gain for the perpetrator. By implication, to deter a behavior, the negative consequences (i.e., costs) of that action must necessarily be perceived as greater than those of other behavioral options (see Gibbs 1986; Williams and Hawkins 1986; Lundman 1986; Paternoster 1987, for general discussions and reviews of evidence and issues).

DATA AND VARIABLES

The major objective of this chapter is to determine how the experience of arrest influences the perceived likelihood and the perceived severity of various consequences of perpetrating wife assault. Some of the consequences can be viewed as legal sanctions in that they are negative reactions on the part of legal officials (i.e., police arrest, court appearance, conviction, jail). Others are extralegal or social in that they are actions taken by people outside the context of the criminal justice system (i.e., police called, partner leaves, friends and relatives disapprove or lose respect for the assaulter, assaulter loses self-respect). The importance of the objective is that by empirically examining how arrest influences perception of such consequences, we can begin to learn how arrest may operate to reduce recidivist wife assault.

A problem we have in accomplishing the objective is that the focus of the analysis is on a sample of arrested repeat wife assaulters (described hereafter). Thus, a non-arrested comparison group is needed. The problem is addressed by using two separate surveys of non-arrested wife assaulters, who were asked questions about the consequences of wife assault identical to those asked of arrested wife assaulters, in the general population: one a national survey of coupled adults in the United States and the other a provincial survey of adults in Alberta, Canada.

General Population Surveys

The U.S. survey of adult couples, utilizing telephone interviews and random-digit dialing, is a national panel study of deterrence and social control of aggression in marital or marriagelike relationships. It builds on the National Family Violence Re-survey conducted in the summer and early fall of 1985 (Straus and Gelles 1989). Assaulters identified in 1985 through the administration of the Conflict Tactics Scale (Straus 1979) and a comparable number of non-assaulters were reinterviewed one year later in 1986 (ever assaulters = 763, never assaulters = 646) and again one year later, in 1987 (ever assaulters = 415, never assaulters = 780). The present analysis is based on data collected from male respondents whose CTS scores as of 1987 show that they repeatedly (two or more times) used some type of physical aggression against their female partners in the previous twelve months (N = 33 of 492 men interviewed in 1987).[1]

Data on the perceived likelihood of legal and social sanctions were obtained by posing the following scenario to respondents:

Suppose you hit your partner. I am going to read a list of things which might happen as a result. Please note the chances of each result on a zero-to-ten scale. You should give a zero if you think it has no chance at all of happening, and a ten if you think it is sure to happen. You can use any number between zero and ten to indicate the chances of each happening.

Respondents were then asked to indicate how bad it would be for them if these things did happen as a result of hitting their partners. Again, a zero-to-ten scale was used, with zero meaning not bad at all and ten meaning extremely bad. The legal sanction used in this procedure is arrest; and the social sanctions include police called, loss of partner, social disapproval, and loss of self-respect. The zero-to-ten scales reflecting perception of the likelihood or severity of these sanctions are used in the present analysis.

The second general population survey used in the present analysis is the Alberta survey conducted in 1987 at the University of Alberta (Kennedy and Dutton 1987, 1989). The Conflict Tactics Scale was administered to adults (eighteen or older) using both face-to-face and telephone interviewing. Face-to-face interviewing was conducted in the city of Edmonton, while telephone interviewing was used in the remainder of the province. For the Edmonton survey, respondents were selected randomly from a computerized list of addresses compiled by Edmonton's Civic Census in 1986. For the remainder of the province, respondents were selected through random-digit dialing.

The Alberta survey used questions identical to those administered in the U.S. survey to obtain data on the perceived likelihood and severity of legal and social sanctions. Moreover, the sanctions incorporated in the Alberta survey were also the same as those in the U.S. survey. Repeat wife assaulters were also identified as those men who reported using some type of physical aggression on the CTS scale against their female partners two or more times during the previous twelve months (N = 30 of 355 men interviewed in 1987).[2]

In short, we have identical data from two independent surveys of two different general populations. From these surveys, we calculate perceptual estimates of the likelihood and severity of legal and social sanctions for men identified as repeat wife assaulters as of 1987. Yet these men have not been arrested for such aggressive behavior. Although we explore the similarities and differences between the estimates reported by repeat wife assaulters in the U.S. and Alberta surveys, the primary objective is to use these perceptual estimates as baselines for non-arrested repeat wife assaulters. Specifically, we compare the perceptual estimates of arrested assaulters to those of these two samples of non-arrested assaulters.

Vancouver Arrested Assaulters

The arrested repeat wife assaulters in the study reported here were sixty men who had been convicted of common assault against their wives and were undergoing treatment with the Assaultive Husbands' Treatment Project (a court-mandated treatment project in Vancouver, B.C.). For purposes of comparability with the U.S. and Alberta surveys, only data for subjects still in intact relationships are reported in this study. Further, the issues we address bear on the perceived consequences of assault within intimate relationships. All subjects and their female partners completed the Conflict Tactics Scale (Straus 1979) to assess the frequency of husband-to-wife physical aggression within the last year. The men self-reported an average of fourteen acts of physical aggression against their wives in the preceding year. Their wives reported an average of twenty-two acts of physical aggression against themselves in the preceding year. Hence, by either report, these men were repeat wife assaulters in the top ninety-ninth percentile, according to North American standards compiled by Straus, Gelles, and Steinmetz (1980). Their average age was 31, and their average education was 12.2 years.

At the beginning of treatment (about four months after conviction in court) and again about one-and-a-half to two years after court and about eight to sixteen months after completing a treatment program, respondents answered perceptual questions developed by Williams and Carmody (1986) and reported by Carmody and Williams (1987). This is the same set of questions used in the U.S. and Alberta surveys, except that the scenario posed to these men was prefaced by the following phrase: "Suppose you reoffend similar to the last time . . . ."

To assess whether answers given on to these questions were influenced by the respondents' tendency to image-manage, the Marlowe-Crowne social desirability scale was also administered. At Time 1 (four months postconviction), these men were still on probation. In most cases their probation orders required them to report to a probation officer and to attend the treatment group. The orders were generally in effect for a one-year probationary period. Time 2 questionnaire administration occurred about one year after the completion of the (four month) treatment group (about twenty months after conviction) and after the end of the term of probation.

Arrested assaulters were also asked to rate the amount of relationship power they and their wives had prior to their arrest. They were also asked to report the extent of social disclosure of aggression, both by themselves and their wives prior to arrest and subsequent to arrest. These are important issues because rectifying a power imbalance in favor of men and making such assaults socially

Table 6.1
Likelihood Scores for Legal and Social Sanctions for Arrested and Non-Arrested Repeat Wife Assaulters

	Non-Arrested		Arrested	Pairwise Comparisons[1]
	(a) U.S.	(b) Alta.	(c) Van.	
Legal Sanctions				
Police arrest	2.6 (12.2)	1.3 (7.9)	8.3 (3.0)	c > a, b
Court appearance	--	--	8.5 (3.4)	--
Conviction	--	--	7.8 (3.5)	--
Jail	--	--	7.4 (3.6)	--
Social Sanctions				
Police called	2.4 (10.2)	1.6 (7.3)	6.3 (3.7)	C > a, b
Loss of partner	3.9 (14.7)	3.1 (7.9)	7.0 (3.6)	C > a, b
Social disapproaval	6.8 (11.7)	4.9 (14.5)	6.9 (3.1)	n.s.
Loss of self-respect	6.8 (13.4)	6.3 (14.0)	7.6 (3.1)	n.s.

Note. SD in brackets. U.S. = United States survey (Williams & Straus, 1986); Alta. = Alberta, Canada survey (Kennedy & Dutton, 1987, 1989); Van. = convicted wife assaulters in Vancouver, Canada; -- = data not available; n.s. = no significant pairwise comparisons. n.s. = no significant pairwise comparisons.

[1]Pairwise comparisons were t-tests. Due to the large number of tests, the familywise Type I error rate (α_{FW}) was held at .05 by testing each comparison at α_T = .05/30 = .002.

visible may reduce the incidence of wife assault. As not all men could be contacted at Time 2, data are reported for thirty-two of the initial sample of sixty. Scores are reported only for men still in their original relationship at Time 2. However, there is no initial evidence of attrition bias here. Specifically, Time 1 scores for the men contacted at Time 2 did not differ significantly from Time 1 scores for the remaining twenty-eight men. Nonetheless, the results should be considered only suggestive, given the high proportional loss of cases.

EMPIRICAL RESULTS

Table 6.1 presents the mean perceived likelihood scores for non-arrested (i.e., U.S. survey and Alberta survey) and arrested repeat wife assaulters. Consider first the scores for the U.S. and Alberta surveys. The means from both of these samples are not significantly different. Thus, for all practical purposes, both surveys can be used for comparative purposes. This is underscored by the fact that the pattern among the mean perceived likelihood scores is similar in both samples, with police called and police arrest perceived as least likely, followed by loss of partner, social disapproval, and loss of self-respect. Thus, despite any socioeconomic, cultural and other differences that may exist between the two nations, a substantial amount of consensus is apparent in the perceived likelihood of these legal and social sanctions.

However, the perceived likelihood of legal sanctions is very low in these general populations. In the United States, repeat assaulters perceive slightly more than a two-out-of-ten chance of arrest, on the average, while the mean perceived likelihood score in Alberta, Canada, is slightly higher than a one-out-of-ten chance of arrest. These men clearly view arrest as a rare result of assault, suggesting that the future threat of arrest as a deterrent may be discounted. Assaulting with impunity (i.e., no arrest experience) is most likely the reason for the finding. This point is supported further by examining the mean perceived likelihood scores for those men who have experienced arrest and prosecution.

Notice that the likelihood scores on police called and police arrest for the Vancouver arrested assaulters are significantly higher than those for either of the general population surveys. The means for both sanctions are relatively high, representing a seven- or eight-out-of-ten chance of happening. Moreover, although comparisons with the U.S. and Alberta surveys cannot be made, the mean perceived likelihood scores on the other legal sanctions (i.e., court appearance, conviction, jail) are also relatively high. The scores for social sanctions are not significantly different from those of the U.S. and Alberta surveys, with the exception of loss of partner.

In sum, the experience of arrest and subsequent prosecution appears to heighten the perceived risk of legal sanctions but not necessarily of social sanctions such as social disapproval or loss of self-esteem. However, the arrest experience also appears to increase the perceived risk of losing one's partner. Perhaps these men perceive the arrest as dramatizing the seriousness of the aggressive behavior to their partners and others (e.g., friends and relatives) and empowering their wives so that any further instances of such behavior would be met with a dissolution of the relationship. Additional supportive evidence of this possibility is reported in Table 6.2, which shows the before and after arrest means on the power and social disclosure measures.

Responses to questions about power distribution in the relationship taken at Time 1 indicate that men perceive their wives as having more relative power in the marriage (and themselves less) after police intervention. Average ratings of their wives' power after police intervention are 5.5 (maximum = 9) compared to 4.9 before, which is a non-significant change. However, men rate their own power in the relationship as significantly dropping from 5.2 before arrest to 3.7 after arrest. More importantly, at this postintervention juncture, men perceive that they have significantly less power in the relationship than their wives (men's

Table 6.2
Reports of Power Differentials and Social Disclosure of Assault before and after Arrest for Wife Assault (N = 60)

Power and Disclosure Variable	Before Arrest	After Arrest (Time 1)	t-value
Power: wives' power	4.9	5.5	
offenders' power	5.2	3.7	4.83*
Disclosure: wives' disclosure	2.2	10.0	8.88*
offenders' disclosure	.3	4.2	9.50*

* p ≤ .01, two tailed test.

power = 3.7, women's power = 5.5, $t = 3.29$, $df = 59$, $p < .001$). At present it is not known whether this perception stems from real alterations in the woman's behavior towards the offender after the arrest. In any event, these data demonstrate another effect of arrest: an alteration of the power relationship in the previously assaultive couple. This, in turn, may result in men believing that their wives will take assertive actions to end their victimization, including dissolving the relationship or notifying the police as well as others.

Responses to the question of disclosure taken at Time 1 indicate that arrest significantly increases the probability that both victims and perpetrators of assault increase the disclosure of the violence after arrest occurs. Wives report telling an average of 2.2 people about pre-arrest assaults compared to 10 people for post-arrest assaults, which is a significant increase. Men report telling an average of 0.3 people about the pre-arrest assault and 4.2 about the post-arrest assaults, which also is a significant increase. The importance of these findings is that men, but even more so women, are likely to make violence known to others. This increased visibility renders assaulters more vulnerable not only to legal intervention but also to any number of social control mobilizations that might take place, ranging from informal (e.g., social disapproval) to formal (e.g., treatment) sanctions. In addition, disclosure can generate social support for the victim, which may make her less likely to introject blame for the assault or to tolerate further assault.

The empirical results thus far pertain to perceptions of the likelihood that legal and/or social sanctions will be imposed as a consequence of arrest for wife assault. Additionally, factors that might explain why arrest elevates such perception have been suggested (i.e., alteration of power in the relationship and increased social disclosure). Now consider perceptions of the severity of these sanctions. Relevant data are presented in Table 6.3.

As with the perceived likelihood scores, a comparison of the mean perceived severity scores in the U.S. and Alberta samples shows that non-arrested repeat assaulters in both surveys perceive severity in a similar fashion. Once again,

Table 6.3
Severity Scores on Legal and Social Sanctions for Non-Arrested and Arrested Repeat Wife Assaulters

	Non-Arrested		Arrested	Pairwise Comparisons[1]
	(a) U.S.	(b) Alta.	(c) Van.	
Legal Sanctions				
Police arrest	5.7 (17.7)	7.3 (7.7)	9.2 (1.5)	c > a
Court appearance	--	--	9.7 (0.7)	--
Conviction	--	--	9.0 (2.1)	--
Jail	--	--	9.4 (2.0)	--
Social Sanctions				
Police called	5.1 (16.5)	4.6 (8.5)	8.6 (2.3)	C > a, b
Loss of partner	7.9 (8.27)	7.2 (11.4)	8.0 (2.9)	n.s.
Social disapproaval	6.4 (14.3)	6.5 (9.4)	7.3 (3.3)	n.s.
Loss of self-respect	7.1 (13.1)	7.4 (11.0)	8.5 (2.6)	n.s.

Note. SD in brackets. U.S. = United States survey (Williams & Straus, 1986); Alta. = Alberta, Canada survey (Kennedy & Dutton, 1987, 1989); Van. = convicted wife assaulters in Vancouver, Canada; -- = data not available; n.s. = no significant pairwise comparisons. n.s. = no significant pairwise comparisons.

[1]Pairwise comparisons were t-tests. Due to the large number of tests, the familywise Type I error rate (p_{FW}) was held at .05 by testing each comparison at p_T = .05/30 = .002.

none of the means are significantly different, suggesting that both samples can be used in comparison with arrested assaulters. Moreover, although repeat assaulters in the Alberta survey rate police arrest as slightly more severe than those in the U.S. survey, men in both samples perceive loss of partner and loss of self-respect as most severe. Arrested repeat assaulters also rated the severity of legal sanctions (police called, police arrest) significantly higher than did non-arrested assaulters.

An important issue is whether this perceived risk of legal intervention is a short-term aberration or is sustained over time. Data bearing on the issue are shown in Table 6.4. It presents the Time 1 (during treatment) and Time 2 (follow-up) means on the perceived likelihood and perceived severity measures for the arrested repeat wife assaulters (i.e., the Vancouver sample). A comparison of these means shows that the perceived likelihood of police called and police arrest

Table 6.4
Perceived Likelihood and Perceived Severity Scores on Legal and Social Sanctions for Arrested Repeat Wife Assaulters (N = 32)

Types of Sanctions	Perceived Likelihood			Perceived Severity		
	Time 1	Time 2	Pairwise Comparison	Time 1	Time 2	Pairwise Comparison
Legal Sanctions:						
Police Arrest	8.5	8.0	n.s.	8.8	9.4	n.s.
Court Appearance	9.6	7.6	1 > 2*	8.4	9.0	n.s.
Conviction	8.8	6.7	1 > 2*	7.3	9.3	2 > 1*
Jail	7.5	4.3	1 > 2**	8.7	9.3	n.s.
Social Sanctions:						
Police Called	7.2	7.0	n.s.	8.4	8.0	n.s.
Loss of Partner	8.1	8.2	n.s.	5.1	9.6	2 > 1**
Social Disapproval	6.6	7.7	2 > 1*	6.7	8.4	2 > 1*
Loss of Self-Respect	7.7	9.3	2 > 1*	8.4	9.5	n.s.

* $p \leq .05$, two tailed test

** $p \leq .01$, two tailed test

Pairwise comparisons were t-tests. Due to the large number of tests the familywise Type I error rate (P_{FW}) was held at .05 by testing each comparison at $p_T = .05/30 = .002$.

remains high and does not significantly change. However, the average perceived likelihood scores for the other legal sanctions significantly decline from Time 1 to Time 2, but not for the mean perceived severity scores. They remain essentially unchanged or slightly increase (see especially the perceived severity of conviction). For the men at Time 2, probation had expired and court-mandated treatment had ended. Perhaps the absence of the ''reminders'' of legal intervention for assault diminishes the perceived likelihood of these legal sanctions.

Concerning social sanctions, observe that the mean perceived likelihood and perceived severity scores remain largely unaltered. However, notice that the perceived likelihood scores for social disapproval and loss of self-respect and severity scores for loss of partner and social disapproval are higher at follow-up than during treatment. This may be a treatment effect. The court-mandated program in which these men have been involved encourages them to assume the responsibility of their actions and to deal more effectively with issues of power and intimacy in their relationships with their female partners (see Dutton 1988). A by-product may well be a greater importance placed on the viability and persistence of the relationship. To the extent this is true, it underscores the importance of making treatment a condition of arrest and prosecution. Treatment may heighten the awareness of the legal and social consequences of assault and prevent the possible anger associated with arrest from being displaced on wives. However, that treatment may be possible only if wife assaulters are arrested.[3]

DISCUSSION

The present study suggests that arrest may reduce recidivism not only through deterrence but, in addition, by altering a power dynamic in the relationship, making the wife appear to have more sanctioning power, and by increasing social disclosure. Questionnaire ratings by males (at Time 1) of their wives' sanctioning power reveal strong perceptions of considerable power in her hands. For example, in response to the proposition that one of their wives could call the police at any time, say that her husband had hit her, and be believed, the men indicated strong agreement ($\overline{X}$ = 3.1 on a nine-point scale where 1 indicates strongly agree and 9 indicates strongly disagree). The same agreement was found for items that indicated that the police would believe the wife and not the husband ($\overline{X}$ = 3.2) and that she could have him arbitrarily arrested ($\overline{X}$ = 3.8). These responses indicate a concern that arrested men have at Time 1 that the criminal justice system is siding with their wives. In effect, the woman derives "power" (vis-à-vis her assaulter) from her perceived support by the criminal justice system. Clearly, this power depends on the woman's perceived willingness to call the police if reassaulted. If the perpetrator perceives her as having this willingness and the criminal justice system as being likely to respond, then the female partner is empowered. Arrest serves to increase this perception.

Furthermore, in the case of wife assault, arrest serves a function of making a private event public. This effect in itself could serve to reduce subsequent violence. Victims of wife assault who do not disclose the assault tend to live with "pluralistic ignorance" of the common nature of wife assault. Hence, they are more likely to attribute the event to some unique aspect of themselves, as they believe the assault to be idiosyncratic (Dutton 1988). Disclosure can serve to alter that attribution by increasing the probability of reciprocal disclosure. Disclosure can also be a first step toward generating informal sanctions from friends and family toward the assaultive male and an empowering support network for the victim. Because arrest makes disclosure more likely, that informal side effect of arrest could serve to reduce recidivism.

These findings modify the interpretation of Sherman and Berk (1984) that arrest reduces recidivism through deterrence. Arrest (when coupled with conviction in court and the beginning of court-mandated treatment) produces a variety of informal "ripple effects" (see Williams and Hawkins 1986, 1989a) that may account for the apparent association of arrest with reduced recidivism. Further research is required to disentangle a "pure" deterrent effect of the legal sanctions themselves (i.e., the threat of the intrinsic consequences of legal sanctions) from possible covarying informal sanctions (i.e., life disruptions resulting from arrest, such as loss of partner or social disapproval).

Although our analysis is only suggestive and exploratory, it points to directions for such research and supports the potential for pro-arrest policies, combined with prosecution and court-mandated therapy, for the reduction of repeat wife assault.

NOTES

The research for this chapter was supported by the following sources: a grant from the Social Sciences and Humanities Research Council of Canada, Don Dutton, Principal Investigator; a grant from the National Science Foundation (SES-852–0232), Kirk R. Williams, Principal Investigator (Murray A. Straus, Co-investigator); and the Population Research Laboratory and the Department of Sociology, University of Alberta, Les W. Kennedy, Principal Investigator.

1. The N for the 1987 sample of males is weighted, as are all of the results reported based on the analysis of the U.S. survey data, because the 1985 sampling design (a national probability sample) was altered, as described, resulting in an overrepresentation of assaulters. A weighting procedure was implemented by Louis Harris and Associates, the data collection agency, so that the sample composition in 1986 and 1987 would correspond to that of 1985. In short, non-assaulters were upweighted and assaulters were downweighted, with the total Ns for each year remaining the same (N = 1,409 in 1986 and N = 1,195 in 1987). This weighting procedure reduces the likelihood of bias due to follow-ups. See Straus and Gelles (1989) and Williams and Hawkins (1989a, 1989b) for more discussion of the technical details of the U.S. survey.

2. As with the U.S. survey, all reported results are based on weighted data, as the final sample consists of an overrepresentation of Edmonton residents and an underrepresentation of Calgary and other provincial residents. Thus, appropriate weights were calculated and used to bring the sample composition in line with the proportional representation of each area to the total Alberta population. See Kennedy and Dutton (1987, 1989) for a discussion of the Alberta survey.

3. Of course, the Time 2 data present an interpretational problem because they are self-selected. Only 32 of the original sample could be contacted at Time 2. Of the remaining 28 men, 16 had moved with no forwarding address. Obviously, self-selection may be based on the non-occurrence of recidivism so that results cannot be generalized to a recidivist population. This type of attrition problem frequently plagues longitudinal studies in family violence. For men in the returning group, self-reports of recidivist violence on the CTS correlated -.56 with overall legal sanctions (i.e., a summary index) at Time 2 and -.57 with overall social sanctions. For this group using the overall summary indexes, legal sanctions did not decrease significantly after the completion of treatment and probation, and the perceived social sanctions increased significantly ($t = 12.6$, $df = 343$, $p < .0001$).

REFERENCES

Bandura, A. 1979. The Social Learning Perspective: Mechanisms of Aggression. In H. Toch, ed., *Psychology of Crime and Criminal Justice*. New York: Rinehart and Winston.

Berk, R. A., and P. J. Newton. 1985. Does Arrest Really Deter Wife Battery? An Effort to Replicate the Findings of the Minneapolis Spouse Abuse Experiment. *American Sociological Review* 50:253–62.

Binder, A., and J. W. Meeker. 1988. Experiments as Reforms. *Journal of Criminal Justice* 16:347–58.

Bowker, L. H. 1983. *Beating Wife Beating*. Lexington, Mass.: Lexington Books.

Carmody, D. C., and K. Williams. 1987. Wife Assaulters' Perceptions of Sanctions. *Violence and Victims* 1:101–24.

Coleman, D. H., and M. A. Straus. 1986. Marital Power, Conflict and Violence in a Nationally Representative Sample of American Couples. *Violence and Victims* 1:141–57.

Crowne, D. P., and D. Marlowe. 1960. A New Scale of Social Desirability Independent of Psychopathology. *Journal of Consulting Psychology* 24:349–54.

Dutton, D. G. 1986a. The Outcome of Court-mandated Treatment for Wife Assault: A Quasi-Experimental Evaluation. *Violence and Victims* 1(3):163–75.

———. 1986b. Wife Assaulters' Explanations for Assault: The Neutralization of Self-punishment. *Canadian Journal of Behavioural Science* 18(4):381–90.

———. 1987. The Criminal Justice Response to Wife Assault. *Law and Human Behavior* 11(3):189–206.

———. 1988. *The Domestic Assault of Women: Psychological and Criminal Justice Perspectives*. Boston: Allyn and Bacon.

Dutton, D. G., B. Fehr, and H. McEwen. 1982. Severe Wife Battering as Deindividuated Violence. *Victimology* 7:13–23.

Dutton, D. G., and C. E. Strachan. 1987. *The Prediction of Recidivism in a Population of Wife Assaulters*. Third National (U.S.) Conference on Family Violence, Durham, N.H.

Fagan, J. 1988. Desistance from Family Violence: Deterrence and Dissuasion. In M. Tonry and L. Ohlin, eds., *Crime and Justice: An Annual Review of Research* (Special volume on family violence). Chicago: University of Chicago Press.

Fagan, J., E. Friedman, S. Wexler, and V. S. Lewis. 1984. *National Family Violence Evaluation: Final Report. Vol. 1: Analytic Findings*. San Francisco: URSA Institute.

Feld, S. L., and M. A. Straus. 1989. Escalation and Desistance of Wife Assault in Marriage. *Criminology* 27:141–61.

Gibbs, J. 1986. Deterrence Theory and Research. In G. B. Melton, ed., *The Law as a Behavioral Instrument*. Nebraska Symposium on Motivation, University of Nebraska Press.

Jaffe, P., and C. A. Burris. 1982. *An Integrated Response to Wife Assault: A Community Model*. Ottawa: Research Report of the Solicitor General of Canada.

Jaffe, P., D. A. Wolfe, A. Telford, and G. Austin. 1986. The Impact of Police Charges in Incidents of Wife Abuse. *Journal of Family Violence* 1(1):37–49.

Kennedy, L. W., and D. G. Dutton. 1987. *The Incidence of Wife Assault in Alberta*. Population Research Laboratory, University of Alberta.

———. 1989. The Incidence of Wife Assault in Alberta. *Canadian Journal of Behavioural Science* 21:40–54.

Lempert, R. O. 1989. Humility Is a Virtue: On the Publicization of Policy-Relevant Research. *Law and Society Review* 23:145–61.

Lundman, R. J. 1986. One-wave Perceptual Deterrence Research: Some Grounds for the Renewed Examination of Cross-sectional Methods. *Journal of Research in Crime and Delinquency* 23: 370–88.

Maiuro, R. D., T. S. Cahn, and P. P. Vitaliano. 1987. Treatment for Domestically Violent Men: Outcome and Follow-up Data. Paper presented at the meeting of the 95th American Psychological Association, New York.

Novaco, R. 1976. The Functions and Regulation of the Arousal of Anger. *American Journal of Psychiatry* 133(10):1124–1128.

Paternoster, R. 1987. The Deterrent Effect of the Perceived Certainty and Severity of Punishment: A Review of the Evidence and Issues. *Justice Quarterly* 4:173–217.

Schulman, M. 1979. *A Survey of Spousal Violence against Women in Kentucky.* Washington, D.C.: U.S. Department of Justice, Law Enforcement Assistance Administration.

Schwartz, M. 1987. Repeated Spousal Assaults in the National Crime Survey. Paper presented at the American Society of Criminology, Montreal.

Sherman, L. W., and R. A. Berk. 1984. The Specific Deterrent Effects of Arrest for Domestic Assault. *American Sociological Review* 49:261–72.

Sherman, L. W., and E. G. Cohn. 1989. The Impact of Research on Legal Policy: The Minneapolis Domestic Violence Experiment. *Law and Society Review* 23:117–44.

Solicitor General of Canada. 1985. *Canadian Urban Victimization Survey: Female Victims of Crime*, Bulletin #4. Ottawa, Canada.

Straus, M. A. 1977. Wife Beating: How Common and Why? *Victimology* 2 (3–4): 443–59.

———. 1979. Measuring Family Conflict and Violence: The Conflict Tactics Scale. *Journal of Marriage and the Family* 41:75–88.

Straus, M. A., and R. J. Gelles. 1989. Physical Violence in American Families: Risk Factors and Adaptations to Violence in 8,145 Families. New Brunswick, N.J.: Transaction Press.

Straus, M. A., R. J. Gelles and S. Steinmetz. 1980. *Behind Closed Doors: Violence in the American Family.* Garden City, N.Y.: Doubleday/Anchor Press.

Williams, K., and D. C. Carmody. 1986. Wife Assault: Perceptions of Sanctions and Deterrence. Unpublished manuscript, University of New Hampshire.

Williams, K., and R. Hawkins. 1986. Perceptual Research on General Deterrence: A Critical Review. *Law and Society Review* 20:545–72.

———. 1989a. The Meaning of Arrest for Wife Assault. *Criminology* 27:163–81.

———. 1989b. Controlling Male Aggression in Intimate Relationships. *Law and Society Review* 23(45):591–612.

Williams, K., and M. A. Straus. 1986. *Panel Survey of Deterrence Processes.* Funded by National Science Foundation, Washington, D.C.

Wilt, M., and J. Bannon. 1977. *Domestic Violence and the Police: Studies in Detroit and Kansas City.* Washington, D.C.: The Police Foundation.

Zimbardo, P. 1969. The Human Choice: Individuation, Reason and Order vs. Deindividuation, Impulse and Chaos. *Nebraska Symposium on Motivation.* Lincoln: University of Nebraska Press.

7

ARREST AS A METHOD TO CONTROL SPOUSE ABUSE

Arnold Binder and James Meeker

Few, if any, single studies have had as much impact on police services as the Minneapolis Domestic Violence Experiment, whose findings were reported by Lawrence Sherman and Richard Berk in a series of articles beginning in 1983. This study, sponsored by the Police Foundation, was published in various forms and for different audiences, including academics, police agencies, and the general public. As described in detail in this chapter, the impact of the Sherman and Berk research was no accident. Efforts to publicize the article were almost unprecedented for a scholarly work in the criminal justice field.

Arnold Binder and James Meeker, after examining the impact of publicity, here demonstrate methodological problems presented by the Sherman and Berk study. These, in turn, raise serious issues of the external and internal validity of the study. Further, Binder and Meeker consider the serious issues of constitutionality and the adverse affects of a pro-arrest policy on the offender, the victim, and the public and on the police as an institution. Perhaps the most significant contribution of this chapter is to illustrate the potential problems of basing public policy on any single study, whether or not it is a pilot study. This chapter has significance not only for the study of the response to domestic violence but also for the formulation of public policy.

The study, known as the Minneapolis experiment or study, that provides the focus of this chapter was devised, funded, and completed in the context of the spirit of raised consciousness discussed in the preceding chapter. To highlight the resonance between the results and the spirit of the times, moreover, publication of the results was accompanied by an informational barrage similar to a process referred to as propaganda in other contexts. The barrage, which included vigorous advocacy of harsher treatment for minor offenders, proceeded despite major weaknesses in the study's methodology and substantial dangers in generalizing its results. That process of information dissemination will be discussed in this chapter after the presentation of the study's features; then it will be argued that the treatment recommended on the basis of the study, though very much in accordance with the popular mood of low tolerance and antipathy, was not supported by scientific evidence as claimed, may produce lasting harmful effects on people other than the abuser, probably violates certain constitutional rights of the abuser, and may be counterproductive, harming the victim more than helping her.

The recommended treatment for misdemeanor-level wife abusers is arrest, a procedure not widely used for minor abusers prior to the early 1980s. Despite that recommendation and its open advocacy, as this book goes to press, we simply do not know whether arrest in response to cases of minor (misdemeanor) wife abuse is more or less effective in reducing recidivism than other available, and less harsh, methods. But we do know that grave doubts about its efficacy have been raised by the research of Dunford, Huizinga, and Elliott (1989, 1990), which was a replication of the Minneapolis study. We certainly do not know the array of consequences, some possibly quite negative, of spousal arrest on, first, relationships and general contentment in the home and, second, the efficient operation of the criminal justice system. Yet, the approach of arrest in calls involving minor spousal abuse has been adopted as expected operating procedure in police departments throughout the country.

THE MINNEAPOLIS STUDY

Features of the Study

The general climate of antipathy toward and desire for vengeance against wife abusers was at a high point in the early 1980s when an article by Sherman and Berk (1984a) appeared in the *American Sociological Review* (*ASR*). The research was theoretical, not evaluational, in providing an empirical test of the deductions from two sociological theories in the context of wife abuse: deterrence and labeling. Deterrence won, leading to the conclusion (1984a:261), "The findings falsify a deviance amplification model of labeling theory . . . and fail to falsify the specific deterrence prediction. . . . "

The method involved comparison, in cases of misdemeanor spousal abuse, of arrest with two alternate possible police responses, mediation and separation, using officers of the Minneapolis Police Department. From an evaluational point of view, those alternatives were far less than optimum, as they were not based on findings from research on the use of paraprofessionals in crisis intervention. In addition, there was no evaluation of the possible impacts of those responses on individuals, families, or the criminal justice system, nor was there any cost-benefit analysis. But the study was adequate for comparing specific deterrence and deviance amplification as concepts, which was the stated motivation for the research and the reason the results were published in *ASR* rather than, say, *Evaluation Review*.

It seems worth mentioning that Sherman (as in Sherman and Cohn 1989:119) has referred to the Minneapolis study in various subsequent discussions as "policy research" despite the mode of presentation in the *ASR* article. It is not clear whether there has been a change of mind or whether the reference attempts to correct an erroneous impression. In either case, it should be pointed out that, if the only consideration in determining length of incarceration were recidivism in policy-oriented research, then, on a probability basis, keeping offenders in prison indefinitely would top all alternatives.

Before demonstrating the extent to which the research results and their implications for policy change were inappropriately advocated to the professional and lay public by at least one of the investigators, we will present an overview of how generally weak the study was from several perspectives. Indeed, in an article published in 1988, we (Binder and Meeker) referred to the research effort as a "pilot study." One may well be surprised to find a social scientist making a clarion sales pitch that may affect many lives profoundly when his or her research produces definitive results that may properly be generalized to the population in question, but it becomes downright alarming when important alternative plausible hypotheses have not been handled adequately, when there is almost no knowledge about side effects, and when there is very limited generalizability. Let us consider various features of the study critically:

The areas selected for the research at the outset were "located in the two Minneapolis precincts with the highest density of domestic violence crime reports and arrests" (Sherman and Berk 1984a:263). Initially, the participation rate was so low from the officers in those areas that further recruiting was necessary, but cooperation from the new officers was equally poor. By the end of the study, approximately 28 percent of the cases were handled by only three of the original officers.

The law in Minnesota allowing probable-cause arrest for misdemeanor domestic assault that occurred in the last four hours, even though the officer did not observe that assault, is not the law in a large number of states, including states as substantial as California. It would seem of interest to point out that Minnesota Laws of 1978 (as amended in 1979 and 1981) provide "Notwithstanding the provisions of Section 629.34 or any other law or rule to the contrary, a peace officer may arrest without a warrant a person anywhere, including at his place of residence if the peace officer has probable cause to believe the person within the preceding four hours has assaulted his spouse . . . although the assault did not take place in the presence of the peace officer." The laws directed at non-spousal arrest for assault are, in contrast, more restrictive (see Section 629.34, which specifies conditions under which arrest may be made without a warrant in assault generally).

The unemployment rate for both victims and suspects was about 60 percent.

If the preceding points are not enough to lead you to question loose recommendations of nationwide adoption of the Minneapolis procedures—that is, from Bellingham, Washington, to Key West, Florida—consider further that almost one-fifth of the victims were Native Americans, 59 percent of the male suspects had been arrested previously, and only about one-third of the relationships were of wife and husband. To illustrate the dangers of generalizing from that sample, the analysis of wife abuse in metropolitan and suburban New York by Roy (1982) led to such conclusions as the following: In most cases the cohabitants were both employed, only 10 percent of the abusive men had criminal records and almost half of those were for wife abuse, and two-thirds of the partnerships involved married couples.

As stated previously, the alternatives compared to arrest, that is, separation and mediation by patrol officers lacking any special training in this area, have been shown to be much less than state-of-the-art treatment responses. In this context, it should be emphasized that it would have taken little effort to strengthen the alternatives by giving the officers minimum training in crisis intervention. [It is of incidental interest to note that Roberts (1982) has pointed out that there was a hotline for abusers in Minneapolis during the period of Sherman and Berk's research; it was operated in cooperation with the Men's Center's Men in Violent Relationships Project. Services were available six days each week from 6:00 P.M. to 2:00 A.M. and could have been used for systematic policy research to examine certain interesting alternatives to the pure police model. That project was not mentioned in any of the Sherman and Berk reports.] Of course, the nature of the alternatives would not be important if one were conducting a study only to test the theoretical constructs of deterrence and labeling theory. However, we argue that the failure becomes very important if one is conducting an evaluative study of policy alternatives from which arguments for policy change will be made.

There is reason to question the validity of the authors' statistical analyses and the conclusions that they generated. As the arguments in support of that statement are much too complex for presentation in this chapter, we refer you to the article by Binder and Meeker (1988) that contains a full statistical critique.

While arrest has been stressed as the determining factor in producing outcomes, that variable was confounded as a result of the policy of the Minneapolis Police Department to keep suspects arrested for domestic assault in jail at least overnight. In fact, according to Sherman and Berk (1984a:268), many were kept in jail for longer than that. In particular, "of those arrested, 43 percent were released within one day, 86 percent were released within one week, and only 14 percent were released after one week or had not yet been released. . . . " Again this issue has increasing importance as one shifts from using the study to compare theoretical propositions to arguing for policy change. The subsequent use of the study's results to argue for a policy of presumed arrest in misdemeanor domestic assault situations largely ignores the possible incarceration effect and completely fails to address what effect mandatory incarceration for such offenses would have on jail systems that are already overcrowded in most areas of the country. Yet, without incarceration following arrest, it is not clear whether any of the claimed results of the study would be duplicated.

There are other sources of alternative plausible hypotheses, and thus weakened internal validity, embedded in the operationalization of the design. For example, in the report of the Police Foundation (Sherman and Berk 1984b:6), there is the following acknowledgement: "There was one factor, however, that seemed to govern the effectiveness of arrest: whether the police showed interest in the victim's side of the story." There was no effect due to arrest when the "showed interest" group was removed from the analysis. The investigators interpreted that to mean "that by listening to the victim, the police 'empower' her with their strength, letting the suspect know that she can influence their behavior"— that is, she can influence the arrest process. But there is an alternative plausible hypothesis that lies in the realm of victim precipitation. Perhaps the special attention given to the woman leads to a change in *her* behavior, behavior that provokes or exacerbates violence. That may even be interpreted as an enhancement of the effect on *her* produced by the police intervention of arrest.

In summary, the investigators of the Minneapolis study focussed on the effects of arrest on recidivism in a comparison that involved weak alternatives. That focus, too, was accomplished without any consideration of the side effects of arrest on children in the household, on employment discrimination, on long-range marital contentment, on the costs to law enforcement, on system capacity, or on any of the numerous other factors that would enter consideration in responsible policy research (see Wright 1985 for a discussion of those factors). In addition, there were so many unique factors in the particular Minneapolis setting and in the limited cooperation from officers that it would be unsound scientifically to generalize whatever results the Minneapolis study produced to most locations where there are police departments in the United States. Finally, it must be emphasized that some scholars have raised serious questions about the design, the procedures as executed, the statistical analyses, and the broad conclusions of the study.

Selling the Study

It seems reasonable to assume that there should be a relationship between the degree of certainty one has in the conclusions drawn from a research effort and the level of activity put into active dissemination of those conclusions. If there are serious questions about internal validity, about side effects, and about generalizability, a scientist would be expected to refrain from active advocacy of changes in policy based on the conclusions and even to do whatever he or she can to control inappropriate dissemination by others. That, we emphasize, is not the same as arguing, as did Lempert (1989), that research studies should be replicated before their results are used to influence policy. There are many definitive studies, such as the polio trials of the early 1950s, where the results are so convincing that policy change becomes desirable or even mandatory in the absence of replication. The emphasis is on the degree of certainty that results from research findings, not on replication, although replication is of course a path toward achieving that degree of certainty.

The principal investigators did indeed show concern about the validity of their results despite their recommendations and subsequent propaganda barrage. In the *ASR* article, we find (Sherman and Berk 1984a:269), "The message should be clear: external validity will have to wait for replications." Moreover, the need for replication was stated, because of the preliminary nature of the results, with the announcement that the National Institute of Justice (NIJ) was planning to fund those replications.

Given that set regarding the weakness of design from the perspectives of policy research, external validity, and internal validity and the reasonable expectation of caution in policy recommendations and advocacy when the evidence is weak, let us consider the handling of the research from the perspective of marketable product. Lest you think that we are overstating or exaggerating the sales job or the effects of that sales job, note that the early details that follow come from an article by Sherman and a colleague (Sherman and Cohn 1989). It is readily admitted in the article that the research was "actively promoted" (1989:120) and that there was an attempt to "orchestrate the release of the experimental results for maximum press coverage" (1989:120). In fact, before the *ASR* article even appeared, there was publication of "preliminary findings" by the Police Foundation (Sherman and Berk, 1983), persuasion of "the Minneapolis area public television station to film a documentary on the research" (Sherman and Cohn 1989:120), and an arrangement for the appearance of "an exclusive story in the *New York Times* Tuesday 'Science' section" (1989:120). Shortly after publication of the article, a column was submitted to the *Wall Street Journal* by Sherman and Bouza (1984) and published there, and the Police Foundation issued Volume 1 of *Police Foundation Reports*, containing a popularized summary of the Minneapolis study (Sherman and Berk 1984b). Mailed to police departments throughout the country, it contained elongated statements of endorsement from no less than James Stewart, Director, NIJ; Patrick Murphy, President, Police Foundation; and Anthony Bouza, Chief of Police, Minneapolis. Here's an illustration of the intensity of those endorsements (1984b:5):

The domestic violence experiment, by demonstrating the efficacy of an arrest policy, influenced the Minneapolis legislature to make necessary changes; reshaped the policies of the Minneapolis Police Department to force more arrests; and reinforced the feminist thrust calling for stricter adherence to an arrest policy in domestic violence cases.

... an important step has been taken and ... this step will influence police handling of domestic violence cases nationally.

Next, there was a press release issued by NIJ, and then (Sherman and Cohn 1989:121):

A ... key decision was [made] to release the final results on the Sunday of Memorial Day weekend. This timing increased the chances that the story would face less competition on a "slow news day" ... , even more so than on Sundays without a three-day weekend. The wire services and over 300 newspapers carried the story. The PBS "McNeil-Lehrer News Hour," which had been notified well in advance, also ran a ten-minute segment on the study, followed by CBS "Evening News" three months later.

Our final illustration from the process by which the arrest of wife abusers was "actively promoted" as the preferred alternative for the police is a bit more indirect. It occurs via a report issued in 1984, the year of the *ASR* article, by a task force of the Attorney General. Catherine Milton, formerly an assistant director of the Police Foundation, was a task force member, and each of the following people appeared as a witness at one of its hearings: Sherman and Bouza in December 1983 and Stewart in February 1984. The report contains the pronouncement that, as therapeutic approaches to spousal abuse were soft-headed (1984:23) and ineffective, it must be treated as a crime with full criminal consequences. The following are examples of statements in the report derived from the findings in Minneapolis:

A strong commitment by law enforcement officials, prosecutors, and courts in responding to family violence as a crime can aid in deterring, preventing, and reducing violence against family members. (1984:11)

Because mediation is most often an inappropriate law enforcement response and because arrest and overnight incarceration . . . have been shown to be an effective deterrent against household assault, arrest must be the presumed response in cases of family violence. (1984:24)

Law enforcement intervention is a critical component of the justice system's effort to break the cycle of violence within the family. Research now *clearly* shows that when a criminal assault has been committed, arresting the offender actually contributes to reducing the recurrence of violence. [italics added] (1984:104).

A related, though more restrained, set of comments and recommendations may be seen in Goolkasian (1986). The active promotion did indeed produce results, to a surprising degree. Clearly that effect did not result only from the considerable skill of the propagandists, as described early in this presentation. Several forces were at work during the early 1980s that made society most receptive to the punitive approach in cases of wife abuse. (The pitch, as emphasized, was *ad populum* in nature.)

As early as 1985, Wright (1985:250) noted:

Although this is only one study, involving a limited number of cases, its effect has been profound. Not only is its conclusion cited and accepted by the United States Attorney General's Task Force on Family Violence, but it is also appearing in local training guides for police departments. The study, coupled with the publicity it has received by the media and other concerned groups, has probably been the most instrumental in influencing a policy of mandatory arrest.

The effects of the publicity efforts were assessed by Sherman and his associates in surveys of police departments in cities of over 100,000 people at three stages: before the *ASR* article appeared but after the preliminary results were released (Sherman with Hamilton 1984), in June 1985 (Sherman and Cohn 1986), and in June 1986 (Cohn and Sherman 1987). Perhaps the central finding of those surveys was stated by Sherman and Cohn (1989:126) as follows, "forty-three police departments reported a change to an arrest policy when respondents accurately knew the experimental results whereas twelve reported such a change when respondents did not accurately know the results."

Further evidence of the effects of the study on public policy and on those who create public policy is shown in the work of Binder and Meeker (1988) and Meeker and Binder (1990). Finally, Buzawa and Buzawa (1990) have reviewed and evaluated the movement toward exacting legislation and ordinances that mandate arrest in cases of spousal abuse, a movement that received considerable stimulation from the Minneapolis results.

THE ISSUE OF CONSTITUTIONALITY

Let us consider the purpose of arrest and the protections against its misuse in American law. The ultimate source of those protections is of course the Bill of Rights, even though the term "arrest" occurs nowhere in the Constitution. Rather, relevant arguments regarding the propriety of arrest procedures are derived from the following statements: "The right of the people to be secure in their persons, houses, papers, and effects against unreasonable searches and seizures shall not be violated" (in the Fourth Amendment); "No person shall . . . be deprived of life, liberty, or property without due process of law" (in the Fifth Amendment); " . . . nor shall any state deprive any person of life, liberty, or property, without due process" (in the Fourteenth Amendment).

The language of the Fourth Amendment also carries requirements of warrants and probable cause prior to seizures of the person as well as searches in reaction to such earlier corruptions as writs of assistance in colonial America and general warrants in England. The issue of warrants has some relevance for the present arguments, but exposition of that relevance would be too complicated for the purposes of this chapter.

The implications for arrest of those phrases from the Bill of Rights are contained in the following quotes presented by LaFave (1965:437): "To be lawful, not only must an arrest be made on a proper occasion but . . . it must be made for the purpose of apprehending the person arrested and taking him before a court or public official"; "It requires a vivid imagination to conceive of an officer making an arrest for the purpose of releasing his prisoner." Moreover, the Supreme Court expressed its concern that arrests for misdemeanors be used without judicial protections only rarely, if at all, in the following manner (*Draper v. United States*, 358 U.S. at 315, 316): "The rule which permits arrest for felonies, as distinguished from misdemeanors, if there are reasonable grounds for believing a crime has been or is being committed . . . grew out of the need to protect the public safety by making prompt arrests. . . . Yet, apart from those cases where the crime is committed in the presence of the officer, arrests without warrants, like searches without warrants, are the exception, not the rule in our society."

A fundamental concept in our justice system is that one is not *punished* without due process of law. A distinguishing function of criminal law, as opposed to civil law, is the punishment of those found guilty, in appropriate court procedures, of violating the law. In fact, the legal presumption is that a defendant is innocent until proven guilty. The major justifications for incarceration before trial are based on the dangerousness of the defendant and prevention of fleeing the jurisdiction.

It is well known that the legal system does not always operate within strictly constitutional bounds. LaFave (1965), for example, has pointed out a common abuse of the arrest process to harrass suspected violators of prostitution, gambling, and liquor laws when no prosecution is intended. Arrests are made strictly for the sake of punishment to deter offenders. The general attitude of La Fave and others is to condemn such practices and certainly not to use them as justifications for advocacy of a similar policy of abuse in other areas. Indeed, the Supreme Court has recognized the threat to the legitimacy of the entire legal system when enforcers abuse the system in order to enforce the law (see *Mapp v. Ohio*, 367 U.S. 643, 1961, where the Court extended to the states the rule excluding evidence that was obtained illegally.)

Sherman and his associates and the task force influenced by them and their work stated their policy recommendation and its effects as follows: "we favor a *presumption* of arrest; an arrest should be made unless there are good, clear reasons why an arrest would be counterproductive" (Sherman and Berk 1984a:270), "the chief executive of every law enforcement agency should establish arrest as the preferred response in cases of family violence" (Attorney General's Task Force on Family Violence, 1984:17), and "Stimulated by efforts to publicize the results of the Minneapolis Domestic Violence Experiment, police departments were persuaded [by us] to adopt an arrest policy for misdemeanor domestic violence" (Sherman and Cohn 1989:117).

Consider, now, carefully, the reasons for those recommendations and the purpose of arrest in cases of misdemeanor spousal abuse. The recommendations stem from a presumed finding in a Minneapolis study that for misdemeanor assaults there was a difference in subsequent abuse between arrested abusers (most of whom were incarcerated) and those treated by separation or mediation. Consequently, the principal purpose in arresting a given suspect is to reduce the probability of recidivism among all people treated in that fashion. The basis is specific deterrence and the means is punishment by the police. There is no consideration of due process, and while there may be hope for prosecution, there is no hint of that as a goal of the arrest process. In fact, the justification for the policy is the deterrence that is presumably created by the punishment, through arrest and incarceration, of suspects by the police, not the courts. Nor is there justification for incarceration based on accepted principles. As policy is directed at misdemeanor assaults, it would be difficult to argue a presumption of incarceration on the issue of dangerousness or a concern about fleeing the jurisdiction.

Sherman and Berk (1984a:270) admit that their policy amounts to punishment by the police without constitutional protections in the following statement, "This [the results of their study] suggests that arrest and initial incarceration alone may produce a deterrent effect, regardless of how the courts treat such cases, and that arrest makes an independent contribution to the deterrence potential of the criminal justice system.'' Similarly, Dunford, Huizinga, and Elliott (1989:1) acknowledge, ''Sherman and Berk specified 'arrest and initial incarceration alone' as deterring continued domestic assault and recommended that the police adopt arrest as the favored response to domestic assault *on the basis* of its deterrent power.''

We will end this section on the relationship between arrest for purposes of deterrence and the requirements of due process with a quote that carries considerable meaning for the trend of our arguments; it is from the *Terry v. Ohio* (392 U.S. at 26, 1967) decision of the U.S. Supreme Court, ''An arrest is the initial stage of criminal prosecution.''

OTHER IMPORTANT CONSIDERATIONS

The essential portions of our final position that the specific recommendations of Sherman and Berk may actually be counterproductive in efforts at control are handled thoroughly in a paper by Hirschel and Hutchinson (1989). The critical arguments of that paper are summarized below.

First, about 75 percent of the calls for service in cases of wife violence do not involve conflicts that can be legally defined as criminal offenses, because of the absence of probable cause. Yet, many of those may be just the cases where early intervention is most critical although arrest is not a possible response.

Second, many cities with preferred arrest policies require the abuser to be present for police to effect an arrest. ''Since male abusers have left the scene approximately half the time before police arrive, an on the scene arrest is not an option . . . '' (Hirschel and Hutchinson 1989:39). (See the findings of Dunford et al. 1989, 1990 for interesting relevant data.)

Third, a policy of ''preferred arrest'' is, as Hirschel and Hutchinson have shown, practically meaningless. Given that direction, actual operations vary greatly state to state, city to city, community to community, and even officer to officer. Moreover, in one area, arrest may lead to no more than an hour in jail, in another it may mean a weekend, and there is no evidence whatsoever linking levels of incarceration with outcomes. In their words (1989:10), ''Thus, to note that a particular police department or some number of departments have a preferred arrest policy may tell us little more than some kind of policy exists.''

Fourth, ''arrest as a preferred response for spouse abusers tends to overlook the great variation which is known to exist in the abusive population. . . . It is quite naive to think [for example] that the simple fact of arrest will have much impact on career criminals'' (1989:40).

And fifth, ''it is myopic to think that this rather straightforward action by the police will have a long term impact on the overall problem'' (1989:40). One must think in terms of community mobilization, not punishment and deterrence, that incorporates the findings of such investigators as Ferraro (1989), Buzawa

(1982, 1988), and even Berk and Newton (1985). Emphasis on arrest alone may delay that mobilization and thus delay processes that lead to effective control.

CONCLUSION

In concluding, it is worth pointing out that an excellent set of guidelines for police officers was written by Nancy Loving (1982) of the Police Executive Research Forum (PERF). Her orientation to the issue is as follows (1982:278): "Formal procedures should represent a balanced combination of acceptable standards of conduct with the rules of law and due process. They should be general enough to allow the officers freedom to exercise their unique talents and skills, but specific enough for them to know what action they should not take."

She does recommend arrest for misdemeanor assaults, but only when "there is evidence of physical harm on the victim" (as in the case of the specification of a felony in California law). Her orientation is multidisciplinary in the recognition that typically ancillary services are available to the police; and it is based on a broad perspective of policy issues, including the welfare of children and the special needs where there has been use of drugs or alcohol or where there is evidence of mental disturbance. Unfortunately, most police departments and policy makers are probably not aware of Loving's work, perhaps primarily because it is not in tune with the punitive tenor of the times and because she has not been driven toward aggressive dissemination.

REFERENCES

Attorney General's Task Force on Family Violence. 1984. *Final Report*. Washington, D.C.: U.S. Department of Justice.

Berk, Richard A., and Phyllis J. Newton. 1985. Does Arrest Really Deter Wife Battery? An Effort to Replicate the Findings of the Minneapolis Spouse Abuse Experiment. *American Sociological Review* 50:253–62.

Binder, Arnold, and James W. Meeker. 1988. Experiments as Reforms. *Journal of Criminal Justice* 16:347–58.

Buzawa, Eve S. 1982. Police Officer Response to Domestic Violence Legislation in Michigan. *Journal of Police Science and Administration* 10:415–24.

———. 1988. Explaining Variations in Police Response to Domestic Violence. In Gerald T. Hotaling, David Finkelhor, H. R. Kirkpatrick, and Murray A. Straus, eds., *Coping with Family Violence*. Beverly Hills, Calif.: Sage.

Buzawa, Eve S., and Carl G. Buzawa. 1990. *Domestic Violence: The Criminal Justice Response*. Newbury Park, Calif.: Sage.

Cohn, Ellen G., and Lawrence Sherman. 1987. *Police Policy on Domestic Violence, 1986*. Crime Control Reports, No. 5. Washington, D.C.: Crime Control Institute.

Dunford, Franklyn W., David Huizinga, and Delbert S. Elliott. 1989. *The Omaha Domestic Violence Police Experiment*. Final Report. Washington, D.C.: National Institute of Justice.

———. 1990. The Role of Arrest in Domestic Assault: The Omaha Police Experiment. *Criminology* 28:183–206.

Ferraro, Kathleen J. 1989. Policing Woman Battering. *Social Problems* 36:61–74.

Goolkasian, Gail A. 1986. *Confronting Domestic Violence: A Guide for Criminal Justice Agencies*. Washington, D.C.: National Institute of Justice.

Hirschel, J. David, and Ira W. Hutchinson III. 1989. The Theory and Practice of Spouse Abuse Arrest Policies. Paper presented at the annual meeting of the American Society of Criminology, Reno, Nev., November.

LaFave, Wayne R. 1965. *Arrest: The Decision to Take a Suspect into Custody*. New York: Little, Brown.

Lempert, Richard. 1989. Humility Is a Virtue: On the Publicization of Policy-Relevant Research. *Law and Society Review* 23:145–61.

Loving, Nancy. 1982. Developing Operational Procedures for Police Use. In Maria Roy, ed., *The Abusive Partner: An Analysis of Domestic Battering*. New York: Van Nostrand Reinhold.

Meeker, James W., and Arnold Binder. 1990. Experiments as Reforms: The Impact of the "Minneapolis Experiment" on Police Policy. *Journal of Police Science and Administration* 17:147–53.

Roberts, Albert R. 1982. A National Survey of Services for Batterers. In Maria Roy, ed., *The Abusive Partner: An Analysis of Domestic Battering*. New York: Van Nostrand Reinhold.

Roy, Maria. 1982. Four Thousand Partners in Violence: A Trend Analysis. In Maria Roy, ed., *The Abusive Partner: An Analysis of Domestic Battering*. New York: Van Nostrand Reinhold.

Sherman, Lawrence W., and Richard A. Berk. 1983. *Police Response to Domestic Violence: Preliminary Findings*. Washington, D.C.: Police Foundation.

———. 1984a. The Specific Deterrent Effects of Arrest for Domestic Assault. *American Sociological Review* 49:261–72.

———. 1984b. *The Minneapolis Domestic Violence Experiment: Police Foundation Reports*, 1. Washington, D.C.: Police Foundation.

Sherman, Lawrence W., and Anthony V. Bouza. 1984. The Need to Police Domestic Violence. *Wall Street Journal*, May 22, p. 28.

Sherman, Lawrence W., and Ellen G. Cohn. 1986. *Police Policy on Domestic Violence, 1985: A National Survey*. Crime Control Reports No. 1. Washington, D.C.: Crime Control Institute.

———. 1989. The Impact of Research on Legal Policy: The Minneapolis Domestic Violence Experiment. *Law and Society Review* 23:117–44.

Sherman, Lawrence W., with Edwin E. Hamilton. 1984. The Impact of the Minneapolis Domestic Violence Experiment: Wave 1 Findings. Washington, D.C.: Police Foundation (unpublished manuscript).

Wright, Carol. 1985. Immediate Arrest in Domestic Violence Situations: Mandate or Alternative. *Capital University Law Review* 14:243–68.

LEGAL CASES

Draper v. United States, 358 U.S. 307 (1959)

Mapp v. Ohio, 367 U.S. 643 (1961)

Terry v. Ohio, 392 U.S. 1 (1967)

III
PROSECUTORIAL AND JUDICIAL RESPONSE

DOMESTIC VIOLENCE: ITS LEGAL DEFINITIONS

James B. Halsted

Professor James Halsted is an attorney who has written extensively about the dynamics of the interactions between legal theories and the reality of courtroom behavior. In this chapter, he uses his background as an attorney to illustrate the practical reality of how domestic violence cases have typically been handled by prosecutors and the courts. Traditionally, these have been shoehorned into various traditional offense categories such as battery, assault, aggravated assault, rape, or murder. Such typologies have failed to recognize the unique challenges presented by domestic violence cases. They begin with the characterization of the crime. Because the offenses tend to be classified as misdemeanor assaults, a very low priority offense, they are trivialized by the judicial institutions. With the exception of marital rape, an assault that must be termed a felony, or misdemeanor assault witnessed by an officer, rigid evidentiary barriers inhibit effective prosecution. Consequently, without a specific effort to surmount such obstacles, the tendency to drop such cases is frequently reinforced.

Halsted suggests that reclassification of relevant offenses could improve the criminal justice system and improve the consistency of its operations. Certainly, a plethora of new statutes have recently been created that are specific to domestic violence offenses. Despite some promise, it is unclear whether reclassification attempts would in fact change the response patterns of criminal justice agencies. Strategies might arise to tacitly recategorize crimes or to increase efforts to divert cases away from the court system. Research is therefore needed to explore whether tendencies to trivialize domestic violence cases are primarily due to inadequacies in legally defining crimes or whether resistant organizations who still do not see domestic violence as a legitimate issue will circumvent new statutes.

John Fidders, enforcement director of the Securities Exchange Commission, was accused of wife beating during a 1985 divorce proceeding. Mrs. Fidders accused him of blackening her eye, punching her, breaking her eardrum with a blow to the head, and permanently injuring her neck by trying to throw her over a balcony. She also testified he attacked her while she was pregnant (Jackson 1985). In another case, a physician in Montgomery County, Maryland, the richest county in the nation, jumped on his wife's spine and caused paralysis because she left the door open and let cool air-conditioned air escape (Barnett 1986). Neither case was processed as criminal.

The first official federal investigation of woman abuse was conducted shockingly after the fact. The U.S. Attorney General's 1984 Task Force on Family Violence discovered that woman abuse was *the* major cause of physical injury to women in the United States and that nearly a third of female homicide victims are killed by husbands or boyfriends. While the task force acknowledged the sheer magnitude of the social problem of woman abuse, its proposed solutions remain contested.

The term "woman abuse" describes more than marital abuse; it includes physical attacks by a person with whom the victim has a relationship involving cohabitation and sexual intimacy. Indeed, 50 percent of the incidents of woman abuse involve persons no longer or never legally married (Anderson 1983).

In the years between 1977 and 1990, significant changes in the legal responses to woman abuse have occurred in the United States. During this period, a grassroots battered women's movements have worked to change existing legislation and to create new laws specifically designed to provide institutional, judicial, and statutory support to abused women. Kathleen L. Ferraro (1989) points out that, historically, efforts to control battering through the law were championed by early religious leaders, feminists, and retributivist politicians. For example, in 1882 Maryland passed a law to punish wife beaters at the whipping post. A similar law was passed in Delaware and Oregon. Yet, as Ferraro points out, records indicate that very few men actually were whipped in public; and this type of punishment was much more likely to be inflicted on black men. United States history also contains numerous accounts of vigilante efforts to control wife beating. During the latter part of the nineteenth century, racist mobs such as the Ku Klux Klan and the White Caps attempted to control wife beating through a series of threats and beatings. Of the eighty targets of the White Caps in one Indiana county in the 1880s, nine were wife beaters. In fact, both the whipping-post legislation and the vigilante responses were attempts more to control lower-class, black, and unconventional groups than to eliminate violence against women. For example, the Ku Klux Klan focussed primarily on slaves and also punished prostitutes and adulteresses.

Progressive Era feminists, such as Elizabeth Cady Stanton, initially worked against male violence; they later relinquished the issue to concentrate on obtaining suffrage, according to Ferraro (1989). During the present century, protection of women from male violence was an issue that the legal system, along with the rest of the culture, chose to ignore until recently.

In the early 1970s feminists again began to organize against this type of battering. The first book published in the United States by Del Martin in 1976 documented the official nonintervention policies of police departments and the subsequent disastrous consequences for women. One of the reasons the battered women's movement began in the United States in the 1970s, with its intense purposefulness, was a keen awareness of the failure of the legal system to protect victims of intimate male abuse. Informed by social science research, which documented the failure of police and courts to provide protection to battered women, the movement surged ahead.

CRIMES OF WOMAN ABUSE

Most of the scholarship on woman abuse seems to refrain from methodically defining legally the exact crimes that may be committed during a woman-battering episode. This omission is significant because, if reformers are to respond holistically to the problem, they must understand the specific laws that are or are not being broken by episodes of woman abuse.

Indeed "woman abuse" is not a legal term. It is a sociological one. However, during a woman-abuse episode, a series of crimes may manifest, depending upon the exact behavior involved. The violent man may be charged with one or more of these traditional offenses: "battery," "assault," "aggravated assault or battery," "rape," "murder," and "voluntary manslaughter." Furthermore, he also may be charged with a series of nontraditional crimes such as: "spouse abuse," "domestic violence," "family abuse," "violation of a protection order," "violation of a temporary restraining order," and "victim/witness intimidation." Finally, certain spin-off crimes might be committed during an official investigation of a woman-abuse complaint. "Disorderly conduct" and "resisting arrest" are the most frequent ones. The time has come to render the legal definition of each of the crimes that may be committed during a woman-abuse episode in order to enlighten those studying the subject on which types of behavior constitute which specific crimes and which types of behavior are in fact abusive but noncriminal.

As Battery

The word "battered" in the term "battered woman" is derived from the crime of "battery," a specific crime in common law for hundreds of years. Battery has been codified as a crime in every state's criminal code. Often people mistakenly believe that the behavior that technically constitutes a battery is instead an assault (see next section). A battery, however, is a more serious crime than an assault. Its legal definition is "The unlawful application of force to the person of another without the consent of the victim" (Dix and Sharlot 1980:44).

Traditionally, no injury to the victim is required for a battery to be complete. No mark need be left on the victim. Also, if the application of force is indirect (for example, by poison or, in some states, by giving the victim a venereal disease), the activity still constitutes criminal battery. Usually the batterer does need not intend to injure the victim. Hence, a man who negligently causes a physical injury to a woman commits a criminal battery (Dix and Sharlot 1980).

The results of some of the research generated by questionnaires administered to abused women provide a wealth of information describing various examples of battery committed on women. Whenever men slap women in the face, hit them on the backside, punch them in the face or arm, commit acts of hairpulling, shoving, arm twisting, choking, scraping, scratching, grabbing, smothering, tying up or handcuffing, pinching the body, kicking, kneeing, burning, holding a woman's head under water, or throwing and hitting her with nonlethal objects, these violent men are in each instance committing a separate crime of battery on the woman (Roy 1977).

Ola Barnett's study tells us much about the nature of criminal battery in the violent home. She reports that shoving is the type of battery men inflict most often. The other types of battery most commonly inflicted on women, according to Barnett's study, in descending order of frequency are as follows: (1) shaken/manhandled, (2) slapped/hit, (3) hit/punched/socked with a fist, and (4) armtwist. Although no injury is required legally for these attacks to constitute a criminal battery, Barnett's research indicates that these women usually incur physical injuries whenever they are battered by their husbands. The most common injuries are bruising, bleeding, and blackened eyes, according to Barnett (1986).

A simple battery perpetrated on wives and intimates in the home or upon strangers outside of the home is a misdemeanor in every state. A misdemeanor is a less serious form of crime that carries as a maximum penalty a jail term of less than one year and usually a fine.

As "Assault"

The crimes of assault and battery traditionally are punishable under the jurisdiction of state and local governments. A man who assaults or batters his intimate usually commits no federal crimes.

Great confusion exists concerning the legal definition of "assault." Many citizens mistakenly assume that, if one person inflicts an actual physical attack upon another and does so with malice and without excuse or justification, the victim has been assaulted. This is not so. Such behavior constitutes the crime of battery and not assault.

Under the common law and in the criminal codes of most states (although some state legislatures mistakenly have defined the behavior constituting a battery as an assault), a criminal assault consists of one of the following types of behavior: (1) an attempted battery and/or (2) intentionally placing another in fear of an immediate injury (Inbau, Thompson, and Moenssens 1983:185). The first type of assault is a crime in all fifty states and in Canada. Less than 50 percent of the states, however, include the second type of assault in their criminal codes (Inbau et al. 1983).

In the violent home a man commits the crime of assault on his intimate whenever he engages in behavior like throwing things at her and coming close to hitting her, or when he pushes at her and misses, or grabs at her and misses, or slaps at her and misses, or tries to kick, bite, or hit her with his fist and fails to do so. In each example, the man is attempting to batter the woman but fails; in doing so he commits the crime of assault.

In many jurisdictions, when a man intimidates his intimate by threatening to hurt her and gestures as if he is going to hurt her so that the woman experiences "reasonable apprehension" that she is going to be injured by his acts and threats, this activity also constitutes the crime of assault on the woman. In a slim majority of the states, however, this behavior is noncriminal.

Little statistical evidence exists to indicate how many women annually are victims of criminal assault by the men living in their households. This ignorance is partially due to the fact that most women simply consider themselves fortunate when they manage to avoid blows or thrown objects and do not report such incidents as criminal assaults.

Another problem in estimating the number of criminal assaults on women in the home lies with the questions asked abused women. Usually the researchers administering questionnaires are also unaware that men who unsuccessfully try to hit women or who make threatening gestures toward them that cause fear and apprehension are committing criminal assaults in many states. Yet instances of men assaulting intimates remain criminal activity whether researchers or the victims recognize them as such or not. Simple criminal assault is punished as a misdemeanor in every state.

As Aggravated Assault or Aggravated Battery

Attacks constituting aggravated assault or aggravated battery are similar to those of simple assault and battery, but they are more serious crimes. A simple assault or battery becomes aggravated when the activity becomes more dangerous or brutal. Generally, "aggravated assault" and "aggravated battery" are defined as one or many of the following types of behavior: (1) an assault or battery where the means or the instrument used to accomplish the injury is highly dangerous, or (2) where the assailant has some ulterior or malicious motive in committing the assault or battery other than the mere desire to have the person punished, or (3) when the assault or battery is committed with a deadly weapon under circumstances not amounting to an intent to murder, or (4) when a simple battery results in significant bodily injury to the woman (Johnson 1980:322).

The statistical research on family violence provides many common examples of aggravated assaults and aggravated battery occurring in violent homes throughout North America. Men are attacking women with guns, knives, lamps, pipes, "objects," chairs, broom handles, and boiling water (Straus, Gelles, and Steinmetz 1980). If the women are struck by these objects, then the men have committed the crime of aggravated battery; if they miss their targets, they commit the crime of aggravated assault.

One national survey revealed that in one of every two hundred couples, one spouse will use a knife or gun on the other (Straus, Gelles, and Steinmetz 1980). If the man initiates an aggravated battery on the woman and the victim dies some time later, the crime is transformed from an aggravated battery into either murder or manslaughter.

As Rape

Common law defines "rape" as "The act of a man who has unlawful sexual intercourse with a woman other than his wife, without her consent" (LaFave 1978:96). Under this definition, it is legally impossible for a husband to rape his wife. The "wife exclusion," which still exists in many jurisdictions in North America and throughout the world, is commonly referred to as "the marital exception." A California state senator expressed it this way, "But if you can't rape your wife, who can you rape?" (Schulman 1980).

During the 1970s a significant number of state legislatures have acted inconsistently in regard to marital rape exemption, either strengthening or diluting it. Some states allow prosecution for rape of a husband who engages in sexual intercourse with his wife without her consent after they have separated and filed for divorce. Yet other states have actually extended the marital rape exemption to couples who cohabitate outside of marriage. In these states it is legally impossible for a boyfriend to rape his live-in girlfriend. Other states allow the marital exemption to be extended even to dates when there have been voluntary sexual relations in the past. It is legally impossible in these states for a man to rape his date if she has slept with him before! Other states are silent on the marital rape exemption (Schulman 1980).

The greatest number of states, however, have enacted legislation to protect women by making it *possible* for a husband to rape his wife in the same way he is legally eligible to rape any woman. The statutory change usually made is to drop the marital exemption. These new statutes do not distinguish the crime of stranger rape from what criminal justice scholars often refer to as "marital rape." However, marital rape is the same crime as rape.

The crime of rape in many states has been redefined as "sexual battery" or "sexual penetration." Raping intimates is frequently a part of the violence committed in American homes. A study by the Battered Woman's Research Center in Denver, Colorado, showed that 34 percent of the 400 battered women studied had been raped in their marriage at least once. Forty-one percent were forced to insert objects into their vaginas, to engaged in group sex, to have sex with animals, or to play bondage games against their will (Armstrong 1983).

Several groups of empirical researchers suggest that marital rape is more common than all other forms of rape combined (Groh and Birnbaum 1979; Walker 1979). Furthermore, additional crimes often are committed during acts of marital rape. Diana Russell says that a husband who often rapes his wife also threatens "not infrequently" to kill her (aggravated assault) if she does not comply (1982).

When is intercourse between a husband and wife marital rape? It is exactly the same as common-law rape (a male's forcing sexual intercourse with a woman without her consent) in states that have dropped the marital exemption. Where it is criminal to commit forceful intercourse with one's wife without her consent, marital rape is conduct like any other rape and often is considered a capital crime (authorizing a maximum sentence of life in the state penitentiary). The California rape statute is typical of the growing minority of states that recognize marital rape as criminal rape. California defines rape as (1) forced intercourse; (2) intercourse obtained by threat or force; or (3) intercourse when consent is impossible because the victim is unconscious, severely drugged, asleep, or in some other way totally helpless (Perkins and Boyce 1989:114).

In the violent home, whenever a woman does not consent to having intercourse with her intimate and clearly communicates this lack of consent to him and nonetheless he forces her to have intercourse with him, he commits the crime of (marital) rape. Furthermore, the woman does not need to have a "good reason" from the man's point of view for not consenting to his demand for intercourse; the law requires only that she communicate her lack of consent to him. Empirical researchers as yet have failed to ask North American marital rape victims specifically why they did not want to have sex when their intimates raped them. However, in a survey conducted in West Germany, some of the reasons listed were (1) chronic discrepancy in sexual desires or needs; (2) being ill, in pain, or fatigued; (3) dislike of being woken for sex; (4) dislike of husband's behavior; (5) disinterest in sex during or after fighting, whereas many husbands appear to be interested in sex at those times; and (6) pre-divorce turn-off (Russell 1982). Hence, if a woman gives such a reason she is saying to the man that she does not consent to intercourse. If he subsequently forces intercourse on her, he has raped her, in states that have criminalized spousal rape.

As Murder or Voluntary Manslaughter

Almost an equal number of wives kill their husbands as husbands kill their wives. When spouses kill spouses, the wife is the victim in 52 percent of the cases, the husband in 48 percent. Apparently men and women are equally inclined toward deadly marital interaction (Lyon and Morrison 1982).

Two types of homicide usually are charged by the states when spouses kill each other, "murder" and "voluntary manslaughter." Murder is the unlawful killing of another human being with malice aforethought. Voluntary manslaughter is a killing that otherwise would be murder but which was committed in response to adequate provocation (Kadish, Scholhofer, and Paulsen 1983:416).

Many killings between men and women who are intimate involve the killer's being provoked into a rage and then killing the provoker. If a jury determines that the events provoking the killer into this rage also would have provoked an ordinary citizen who acts with prudence and caution in his daily affairs into a rage (one called by law "the reasonable person") then the killing is considered less serious and is classified as voluntary manslaughter. Examples of adequate provocation are witnessing one's spouse commit adultery, receiving a violent and painful blow from one's spouse, and engaging in mutual combat in which both man and woman voluntarily participate. An intimate provoked by any of these events into killing the other commits the crime of voluntary manslaughter. Also, some courts have ruled that when a woman kills her intimate while believing she is doing so in self-defense, even if legally her situation is *not* self-defense, she has not committed murder but rather voluntary manslaughter (Perkins and Boyce 1989).

Killing an intimate is murder, not voluntary manslaughter, when an enraged spouse kills the other after being provoked by such things as the other's insults, or name-calling, or threats, or naggings, or verbal attacks, or the dinner not being ready on time, or her not submitting to his sexual demands, or financial arguments, or similar lesser provocations. These killings would never be considered as a matter of law to have been adequately provoked. Hence all such killings are murder (Perkins and Boyce 1989).

The family homicides of murder and voluntary manslaughter are felonies in every state. Murder, especially if premeditated, is punishable by death in the majority of states. Life imprisonment is a common alternative to a death sentence in husband-wife murder cases. Usually, criminal courts can authorize no lesser sentence than life imprisonment for a conviction of murder. Voluntary manslaughter, on the other hand, is punished less severely. Intimates convicted of voluntary manslaughter have received punishment as minimal as probation and as severe as sentencing to fifty years in prison.

As Spouse Abuse

A man who assaults his intimate woman commits a misdemeanor. A husband who batters his wife also should be charged with a misdemeanor. If the attack constitutes an aggravated assault or battery, he should be charged with a felony. The same is true if he rapes her in certain states. Although these crimes all have been referred to here as the crimes of "woman abuse," they constitute a series of separate and distinct criminal charges in North America. Such has been the case throughout the twentieth century. Yet despite this legal fact, many criminal investigators responding to family disturbances, as well as the lawyers prosecuting them or the judges adjudicating them, still continue to believe that assaults, batteries, aggravated assaults, aggravated batteries, and rapes perpetuated against women by the intimate men in their lives are *not* crimes but instead constitute "civil matters" (Attorney General's Task Force on Family Violence 1984).

As a consequence, significant changes in statutes related to domestic violence have occurred in many states. These legislatures have enacted substantive changes to the states' criminal laws. At least eight "domestic violence statutes" have been legislated, thereby creating a separate domestic violence criminal offense (sometimes called "spouse abuse" or "family abuse"). At first these new crimes may appear superfluous, as every state enacting them already had laws sanctioning the crimes of women abuse. But as Buzawa (1990) points out, this new legislation may nonetheless have several key advantages.

First, it directs law enforcement to the elements of a particular crime specific to domestic violence, not to the generalized laws of assault and battery. This may encourage a more active police response either because of enhanced knowledge of the law or enhanced exposure to civil liability if a specific domestic violence statute is not enforced.

Second, statutes allowing misdemeanor warrantless arrests usually have procedural requirements that may limit the ability of law enforcement to effect the arrest (for example, time limits may have passed or the required evidence of visible injury to the victim may not be available). Creating a new statute might give the legislature a chance to break out from such restrictions.

Third, such legislation makes it far easier for the state to retain better records of reported domestic violence incidents and of case disposition. When such cases are lumped into the generic category of assault and battery, it is difficult for outside observers to determine with any degree of accuracy whether domestic violence cases are being prosecuted with the same vigor as battery cases involving unrelated parties.

Fourth, because the domestic violence violation is a specific offense, courts imposing sentences may have the ability to impose more tailor-made punishments than in standard criminal law cases, which usually are limited to fine, probation, or jail. For example, a sentence may include the imposition of injuction-like conditions upon release from jail, the continuing threat of deferred prosecution for a number of months, and forced assignment to a counselling program.

Buzawa (1990) reports further that the following eight states have made various aspects of domestic violence a separate offense: Arkansas (relates to abuse by husbands only), California, Hawaii, North Carolina (covering spouses and persons who have lived "as if married"), Ohio (but only as to members of the same household related by blood or marriage), Rhode Island, South Carolina (including violence between parents, children, spouses, and persons cohabitating or formerly cohabitating), and Tennessee.

Also, a number of states, while not specifically adding domestic violence as a separate criminal offense, have enacted legislation allowing law enforcement to cross-reference existing assault and battery laws into their new domestic violence statutes. This technique was apparently legislated to emphasize to police and prosecutors that these statutes should be considered in appropriate domestic violence cases.

In summary, although as a matter of legal fact these new crimes ("spouse abuse," "domestic violence," and "family abuse") are redundant to crimes already on the books in these eight states, their potential significance cannot be overstressed. The legislative intent behind the enactment of these new crimes is to impress upon law enforcement authorities the criminality of such cases. The South Carolina criminal code best exemplifies this separate crime of "spouse abuse," in calling it "domestic criminal violence." The statute makes unlawful the following acts: (1) To cause harm or injury to his family or household member, or (2) To offer or attempt to cause physical harm or injury to his or her family or household member with apparent present ability under circumstances reasonably creating fear of imminent peril (516, Ch 25 S.C.C.L.).

If a redundant law has the effect of inspiring the criminal justice system to recognize and respond to the crimes of domestic violence as actual crimes, thereby affording greater protection to abused women, then the more such redundant statutes the better.

As Violation of a Protection Order

Simply charging an abusive man with a misdemeanor (a battery on his wife, for example) usually results in his being freed on bail, certainly before his court date and probably within twenty-four hours of his arrest. If he is out on bail, then the accusing woman probably is still in peril even though the criminal justice system has taken over her case. A significant number of men out on bail present a real danger to the women responsible for their facing a court date; if not dangerous, they may be manipulative. Recognizing this danger, the legal system has attempted to provide a vehicle by which, in theory at least, a woman may attempt to insure her own safety. This vehicle is called a "protective order" (or a TRO, a temporary restraining order).

Theoretically, a woman can apply to a judge (usually a civil judge) for a protection order by testifying to the judge that the man who battered, assaulted, or raped her will be dangerous to her in the future. The man could be ordered by the judge to stay away from the woman. If afterwards he harasses, visits, batters, or rapes her while subject to the protection order, he "violates the terms" of the protection order. Theoretically, he then is rearrested and "held in contempt of court" until the judge is convinced he will not violate the order again.

Violation of a protection order technically is not one of the crimes of woman abuse. It is civil contempt of court. Yet as it sometimes results in the incarceration of abusive men, it should be considered here.

The judge's power to issue injunctive orders preventing undesirable conduct is considered to be ancillary to the court's substantive powers. Because the issuance of such orders is not one of their primary purposes, courts tend to issue injunctive orders sparingly, primarily as a response to inappropriate conduct or serious threats by the person being restrained. Typically, the court will try to have both sides represented at a "TRO hearing" prior to issuing an injunction. However, if the matter is urgent, such as the threat of immediate violence, exparte orders may be issued where only the complainant is present. Subsequent violations of these protective orders may, depending on the applicable statutes,

constitute independent grounds for arrest (in nineteen states) or simply be punished as contempt of court (Buzawa 1990).

The scope of civil protective orders theoretically provides a legal tool that
could assume a central role in the arsenal of legal responses to domestic violence,
according to Buzawa, for three reasons.

First, the courts have a wide power to fashion injunctive relief, unlike the
relatively strict restraints on them when imposing sentencing in criminal cases.
For example, courts often issue the following protective orders in domestic
violence cases:

1. An offender is ordered to move out of a domicile or not to use certain property like
   a car, even if the title to the property is in the name of the offender.

2. An offender is ordered to refrain from further physical or psychological abuse.

3. An offender is ordered to refrain from any contact with the victim.

4. An offender is ordered to enter counselling to finish the program.

5. An offender is directed to pay support, restitution, or attorney fees.

6. Provisional custody of minors is granted to the victim and drafted onto the protective
   order.

Second, the court's protective order has the effect of increasing the leverage
of the victim. Specifically, she may obtain relatively unfettered control over the
home or other essential assets. In addition, the knowledge that a protective order
can be enforced by the local police department may make her more secure and
the offender less likely to initiate abuse.

In addition, the victim (with the assistance of a knowledgeable advocate) has
the potential for far more control over the situation than in a normal criminal
prosecution. After obtaining a protective order, she can better overcome the
indifferent attitudes of police officers, the prosecution, and court personnel (if
not judges). Also, she can restrain overzealous criminal prosecution and thereby
not let the system take control in jurisdictions with mandatory arrest policies.

Third, the use of protective orders gives police departments a method for
recognizing when an offender is a recidivist, thereby requiring the police to take
a more activist approach. In addition, the enforcement of the protective order
provides a vehicle for preventing abuse.

Finally, if somewhat more cynically, when the police respond to a domestic
violence incident where a protective order is in existence, they may be more
inclined to take an activist role, as the order may establish a legal duty of care
that the officer owes to the victim. Breach of this duty could make him or the
police department civilly liable if the order is not enforced (1990).

Despite the important potential for the use of general civil-law protective
orders, to date they have not been used as extensively as possible in domestic
violence cases. Four reasons exist for this sparing use, according to Buzawa.

First, because courts consider injunctive relief as a serious restriction on personal liberty and as ancillary to their primary duties, they usually require an initial act of domestic violence before seriously considering issuing such an order.

Second, the process of obtaining an order must be initiated and pursued by the continued affirmative action of the victim, often in the face of procedural requirements and the indifference or even hostility of court personnel and/or the judiciary.

Third, issuance of an order is, with few exceptions, at the discretion of the judge in question. Judges usually do not issue such orders as a matter of course, as has often been noted.

Fourth, police departments must obtain copies of the order to have it enforced. Although the victim can keep a copy, the best system requires active notification by the court clerks to the relevant police departments. This action again is subject to many slowdowns and/or the indifference of both court personnel and the police personnel assigned to monitor the existence of such orders (1990).

Two types of protective orders have become common: general civil protection orders or TROs, and an order ancillary to divorce proceedings. The only states lacking such protective orders are Arkansas, Hawaii, and Idaho.

As Victim/Witness Intimidation

Recognizing the frequent failure of protection orders to provide safety to the woman victim before the man's trial for woman abuse, some state legislatures have enacted additional specific legislation making victim/witness intimidation a crime. These laws are aimed in part at men who extort or abuse the woman victim from pressing charges or testifying against him. These laws make criminal any activity that interferes with a citizen's seeking redress through the criminal justice system or interferes with any witness to a crime. This legislation unfortunately is rarely enforced.

As Spin-off Crimes: Disorderly Conduct or Resisting Arrest

Often a man arrested after the police intervene in a domestic disturbance is charged with crimes additional to the ones related to his abuse of the woman in the home. Police entering a domestic disturbance crime scene may discover men who are enraged, quite often drunk, and also angry at the police for invading their "castle." Some woman abusers become so irate at the police for questioning the way they "handle" their women that these men turn their rage against the investigating officers in the home, in the yard, or in the squad car.

Although the police may initially be hesitant to file criminal charges against a man for beating a woman, the same reluctance will not be seen when the police themselves become victims of the man's rage. Behavior such as yelling, profanity, lack of cooperation, or committing an assault or battery on the police are most often met with the full force of the law. These abusive men are usually booked, fingerprinted, photographed, and charged with "disorderly conduct," "resisting arrest," "assaulting a police officer," "interference with a police officer," or any combination of these spin-off crimes and then promptly jailed. In such instances, the abusive man is often charged with crimes against the woman in order to provide the original arrest that he is held to have resisted.

THE LAW OF ARREST

The traditional attitudes of society toward woman abuse often are responsible for the historical lack of aggressive police responses to family disturbance calls. Violence against family members long has been considered something less than a real crime by the police (Langley and Levy 1977). Traditional criminal justice practice has been based on the assumption that the crimes of spouse abuse in reality are not crimes at all but instead constitute a mere "family disturbance" and that family disturbances do not require an arrest.

Although patrolmen responding to the crime scene are called upon to stop the immediate violence at hand, law enforcement historically has not been encouraged by any component of the criminal justice system or social service systems to intervene with a formal arrest (Attorney General's Task Force on Family Violence 1984). So hesitant has the traditional officer been to arrest the woman abuser that in many cases the abuser has not been arrested even when a homicide is imminent.

The traditional police approach to family calls may have stacked the situation in favor of the attacker. The net effect of the failure of police to arrest husbands when called to investigate domestic disturbances is that the wives' cries for help have for the most part been rejected. The refusal to arrest tells the victim that her beating is not a real problem and thereby reinforces the man's position, saying to him, "We're here because we were called, but we don't think this is serious. We're here to patronize your wife." For years such a response by the majority of police departments in the United States has affixed an official stamp of approval to the husband's behavior. Historically the traditional police response to domestic violence calls has implied to the abusive husband that it is acceptable for him to beat his wife, but recently the situation is changing somewhat.

In many states, the reason for police failure to arrest the abusive husband is that the officers did not have the power to do so. In certain states, statutes forbid a police officer from making a warrantless arrest for a simple battery unless the offense occurred in the officer's presence. In these states, when an officer has probable cause to believe a man has battered a woman, the officer cannot arrest him unless the officer witnessed the violence. In such circumstances, the only way the officer can legally arrest the abusive man is for the battered woman to file a formal complaint. Most often, she must do so in person at the police station. Even though she may have called the police in the first place, for many reasons abused women are extremely reluctant to sign criminal papers on their intimates.

The procedural requirements for a warrantless arrest in cases of domestic violence misdemeanor battery is in a stage of significant transition. Prior to the early 1970s, all but fourteen states required that an officer witness a misdemeanor's occurrence before he legally could make a valid warrantless arrest. Since then the law in this area has evolved rapidly. As recently as 1987, only eleven states did not provide such warrantless arrest powers to their police. Presently forty-eight states (all but Alabama and West Virginia) have enacted some form of statute authorizing warrantless arrests for domestic violence related misdemeanors. It must be noted that these statutes are not uniform and many contain exception or procedural requirements that effectively limit their applicability. These exceptions may limit warrantless arrests to cases in which the officer observes that a victim has been injured or that only a short time has elapsed between the act of abuse and the call to the police (Victim Services Agency 1988). The reasons for these exceptions appear to follow general criminal law precepts, that is, requiring visible injury is intended to separate out "garden variety" disputes from serious battery requiring police action. Similarly, requiring a short time frame may parallel other warrantless arrest exceptions, such as the doctrine of hot pursuit. Finally, the exceptions may occur as a result of legislative compromise between advocates of change and those fearful of overzealous police enforcement and the intrusion of the police into "family life" (Victim Services Agency 1988).

The recent concern and legislative movement over facilitating police ability to arrest woman abusers was initiated in part by scholarly research that concluded that an arrest was the best deterrent of future woman battering. This experimental study, conducted in Minneapolis, concluded that, among arrest, separation, and mediation, arrest is the most effective deterrent to future woman abuse (Sherman and Berk 1985). These findings, while not conclusive, have been incorporated into most of the scholarly discussions about the desirability of a pro-arrest stand to protect abused women from violent men.

Recently, in response to frustration over low arrest rates and the tentative findings of Sherman's study that suggest arrest as the best police deterrent of women abuse, many states have adopted or are considering legislation that would force mandatory arrests at all homes where probable cause suggests participation in acts of domestic violence (see Figure 8.1). The use of a mandatory arrest statute is highly unusual in criminal procedure and can readily be seen as a somewhat desperate reaction to the perceived inadequacies of the historical police response to domestic violence.

As of mid-1988, nine states have enacted such mandatory arrest statutes; all such statutes apply to cases of felonies and eight to misdemeanors (see Table 8.1). As is common in this area, the statutes do not parallel each other, with some requiring evidence of injury or another condition before an arrest becomes mandatory.

In addition, Iowa goes one step further by limiting the prosecutor's ability to decline prosecution in domestic violence cases. At this time, Iowa is the only state known to adopt this position.

Figure 8.1
Domestic Violence Arrest Legislation: Status of the States

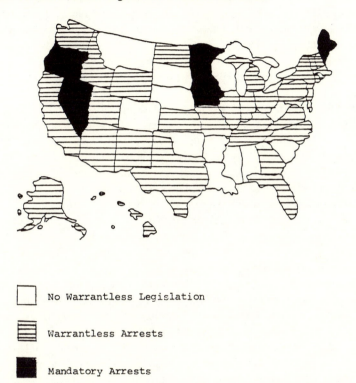

☐ No Warrantless Legislation

▤ Warrantless Arrests

■ Mandatory Arrests

Source: Buzawa, E. 1990. *Criminal Justice Responses to Domestic Violence*. Beverly Hills, Calif.: Sage Publications.

Table 8.1
Mandatory Arrest States

State	Felony	Misdemeanor
Connecticut	*	*(if crime fresh)
Iowa	*	*
Louisiana (only if victim in danger)	*	*
Maine	*	--
Nevada	*	*
New Jersey	*	*
Oregon	*	*
Washington	*	*
Wisconsin (only if victim in danger)	*	*

Source: Law Enforcement Response to Domestic Violence, Victim Services Agency, 1988.

By the winter of 1984, American police departments in the forty-four states that do not mandate arrest were aware of the results of the Sherman research that suggested that arrest in domestic calls is two-and-one-half times more effective as a deterrent than is intervening by mediation or separation. However, few of the nation's police organizations implemented any mandatory arrest policies in domestic violence cases (Benedetto 1986). Only after the verdict in Tracey Thurman's case in 1985 did police departments change their policies significantly.

Consider what happened when the police did not arrest Charles "Buck" Thurman in Torrington, Connecticut. Between October 1982 and June 1983, Buck's abused wife, Tracey, made seven or eight calls and visits to police headquarters begging for protection from her estranged husband. She signed several sworn complaints against him. But because it was a "family matter," the officers did not treat her complaints as seriously as they would have in ordinary nondomestic situations.

In the final beating, which took place outside of the house, Tracey was stabbed repeatedly just as a police officer she had called earlier arrived. His response was delayed twenty minutes while he went to the station to "relieve himself." After arriving at the bloody scene the officer first asked Buck for the knife but did not arrest or try to handcuff him. Buck gave him the knife but then proceeded to stomp on his wife's face and then run into the house. Buck soon returned with their young son, and in front of the boy and the officer Buck cursed and kicked Tracey in the head, leaving her partially paralyzed.

Eventually six officers arrived at the scene. But, according to Tracey's testimony, the husband still was not arrested. He was apprehended only after he headed for Tracey again as she lay on the ambulance stretcher.

Tracey sued the Torrington Police Department as well as twenty-four officers separately and individually. All these officers at one time or another had been contacted about Tracey's beatings and had failed to act. She alleged in her lawsuit that the police officers had been negligent in not arresting Buck and had violated her constitutional rights to equal protection under the law.

The federal judge in this case ruled that, when the police treat victims of violence differently according to their relationship to the abuser (intimate versus stranger), such policies and actions violate the victim's guarantee of equal protection under the law. Furthermore, the judge ruled on June 4, 1985:

A man is not allowed to physically abuse or endanger a woman merely because he is her husband. A police officer may not knowingly refrain from interfering and may not decline to make an arrest simply because the assailant and the victim are married. Such an action on the part of the officer is a denial of equal protection of the law.

The jury found the twenty-four officers negligent in that they had violated Tracey Thurman's civil rights. The jury awarded her $2.3 million in compensatory damages. The Torrington police department's insurance company paid the settlement but stated that it might thereafter refuse to cover any police departments that had not educated their officers about domestic violence intervention (Buddy and Taylor 1986).

What actions will best motivate the police and others in the criminal justice system to better protect abused women—the results of scholarly research or legislation mandating mandatory arrest or possibly the threat of economic sanction? History often demonstrates the latter to be the most powerful motivation.

I believe it to be no coincidence that, after the Sherman study (1984–85) but before the *Thurman* verdict and its attendant publicity, the percentage of the nation's police organizations that had mandatory arrest polices in domestic violence cases remained where it had been for about the past five years, at 10 percent (Benedetto 1986). Yet after *Thurman v. Torrington*, police department policies requiring mandatory arrest in domestic violence cases increased dramatically to 31 percent nationally (Benedetto 1986).

What is the lesson to be learned here by those trying to reform domestic violence statutes and policies? What can those who directly interact with the problem—by being employed in one of the social services responding to domestic violence, or by collecting data and conducting scholarly research on the subject, or by enforcing the laws or by writing the statutes—do to effect reforms to better protect abused women? A new point of view may be called for. It seems that legal actions that significantly threaten the pocketbooks of the enforcement, adjudication, and protection agencies might well be the ones that will receive primary consideration. Lawyers always have known that nothing makes a doctor a better physician than the threat of a medical malpractice lawsuit. I believe the same would be true for law enforcement personnel or prosecutors charged with protecting battered women from their abusive intimates. The threat of criminal justice malpractice lawsuits may be the best reform for the plight of abused American women as they desperately struggle for safety and self-esteem in the 1990s.

REFERENCES

Anderson, K. 1983. Private Violence. *Time*, 122(10):18–30.

Armstrong, L. 1983. *The Home Front: Notes from the Family War Zone*. New York: McGraw-Hill.

Attorney General's Task Force on Family Violence. 1984. *Final Report*. Washington, D.C.: Department of Justice.

Barnett, O.W. 1986. Quantitative Aspects of Battering. Paper presented at the meeting of the Academy of Criminal Justice Sciences, Orlando, Fla.

Benedetto, R. 1986. Police File More Charges, Talk Less in Domestic Cases. *USA Today*, February 17, pp. 2, 7.

Buddy, M., and K. Taylor. 1986. Please Somebody Help Me. 20/20, January 23, 1986.

Buzawa, E. 1990. *Criminal Justice Responses to Domestic Violence*. Beverly Hills, Calif.: Sage.

Dix, M., and Sharlot, R. 1980. *Criminal Law Cases and Materials*, 2d ed. St. Paul: West Publishing Co.

Ferraro, K. 1989. Policing Woman Battering. *Social Problems* 36(1):61–74.

Groh, A. N., and H. I. Birnbaum. 1979. *Men Who Rape: The Psychology of the Offender*. New York: Plenum.

Inbau, F., I. Thompson, and A. Moenssens. 1983. *Criminal Law*, 3d ed. New York: Foundation Press.

Jackson, B. 1985. John Fedders of SEC Is Pummeled by Large and Personal Problems. *The Wall Street Journal*, February 25, pp. 1, 24.

Johnson, P. 1980, *Criminal Law, Cases, Materials and Text on the Substantive Criminal Law and Its Procedural Context*. 2nd ed. St. Paul, Minn.: West Publishing Co.

Kadish, S., S. Scholhofer, and M. Paulsen. 1983. *Criminal Law and Its Processes*, 4th ed. Boston: Little Brown.

LaFave, W. 1978. *Modern Criminal Law*. St. Paul: West Publishing Co.

Langley, R., and R. Levy. 1977. *Wife Beating: The Silent Crisis*. New York: E. P. Dutton.

Lyon, A., and H. Morrison. 1982. Self-defense and Battered Spouse Syndrome: A Legal and Psychological Perspective. *National College of Criminal Defense Lawyers* 9:8–16.

Perkins, R., and R. Boyce. 1989. *Criminal Law and Procedure*, 7th ed. Mineola, N.Y.: Foundation Press.

Roy, M. 1977. *Battered Women*. New York: Van Nostrand Reinhold.

Russell, D.E. 1982. *Rape in Marriage*. Riverside, N.J.: Macmillan.

Schulman, J. 1980. The Marital Rape Exemption in the Criminal Law. *Clearinghouse Review* 14(6).

Sherman, L., and R. Berk. 1984. The Specific Deterrent Effects of Arrest for Domestic Assault. *American Sociological Review* 49:261–72.

———. 1985. *The Minneapolis Domestic Violence Experiment*. Washington, D.C.: Police Foundation Reports.

Straus, M. A., R. J. Gelles, and S. Steinmetz. 1980. *Behind Closed Doors*. Garden City, N.Y.: Anchor Press/Doubleday.

Victim Services Agency. 1988. *The Law Enforcement Response to Family Violence: A State by State Guide to Family Violence Legislation*. Law Enforcement Training Project. New York: Victim Services Agency.

Walker, L. 1979. *The Battered Woman*. New York: Harper and Row.

9

INNOVATIVE APPROACHES TO THE PROSECUTION OF DOMESTIC VIOLENCE CRIMES: AN OVERVIEW

Naomi R. Cahn

The following chapter by Naomi Cahn covers innovations in prosecutorial treatment of offenders throughout the country. Traditionally, prosecutor offices have been major impediments to an activist approach in handling domestic violence. They do not take such incidents as seriously as crimes that ''affect the public order''; they are pessimistic about the effect of intervention into abusive relationships; and, despite their legal training, they often have misunderstood the legal options available for prosecution. For these reasons, prosecutorial staff have often used their wide discretion to discourage the filing of complaints or to divert incidents away from the criminal justice system by encouraging and at times even forcing victims into mediation or reconciliation programs.

As Cahn demonstrates, this formerly impenetrable wall has been breached. Pressure from women's groups and the development of mandatory arrest or at least pro-arrest policies have meant that a far greater number of such cases have reached the attention of prosecutors. Concomitantly, pressure to handle such cases effectively is increasing. Prosecutors can go in one of two directions: ever more dismissals at an early stage or the development of innovative procedures to handle such cases effectively and lessen recidivism.

This chapter presents a critical examination of several different model prosecution programs. Cahn reviews the case screening method used in Denver and the District of Columbia; prosecutorial management policies, including ''no drop'' policies; conditional pretrial releases; efforts to support victims by encouraging cooperation in order to enhance case survival rates (and gain additional valuable evidence); and new trial techniques to preserve evidence, use experts, and develop a more effective range of sentencing options.

Cahn's conclusion that innovative prosecutorial approaches may increase the number of cases prosecuted and ultimately decrease recidivism presents a significant finding. It suggests strongly that prosecutors should focus more attention on case progression. It also suggests that further research is needed to determine which of these innovations are most cost effective and best able to limit recidivism. In addition, any innovations need to be seen as part of a coordinated public policy when matched with a system featuring effective police responses and appropriate sentencing by the judiciary.

INTRODUCTION

When a woman is abused, her first call within the criminal justice system is generally to the police. However, it is the prosecutor's office that is then responsible for pursuing any further criminal action against the abuser. The prosecutor's office decides whether to bring to court an abuser who has been arrested; if it decides to do so, the prosecutor's office then has control over trial preparation, plea negotiations, and the trial itself.

For battered women[1] and their advocates, prosecutors' offices have often been a major impediment to improving the overall response of the criminal justice system. Indeed, some prosecutors admit that they simply do not take domestic violence as seriously as other crimes. For example, one supervisor in the District of Columbia prosecutor's office explained that his office prosecutes domestic violence less vigorously than other crimes because, "*[i]nteraction* between people who know each other is really different in kind than *violent behavior* directed toward strangers" (Gellman 1989, emphasis added). In many of the states that have established commissions to study gender bias in the courts, the commissions have found prosecutorial attitudes and practices that similarly inhibit processing domestic violence cases, such as prosecutors who misunderstand the legal options available to a victim, discourage the filing of complaints, and encourage mediation or reconciliation (Minnesota 1989; Nevada 1989; Utah 1990).

As their underlying justification for failing to pursue aggressively domestic violence cases, prosecutors assert that they have the discretion to choose which cases to process. This discretion, which is virtually unlimited, originates in the constitutional separation of powers (Friedman 1982). Prosecutors are part of the executive branch of government and, as such, have the authority to determine how laws are to be implemented or administered to obtain their goals. Although statutes or judicial review may set some outside limits on prosecutorial discretion, for the most part prosecutors have great latitude and little accountability in deciding which cases to pursue and how to pursue them (Friedman 1982). Prosecutorial discretion is also defended for other reasons: it permits individualized treatment of defendants; it allows prosecutors to interpret statutes that may be vague; and it allows prosecutors to set priorities in handling their caseload, a necessity given the sheer number of criminal cases (Ellis 1984).

But why do prosecutors choose to exercise this discretion not to proceed in domestic violence cases? First, prosecutors have traditionally assumed that domestic violence is trivial, that women provoke the abuse against them, or even that women like being beaten (Lerman 1981). Second, prosecutors explain that, because victims simply do not follow through in domestic violence cases, there is no need to waste precious prosecutorial resources on them. One study of the reasons that prosecutors decided not to charge domestic violence cases found that, in 45 percent of the cases, the primary reason for the failure to go forward was the victim's wishes (Schmidt and Steury 1989).[2] Generally, because no one else has seen the violence, the victim is the only witness, making the case almost impossible to prove if she is unwilling to testify. Unfortunately, as one source explains, "[m]isunderstandings" based on the reluctance of some battered women to pursue prosecution have resulted in a systemic bias against all battered women seeking legal help (Nevada 1989).

It is true that the crime of domestic violence differs in one significant way from most other crimes, in that the lives of the aggressor and the victim are intertwined. The two may live together, be married, have been married at one time, and may have children. Consequently, unless there are special procedures to promote victim cooperation and a special unit to advocate for the victim, the victim may be unwilling to testify against the abuser and so may be an uncooperative witness.

The outcome is a vicious circle, in which prosecutors do not prosecute and victims continue to be uncomfortable with prosecutorial procedures. The resulting prosecutorial inaction, however, simply perpetuates the same problems that have caused prosecutors to treat these cases differently and fails to protect adequately the victims of domestic violence who need action from the criminal justice system. Because of the attitudes and actions of prosecutors towards these cases, abusers learn that the criminal justice system does not take seriously their actions and so continue the abuse. Unless abusers are adequately prosecuted, their violence usually continues and may escalate, further damaging the victim and her children (Cahn and Lerman 1991; Waits 1985). Victims learn not to rely on the criminal justice system for help. Although civil orders of protection can provide some help to the victim, they also depend on the criminal justice system for enforcement (Brown 1988). Only through strong and effective intervention by police, prosecutors, and the courts will the violence stop.

In many communities, primarily as a result of pressure from battered women's groups, the police are acting more aggressively in domestic violence cases. As police departments adopt mandatory or pro-arrest policies, the number of arrests increase dramatically. For example, after the state of Washington implemented a mandatory arrest law in domestic violence cases in 1984, there was a 520 percent increase in arrests in Seattle in the first six months of 1985 over the same period in 1984, and the number of successful prosecutions jumped by 300 percent (Ferguson 1987). In Alexandria, Virginia, in the two years following the institution of a domestic violence mandatory-arrest policy, 83 percent of the incidents to which police responded resulted in an arrest (City of Alexandria 1990).

This increase in arrests results in more arrestees for the prosecutors to process.

Prosecutors have two choices: they can either develop innovative procedures to handle the increased caseload or dismiss more cases. In some cities over the past two decades, often as a result of working with battered women's advocates, prosecutors have chosen this first alternative. They have undertaken to take more seriously their responsibility to stop domestic violence crimes by developing and adopting policies that help end the violence. Their goal is to increase the number of successful prosecutions and reduce offender recidivism by encouraging victim participation and establishing procedures to overcome prosecutors' myths about domestic violence. As a result, these offices have developed policies that are more responsive to the specific needs of victims of domestic violence.

As they obtain more experience with implementation of these policies, prosecutors and battered women's advocates have learned that some strategies are more successful than others. Prosecutors' offices are most likely to have an impact on domestic violence recidivism if they both develop goals for handling domestic violence cases that emphasize to the public, victim, and defendant that domestic violence is a crime and that it is the prosecutors' responsibility, not the victim's responsibility, to prosecute and work together with other criminal justice agencies to develop procedures that keep the defendant under the control of the criminal justice system in some effective manner (avoiding mere wrist slapping) (Mickish and Schoen 1988). Although there are few studies on the effectiveness of prosecution, it does appear that prosecution deters subsequent offenses, at least for abusers with a low level of serious violence (Elliott 1989).

This chapter critically highlights policies from some of the different "model prosecution" programs throughout the country. These programs were chosen as representative of the most innovative in the country, based on recommendations from battered women's advocates. The areas for comparison are in accordance with the stages of the criminal justice system, beginning with case screening and complaint filing and proceeding through prosecutorial management policies, victim support, trial techniques, and sentencing programs. These innovations show that prosecutors who work with battered women's advocates and implement special policies to handle domestic violence cases are able to increase the number of cases prosecuted and to decrease the recidivism rate.

STAGES OF PROSECUTION

Although specific procedures vary from jurisdiction to jurisdiction, there are, in most places, several distinct stages to any prosecution. At each step, prosecutors can exercise their discretion to dismiss cases or to proceed (Kamisar et al. 1990). The first stage is case screening. This is when prosecutors first see the cases and make the initial decisions of whether to file charges. Reasons for not filing at this stage include a lack of evidence, caseload concerns, the victim's desire not to prosecute, and the arrestee's good reputation and lack of prior record (Kamisar et al. 1990). If a charge is filed, then the state (or city), not the victim, is the party.[3]

The next stage is arraignment, at which the defendant is formally notified of the charges against him, counsel is appointed in appropriate cases, and a judge (or magistrate) sets bond. The amount of bond depends on the danger posed by the defendant to the community, the arrestee's record, and the likelihood that the defendant will flee (Atkins and Pogebrin 1982). In many cases, including felonies (generally defined as crimes punishable by more than one year in prison), a hearing is held before arraignment in front of a grand jury to see if there is probable cause or reason to believe that the arrestee committed the crime. Regardless of the charge, at the arraignment the defendant enters a plea of innocent, guilty, or nolo contendere.

Between charging and trial, the prosecutor and defense attorney may plea bargain, allowing the defendant to plead guilty to a less serious charge; guilty pleas may be accompanied by certain conditions, such as a requirement that the defendant participate in counselling or be placed on probation. If there is a plea bargain, the defendant must still appear in court so that the judge can determine that the plea was voluntary. If there is no plea bargain, the defendant is entitled to a jury trial (for all but certain misdemeanors); if the jury finds the defendant guilty, there is a sentencing hearing. Finally, the defendant can appeal his finding of guilt.

In domestic violence cases, prosecutors have modified virtually every stage in this typical procedure to take into account the special circumstances of domestic violence cases.

CASE SCREENING AND CHARGING POLICIES

Case Screening

Case screening is the first point at which a case can enter the prosecutor's office. It is the control point; if a case is screened but not filed, there can be no further action on the case. An office committed to increasing the pool of cases for prosecution must ensure that cases do not drop out at this early stage (Cahn and Lerman 1991). Thus, offices have developed different methods to ensure adequate initial processing of domestic violence cases.

Cases enter most frequently through police action, such as arrest; rarely, cases may enter through a victim-initiated procedure, as through a local citizens' complaint center. In some programs, such as Denver's, the police fill out special domestic violence incident reports, and prosecutors review those reports (Goolkasian 1986a). In other jurisdictions, such as Alexandria, prosecutors review all police calls to see whether there have been any domestic violence calls. The office determines which cases need further investigation. It is important that prosecutors and victim advocates work closely with the police to review domestic violence calls as soon as they occur.

When cases enter through victim initiation, the police are not involved and the prosecutor has the opportunity to interview the victim directly as a basis for an evaluation of the case. One study found that prosecutors appear to file charges less often in these cases than in cases which enter through police action, even when the cases were comparable in seriousness of injuries (Schmidt and Steury 1989). In the District of Columbia, where prosecutors hold hearings on victim-initiated complaints to determine whether there is probable cause to issue an arrest warrant, prosecutors rarely initiate arrest warrants. The District of Columbia had an estimated arrest rate of less than 5 percent in domestic violence cases (Baker, Cahn, and Sands 1989), and prosecutors issued only 112 arrest warrants in cases referred to the local citizens' complaint center, even though they scheduled hearings in 3,650 of the cases (District of Columbia Citizens' Complaint Center 1989). Such hearings seem to be a way for prosecutors to take some action in a case, but not to take serious steps resulting in prosecution. Unfortunately, few offices have developed procedures to improve their response to victim-initiated complaints; this results in prosecutors losing many cases at their potential entry point.

Filing Charges

The next step is to formally charge the defendant with a crime. In the past, victims were often required to sign charges in domestic violence cases, unlike in most other cases, to show that they were willing to cooperate with the prosecution (Lerman 1981). When the prosecutor is responsible for signing the charge, a stronger message goes to the abuser, making it clear that his action is a crime against both society and the victim, not just the victim, as in any other crime. Indeed, "It is contrary to the principles of th[e criminal justice system] to even indirectly hold victims of domestic violence responsible for law enforcement in the area of their victimization" (Minnesota 1989). The victim should then become like any other witness, with little control over the prosecutorial process. Accordingly, in many offices for which domestic violence crimes are a priority, it is the prosecutors who make the filing decisions, and who proceed even if this action goes against the victim's expressed wishes (Denver 1986; Los Angeles City Attorney 1988). They recognize that making the filing decision the victim's responsibility provides an opportunity for the abuser to intimidate her and keep her from pursuing charges. By contrast, in Portland, Oregon, prosecutors believe that a policy that places filing responsibility on the victim has resulted in the prosecutor's office filing a comparatively low number of charges (Lambert 1990). Some offices have developed elaborate guidelines on when to file charges. In Los Angeles, there are three possible outcomes for a case: filing is the most serious outcome; less serious is scheduling a hearing (this is supposed to be used for minor incidents to warn the abuser or in instances where the victim is unwilling to prosecute); and the least serious outcome is rejection of the case altogether. The attorney should file charges if:

1. The report presents the elements of a crime and describes more than a minor or technical violation of the law; and

2. There is at least moderate injury.
3. If the victim is unwilling to prosecute, there must be corroboration of the incident. Corroboration is *not* required if the injury is serious. (Los Angeles City Attorney 1988)

There are similarly detailed requirements for hearings and rejections. If the crime fits under two sets of guidelines, it is supposed to be treated under the more serious guidelines. Prosecutors are admonished that the decision to file is their responsibility, not the victim's.

Although the Los Angeles office is committed to prosecution, there are still problems with establishing criteria that allow prosecutors to hold hearings. The hearings can turn into a dumping ground for domestic violence cases.

In San Francisco, unlike Los Angeles, the prosecutor's office has established protocols only for when to prosecute or to decline cases. Although there are separate protocols for misdemeanors and felonies, the criteria are substantially the same and require the district attorney to look at the following factors in deciding whether to charge the abuser: the extent or seriousness of injuries . . . , use of a deadly weapon, defendant's prior criminal history, and past history of violence (San Francisco District Attorney's Office 1985). The felony protocol also requires the prosecutor to consider the "potential lethality of situation" (San Francisco District Attorney 1983). After the felony protocols were implemented in 1983, filing in domestic violence cases increased by 136 percent (San Francisco 1988). Positive dispositions, in which the court retained jurisdiction over the defendant, increased by 171 percent.

In Seattle, the city attorney files charges whenever there has been a domestic violence call leading to an actual arrest (Goolkasian 1986a). Under state law, the police must forward to the prosecutors an incident report for which there was probable cause to arrest within ten days of the domestic violence call, unless the case is being investigated (Washington 1990). This ensures that prosecutors have ready access to the pool of domestic violence cases. However, if there is a report but no arrest, the prosecutor contacts the victim to explain her legal options, which include initiating prosecution (Goolkasian 1986a).

Detailed criteria for when to file charges and for whether to charge cases as misdemeanors or felonies are critical to improving prosecutors' response by increasing the number of charges filed. They provide a checklist that ensures that appropriate cases will be prosecuted for the actual crimes committed, and they establish accountability, so that prosecutors must explain decisions not to file. Although prosecutors still have discretion over which cases to pursue, office guidelines set up limits on this discretion, ensuring that more cases get filed. Moreover, explicit charging guidelines can help to ensure that the responsibility of whether to file is placed on the prosecutor, not on the victim.

No-Drop Policies

As part of the policy that prosecution is the prosecutor's responsibility, many offices have also decided to adopt no-drop policies, which emphasize that the prosecutors control decisionmaking by precluding the victim from deciding to drop charges. For example, the King County, Washington, prosecuting attorney's office explains to victims that they are witnesses for the state and that, even if they reconcile with the defendant, the state will not drop charges (King County 1989). There are variations on these policies: Alexandria and Brooklyn have "soft" no-drop policies that allow victims to drop charges after counseling and appearing in front of a judge or counselor to explain why they are dropping the charges (Holtzman 1988).

Proponents of strong no-drop policies assert that precluding victims from influencing prosecution forces prosecutors to take these cases seriously and establishes that domestic violence is a crime against society; opponents argue that battered women have the right to decide whether they want intervention from the criminal justice system (Goolkasian 1986a). The experience of Duluth with its drop policy is illuminating. Duluth initially decided not to adopt a hard no-drop policy, but to use a case-by-case approach and develop other methods to encourage prosecution (Pence 1983). However, after several years of experience with this policy, during which it discovered that the abuser was intimidating the victim and thereby controlling the charging decisions, Duluth adopted a hard no drop policy (Duluth City Attorney 1990). In contrast to the Duluth experience, a controlled study in Indianapolis concluded that, in cases where the victim initiated the prosecution, recidivism decreased when victims had control over whether to drop charges and decided not to drop charges (although a victim who did drop charges was more likely to be battered again) (Ford and Regoli, this volume).

Some offices have taken the no-drop policy to extremes by jailing victims for refusing to testify (Waits 1985). Although it is a good idea to subpoena victims, because this shows that the victim has no control over the process, it is punitive for victims who may face extreme threats and intimidation from their batterers. Thus, while offices should adopt variations on a no-drop policy and study its effects, they should also develop witness protection programs and not punish victims who refuse to testify.

PRETRIAL RELEASE

Although most domestic violence defendants are released before trial, generally on their own recognizance (Goolkasian 1986b), prosecutors can ask that the court set a bail amount comparable to that of other crimes and that conditions be set on the abuser's release (Waits 1985). Many states allow prosecutors to impose conditions on pretrial release in domestic violence cases (Lerman 1981). The National Council of Juvenile and Family Court Judges recommends the following:

1. Setting bail consistent with other assault offenses.
2. Releasing the alleged offender conditioned upon having no contact with the victim.

3. Imposing other special conditions of release which protect and maintain victims and family members.

4. Ensuring that the victim will be notified of a pending release and that adequate provisions will be made for the victim's safety.

5. Ensuring that release conditions will be monitored and acted upon. (National Council of Juvenile and Family Court Judges 1990)

The most important concerns are separating the parties and protecting the victim (Lemon 1990).

The policy of the Los Angeles City Attorney is that protective orders should be sought as a condition of release in any situation where there is a reasonable likelihood that the abuser may try to harm the victim (Los Angeles City Attorney 1988). The office estimates that 75 to 80 percent of victims receive this type of order at arraignment. In San Francisco, the prosecutor automatically requests a stay-away order at the defendant's first appearance, unless the victim specially indicates she does not want one (San Francisco District Attorney 1983). These pretrial release conditions let the batterer know that he cannot continue his behavior with impunity, and they may strengthen the victim's cooperation because she knows that the prosecutor's office will protect her. It is important that offices establish standard procedures so that they automatically seek protection orders and other appropriate pretrial release conditions.

VICTIM SUPPORT PROGRAMS

Because of the unique situation of victims of domestic violence crimes, many prosecutors work closely with outside victim advocacy programs or have established such programs internally. The goal of these programs is to provide support for victims, to encourage victim cooperation with programs, and to enhance case survival rates. Advocates at the projects may help prosecutors by getting additional information on the history of abuse and the nature of the violence; they may provide counseling to the victim; they may explain the criminal justice system to the victim; and they often accompany the victim to court (King County Prosecuting Attorney 1988). Judges and lawyers both believe that these programs are effective in reducing dismissals (Minnesota 1989). The Los Angeles district attorney's office estimates that 70 percent of all victims cooperate with prosecution once they have the assistance of victim advocates (Lemon 1990).

There are two models for these programs: in one model, the projects are independent organizations that coordinate closely with the prosecutor's office; under the other model, the projects operate as an internal division of the prosecutor's office. The Duluth Domestic Abuse Intervention Project (DAIP) is an example of the first model. DAIP, which is actually the coordinating agency for nine criminal justice and human service agencies, trains victim advocates who are not affiliated with the prosecutor's office (Pence 1983). The advocates begin working with each victim at the time of initial contact with the prosecutor's office. ''The role of the advocate is to assist victims in making the determination whether to press charges, to prepare the victim for the court process, to provide the prosecuting attorney with information concerning the case and assistance in evidence gathering, and to assist the prosecutor in making decisions regarding the case'' (Pence 1983). DAIP also organizes battered women's groups to provide support to help victims end the violence against them (Pence and Shepard 1988). DAIP staff coordinates treatment programs for the abuser; and DAIP, not the victim, is responsible for monitoring the abuser's compliance with probation conditions (Pence 1983).

Seattle and Baltimore have established victim support projects that are within the prosecuting attorneys' offices. In Baltimore, the Domestic Violence Unit is part of a citywide cooperative effort to respond to domestic violence (Baltimore City Domestic Violence Policies and Procedures 1989). The process begins after the police, commissioners, and court clerks identify domestic violence cases, when the unit sends out a letter to the victim requesting that she schedule an interview. The Baltimore unit then provides the following services:

—supportive counseling and empathic listening to meet the victim's emotional needs regarding criminal prosecution or use of the legal system.
—referral to other services such as shelter, social services and community or mental health agencies for ongoing counseling.
—information about how to obtain criminal and civil legal remedies.
—preparing victims and witnesses for court, court accompaniment.
—obtaining documentation of the crime, i.e., medical records, police reports.
—advocacy on behalf of the client within the legal system.
—communication with other agencies on behalf of the client. (Young 1990)

In Seattle, the Victim Assistance Unit of the prosecutor's office provides direct advocacy services to victims of misdemeanors (King County Prosecuting Attorney 1988). The unit contacts the victim and interviews her as soon as possible after the assault. Staff then follow up by mailing the victim a detailed information packet on court procedures and protections available to domestic violence victims. There is also a special volunteer program that accompanies the victim to court. In felony cases, these services are instead provided by the office's Special Assault Unit, which has its own victim coordinator. This unit, which handles all felony sexual violence and domestic violence cases and uses vertical prosecution in combination with a special victim center, appears to be as effective as a special domestic violence unit (Baird 1990).

There are no empirical studies of whether independent or internal programs are more effective. Both models, of course, provide victims with some of the support they need to encourage follow-through with prosecution. However, many domestic violence advocates believe that programs that are independent of prosecutors' offices can be more responsive because their primary purpose is to work with victims; internal programs have additional responsibilities, such as providing investigative and litigation support for the prosecutors (Brygger 1990).

As a final reason for providing adequate victim support, prosecutors' offices may be legally liable for injuries to victims if they establish a legally recognized "special relationship." A woman who was supposed to testify that her husband had abused their six-month-old son by beating him and burning him with a cigarette repeatedly told prosecutors that her husband had threatened—verbally and in writing—to kill her, and she even asked for an escort to the trial (Resnick 1990). Before she could testify, her husband set her on fire. A jury awarded her $2.3 million (she can receive only a small portion of that under the state's liability cap).

CASE MANAGEMENT

Prosecutors' offices make a series of general decisions on case administration that have a significant impact on continuation of cases, including whether to use "vertical" prosecution (the case is followed from charging to sentencing by the same attorney), whether to establish a special domestic violence unit, and whether to handle misdemeanors and felonies in different offices. The decisions may be based on economic concerns or office goals. For example, prosecutors may choose to focus only on felony cases, because they are more serious crimes, or on misdemeanors, because they are more numerous and may have additional evidentiary problems and because prosecution may prevent escalation to the felony level (Goolkasian 1986a). The choices then have ramifications for the support provided to victims.

In Baltimore, Maryland, a special domestic violence unit handles all misdemeanor cases, although there is no comparable unit for more serious crimes. The special domestic violence unit in the State's Attorney's office, which has two prosecutors and two paralegals, provided services to more than seven thousand victims in 1988–89 (Young 1990). However, it is simply unable, because of limited staff, to offer special services to victims in domestic violence felony cases and in misdemeanor cases where the defendant requests a jury trial (Young 1990). Thus, while the unit offers benefits to many victims, its services are unavailable to victims who foresee lengthy trials and to those with more serious injuries (felony cases).

By contrast, in San Francisco, the Family Violence Project concentrates on felony cases, although it will take serious misdemeanor cases, such as those which were originally filed as felonies (San Francisco District Attorney 1985). Because there is vertical prosecution, the same "Domestic Violence Assistant District Attorney" handles the case from arraignment through sentencing. Vertical prosecution and special domestic violence units provide case continuity for victims and also ensure that prosecutors have expertise in handling domestic violence cases (Attorney General's Task Force on Family Violence 1984).

POSTCHARGE DIVERSION OPTIONS

Diversion programs are an alternative to traditional criminal prosecution and sentencing through which case processing is suspended while the defendant completes a treatment program (Goolkasian 1986a; Lerman 1981). There are, essentially, two types of diversionary programs based on when the defendant is diverted out of the proceedings: (1) postcharge but pretrial, so that the batterer is referred to counseling before the trial even begins and, if he completes the counseling, the charges are not otherwise prosecuted and (2) postplea, where the defendant actually enters a guilty plea, but his sentence is stayed if he complies with a counseling program (this is also called probation).

The decision as to when diversion should occur is controversial (Cahn and Lerman 1991). Proponents of pretrial diversion argue that it is a quick way to get a batterer into a counseling program and avoids problems with witness cooperation because it is so early in the proceeding. On the other hand, opponents maintain that the batterer may not take the counseling program as seriously if he has not had to admit guilt; also, batterers who fail to follow through with the diversionary process are rarely prosecuted. Moreover, diversion extends the time that a case is held open so that, if there is a violation, testimony about the violence will not be as fresh (Waits 1985; Lerman 1984).

Proponents of postplea diversion argue that, because a batterer must admit guilt, diversion sends a strong message to the abuser and that prosecutors are more likely to enforce diversion agreements if an abuser violates the diversion conditions. Depending on when the abuser enters into diversion, however, postplea diversion may require much more victim cooperation, and a long time may elapse between the time when the initial charge is filed and the time when the defendant enters a diversionary program.

To prevent abuse of the diversionary process, prosecutors have developed strict eligibility guidelines for when diversion is appropriate. In San Francisco, pretrial diversion can be used only in certain misdemeanor cases:

the defendant has no convictions for any offence involving violence within the past seven (7) years. . . .

(c). the defendant's record does not indicate that probation or parole has ever been revoked without thereafter being completed;

(d). the defendant has not been diverted to domestic violence within the last five (5) years. . . .

(e). the crime charged was not a corporal injury resulting in a traumatic condition . . . or an assault with a deadly [*sic*]. . . .

Oppose referral where the defendant does not appear to be a suitable candidate. . . .

Suitability for diversion should be evaluated in light of:

(a). Repeated history of violent conduct (reported or unreported within the past year but especially where medical attention was sought);

(b). the victim's lack of reasonable objections;

(c). the defendant's demonstrable motivation and agreement to comply with the terms and conditions of diversion. (San Francisco District Attorney 1985).

The diversion program involves counseling once a week for a period of six months to one year. While pretrial diversion is not optimal, San Francisco has taken steps to prevent it from being used inappropriately. Guidelines can help deter prosecutors from using pretrial diversion as a means to manage their case dockets or to overcome problems with uncooperative witnesses, but it may not decrease the recidivism rate if the defendant believes that he is "getting off" his criminal charges, because he may not get the message that domestic violence is a crime (Adams 1990).

Denver has adopted postplea diversion, under which defendants must plead guilty but judgment and sentencing are deferred (Denver Domestic Violence Manual Task Force 1986). Defendants are first screened for eligibility (abusers with previous convictions for domestic violence cannot participate) and then are evaluated for suitability.

Given the controversy over diversion programs, the National Council of Juvenile and Family Court Judges recommends that: "[d]iversion should only occur in extraordinary cases, and then only after an admission before a judicial officer has been entered." The organization notes that diversion is inappropriate when "it is used as a calendar management tool, when first offenders are long term abusers, when the required treatment is only of brief duration and is not monitored, and, perhaps most important, when the use of diversion is perceived as a less than serious response to the crime" (National Council of Juvenile and Family Court Judges 1990).

If diversion is used, there are certain fundamental guidelines on the appropriate type of treatment. First, the best type of program provides specified batterer's counseling. Treatment that focusses solely on anger management tends to put the blame on women for provoking the batterer and does not address the root problems of the batterer (Adams 1988; Ganley 1986). Similarly, joint counseling with the victim or mediation suggest that the victim played some role in precipitating the violence and that she also needs to change her behavior (Adams 1988). Instead, batterer's counseling needs to increase the abusers' responsibility for their battering, decrease abusers' dependence on their victims, and teach abusers how to control their behavior (Ganley 1986). Second, diversion should occur postplea, so that the batterer admits responsibility for his actions. Third, the treatment should be mandatory for a specific period of time. Finally, the batterer's attendance should be carefully monitored so that, if he fails to attend, prosecution can continue or a sentence can be imposed. Indeed, California, where a statute authorizes pretrial diversion in misdemeanor cases, is considering replacing the current law with one that allows only postconviction diversion, in large part because of ineffective monitoring (Heisler 1990).

TRIAL PROCEDURES

Because of the variation between states in evidentiary and procedural rules, prosecutors have developed different trial techniques where battered women are the victims to overcome evidentiary problems such as uncooperative victims and the admissibility of expert testimony.

Evidentiary Techniques

To preserve testimony when it is fresh, as well as to ensure that prosecution can proceed without testimony from the victim, the Indianapolis prosecutor videotapes the initial victim interview (Cahn and Lerman 1991). In Miami, the prosecutor obtains a sworn statement from the victim at the initial case screening. Later in the proceedings, offices use a variety of sources for additional evidence (Rosenbaum 1990). Los Angeles uses 911 tapes (Los Angeles City Attorney 1988). Other offices rely on police officer testimony, medical records, or family members who witnessed the violence as evidence when the victim is hostile. These techniques make the case stronger and decrease the office's dependence on the victim's testimony; they can also help impeach the victim's testimony if she recants on the stand.

Expert Testimony

Juries may not believe that abuse occurred if a victim returned to her abuser and so may not convict an abuser. Advocates for battered women who have killed their abusers have used expert testimony on the battered women's syndrome for more than a decade (Schneider 1986); prosecutors are now using such testimony to help convict batterers. Expert testimony is generally admissible in court if it will help the judge or jury (Federal Rules of Evidence). Expert testimony on battered women's syndrome frequently discusses the pattern of psychological and physical abuse and the psychological effects of the economic and social problems attendant on battering, such as the victim's financial dependence on the abuser and the lack of emotional support she may receive from family and friends (Schneider 1986). Commonly, experts testify about Lenore Walker's research on a three-stage cycle of violence from which a victim feels she cannot escape (Walker 1984).

In *State v. Ciskie*, the prosecutor introduced expert testimony in a rape case between a former boyfriend and girlfriend to explain why the victim did not promptly report four instances of rape and why, despite the abuse, she did not leave the relationship (*State v. Ciskie* 1988). In Denver, shelter personnel are called in to testify about how the battered women syndrome might cause a woman to recant earlier testimony when she appears at trial (Larson 1990). Similarly, Los Angeles uses shelter personnel, rather than psychologists, to testify about battered women's syndrome (Bowman 1990).

In another innovative use of expert testimony, New Hampshire prosecutors called a psychological expert to testify about the abuser, who claimed that he had assaulted his wife because of insanity (*State v. Baker* 1980). The witness explained that battered woman's syndrome might characterize the defendant's marriage and explain his actions, thus providing an alternative to mental illness as the basis for the assault. At least one California prosecutor has introduced similar testimony (Lemon 1990).

This creativity in overcoming evidentiary problems is a promising innovation. These techniques show how prosecutors can develop trial procedures to increase conviction rates.

SENTENCING OPTIONS

There are two possibilities after a guilty plea or finding of guilt at trial: probation and/or fine or imprisonment. Probation conditions generally include participation in counseling or other diversionary programs (see the earlier discussion on diversion). As with pretrial diversion, offices need to set up stringent monitoring to ensure that batterers comply with their probation conditions. In Denver, if defendants are not eligible for diversion, they may still apply for probation (Denver Domestic Violence Manual Task Force 1986). An elaborate procedure for presentence investigations includes administering the Minnesota Multiphasic Personality Inventory (MMPI). The probation office then makes a recommendation, which requires at least a partially suspended jail sentence.

Too often, batterers are not imprisoned (Waits 1985). Prosecutors can request tougher sentences, thereby educating both the abuser and the court to the seriousness of the crime. In California, prosecutors who receive special funding for spouse abuse units must make all reasonable efforts to persuade the court to impose the most severe authorized sentence on a person convicted as a spouse abuser (California 1990). The Judicial and Probation Guidelines in Duluth set out a presumptive sentencing recommendation for misdemeanor offenses, beginning with thirty to sixty days in jail, suspended upon conditions that protect the victim and rehabilitate the defendant, for the first offence (Goolkasian 1986a). Requiring prosecutors to recommend sentences commensurate with other crimes helps send abusers the message that they have committed a serious crime.

MONITORING

The prosecutorial programs just discussed were developed to overcome traditional evidentiary problems and myths about victims in domestic violence cases. Some prosecutors have worked closely with community members to implement policies that respond adequately. The question is: are these programs effective in increasing victim cooperation and reducing recidivism?

Responding is somewhat problematic because there is often no formal monitoring process within each office, and there are few statistics that compare the impact of different policies. Nonetheless, many of the studies confirm that changed prosecution policies do help end violence. One study, for example, found that court-mandated counseling does reduce recidivism (Dutton 1987). Another study found that the chance that an abuser will commit further violence decreases upon the abuser's contact with the prosecutorial and judicial systems (Ford and Regoli, this volume).

Moreover, individual programs show dramatic increases in the numbers of arrests and prosecutions following implementation of these programs and also show victim satisfaction with their treatment. Statistics from the Duluth project, which was implemented in 1982, show the success of these programs: The conviction rate for domestic violence abusers was 20 percent in 1980, compared to 82 percent in 1982 (Minnesota 1989). A one-year follow-up study in Duluth found that approximately 70 percent of the victims reported no recent physical abuse; another study found that 80 percent of the victims believed that the response by DAIP and other criminal justice agencies was helpful (Pence and Shepard 1988). Los Angeles reported that, before it developed a special prosecution unit, 55 percent of defendants were found to be, or pled, guilty; following implementation of a special unit, it now has a 77 percent guilty rate (Bowman 1990). Miami dramatically increased the number of felonies charged, from 25 percent to 40 percent, after it established a special domestic violence unit (Rosenbaum 1990).

These studies show that new programs can increase the pool of cases, the total number of prosecutions, and the number of convictions and decrease recidivism. Because of the relatively limited data from follow-ups to determine the effectiveness of criminal justice intervention, there needs to be more research and monitoring (Elliott 1989). Individual programs should, at the least, report the following statistics: the number of domestic violence calls to the police and the number of incident reports and arrests; the disposition of all incidents and arrests such as the number of cases dismissed, diverted, plead out, with reduced charges; types of sentences imposed; repeat offenses within six months, one year, and two years; and treatment completion rates. These statistics should be monitored by outside agencies to ensure accurate reporting. Improved research and monitoring of domestic violence programs will result in increasingly effective practices.

CONCLUSION

Prosecutorial practices and policies are a key factor in whether domestic violence cases progress through the criminal justice system and are responsible for the variable rates of prosecution in different jurisdictions (Minnesota Supreme Court Task Force for Gender Fairness in the Courts 1989). Consequently, prosecutors report that the critical components of any program to increase the effectiveness of domestic violence case processing are commitment by the office and changes in the attitudes and actions of individual prosecutors (Cahn and

Lerman 1991). When special attention is directed to implementing new policies, this can increase the number of prosecutorial actions; without such a focus, the process will revert (Rauma 1984). Cooperation by victims can increase dramatically with appropriate prosecutorial support and policies. Thus, the most effective programs have policy statements and goals that recognize that domestic violence is a crime and that abusers must take responsibility for their actions. They can then support police in their efforts, help to break the cycle of violence, and control the abuser.

To do this, prosecutors' offices need training. While most prosecutors' offices do not require special instruction to handle domestic violence cases, such training may be necessary in order to implement office policies. Just as police departments are now requiring domestic violence training (as in the District of Columbia), so too should prosecutors' offices.

Finally, prosecutors need to understand that they must work together with other criminal justice agencies. Prosecutors can take actions by themselves that will improve the system; but the impact of new policies is much more significant if police, social service agencies, and court administrators adopt comparable policies (Finn and Colson 1990).

NOTES

I would like to thank Chris Jacobson for her skillful research assistance, and Mary Pat Brygger, Tony Gambino, and Lisa Lerman for their suggestions.

1. Battered women are most often the victims of domestic violence. Although men are also battered, the term "battered women" is used interchangeably with "victims."

2. The study also found, however, that prosecutors did not file charges in more than half of the cases in which the victim sought such an action.

3. In criminal cases, the case is, of course, between the state and the defendant. It is the state that brings charges and pursues the case against the defendant; typically, the victim's only roles are to provide information to the prosecutor and to testify in the case.

REFERENCES

Abraham, L. 1987. Deputy District Attorney for Multomah County. Domestic Violence Unit Procedures Manual. Portland, Ore.

Adams, D. 1988. Treatment Models of Men Who Batter: A Profeminist Analysis. In K. Yllo and M. Bograd, eds., *Feminist Perspectives on Wife Abuse*. Newbury Park, Calif.: Sage.

———. 1990. Executive Director of Emerge. Letter to Washington, D.C. Council Member W. Rolark, June 15.

Atkins, B. and M. Pogebrin. 1982. Discretionary Decision-making in the Administration of Justice. In B. Atkins and M. Pogebrin, eds., *The Invisible Justice System: Discretion in the Law*, 2d ed. Cincinnati: Anderson Publishing Co.

Attorney General's Task Force on Family Violence. 1984. *Final Report*. Washington, D.C.: Department of Justice.

Baird, R. 1990. Victim Advocate, King County Victim Assistance Unit. Telephone call, August.

Baker, K., N. Cahn, and S. J. Sands. 1989. Report on District of Columbia Police Response to Domestic Violence. Unpublished manuscript. Washington, D.C., November 3.

Baltimore City Domestic Violence Policies and Procedures. 1989. City of Baltimore: Office of the Mayor.

Bowman, A. 1990. Prosecuting Attorney, Los Angeles City Attorney's Office. Telephone call, July.

Brown, G. R. 1988. Battered Women and the Temporary Restraining Order. *Women's Rights Law Reporter* 10:261–67.

Brygger, M. P. 1990. Director, National Woman Abuse Prevention Project. Telephone call, August.

Cahn, N., and L. Lerman. 1991. Prosecuting Woman Abuse. In M. Steinman, ed., *Woman Battering: Policy Responses*. Cincinnati: Anderson Publishing.

California. 1990. *Deering's Penal Code Annotated of the State of California*, § 273.84(b), 1990 Supplement. San Francisco: Bancroft-Whitney.

City of Alexandria, Virginia. 1990. Domestic Violence Intervention Project: February 1, 1988–January 31, 1990.

Denver Domestic Violence Manual Task Force. 1986. *The Denver Domestic Violence Manual*. Denver, Colo.

District of Columbia Citizens' Complaint Center and D.C. Mediation Service. 1989. Workload and Activity Information.

Duluth City Attorney. 1990. Prosecution Guidelines for Domestic Abuse Cases. Duluth, Minn.

Dutton, D. G. 1987. The Criminal Justice Response to Wife Assault. *Law and Human Behavior* 11:189–206. Actual study in D. G. Dutton, The Outcome of Court-Mandated Treatment for Wife Assault: A Quasi-Experimental Evaluation. *Violence and Victims* 1, no. 3 (1986): 163–75.

Elliott, D. S. 1989. Criminal Justice Procedures in Family Violence Crimes. In L. Ohlin and M. Tonry, eds., *Family Violence*. Chicago: University of Chicago Press.

Ellis, J. 1984. Prosecutorial Discretion to Charge in Cases of Spousal Assault: A Dialogue. *Journal of Criminal Law and Criminology* 75:56–102.

Federal Rules of Evidence, Rule 702.

Ferguson, H. 1987. Mandating Arrests for Domestic Violence. FBI Law Enforcement Bulletin. Washington, D.C., April.

Finn, P., and S. Colson. 1990. *Civil Protection Orders: Legislation, Current Court Practice, and Enforcement*. Washington, D.C.: National Institute of Justice.

Friedman, L. 1982. Discretion and Public Prosecution. In B. Atkins and M. Pogebrin, eds., *The Invisible Justice System: Discretion and the Law*, 2d ed. Cincinnati: Anderson.

Ganley, A. 1986. Perpetrators of Domestic Violence: An Overview of Counseling the Court-mandated Client. In D. Sonkin, ed., *Domestic Violence on Trial: Psychological and Legal Dimensions of Family Violence*. New York: Springer.

Gellman, B. 1989. In the District, Justice vs. Management: Prosecutors' Role in "Papering" Cases before They Reach Court. *Washington Post*, June 8, p. Cl.

Goolkasian, G. 1986a. *Confronting Domestic Violence: A Guide for Criminal Justice Agencies*. Washington, D.C.: National Institute of Justice.

————. 1986b. *Confronting Domestic Violence: The Role of Criminal Court Judges.* Washington, D.C.: National Institute of Justice.

Heisler, C. 1990. Assistant District Attorney, Domestic Violence Prosecution Unit, San Francisco, Calif. Letter to Washington, D.C., Council Member W. Rolark, June 14.

Holtzman, E. 1988. King County District Attorney. The Legal Needs of Battered Women. Testimony before the New York City Council, Committee on Women, March 15.

Kamisar, Y., W. R. LaFave, and J. H. Israel. 1990. *Basic Criminal Procedure: Cases, Comments and Questions*, 7th ed. St. Paul: West Publishing Co.

King County Prosecuting Attorney. 1988. *Status Report.* Seattle: Victim Assistance Unit, May 10.

————. 1989. *Domestic Violence Information Packet.* Seattle: King County Prosecuting Attorney.

Lambert, G. 1990. Victim Advocate, Domestic Violence Unit of the Victim's Assistance Program, Multnomah County District Attorney, Portland, Ore. Telephone call, June.

Larson, D. L. 1990. Project Safeguard, Denver, Colo. Telephone call, July.

Lemon, N. 1990. *Domestic Violence: The Law and Criminal Prosecution.* San Francisco: Family Violence Project.

Lerman, L. 1981. *Prosecution of Spouse Abuse: Innovations in Criminal Justice Response.* Washington, D.C.: Center for Women Policy Studies.

————. 1984. Statute: A Model State Act: Remedies for Domestic Abuse. *Harvard Journal on Legislation* 21:61–143.

Los Angeles City Attorney. 1988. Domestic Violence Prosecutions. Los Angeles: Office of the Los Angeles City Attorney, April.

Mickish, J., and K. Schoen. 1988. Domestic Violence: Developing and Maintaining an Effective Policy. *The Prosecutor* (Winter): 15–20.

Minnesota Supreme Court Task Force for Gender Fairness in the Courts. 1989. Report. *William Mitchell Law Review* 15:825–948.

National Council of Juvenile and Family Court Judges. 1990. *Family Violence: Improving Court Practice.* Reno: Family Violence Project.

Nevada Supreme Court Gender Bias Task Force. 1989. Justice for Women. First Report of the Nevada Supreme Court Task Force on Gender Bias in the Courts. Carson City, Nev.

Pence, E. 1983. The Duluth Domestic Abuse Intervention Project. *Hamline Law Review* 6:247–75.

Pence, E., and M. Shepard. 1988. Integrating Feminist Theory and Practice: The Challenge of the Battered Women's Movement. In K. Yllo & M. Bograd, eds., *Feminist Perspectives on Wife Abuse.* Newbury Park, Calif.: Sage.

Rauma, D. 1984. Going for the Gold: Prosecutorial Decision Making in Cases of Wife Assault. *Social Science Research* 13:321–51.

Resnick, R. 1990. Prosecutor Held Liable in Florida. *National Law Journal*, August 13, p. 3.

Rosenbaum, M. 1990. Prosecuting Attorney, Miami State Attorney's Office. Miami, Fla. Telephone call, June.

San Francisco District Attorney. 1983. Domestic Violence Felony Prosecution Protocol. San Francisco: Family Violence Project, 1983.

————. 1985. Misdemeanor Protocol for Domestic Violence Cases. San Francisco, Calif.

————. 1988. *Prosecution of Domestic Violence Cases in San Francisco*. San Francisco: Family Violence Project, June.

Schmidt, J., and E. Steury. 1989. Prosecutorial Discretion in Filing Charges in Domestic Violence Cases. *Criminology* 27(3):487–510.

Schneider, E. 1986. Describing and Changing: Women's Self-defense Work and the Problem of Expert Testimony on Battering. *Women's Rights Law Reporter* 9:195–225.

Utah Task Force on Gender and Justice, March 1990. Report to the Utah Judicial Council. Salt Lake City, Utah.

Waits, K. 1985. The Criminal Justice System's Response to Battering: Understanding the Problem, Forging the Solutions. *Washington Law Review* 60:267–329.

Walker, L. 1984. *The Battered Woman Syndrome*. New York: Springer.

Washington. 1990. *Revised Code of Washington Annotated*, Title 10, Chapter 10.99, 1990 Supplement. St. Paul: West Publishing Co.

Young, R. 1990. Director, Domestic Violence Unit. Statement to Senate Judiciary Committee. Baltimore, Md., June 18.

LEGAL CASES

State v. Baker, 120 N.H. 773, 424 A.2d 177 (1980)

State v. Ciskie, 110 Wash. 2d 263, 751 P.2d 1165 (1988)

THE PREVENTIVE IMPACTS OF POLICIES FOR PROSECUTING WIFE BATTERERS

David A. Ford and Mary Jean Regoli

David A. Ford and Mary Jean Regoli report on the effectiveness of various prosecutorial responses to battered women. Their study is a unique effort to test empirically which of four potential responses—no prosecution, pretrial diversion, prosecution and rehabilitation, and prosecution and other sanctions (such as time in jail)—will prove to be the most effective in preventing future acts of violence. It uses a randomized field experiment to test the effects of these treatment alternatives over a large population of offenders. The 678 cases represented virtually all offenders in Marion County, Indiana, the county including the city of Indianapolis. Although treatment recommendations were voluntary, unlike those in the original Sherman and Berk study in Minneapolis, it appears that prosecutors were willing to abide by these recommendations, allowing the researchers to develop a more reliable measure of relative efficacy.

The findings suggest that prosecutors' actions may have a dramatic effect on future rates of recidivism. The authors report that the simple course of accepting charges and proceeding through the initial hearing was found to decrease future acts of violence. However, their review of the differential impact of the four courses of treatment strongly suggests that the interaction between the options chosen and future violence may not be clear-cut. For example, the victim's ability to charge the offender, even if such charges are later dropped, appears to affect rates of future violence. As such, empowering the victim to control the process may be more significant than actually maintaining the prosecution of the offender. In turn, this finding appears to confirm a significant potential role for victims in developing an effective method to control domestic violence in their lives. The interesting findings of the study suggest that research may profitably address the proper role for "victim advocates." Also, the spread of "no-drop" policies that limit the autonomy of victims may have some adverse consequences.

This chapter reports research findings on the effectiveness of policies for prosecuting wife batterers in protecting women from future violence. It describes the Indianapolis Prosecution Experiment,[1] the first randomized field experiment to evaluate the specific preventive impacts of prosecution and adjudication in cases of wife battery. It introduces the research by specifying what is meant by a criminal justice effect and by discussing prior research on such effects. Then, focussing on prosecution as it operates in Indianapolis, it describes the experiment as designed to evaluate the preventive impacts of prosecution policies. Later sections explain the procedures for randomizing policies, report baseline sample characteristics, and present the data analysis and findings. Finally, the findings are examined as they apply generally to criminal justice and to the victimization of women in violent relationships.

CRIMINAL JUSTICE EFFECTS ON WIFE BATTERY

To say that criminal justice has an effect here means that it can reduce the chance that a batterer will commit new violence against a given victim, within at least six months of an initial incident addressed by law enforcement. We refer to this as a "specific preventive" impact or effect. The effect may be due to punishment and deterrence, to officially mandated rehabilitative interventions, to informal processes facilitated by either threatened or actual formal criminal processing.

Research suggests that police intervention can prevent habitual wife battering. Langan and Innes (1986) presented evidence from the National Crime Survey that 41 percent of battered married women who did not call the police suffered a recurrence of violence by their husbands within six months, compared to 15 percent of those who did call the police. This finding says nothing about what the police did upon arriving at the scene of a violent domestic disturbance. We may assume, however, that for the survey period (1978–1982), few police departments had aggressive strategies for responding in the interest of victim protection (see for example Berk and Loseke 1980–81; Ford 1983; Loving 1980), as frequently noted for earlier periods (Bannon 1975; Bard and Zacker 1974; Field and Field 1973; Gregory 1976; Martin 1976; Parnas 1967, 1970; Paterson 1979; Roy 1977). Thus, by merely "showing up" the police reduced the chance of repeat violence.

The Minneapolis Experiment (Sherman and Berk 1984) found that police can deter continuing abuse by arresting suspects in violent domestic disturbances. The impact held for arrest per se, as few of the cases were prosecuted. Other research guided by less rigorous designs have reached similar conclusions (Berk and Newton 1985; Jaffe et al. 1986).

But the effectiveness of arrest is not universal. The Omaha Police Experiment, (Dunford, Huizinga, and Elliott 1989) failed to detect a deterrent impact for warrantless arrest. On the other hand, when a suspect fled the scene before the police arrived but was arrested later under a police-initiated warrant, he was significantly less likely to batter again the same victim within a one-year follow-up period. Unlike Minneapolis, most of the Omaha cases were prosecuted; 64 percent of the suspects arrested in the Omaha experiment were ultimately convicted (compared to 2 percent in Minneapolis). Prosecution and adjudicated guilt likely confound the impact of arrest alone.

The police studies show (though with some equivocal results) that police intervention of some sort can prevent the recurrence of conjugal violence. Should we not expect an even greater impact when suspects are formally punished through prosecution with court sentencing?

Elliott's (1989) search for research findings on the effectiveness of prosecution and judicial processing found only one study with sufficient methodological rigor to allow even tentative conclusions to be drawn on preventive impacts. Fagan (1989, et al. 1984) studied 270 victims self-selected as participants in five federally funded criminal justice intervention programs. Overall, 29 percent of the victims reported subsequent incidents of violence. Prosecution was ''attempted'' in seventy-four cases, and eighteen defendants were convicted and sentenced. Fagan compared men who were prosecuted with those who were not. He also compared those who were convicted with those who were not. He found no statistically significant differences in the percentages of men persisting in violence toward the same victims. Although Fagan argues that ''criminal justice interventions'' were most effective in reducing the incidence of repeat violence in cases where defendants had a history of less severe violent behavior, his data do not support the conclusion for the cases prosecuted.

Prosecutors and judges may use a broad range of legal tools for processing cases of domestic violence. They have discretion to enact a variety of policies, ranging from dismissing a case through prosecuting to conviction with harsh punishment. They also can recommend and implement sentences not specifically prescribed by statute but allowed as conditions of probation. For example, defendants may be required to participate in rehabilitative treatment programs as a requirement of probation.

Dutton (1986) attempted to evaluate the impact of postconviction, court-mandated treatment for batterers by comparing recidivism rates for a sample of fifty men who completed a program with a matched sample of fifty men who either failed to complete or never entered the program. He reported significant differences—4 percent versus 40 percent recidivism—favoring the effectiveness of batterer treatment in reducing subsequent violence. Unfortunately, Dutton's design has several obvious sources of bias favoring inflated treatment success. Defendants were selected into treatment by some criterion of suitability, which generally means rejecting likely failures; some men in the ''untreated'' group actually received some program treatment and could have been rejected because of failure; the time on probation (regardless of treatment) and the length of the follow-up period were not controlled to minimize treatment-related surveillance effects and opportunities to recidivate. Although quasi-experimental designs can yield important findings, the difficulties with Dutton's efforts demonstrate a clear need for a randomized experiment.

THE PROSECUTION PROCESS IN INDIANAPOLIS

The range of statutory options and creative discretionary alternatives challenges our ability to evaluate all policy-relevant strategies for processing conjugal violence cases. Nevertheless, guided by policy concerns, we can categorize outcomes under four sets: no prosecution (as may occur when victims are permitted to drop charges), pretrial diversion of defendants to treatment under batterer rehabilitation programs, prosecution to conviction with sentencing to rehabilitative treatment as a condition of probation, and conviction with other conditions, including the possibility of jail.

Figure 10.1 summarizes the prosecutorial and judicial processes for handling cases of wife battery brought to the prosecutor's office in Marion County, Indiana. After a violent attack on a woman, someone may or may not call the police to the scene. If the police are at the scene, they are expected to investigate for evidence to support probable cause for a warrantless arrest. If it exists, they may arrest at their discretion. Upon making such an on-scene arrest, officers fill out a probable cause affidavit and slate the suspect into court for an initial hearing. When the police are not called, or if they are called but do not arrest, a victim may initiate charges on her own by going to the prosecutor's office and swearing out a probable cause affidavit with her allegation against the man. Following a judge's approval, the alleged batterer may either be summoned to court or be arrested on a warrant and taken to court for his initial hearing.[2]

At the time of initial screening, the prosecutor determines a track for processing a case according to what outcome should be pursued. Although there are many variations, Figure 10.1 depicts the four general prosecutorial tracks discussed. This early judgment guides future discretionary actions as the case moves to court. A prosecutor's decisions throughout the process rely not only on legal considerations (including convictability and procedural convenience) but also on guesses about what might be in the victim's best interests. Those decisions have traditionally reflected both personal biases and prosecutorial lore (e.g., Ford 1983; Rauma 1984). Given the absence of research findings pointing toward an effective track, prosecutors' decisions today are likely to be informed by guides to action such as offered by Lerman (1981), the Attorney General's Task Force report (1984), or Goolkasian (1986). Each calls for greater consideration of victim security by advocating policies presumed to "work" in the same sense that arrest "works"—batterers processed under the guidelines should be less likely to repeat their violence than they would otherwise.

Figure 10.1
Overview of the Prosecution Process

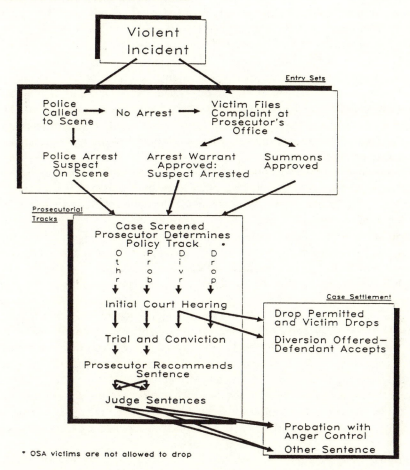

* OSA victims are not allowed to drop

THE INDIANAPOLIS PROSECUTION EXPERIMENT

The Indianapolis Prosecution Experiment (IPE) was designed to discover which policies work as cases move beyond the police into the realm of prosecutorial and judicial action. It examines the alternatives for processing cases of wife battery depicted in Figure 10.1, depending on whether a case enters the criminal justice system by victim-initiated complaint or by on-scene police arrest.[3]

The "drop permitted" track anticipates victims dropping charges, contrary to the more widely advocated "no-drop" policy. Responding to victim advocates who called for denying victims the opportunity to drop charges (e.g., Lerman

1981), the Marion County prosecutor's office had previously implemented a no-drop policy under the assumption that it would provide victims greater protection from continuing abuse. Though eagerly accepted as an appropriate policy, it has never been shown to have a preventive impact; and some have argued that it may function to disempower victims, thereby placing them at greater risk (Ford 1984; also see Fields 1978).

The drop-permitted policy was available only to cases initiated by victim complaint to the prosecutor. When the IPE began, the law enabling warrantless probable cause arrests for misdemeanor battery had just been implemented. All agencies participating in the experiment agreed that to allow victims of on-scene arrest cases to drop charges brought by a police officer would hurt their efforts to encourage arrest.

If a woman is denied the opportunity to drop charges (or if she has permission but elects to proceed), any of three other broad prosecution policies may be activated. The first is also a "no prosecution" alternative offered to a defendant in the form of "pretrial diversion" to a counseling program. If he is willing to admit his guilt and to participate in an anger-control program for batterers, his trial date is deferred to allow time for him to complete the program. Successful completion of the program results in the dismissal of charges. Committing new violence or failing to abide by the terms of the agreement results in the case going to trial.

The second policy option calls for prosecuting to conviction with a request for sentencing to anger-control counseling as a condition of probation (the same batterer treatment program offered under diversion). We call this "probation with counseling." The final prosecution policy option is to seek a conviction with sentencing to fines, probation, and jail, our "other" category. In practice, "other" was a residual category within which a variety of traditional sanctions might be exercised. The analyses presented hereafter use "other" as an experimental control or base category against which the remaining categories are compared.

Cases in the IPE study were selected from all cases of misdemeanor battery or criminal recklessness brought to the attention of the Marion County prosecutor's office between 30 June 1986 and 10 August 1987. To qualify for the study, a defendant had to be an adult (aged eighteen years or older) male alleged to have physically victimized a female conjugal partner. Also, at the time of the study incident, the couple had to fit one of the following relationships: married, previously married, cohabiting, previously cohabiting, or having a child together. The only cases rejected from the study were those in which the suspect fell into one or more of the following categories: he had previously been convicted of felonious violence (e.g., criminal homicide, robbery, burglary with injury, rape, arson with injury, aggravated assault); he had previously been convicted or had a warning letter sent or had a pending case for an act of violence against the same victim as in the new case; he was known to be on probation and was subject to a judgment of violation for the new offense, and the prosecutor wanted that judgment. Cases were also rejected if, prior to randomization and in the judgment of the prosecutor, the defendant posed such danger to the victim that he should be arrested immediately and given no chance of less than rigorous prosecution with harsh punishment.

A total of 678 cases were identified for study. Of those, 480 cases (71 percent) were brought by a victim's direct, in-person complaint to the prosecutor; 198 cases (29 percent) entered the prosecution process following warrantless, on-scene police arrests of suspected batterers.[4] Within each of these "Entry Sets" (i.e., entry by Victim Complaint [VC] or by On-Scene Police Arrest [OSA]), cases were randomly assigned recommendations for prosecutorial treatment (as described hereafter). In addition, the Victim Complaint cases were randomly assigned to either a warrant or a summons condition as the means of bringing a defendant to court.

The study followed each case through the prosecution process until six months following its settlement in court. Outcome measures were obtained from official records, personal interviews with victims and defendants, and direct observation in court. Victims were initially interviewed as soon as possible after the case came to the attention of the prosecutor. Each was interviewed again shortly after the case was settled in court and finally six months after settlement. Defendants were interviewed after their cases were settled. The present analysis focuses on those cases with completed initial and six-month follow-up victim interviews, those which allow an assessment of the impact of prosecutorial and judicial actions on further violence against the victims.

RANDOMIZATION OF RECOMMENDED PROSECUTORIAL TRACKS

The Indianapolis experiment used a "discretion-dependent" design whereby each case entering the study was randomly assigned to a treatment condition that was recommended to a deputy prosecutor for consideration as a prosecution goal. The experiment did not apply any direct treatment; its influence was mediated by prosecutorial and judicial discretion. The normal prosecution policy prior to the experiment was to prosecute every case to conviction with the goal of attaining presumptive sentencing, that is, fines, probation, and executed jail time. Pretrial activities set each case on a course toward that end, what we have been calling a "prosecutorial track." With the implementation of the IPE, other less-punishing treatments were designated as possible outcomes. Cases in the IPE had a greater chance of receiving a less-punishing outcome, as each case now had an equal opportunity of being tracked toward one of three other outcomes.

In effect, the prosecutor was asked to let chance govern her discretion so that each defendant was equally likely to receive any one of the treatments, including less punitive alternatives.[5] For example, under the IPE, a case might be randomly assigned to a pretrial diversion treatment. Diversion would be recommended to

Figure 10.2
Randomization and Prosecutorial Tracks toward Court Outcomes

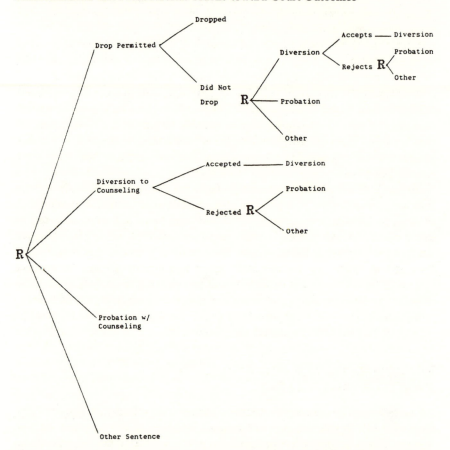

the prosecutor in the hope that she would offer the defendant an opportunity to participate in a batterers' anger-control program instead of prosecution. If she had no reason to argue against the IPE recommendation, the prosecutor would endorse it by entering it as her recommendation on a standardized form in the case file. The success of the experiment rested with the prosecutor's willingness to set aside common biasing factors (including personal values and prosecutorial lore) that might otherwise guide her discretion.

Figure 10.2 shows the design for randomizing prosecutorial tracks. Notice that the process is complicated by the opportunities for victims and defendants to make decisions that could "untrack" them. In those cases, new randomized tracks were recommended to further control for biases in the policy selection process.

The experiment had remarkable success, thanks to cooperating prosecutors, in attaining near perfect agreement between randomized treatment recommendations and the prosecutor's decision, upon screening a case, to track it toward the designed outcome. In only one case did the prosecutor choose to override a randomized prosecution recommendation.[6] That nearly 100 percent of the cases were tracked as recommended demonstrates the prosecutor's commitment to learning what prosecution policy "makes a difference."

The initial tracking decisions provide the principal basis for evaluating policy. Successful randomization assures the most rigorous evaluation of policy possible. Of course, there is no guarantee that stated policy will be implemented as intended. By the time a case comes to court, some months later, a prosecutor may have reason to ignore the initial tracking recommendation. Perhaps the defendant has harassed or committed new violence against the victim and thereby motivated the prosecutor to seek a harsher punishment than recommended. Perhaps a plea bargain is struck that might ensure a conviction with punishment other than recommended, in the interest of guaranteeing at least the conviction. A victim, a defendant, or his attorney may argue successfully against the prosecutor's recommendation. Perhaps the trial prosecutor simply does not like the screening prosecutor's recommendation and chooses to ignore it. Beyond prosecution policy, a judge may choose not to hear or to ignore a prosecutor's recommendations or request for disposing of a case. All such "failures" of policy implementation meant failures in the implementation of experimental treatments.

Indeed, successful ultimate delivery of experimental treatments as designed depended not only on the discretion of actors in the criminal justice process but also on the wishes of victims and defendants. In particular, the Drop Permitted and Diversion conditions call for the prosecutor to offer those opportunities to a victim and/or defendant. If the opportunity is rejected, it represents another failure in implementation of experimental treatments.

SAMPLE CHARACTERISTICS AND BASELINE DATA

This report of the IPE study relies primarily on victim interviews for evaluating effects. As we were unable to obtain interviews for all victims, our claim of "experimental findings" is only as good as the representativeness of the interview subsample. Accordingly, we expect the interview cases to reflect the distribution of overall sample characteristics; we expect the percentages of interviews completed under each treatment to match the distribution of total sample cases; and we expect to find no difference in the randomization of interview cases in comparison to the total sample.

Table 10.1 summarizes basic case characteristics by Entry Set and, where data are available, by Interview and Total samples within Entry Sets. It shows that within Entry Sets, characteristics of the interview samples are virtually the same as those of the total sample. Although entry by victim complaint versus On-Scene Arrest was not randomized, there are few differences in case characteristics

Table 10.1
Characteristics of Victims and Defendants by Entry Set

	Intake Set			
	Victim Complaint		On-Scene Arrest	
	Interview Sample	Total Sample	Interview Sample	Total Sample
Defendant Race				
White	54%	54%	58%	60%
Non-white	46	46	42	40
	(324)	(480)	(106)	(198)
Victim Race				
White	55%	55%	59%	61%
Non-white	45	45	41	39
	(324)	(480)	(106)	(197)
Defendant Mean Age	30.7	30.8	30.6	30.9
	(324)	(480)	(106)	(198)
Victim Mean Age	28.7	28.7	28.0	28.2
	(324)	(479)	(104)	(194)
Conjugal Status				
Married, Cohabiting	31%		41%	
Married, Separated	8		7	
Divorced	9		5	
Unmarried, Cohabiting	20		27	
Previously Cohabited	25		14	
Children Only	6		7	
	(324)		(106)	
Couple has One Child or More	61%		61%	
	(324)		(106)	
Defendant Non-HS Graduate	41%		40%	
	(306)		(101)	
Victim Non-HS Graduate	36%		42%	
	(324)		(106)	
Defendant Unemployed	24%		31%	
	(324)		(106)	
Victim Unemployed	41%		48%	
	(324)		(106)	
Defendant Criminal History				
No Criminal History	24%	26%	23%	26%
Violent Crimes	20	20	19	23
Other Crimes only	56	54	58	51
	(324)	(480)	(106)	(198)

Note: Figures in parentheses are the base Ns for the corresponding statistics.

Table 10.2
Percentage of Victims Interviewed, by Randomized Recommendations for Prosecutorial Action

Intake Set	Randomized Recommended Prosecutorial Track			
	Drop Permitted	Diversion w/counseling	Probation w/counseling	Other Sentence
Victim Complaint	68.3% (120)	69.2% (120)	67.5% (120)	65.0% (120)
On-Scene Arrest	---	66.7% (66)	50.0% (66)	43.9% [1] (66)

[1] The computed chi square is 7.35 [p(2df)=.025] for the 2 x 3 table from which this row is taken, with the other row combining cases that could not be obtained along with refusals under each prosecution track. When cases that could not be obtained are excluded, chi square = 4.03 [p(2df)=.13]. When refusals are excluded, chi square = 5.36 [p(2df)=.07].

across Entry Sets. What differences exist support the need to conduct separate analyses later.[7]

Table 10.2 gives percentages of completed initial and follow-up victim interviews, by recommended prosecutorial tracks. Each figure is computed on a base count that includes cases never brought to court (the defendant "disappeared"), as well as cases where the defendant was found not guilty. The table shows that approximately equal proportions of victims whose charges were initiated by complaints to the prosecutor's office were interviewed at both stages under each treatment. What differences exist occur among victims from On-Scene Arrest cases. These women were generally more difficult to locate than were those who initiated charges on their own. Some had not wanted their abusers arrested and resented any contact with the criminal justice system. Undoubtedly, some victims saw our interviewers as people who were sufficiently close to the system that they should be avoided (after all, the researchers had access to police records that enabled them to identify domestic violence cases).

Tables 10.3 and 10.4 show, for each Entry Set, how cases were ultimately "settled" in court under the recommended treatments. The pair of figures in each cell allows comparison of outcomes for the interview subsample with those for the total sample. The close correspondence between pairs of percentages in each cell demonstrates that the cases in the interview subsample represent the same implementation of randomized treatments as does the total sample. The tables support our contention that the cases with completed interviews constitute a representative and suitably randomized subsample of cases, at least of Victim Complaint cases.

The tables also provide a complete picture of expected outcomes under policies enacted in Marion County. They show the effects of randomized policy tracks

Table 10.3

Case Outcomes upon Settlement in Court by Randomized Recommendations for Prosecutorial Action to Track Cases Initiated by Victim Complaint toward Specified Outcomes (Showing Within-Cell Comparison of Interview versus Total Sample)

	Randomized Recommended Prosecutorial Track			
Court Settlement	Drop Permitted	Diversion w/counseling	Probation w/counseling	Other Sentence
Case Dismissed	1% 9%	1% 4%	9% 16%	9% 12%
Permissible Victim Drop	46 45	0 0	0 0	0 0
Diversion w/counseling	17 14	82 75	4 3	1 2
Probation w/counseling	10 12	6 8	69 64	8 8
Other Sentence	20 15	8 8	6 7	78 74
Not Guilty	6 5	2 4	12 11	4 4
Interview Sample Total Sample	(82) (112)	(83) (112)	(81) (116)	(78) (112)

on case settlements. For example, when prosecutors allow victims to drop charges but otherwise encourage and support victim efforts to prosecute, 46 percent will actually drop. In brief, the tables show what will happen to a case in the "real world," given specific prosecution policies.

After an average of 141 days leading up to settlement in court, there is bound to be considerable discrepancy between the randomized treatment recommendation and the actual case outcome. About 7 percent of all cases were found "not guilty." Another 7 percent were dismissed for reasons other than a direct victim request, as permitted under the experimental drop condition. Generally these were dismissed because the victim failed to appear as a witness (typically after at least one continuance to find her) or because the victim outright refused to cooperate in the prosecution of her abusive partner. The overall correspondence between designed and ultimately delivered treatments approaches 70 percent.

ANALYSIS AND FINDINGS

In this section we analyze the effectiveness of the four prosecution policies in reducing the chance of new violent episodes during two distinct time frames,

Table 10.4
Case Outcomes upon Settlement in Court by Randomized Recommendations for Prosecutorial Action to Track Cases Initiated by Warrantless On-Scene Arrest toward Specified Outcomes (Showing Within-Cell Comparison of Interview versus Total Sample)

Court Settlement	Drop Permitted	Diversion w/counseling	Probation w/counseling	Other Sentence
		Randomized Recommended Prosecutorial Track		
Case Dismissed	--	9%	24%	14%
	--	13%	27%	21%
Permissible Victim Drop	--	--	--	--
	--	--	--	--
Diversion w/counseling	--	73	0	0
	--	67	2	2
Probation w/counseling	--	7	61	3
	--	6	48	6
Other Sentence	--	7	15	63
	--	5	14	59
Not Guilty	--	5	0	21
	--	10	9	13
Interview Sample		(44)	(33)	(29)
Total Sample		(63)	(64)	(63)

before settlement and six months after settlement of the case in court. We refer to three different measures of violence: official records, victim reports in response to a direct interview question, and victim reports in response to items on the Conflict Tactics Scale (CTS) (Straus 1979; see the Appendix for a description of CTS violence measures).

Primary analyses rely on interview responses. We found the official reports to be least satisfactory for statistical purposes because there are relatively few such reports and because the opportunity to report is related to the treatments. For example, a victim who drops charges has severed her formal tie to the criminal justice system and cannot expect more aid short of initiating new charges. In contrast, a victim whose batterer is on probation will generally feel protected by the system insofar as a new complaint can be acted on by the probation department without her having to file new charges.

A major finding emerges from initial analyses: In Indianapolis, prosecutorial action on a case, that is, accepting charges and proceeding through an initial hearing in court, significantly reduces the chance of further violence within six months of the time that the case is settled (by dismissal, by acceptance of diversion agreement, by conviction, or by a finding of not guilty). Table 10.5

Table 10.5

Percentage of Interviewed Victims Reporting a History of Defendant Violence against Them, by Entry Set

	Intake Set	
	Victim Complaint N - 324	On-Scene Arrest N - 106
Victim Report of Any Previous Violence		
In 6 months prior to intake	72%	75%
Ever during relationship	91%	86%
Victim Report of CTS Violence[1]		
In 6 months prior to intake	96%	94%
Ever during relationship	98%	96%
Victim Report of Severe CTS Violence[2]		
In 6 months prior to intake	86%	81%
Ever during relationship	90%	85%

---

[1] Conflict Tactic Scale Violence -- victim responded to at least one item from the total scale set (see Appendix).

[2] Severe Conflict Tactic Scale Violence -- victim responded to at least one item from the "severe" subset (see Appendix).

gives baseline violence data both for the entire relationship and for the six-month period leading up to the violent study incident. The rates demonstrate that over 85 percent of IPE victims had experienced violent episodes prior to the study incident, regardless of how the violence is measured. In the six months prior to the study incident, no less than 70 percent of the women were victimized. And when measured by the CTS, over 90 percent experienced some violence, with over 80 percent reporting severe CTS violence.

Based on rates of violence in the six months preceding the incident prosecuted, there is at least a 50 percent reduction in the prevalence of violence committed by IPE defendants in the six months following case settlement, disregarding specific treatments and Entry Sets. More notably, for cases initiated by victim complaints, there is a 66 percent reduction in general CTS violence and a 78 percent drop in severe CTS violence committed by defendants. The corresponding figures for cases entering the system by on-scene arrest are 59 percent and 68 percent. Bringing a defendant to court, even if his case is not adjudicated, provides his victim with a lower risk of recurring violence within six months of case settlement than expected, given her preprosecution experience. The preventive effect is even greater, given prior experience with severe CTS violence.

We now turn to an analysis of specific prosecutorial tracks in order to determine whether one prosecution policy is more effective than another, within specified time frames, Pre-Settlement (the time between filing and settlement in court) and Six Months Post-Settlement (the six-month period following settlement).

Pre-Settlement Violence

Incredibly, victims reported that over 30 percent of the VC defendants and 20 percent of the OSA defendants facing adjudication had committed new acts of violence even before their cases had gone to trial. Can any policy reduce the chance of pre-settlement violence?

Alternative prosecution tracks create different conditions and opportunities for renewed violence, even before a case is settled. This is due in part to the amount of information available to a defendant concerning the likely outcome of his case. Under a Drop Permitted policy, a victim may acknowledge her ability to drop charges in the course of bargaining with the defendant for her security (Ford 1984). Under the Diversion policy, a prosecutor will generally offer the opportunity for diversion by letter or at the defendant's initial hearing in court. Other tracked outcomes may be revealed during plea negotiations. Not surprisingly, therefore, we find that the chance of pre-settlement violence varies by prosecutorial policy, as shown in Table 10.6.

For VC cases, the Drop Permitted policy results in the lowest rate of pre-settlement violence, followed closely by Diversion, for any measure of violence. There are no such significant differences by Prosecutorial Tracks for OSA cases.

The pre-settlement experience has treatment-related impacts other than violence. There are circumstances in a couple's relationship susceptible to influence by prosecutorial policy and related to violence. For instance, alternative policies result in differences in the number of court continuances and thus in the numbers of days from case filing to settlement. The longer a case is awaiting court action, the more opportunity there is, in terms of available time, for violence. The more court appearances, the more attention, forced contact, and perhaps resentment between the victim and defendant, all of which raise the potential for violent conflict. Above all, different prosecution policies may have a direct impact on whether or not a couple chooses to cohabit prior to case settlement. Although cohabitation is not a necessary condition for violence, it enhances the chance of violence by simply providing the time for victim-defendant exposure in face-to-face situations. If they do live together for any time, the greater the chance of renewed violence.

To adjust for these intervening factors, we included them in logit analyses specified to model the policy impacts on the chance of pre-settlement violence. Separate analyses for Entry Sets revealed, as expected, that the chance of pre-settlement violence is a function of both opportunity and prosecutorial policy, as seen in Table 10.7. In terms of opportunity, those victims who cohabit with their suspected abusers at any time after filing and prior to settlement are at

Table 10.6
Percentage of Cases with Reports of Violence prior to Settlement in Court, by Entry Sets for Cases Settled

Source of Report	Intake Set	Randomized Recommended Prosecutorial Track			
		Drop Permitted	Diversion w/counseling	Probation w/counseling	Other Sentence
Official Record:					
Total Sample	VC	3.6% (112)	6.3% (112)	8.6% (116)	9.8% (112)
	OSA	--	1.6% (63)	6.3% (64)	7.9% (63)
Interview Sample	VC	4.9% (82)	6.0% (83)	6.2% (81)	10.3% (78)
	OSA	--	2.3% (44)	3.0% (33)	10.3% (29)
Victim Interview:	VC	12.2% (82)	14.5% (83)	29.6% (81)	35.9% [1] (78)
	OSA	--	18.2% (44)	15.2% (33)	27.6% (29)

[1] Chi square = 18.25, 3df, p<.001

Table 10.7
Logit Analysis of the Effect of Recommended Prosecution Tracks on the Likelihood of Pre-Settlement Violence, by Entry Sets

Variable	Victim Complaint			On-Scene Arrest		
	Coef.	t	p(t)	Coef.	t	p(t)
Drop Permitted	-1.21	-2.81	.005			
Diversion-coun.	- .96	-2.34	.020	.007	0.01	.991
Probation-coun.	- .31	-0.88	.381	- .53	-0.76	.450
Cohabited	1.09	3.81	.000	1.16	2.03	.045
Days to Settle.	.004	2.59	.010	.009	2.35	.021
intercept	-1.73	-4.29	.000	-3.11	-3.62	.000
Chi square =		38.46			10.73	
p(chi square) =		.000			.030	
N =		323			105	

Figure 10.3
Predicted Probability of Pre-Settlement Violence by Victim-Complaint
Defendants for Alternative Prosecutorial Tracks, by Days to Settlement

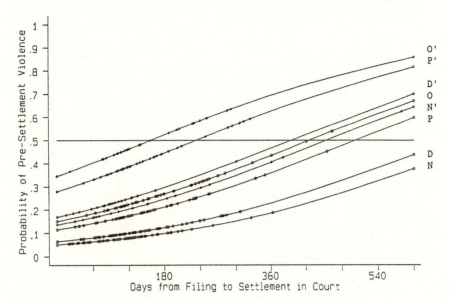

KEY: N — Drop Permitted and Did Not Cohabit During Process
     D — Diversion and Did Not Cohabit During Process
     P — Probation and Did Not Cohabit During Process
     O — Other Sentence and Did Not Cohabit During Process
     N' — Drop Permitted and Cohabited During Process
     D' — Diversion and Cohabited During Process
     P' — Probation and Cohabited During Process
     O' — Other Sentence and Cohabited During Process

NOTE: Points plotted at 0 and at 600 days are included only to
       identify policies.

significantly greater risk of new violence. The chance is further enhanced as the
length of time before case settlement is extended.

Controlling for these opportunity variables, we find that only among cases
initiated by victim complaint is there any significant policy impact. In the pre-
settlement time frame, allowing victims to drop charges or offering defendants
the opportunity to enter a batterers' anger-control program under a diversion
agreement will have a significant preventive impact prior to formal action on
their respective choices. Figure 10.3 illustrates the persistence of these relative
policy impacts for VC cases, even as the rates of pre-settlement violence predicted
by the model increase with time.

Each policy is displayed with two probability plots—one to show the chance
of violence when the couple remains apart throughout the pre-settlement period

Figure 10.4
Predicted Probability of Pre-Settlement Violence by On-Scene-Arrest Defendants for Alternative Prosecutorial Tracks, by Days to Settlement

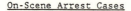

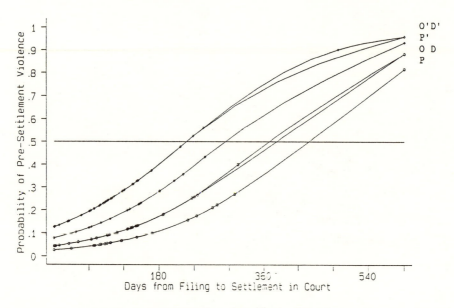

KEY: D = Diversion and Did Not Cohabit During Process
     P = Probation and Did Not Cohabit During Process
     O = Other Sentence and Did Not Cohabit During Process
     D' = Diversion and Cohabited During Process
     P' = Probation and Cohabited During Process
     O' = Other Sentence and Cohabited During Process

NOTE: Points plotted at 0 and at 600 days are included only to
       identify policies.

and one for the chance of violence when they cohabit for any time. Although the predicted risk is higher with cohabitation, Drop Permitted and Diversion are still relatively more effective in preventing pre-settlement violence.

Figure 10.4 shows a somewhat different pattern of effects for defendants arrested on-scene by the police. First, we see the chance of violence increasing given a longer pre-settlement time frame. But recalling that OSA cases have no Drop Permitted track and that the other tracks were not significantly different in their effects (Table 10.7), only the influence of cohabitation is significant.

Six-Month Post-Settlement Violence

Do the pre-settlement policy effects continue through the six-month period following settlement in court? Or does the court experience with its actual sanc-

Table 10.8
Percentages of Cases with Reports of Violence within the Six Months
Following Settlement in Court, by Entry Sets

| | | Randomized Recommended Prosecutorial Track | | | |
Source of Report	Intake Set	Drop Permitted	Diversion w/counseling	Probation w/counseling	Other Sentence
Official Record:					
Total Sample	VC	1.8% (112)	5.4% (112)	2.6% (116)	2.7% (112)
	OSA	- -	1.6% (63)	1.6% (64)	6.4% (63)
Interview Sample	VC	2.4% (82)	3.6% (83)	3.7% (81)	3.9% (78)
	OSA	- -	2.3% (44)	3.0% (33)	6.9% (29)
Victim Interview:					
Direct question	VC	23.2% (82)	26.5% (83)	29.6% (81)	35.9% (78)
	OSA	- -	34.1% (44)	45.5% (33)	34.5% (29)
CTS-Any Violence	VC	25.6% (82)	36.1% (83)	30.9% (81)	38.5% (78)
	OSA	- -	34.1% (44)	51.5% (33)	31.0% (29)
CTS-Severe Viol.	VC	17.1% (82)	18.1% (83)	14.8% (81)	25.6% (78)
	OSA	- -	20.5% (44)	36.4% (33)	20.7% (29)

tions result in different outcomes? Table 10.8 presents the answer for data from all sources on incidents of repeat violence, by randomized prosecution policies. As before, those women who are permitted to drop charges are least likely to experience an episode of new violence in the follow-up period. Otherwise, there is no consistent pattern of policy differences for either VC or OSA cases.

The chance of repeat violence six months after a case is settled in court is presumed to vary not only with how the case was tracked prior to settlement but especially with how it is ultimately settled, given a particular policy. Our task now is to analyze further the policy effects, recognizing that the recommended treatment may not be delivered in court (refer to Tables 10.3 and 10.4). We proceed first by examining the impacts of actual delivered outcomes alone and then by treating the actual outcomes delivered in court as intervening variables

Table 10.9
**Logit Analysis of the Effect of Recommended Prosecution Tracks on the
Likelihood of CTS-Measured Follow-Up Violence, by Entry Sets**

Variable	Victim Complaint			On-Scene Arrest		
	Coef.	t	p(t)	Coef.	t	p(t)
Drop Permitted	-1.34	-2.14	.033			
Diversion-coun.	.23	0.61	.542	.31	0.54	.589
Probation-coun.	- .41	-1.04	.302	1.39	2.28	.025
Drop OK x Drop.	2.01	3.01	.003			
Cohabited	1.89	6.61	.000	1.03	2.20	.030
Pre-Set. Viol.	1.52	4.74	.000	2.03	3.39	.001
intercept	-1.80	-5.36	.000	-2.05	-3.56	.001
Chi square =		87.36			22.18	
p(chi square) =		.000			.000	
N =		323			106	

in the relationship between randomized policy recommendations and incidents of follow-up violence.

An initial set of logit analyses for both VC and OSA cases shows the delivered treatments alone have no statistically significant effect on six month follow-up violence. Nor do the delivered treatments serve to influence the effects of prosecution tracks as significant intervening variables. The only theoretically relevant and statistically significant influence of a delivered treatment is in the form of the interaction between the Drop Permitted policy and victims actually dropping charges. We control for its effect by including a dummy interaction variable for cases in which victims were permitted to drop and did so by formal request to the prosecutor. We also include dummy variables for pre-settlement violence and post-settlement cohabitation as controls in modelling the chance of follow-up violence.

The alternative six-month violence measures (direct question, General CTS, and Severe CTS) reported in victim interviews were used in each of several analyses conducted to evaluate prosecutorial and judicial effects.[8] With only minor differences, they result in essentially the same picture. In the analysis presented here, we use the general CTS violence measure because it appears to be sensitive to more violence than the direct question. It also reflects findings associated with more severe CTS violence.

Table 10.9 shows the results of the VC and OSA logit analyses for the impacts of prosecutorial policy, controlling for opportunity (''Cohabited''), predisposition toward violence (''Pre-settlement Violence''), and the interaction of Drop Permitted and Actually Dropping charges (''Drop OK × Dropped''). Within each model, the first two of these control variables can be seen to have significant promotive impacts: a woman who cohabits with her abuser for any time during the six-month follow-up period is more likely to be battered anew during that period; and a woman who has already experienced at least one new episode of

Figure 10.5
Predicted Probability of Violence by Victim-Complaint Defendants within Six Months Following the Settlement of a Case in Court

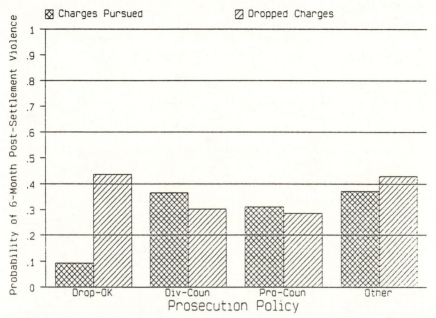

violence prior to case settlement is significantly more likely to be victimized during the follow-up period.

Defendants brought into the prosecution process following victim complaints are less likely to batter again within the follow-up period when the woman is permitted to drop charges. However, if the woman is permitted to drop and does so, she is significantly more likely to be battered again during that time.[9] No other prosecution policy results in a significant effect on these defendants' violence.

Figure 10.5 charts the expected probabilities of new violence for each VC prosecution track after adjusting for the intervening variables. Partialing for permissible drops, we see that the recidivism rate under a Drop Permitted policy is less than 10 percent. Put differently, victims who are permitted to drop but follow through with prosecution have less than a 10 percent chance of being battered again within six months of settlement.

Figure 10.6 breaks down the predicted VC tracking effects by post-settlement cohabitation and pre-settlement violence. While the general pattern of relative effects holds across all breakdowns, it is clear that either having already experienced new violence prior to settlement or living together for any time after settlement contributes substantially to the chance of follow-up violence. It is

Figure 10.6
Predicted Probability of Violence by Victim-Complaint Defendants within Six Months Following the Settlement of a Case in Court, by Pre-Settlement Violence and Post-Settlement Cohabitation

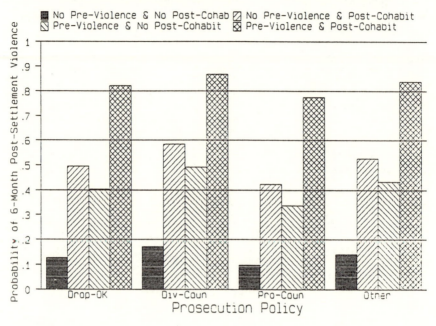

especially remarkable that cohabitation carries a higher risk than having been battered by a man "under the control" of the prosecution process.[10]

Referring again to Table 10.9, we find quite a different result for defendants who entered the system by an on-scene police arrest. After controlling for cohabitation and pre-settlement violence, only Probation with Counseling is found to have a significant impact, and its effect is in the direction of *promoting* new violence. That is, a suspect arrested by the police at the scene of his crime who is then prosecuted with the goal of getting a conviction with sentencing to anger-control counseling is significantly more likely to batter his partner within six months of his case being settled in court than had he not been so processed.[11]

Figure 10.7 shows the predicted chance of new violence given pre-settlement violence and/or post-settlement cohabitation, by prosecution policy. Although the chance of new violence associated with cohabitation appears to be somewhat lower than for VC victims, the OSA women do risk a chance of follow-up violence which approaches or exceeds 80 percent regardless of prosecution policy.

As we turn to discuss some implications of Indianapolis Prosecution Experiment findings, several caveats are in order. First, our evaluation of prosecution policies does not address the actual treatments experienced by a defendant. When

Figure 10.7
Predicted Probability of Violence by On-Scene-Arrest Defendants within Six Months Following the Settlement of a Case in Court, by Pre-Settlement Violence and Post-Settlement Cohabitation

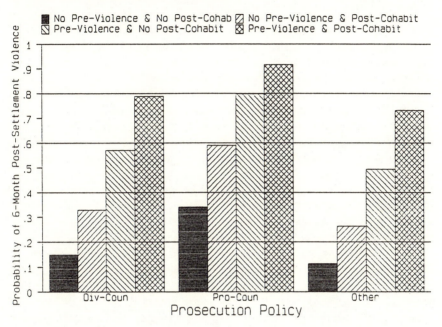

we describe the impact of a policy calling for prosecution to conviction, we are talking about the prosecutor's intention to seek that end. In fact, the policy may not result in prosecution at all, as we saw in Tables 10.3 and 10.4. "Real-world contingencies" result in misimplementation of policy, i.e., an untracking of prosecutorial plans. The finding that some policies will have low rates of implementation is itself a notable outcome.

Second, and closely related as an evaluation concern, treatment content may not be what was intended. For example, we have found that a policy calling for counseling as a condition of probation is relatively ineffective. This does not necessarily mean that counseling under probation is ineffective as a rehabilitative treatment. Even after sentencing, a defendant may never receive treatment because program space is unavailable, his probation term is less than the treatment period, or he simply fails to comply and no one pays attention.

Finally, though it is tempting to compare the relative effects for Victim Complaint cases against those for On-Scene Arrests, we have not tried to establish equivalency as we might under a quasi-experimental design. The extent of our comparative findings is that within Entry Sets there are no significant effects among the No-Drop policy alternatives. Moreover, it must be emphasized that we have not evaluated a Drop Permitted policy for On-Scene Arrests. We cannot extrapolate from the finding for VC cases to OSA cases.

DISCUSSION

Is prosecutorial and judicial action effective in preventing wife battery? Yes. Even if a suspected wife batterer is only brought to court for an initial hearing, the chance of his committing new violence six months after his case is settled will decrease, no matter which specific interventions he may experience. Of course, this does not mean that every defendant will be so deterred. Some may retaliate; others may be unaffected. But given the high proportion of cases with violence in the six months before intervention, we would have predicted much higher rates of new incidents than occurred in the six months after settlement.

Is prosecution tracked to adjudication more effective in preventing violence than offering victims or defendants opportunities to avoid a trial? Apparently not, except in the limited case of a woman filing charges under the Drop Permitted policy and not dropping. That she is at lower risk following adjudication than victims who could not drop suggests that the preventive policy impact derives from her power to drop rather than from judicial action. Although we have argued elsewhere that victims are empowered when they are permitted to drop, we do not claim to understand the mechanism responsible for the effect found in this analysis. There is a clear need for more research on the dynamics of the victim-defendant-system triad, not only to learn why those who follow through gain security but especially to learn why those who drop are at greater risk.

To that end, we speculate that victims are empowered not only by their ability to drop charges but also by their alliance with criminal justice agencies. Threatened sanctions for continuing abuse, whether made explicitly by victims or implicitly by the attention of the state, are made credible by the state's willingness to exercise its power. As long as the alliance holds, as when a victim does not drop charges, she should find protection. But the alliance must also be potent, as would be demonstrated, for example, by a decisive system response on behalf of a victim battered prior to case settlement.

A decisive system response to any violation of conditions for pretrial release, including of course new violence, should serve notice that the victim-system alliance is strong. It tells the defendant that the victim is serious in her resolve to end the violence and that the system is unwavering in its support of her interest in securing protection. We have seen that pre-settlement violence predicts post-settlement violence. To protect victims, it is incumbent on the police, prosecutor, and courts to take such incidents seriously. The policy impacts after settlement may depend on how well agencies can control batterers while they are in the system. Control need not be effected through reactive sanctions. The prosecutor and court can remove opportunities for continuing violence through such actions as ordering conditions for child visitation and confiscating weapons.

The risk associated with cohabitation is at once obvious and distressing. If one assumes that, given the opportunity, a batterer will continue battering a victim, one should expect cohabitation to bring more violence. Of course, women who long ago left their abusers may still be subject to violence. But for Indianapolis victims who seek relief through criminal justice intervention, continued cohabitation carries the higher chance of new violence. This is not to advocate that women leave their abusers. The act of separating may carry such a high risk for fatal violence that only a victim in her unique circumstances can know the impact of leaving. Our findings, however, suggest that women who have already left and have appealed to criminal justice agencies for protection should be supported for their decision and not encouraged to return.

Indeed, the system may both enable and facilitate separation through such means as issuing and enforcing protective orders both before and after case settlement. Such orders may prohibit contact in person or by phone at the victim's home, her workplace, or even in public places and can be written to cover her family and close friends. Victim advocates can assist by making certain that a woman is fully aware of all the services available in her community to help her live apart from an abusive partner. These include emergency shelters, government assistance programs, and long-term housing.   Results of this experiment have direct relevance to policy for prosecuting cases of wife battery in Indianapolis. They may not generalize directly to other cities. Nevertheless, we believe that consideration of the general issues of system responsiveness and victim empowerment can guide policy-making preceding further research. A battered woman needs the opportunity to make decisions on her own life course with guidance, cautionary information, and support from the agencies she trusts for protection.

NOTES

1. Though called the "Indianapolis Prosecution Experiment," the study covers all of Marion County, Indiana, most of which is Indianapolis.

2. A summons is an official notification to a suspect that he is scheduled for a court appearance on a particular date, usually about a month from the time it is issued. A summons is hand-delivered to the suspect by a civil sheriff. In contrast, a warrant is served in person, and the man is immediately arrested. However, if a suspect knows that there is an outstanding warrant for his arrest, he may avoid arrest by turning himself in at the Prosecutor's Office or at court.

3. Police in Indiana have discretionary arrest powers in cases of misdemeanor violence. Under the Indiana Criminal Code, a police officer may arrest for a misdemeanor battery that did not occur in his or her presence if the officer has probable cause to believe that a battery resulting in injury (Class A misdemeanor) has occurred and that arrest is necessary to prevent a recurrence.

4. The percentage distribution of alternative entry sets is an artifact of the experimental design, which called for a fixed distribution of cases to treatment cells. The study continued until all cells were filled under both entry sets. The total count of on-scene arrest cases is no doubt somewhat higher than obtained because further investigation of potential cases was terminated when all cells were filled. We estimate that about fifteen cases were

"lost" because they could not be identified as eligible prior to satisfying the designed count.

5. The term "prosecutor" is used throughout to describe any one of many deputy prosecuting attorneys who might have some involvement with a study case. As virtually all of the initial screening of cases was done by a female prosecutor, the pronoun "her" is used in this section.

6. That case called for "probation with counseling" but was tracked for supposedly harsher treatment under "other" presumptive sentencing.

7. The Entry Sets (VC and OSA) were not randomized and would not normally enter the experimental analysis together.

8. Reports of violence recorded in official records were relatively rare and thus not amenable to statistical analysis.

9. See Ford and Regoli (1990) for a complete discussion of this finding.

10. Whether or not the man and woman live together for any part of the follow-up period is not affected either by treatment or by pre-settlement violence.

11. This is the result of the relatively high proportion of cases dismissed under the Probation track. When we control for dismissals, we find a slight (nonsignificant) promotive Probation impact enhanced by the promotive impact (albeit nonsignificant) of cases being dismissed under this treatment.

REFERENCES

Attorney General's Task Force on Family Violence. 1984. *Final Report*. Washington, D.C.: U.S. Government Printing Office.

Bannon, J. 1975. Law Enforcement Problems with Intra-family Violence. Speech presented at the annual meeting of the American Bar Association, Montreal, Canada, August 12.

Bard, M., and J. Zacker. 1974. Assaultiveness and Alcohol Use in Family Disputes: Police Perceptions. *Criminology* 12:281–92.

Berk, S. F., and D. R. Loseke. 1980–81. "Handling" Family Violence: Situational Determinants of Police Arrest in Domestic Disturbances. *Law & Society Review* 15:317–46.

Berk, R. A., and P. Newton. 1985. Does Arrest Really Deter Wife Battery? An Effort to Replicate the Findings of the Minneapolis Spouse Abuse Experiment. *American Sociological Review* 50:253–62.

Dunford, F. W., D. Huizinga, and D. S. Elliott. 1989. The Omaha Domestic Violence Police Experiment. Final Report submitted to The National Institute of Justice for Research.

Dutton, D. G. 1986. The Outcome of Court-mandated Treatment for Wife Assault: A Quasi-Experimental Evaluation. *Violence and Victims* 1:163–75.

Elliott, D. S. 1989. Criminal Justice Procedures in Family Violence Crimes. In L. Ohlin and M. Tonry, eds., *Family Violence*. Chicago: University of Chicago Press.

Fagan, J. 1989. Cessation of Family Violence: Deterrence and Dissuasion. In L. Ohlin and M. Tonry, eds., *Family Violence*. Chicago: University of Chicago Press.

Fagan, J., E. Friedman, S. Wexler, and V. L. Lewis. 1984. *National Family Violence Evaluation: Final Report. Volume 1: Analytic Findings*. San Francisco: URSA Institute.

Field, M. H., and H. F. Field. 1973. Marital Violence and the Criminal Process: Neither Justice nor Peace. *Social Service Review* 47:221–40.

Fields, M. D. 1978. Wife Beating: Government Intervention Policies and Practices. In *Battered Women: Issues of Public Policy*. Washington, D.C.: U.S. Commission on Civil Rights.

Ford, D. A. 1983. Wife Battery and Criminal Justice: A Study of Victim Decision-making. *Family Relations* 32:463–75.

———. 1984. Prosecution as a Victim Power Resource for Managing Conjugal Violence. Paper presented at the annual meeting of the Society for the Study of Social Problems, San Antonio, Texas, August 26.

Ford, D. A., and M. J. Regoli. 1990. Empowering and Protecting Battered Wives through Prosecution Policy. Paper presented at the annual meeting of the American Sociological Association, Washington, D.C., August.

Goolkasian, G. 1986. *Confronting Domestic Violence: A Guide for Criminal Justice Agencies*. Washington, D.C.: National Institute of Justice.

Gregory, M. 1976. Battered Wives. In M. Borland, ed., *Violence in the Family*. Atlantic Highlands, N.J.: Humanities Press.

Jaffe, P., D. A. Wolfe, A. Telford, and G. Austin. 1986. The Impact of Police Charges in Incidents of Wife Abuse. *Journal of Family Violence* 1:37–49.

Langan, P. A., and C. A. Innes. 1986. *Preventing Domestic Violence against Women*, Bureau of Justice Statistics Special Report. Washington, D.C.: U.S. Department of Justice.

Lerman, L. G. 1981. Criminal Prosecution of Wife Beaters. *Response to Violence in the Family* 4(3):1–19.

Loving, N. 1980. *Responding to Spouse Abuse and Wife Beating: A Guide for Police*. Washington, D.C.: Police Executive Research Forum.

Martin, D. 1976. *Battered Wives*. San Francisco: Glide Publications.

Parnas, R. I. 1967. The Police Response to Domestic Disturbance. *Wisconsin Law Review* 31:914–60.

———. 1970. Judicial Response to Intra-family Violence. *Minnesota Law Review* 54:585–644.

Paterson, E. J. 1979. How the Legal System Responds to Battered Women. In D. M. Moore, ed., *Battered Women*. Beverly Hills, Calif.: Sage.

Rauma, D. 1984. Going for the Gold: Prosecutorial Decision Making in Cases of Wife Assault. *Social Science Research* 13:321–51.

Roy, M. 1977. Some Thoughts Regarding the Criminal Justice System and Wife Beating. In M. Roy, ed., *Battered Women: A Psychosociological Study of Domestic Violence*. New York: Van Nostrand/Reinhold.

Sherman, L. W., and R. A. Berk. 1984. The Specific Deterrent Effects of Arrest for Domestic Assault. *American Sociological Review* 49:261–72.

Straus, M. A. 1979. Measuring Intrafamily Conflict and Violence: The Conflict Tactics (CT) Scales. *Journal of Marriage and the Family* 41:75–88.

Appendix: Conflict Tactics Scale

QUESTION: And how about [MAN]? Tell me whether or not <u>he</u> has done any of
these things in a dispute with you in the six months following the case
outcome.

		yes	no	(IF YES) How many times in 6 months?	
a.	When you had a dispute, has <u>he</u> ever discussed the issue calmly?	1	2	_____	
b.	Brought in or tried to bring in someone to help settle things	1	2	_____	
c.	Insulted or swore at you	1	2	_____	
d.	Sulked and/or refused to talk about it .	1	2	_____	
e.	Stomped out of the room or house (or yard)	1	2	_____	
f.	Did or said something to spite you . .	1	2	_____	
g.	<u>Threatened</u> to hit or throw something at you	1	2	_____	
h.	Thrown or smashed or hit or kicked something	1	2	_____	
i.	Has he ever thrown something <u>at</u> you? . .	1	2	_____	General CTS Violence
j.	Pushed, grabbed, or shoved you	1	2	_____	
k.	Slapped you	1	2	_____	
l.	Kicked, bit, or hit you with a fist . .	1	2	_____	
m.	Hit or tried to hit you with something .	1	2	_____	
n.	Beat you up	1	2	_____	Severe CTS Violence
o.	<u>Threatened</u> you with a knife or gun . .	1	2	_____	
p.	Used a knife or gun	1	2	_____	
q.	Is there anything else he might typically do?	1	2	_____	
	(specify) _____				

11

THE COURT'S RESPONSE TO INTERPERSONAL VIOLENCE: A COMPARISON OF INTIMATE AND NONINTIMATE ASSAULT

Kathleen J. Ferraro and Tascha Boychuk

Kathleen Ferraro and Tascha Boychuk examined case declinations in 1987–88 for Maricopa County, Arizona (Phoenix), a jurisdiction where the state's attorney may refuse to take cases for prosecution. The authors believe that efforts to control battering must be placed in the context of the sociopolitical analysis of the nature of law. According to their analysis, the law tends to maintain a patriarchal authority with distinct race and class boundaries. Violence that does not disturb these boundaries is less threatening to the dominant social order than violence that crosses them and consequently is less likely to be negatively sanctioned. They believe that violence between intimates is punished less than other crimes not because of a sexual hierarchy but because of the typical social and racial homogeneity of victim and offender, compared to those who explicitly challenge the dominant social order.

Efforts to criminalize domestic violence may be doomed to failure because, they assume, crimes committed against those of the same racial and class background as offenders are not responded to as serious threats to social order. If this perspective of maintenance of the social order is proven correct in later research, pressures to increase the severity of responses to domestic violence crimes is likely to fail through informal methods of case dismissal, that is, by call screening as described in the Manning and Pierce and Spaar chapters, by diversion, or by the lenient sentences that Ferraro and Boychuk describe. The methods chosen to test this theory compare the treatment accorded to suspects accused of crimes between intimates with the treatment accorded to those accused of having perpetrated a crime against strangers. They find very little effective difference in case distinctions.

Instead, the authors report their belief that violent acts between people of similar class and racial status are generally treated comparatively leniently in our society. They also believe that domestic violence may serve the unintended function of keeping the system safe by venting anger and frustration onto those closest at hand rather than against the structural sources of unemployment, poverty, and patriarchy.

The absence of protection for battered women within the criminal justice system has been a central concern of those working to end violence against women (Hanmer, Radford, and Stanko 1988; Martin 1976; Dobash and Dobash 1979, 1992; Schechter 1982). Between 1975 and 1990, police training and policies, state legislation, and civil suits challenged the traditional practice of nonenforcement of assault laws in cases of battering (Buzawa and Buzawa 1985; Ferraro 1988, 1989). Within shelter programs and in the literature on battering, women have been encouraged to call the police and to follow through with complaints against men who batter. Efforts to enhance the legal protection afforded to battered women have rested on several implicit and untested assumptions about the criminal justice system and the transformative potential of law. These assumptions are complex and interrelated and require a systematic analysis beyond the scope of this chapter. Our focus here is on the assumption that the enforcement of violent crime statutes in nonintimate cases is more swift, certain and severe than enforcement of cases involving intimates. The call to treat "domestic violence"[1] as a crime is premised on a presumption that other forms of violence are viewed as a threat to social order and typically result in sanctions against offenders. Explicit refusals by police and prosecutors to sanction wife beaters has created the belief among battered women's advocates that wife beating is not viewed as a similar threat and therefore is not treated with equal force of the law. Apart from some anecdotal evidence presented in the 1970s, there has been little empirical work comparing battered women with victims of strangers at the level of adjudication and sentencing. This chapter examines the presumption that nonintimate violence is treated more seriously than intimate violence in terms of prosecution, case disposition, and sentencing. We present data comparing case declinations for intimate and nonintimate cases. We then examine characteristics of cases filed, including relationships between victim and offender, cases involving sexual assault, and sex of offenders. We then present case dispositions and sentences, comparing various levels of seriousness, prior criminal records, and evidence with case outcomes. Finally, we return to the issue of efforts to "treat domestic violence as a crime" within the context of the contemporary criminal justice system in the United States.

METHODOLOGY

The Maricopa County, Arizona, County Attorney's office provided information on case declinations for 1987 and prosecutions for 1987 and 1988. A computer printout generated from the felony offenses filed between June 1987 and February 1988 by the county attorney listed 104 cases of violent crimes between adult intimates. These comprised the sample of violent intimate offenses. One hundred cases of nonintimate violent crimes were selected from an alpha-

Table 11.1
Sex, Age, Race, and Occupation of Offenders (N = 204)

SEX		OCCUPATION	
MALE	174 (85.3)	LABORER	29 (14.2)
FEMALE	30 (14.7)	SERVICE	8 (3.9)
		SALES/CLERICAL	11 (5.4)
		OPERATIVES	9 (4.4)
		TRADES	26 (12.7)
		TECH/SEMI/PROS	7 (3.5)
		UNEMPLOYED	69 (33.8)
		UNKNOWN	45 (22.1)
AGE		**RACE**	
17-25	76 (37.3)	WHITE	98 (48.0)
26-35	85 (41.6)	BLACK	26 (12.7)
36-45	27 (13.3)	HISPANIC	69 (33.8)
46-64	16 (7.8)	INDIAN	11 (5.4)

Table 11.2
Sex, Age, Race, and Occupation of Victims (N = 204)

SEX		OCCUPATION	
MALE	81 (39.9)	LABORER	11 (5.4)
FEMALE	117 (57.6)	SERVICE	23 (11.3)
MULTIPLE	6 (2.5)	CLERICAL/SALES	24 (11.8)
		OPERATIVES	3 (1.5)
		TRADES	5 (2.5)
		TECH/SEMI/PROS	33 (16.2)
		UNEMPLOYED	63 (30.9)
		UNKNOWN	42 (20.6)
AGE		**RACE**	
2-18	30 (14.9)	WHITE	114 (55.9)
19-25	57 (28.0)	BLACK	18 (8.8)
26-35	68 (33.3)	HISPANIC	54 (26.5)
36-45	27 (13.5)	INDIAN	10 (4.9)
46-90	14 (7.0)	UNKNOWN	8 (3.9)
UNKNOWN	8 (3.9)		

betized listing, matching as closely as possible the types of crimes involving intimates. There were nine categories of crimes including murder, kidnap, sexual assault, arson, aggravated assault, resisting arrest, criminal damage, interfering with judicial proceedings, and disorderly conduct. The last four categories, misdemeanor offenses, were lesser included offenses that became the final charge in bargained cases. Most of the cases (78.4 percent) were aggravated assaults. The prosecutors' files from these cases were then examined. The files included a summary of the outcome of the cases, prosecutor statements, police reports, victim statements, and, in some cases, photographs of scenes and victims. From these files, fifty-five legal and extralegal variables were coded concerning offense, offender, and victim characteristics and case outcome. The sex, age, race, and occupation of offenders and victims are presented in Tables 11.1 and 11.2. The variation in sentence outcome was too small to permit multivariate analyses.

Table 11.3
Domestic Violence and Nondomestic Case Declinations

MIDYEAR 1987 NONDOMESTIC		CALENDER YEAR 1987 DOMESTIC VIOLENCE		REASONS
280	(36.2)	188	(35.7)	SENT TO CITY
25	(3.3)	14	(2.7)	AID TO PROSECUTION
43	(5.6)	34	(6.5)	SELF DEFENSE
112	(14.6)	54	(10.3)	NO REASONABLE LIKELIHOOD OF CONVICTION
51	(6.6)	24	(4.6)	LIMITED RESOURCES
47	(6.1)	33	(6.3)	DR INCOMPLETE
51	(6.6)	19	(3.6)	DR NEEDS CLARIFICATION
20	(2.6)	69	(13.1)	V/W RELUCTANCE/REFUSAL TO PROSECUTE
47	(6.1)	19	(3.6)	LOCATE & INTERVIEW VICTIM
13	(1.7)	7	(1.3)	INADEQUATE EVIDENCE OF CORPUS
13	(1.7)	3	(0.6)	V/W CREDIBILITY PROBLEMS
0	(0.0)	29	(5.5)	COOLING OFF PERIOD
67	(8.9)	33	(6.0)	ALL OTHER REASONS
769	(100.0)	526	(100.0)	

Unfortunately it is impossible to dissect the respective contributions of legal and extralegal variables to the final case outcome. Variables were cross-tabulated and chi-squares and t-tests computed for selected variables.

DECLINATIONS TO PROSECUTE

At our request, the statistician for the county attorney generated a list comparing aggravated assault case declinations for domestic violence and stranger cases.[2] When declining cases, attorneys indicate which of thirty-eight reasons apply to their decision not to file (see Table 11.3). The figures provided did not specify the total number of cases submitted for either intimate or nonintimate cases, but only the number of intimate cases declined for the year (526) and the number of nonintimate cases declined at midyear (769). The most common reason given was that the case was sent to the city prosecutor. For intimate cases, 35.7 percent were rejected for this reason; for nonintimate, 36.4 percent were sent to the city. The bifurcated system in Maricopa County tries misdemeanor assault cases in the city court system and felonies at the county level. Over a third of the assault cases submitted were determined to be at a misdemeanor rather than a felony level. In Arizona, felony assaults are those resulting in serious and permanent injury or use of a weapon in commission of the crime. Although trying a case at the appropriate level enhances the possibility of conviction, the maximum penalty resulting from misdemeanor conviction is one year in jail, with the vast majority of cases receiving probation. At the city level, probation is unsupervised and therefore relatively meaningless.

The second most common reason given was "no reasonable likelihood of conviction.'' This was the stated reason for 10.3 percent of intimate and 14.6 percent of nonintimate assaults. This category seems to be a convenient catchall for cases that are weak for a variety of reasons. As the rest of the categories are specific in identifying weak points, this category must represent cases that prosecutors perceive as lacking in sufficient seriousness and evidence to warrant prosecution (see Littrell 1979). The next most common reason given referred to the inadequacy of police reports. For 10 percent of intimate and 12.7 percent of nonintimate assaults, prosecutors viewed police reports as incomplete or in need of clarification.

Despite inadequacy of police reports, inability to prosecute is blamed on the victim. The difference between intimate and nonintimates on victim reluctance to prosecute was larger than for any other category, 13.1 percent of intimates and 2.6 percent of nonintimates. Less than 1 percent gave unavailability of victim as a reason for either group. The lack of victim cooperation in cases of intimate assault is frequently cited as the overriding problem with prosecution. Yet this problem is about as frequent as inadequate police reports, a problem seldom mentioned in accounts of low rates of prosecution.

Victim cooperation in cases of domestic violence is viewed as such a typical problem that prosecutors have established a ''cooling off'' period for such cases. Rather than file the case immediately, prosecutors hold the case until they are sure victims will follow through with testimony. This procedure was completely lacking in nondomestic violence cases, but was the formally given reason in twenty-nine cases of domestic violence (5.5 percent). In our data, the majority of intimate victims were cooperative with prosecution (49 percent). However, a large proportion of intimate victims did request for charges to be dropped once filed (39 percent). The reticence of victims to follow through with criminal prosecution of husbands, ex-husbands or lovers may be increased by a time period during which the offender, his friends, and relatives can put direct and subtle pressure on the victim to drop charges. If a cooling-off period is valid, it should also be implemented for stranger assaults, since stranger victims were unavailable in 27 percent of cases and requested that charges be dropped in 6 percent. If, however, it is a bureaucratic technique for eliminating the difficulty of working with victims who are emotionally and financially tied to their assailants, it would be helpful to provide assistance for the problems rather than discourage prosecution.

At the time of our research, the County Prosecutor's Victim Witness program was so overburdened that advocates could only be assigned to sexual abuse of children and severe adult sexual assault cases. There were not enough advocates to work with battered women. From these files, it is apparent that women worried about financial stability, social stigma, and violent retribution for their participation in prosecution. These concerns are absent for victims of stranger assault. The reasons for victims' reluctance to prosecute, however, are rarely addressed. The reluctance is simply assumed to be an inherent aspect of prosecuting cases of domestic violence.

As the decision to file charges was not the focus of this study, detailed information on the process is not available. However, the bureaucratic response categories checked by prosecutors suggest a high degree of similarity between declinations of intimate and nonintimate assaults. Similar proportions are sent to lower courts, turned away because they are "bad" cases, or rejected because of poor quality police reports. The only area in which there is difference is in the availability and cooperation of victim witnesses. We now turn to the characteristics of cases that were filed for prosecution.

RELATIONSHIP BETWEEN VICTIM AND OFFENDER

The primary independent variable of interest was the type of relationship between victim and offender. We categorized relationships as either intimate or nonintimate. Intimate refers to relationships where victim and offender were or had been married, living together, or involved in an ongoing sexual and romantic relationship. Immediate family members were also included as intimates. Nonintimate relationships were those in which neither blood ties nor sexual or marital bonds existed. Police report forms have a box that is checked for cases officers perceive as domestic violence. These perceptions, however, could not always be relied upon for our purposes, as officers frequently did not code lovers or former lovers as domestic violence cases. The separation of cases into intimate and nonintimate categories was not straightforward. Many of the cases coded as nonintimate involved individuals who were known to each other prior to the offense. Only 31 percent of all cases involved individuals who were complete strangers at the time of the crime. Of these cases, about half were assaults on police officers (15.7 percent of total). This tended to cloud the distinction between intimate and nonintimate. From the police reports, it was apparent that many of these offenses originated as assaults against a female intimate by her lover or husband. In the course of intervention, a police officer was verbally or physically assaulted. When the original victim displayed reticence or ambivalence about prosecution, the case was filed as an assault on the officer. These cases were considered nonintimate because the court ruled on the assault against the officer, not the woman. Another ambiguous category involved people arrested for assaulting someone romantically involved with a former partner (3.9 percent). These cases are related to domestic violence, as they were usually violent demonstrations of a man's need to control and possess a former partner by assaulting her new lover. Still, as the relationship between victim and offender was not of an intimate nature, these cases were included as nonintimate. Neighbors (6 percent), acquaintances (6 percent), and others (1 percent) made up the remainder of the nonintimate category. The intimate category also included some relationships that did not fit with our focus on adult sexual relationships. Family-member victims included three mothers, a grandmother, a stepfather, a daughter, and three brothers. We included these cases to determine whether there was a difference between the way crimes against family members and crimes against adult sexual partners were treated. The small number and diverse types of cases precluded a statistical analysis of this question. However, the longest sentence imposed on any offender was a seventeen-year prison sentence for a young man who shot and killed his stepfather. This offender was nineteen years old at the time of the offense and had no prior record of crimes. He and his friends claimed that his stepfather was abusive to his mother. He stood trial in front of a jury and was convicted of second-degree murder. All of the other cases involving nonspousal family members resulted in dismissal, probation, or brief jail time. A daughter who attempted to kill her mother was civilly committed, judged unfit to stand trial. Of the two young men who assaulted their mothers, one received three years' probation and the other's case was dismissed. The case against the young man who assaulted his grandmother also was dismissed. Of three assaults involving brothers, all received three years' probation, one received six months in jail and another, three months. These brother assaults were severe, resulting in a broken jaw, stab wounds, and severe head and body lacerations. Given the patriarchal ordering of the United States, we expected that patricide would result in the most severe punishment of all crimes. The one case in our sample was in fact punished much more severely than other homicides and other forms of violent crime including gang rape.

As in most crimes, the violent offenses in our sample were primarily intraracial. The majority of offenders were white (48 percent), and their victims were white in 86 percent of cases. Hispanic offenders made up 34 percent of the sample, and their victims were Hispanic in 58 percent of cases. Of all victims, Native Americans were most likely to be victimized by offenders of other races, with only 50 percent attacked by other Native Americans. Since half of the sample consisted of intimate relationships, and the majority of such relationships remain intraracial in the United States, the racial composition of the victim-offender relationship is confounded with the intimacy of relationships.

SEXUAL ASSAULT

Previous research on the processing of sexual assault cases has shown that cases in which there has been a prior sexual relationship are unlikely to lead to successful prosecution (Estrich 1987; Randall and Rose 1981; LaFree 1989). In fact, until recently marital rape was not illegal. In approximately 33 states, marital rape is now illegal under certain circumstances. In two states, however, the marital rape exemption has been extended to voluntary social companions (Searles and Berger 1987). In Arizona in 1987 and 1988, marriage was a complete defense to the charge of sexual assault, except when the couple were legally separated. In 1989, a marital rape law was added to the statutes. In our sample, there were fifteen cases of sexual assault or sexual abuse, six involving intimates and nine involving strangers. The intimate cases are unusual in that they passed through the stages of arrest and filing. They all involved some level of violence. None of these cases was dismissed. One case was the only case in the sample to result in a verdict of not guilty by jury. This was a case of a battered woman who had left her husband, stayed in a shelter, and then moved into an apartment. When she attended a birthday party for her son, her husband kidnapped her at gunpoint, locked her in his house, said he would kill her, and raped her. One of their children testified that their father pointed a gun at them and that she had helped her mother escape through a window after he fell asleep. The woman had a valid order of protection at the time of the assault. The man had a prior charge for aggravated assault. Both husband and wife were Mexican. A local magistrate testified that the husband had a high moral character. The jury found him innocent on charges of kidnapping, sexual assault, and aggravated assault. This case indicates that even when police, prosecutors, and judges attempt to impose criminal sanctions for marital rape, juries may still view sexual intercourse as a husband's prerogative, despite a valid order of protection, a credible witness, and the use of a gun in the commission of the crime. The three other cases of marital rape in our sample were plea bargained. Two of the men were sentenced to three years' probation, and the other to five years' probation. In all three cases, violence and/or weapons were used, and there was evidence of sexual assault. In one case, there was a tape recording of a call the husband made to the police department saying, "I'm going to kill my wife." In two cases the men had no prior records, and in the other the man had only minor convictions with fines and a short jail term for battery of a police officer. Two of the couples were Anglo and one was Mexican. They were all separated at the time of the offense. One victim specifically stated that she did not want the offender to go to prison because she needed the money from child-support payments. The other two victims requested counseling for their rapists.

Only one intimate case resulted in a prison sentence. A man was sentenced to ten years for sexually assaulting his live-in girlfriend. This man had a lengthy criminal record, including three years in prison for burglary, and five years' probation for terrorist threats. Earlier in the year, he had been psychologically evaluated and determined to require residential treatment for chronic polysubstance abuse and a passive-dependent personality disorder. On the day of the crime, he picked up his girlfriend from work and began beating her in the car. When they got home, he tied her with electrical cords, poured cough syrup over her and flicked his lighter about her head while he punched her and forced her to fellate him. Neighbors called police when they heard her screams. Police found the victim naked, bound and bloody, and the offender still in the apartment. The victim was pregnant with the offender's child at the time of the assault. Both man and woman were Anglo. The man took an Alford plea to the charge of attempted sexual assault. The woman first requested a lengthy prison sentence and later asked for help for her rapist. She received letters from the offender from jail describing the pain she had caused him and using the most foul language to degrade her. He also sent letters to his father asking him to convince the victim to drop charges, explaining how he would kill himself or be killed in prison. These letters were turned over to the prosecutor and were part of the file. In this case, the pressure and intimidation by the rapist was documented. Nevertheless, there was a note from the prosecutor in the file suggesting that the victim's request for help for her assailant was related to her earlier "exaggeration of events" in spite of the abundance of evidence to the contrary. In the other cases, where victims first stated a desire for a prison sentence and then requested counseling, it is impossible to know what kinds of pressures were exerted by the offender, other family members, and economic circumstances. Efforts to contact these women, and the others in our sample, were unsuccessful. The majority of our letters were returned with no forwarding address. The few women we were able to contact (ten) were either unwilling to be interviewed or were too busy to arrange time with us.

The other case of intimate sexual assault resulted in five years' probation, one year in jail, and registration as a sex offender. The offender was a junior high school boyfriend of the victim. Their relationship lasted only a few weeks. Ten years later, the offender came to the victim's home and begged to talk to her about his father's death. She allowed him into her house, and he then beat, choked, and raped her. She immediately reported the assault and had a hospital exam that confirmed the rape and the offender through blood, semen, and hair. She was also found to have a perforated eardrum from the beating. Both victim and offender were black. He was unemployed, and she worked as a professional. He had no prior criminal record. She fully cooperated with prosecution and asked that he receive a prison sentence. She moved to protect herself from him upon his release.

The sexual assaults committed by strangers are difficult to compare to the intimate cases because four out of nine involved fondling, one was part of a sting operation to arrest male homosexuals, two were threats, one was a violent rape, and one was a violent gang rape. It is interesting, however, to compare the sentences in marital rape cases with those for the one comparable stranger rape and one of threatened rape.

The second longest sentence given in the entire sample was a fifteen-year prison sentence for a violent stranger rape. A 26-year-old Anglo man broke into the apartment of a 19-year-old Anglo woman while she was sleeping. He hit her with a wooden club and raped her. He had no prior record. The woman immediately called the police after he left her apartment. They found the offender wandering in the parking lot carrying a bloody club. The woman received a hospital exam that confirmed sexual assault. The case went to trial, and he was acquitted of two counts of sexual assault and found guilty of aggravated assault.

A twelve-year prison sentence was given to a 27-year-old Mexican man who was originally charged with kidnap, two counts of sexual assault, and aggravated assault in the gang rape of an 18-year-old Native American woman. The man had one prior charge for assault and endangerment, with no disposition recorded. The young woman reluctantly accepted a ride home from three men. They drove her to a remote area, and each had intercourse with her twice while beating her with fists and stabbing her with a screwdriver. She was found wandering in a daze by a motorist who took her to the fire department. She received a hospital exam that confirmed the sexual assault, multiple contusions and lacerations, and a broken mandible. She identified one assailant in a lineup. He confessed and identified the other two assailants, who fled the country to avoid prosecution. This man pled to one count of aggravated assault and received twelve years of hard time.

The only other prison term imposed for a stranger sexual assault was for a threatened rape. A 27-year-old Mexican man lured a 25-year-old Anglo real estate agent into his home with the promise that his mother was inside and was interested in listing her house. Once inside the house, the offender locked the victim in a bedroom, threw her on the bed, and said, "You're going to get raped." The victim convinced him that the neighbors would know what was going on and that he would not get away with the rape. She was released and fled the house. The offender had prior convictions for fraud, theft, criminal damage, domestic violence assaults, and promoting prison contraband for which he received one year in prison. It is interesting that this single case of a minority male threatening sexual assault against an Anglo female resulted in a much more serious sentence than the violent rape of a black woman by a black man whom she had dated in junior high. It is also much more serious than the sentences given to men who violently raped their wives. Although this is a very small, nonrepresentative sample, the cases provide further support for the relationships between sentence severity, victim-offender relationship, and racial composition of the victim-offender pair. For sexual assault, in this sample, similar stranger assaults resulted in more serious penalties than assaults against intimate partners.

FEMALE OFFENDERS

Women's contribution to violent crime has remained stable for over twenty years, representing about 10 percent of total arrests (Pollock-Byrne 1990). In our sample, 30 offenders (14.7) percent were female. Women were victims in 57 percent of cases. Consistent with prior research, most women assaulted other women (Stanko and Hahn-Rafter 1982). Six intimate cases out of 104 involved female offenders. Twenty-five percent of victims were wives or ex-wives, and 2 percent were husbands. This is more evidence that women do not batter as often as men (see Yllo and Bograd 1988).

None of the intimate assaults committed by women resulted in prison sentences. Only one of the male victims desired prosecution and cooperated with attorneys. There was one homicide committed by a wife against a husband. The woman was 18 years old, her husband was 26. They were both Mexican, and both unemployed. The offender had no prior criminal record. In the course of an argument, the woman stabbed her husband in the shoulder. She did not think he was seriously injured and waited an hour before calling for help. He died from loss of blood. She pled to a charge of manslaughter and was sentenced to five years' probation, one year in jail, funeral expenses, and 100 hours of work.

Two other cases of threatened assault with a weapon resulted in sentences of probation. In one case, a woman claimed that her husband had beaten her two days earlier and she was tired of his abuse. She threatened him with a knife. She was 19 years old, he was 23, and they were both Mexican. Both worked as sales clerks in a convenience store. She had no prior record. She pled to a misdemeanor assault and was sentenced to two years' probation. In the other case, a 28-year-old Anglo woman pointed a gun at her 40-year-old Anglo husband. They were both unemployed, and she had no prior record. She pled to endangerment and received a sentence of three years' probation.

The three other cases involving female intimate offenders were dismissed. One was the only case of lesbian abuse in the sample. A woman called the police when her lover beat her. The victim did not receive serious injury, and the offender had no prior record. The victim did not wish to pursue prosecution, and charges were dropped. In another case, a 21-year-old Anglo woman broke a bottle over her Anglo ex-boyfriend's nose. She had no prior record and worked as a sales clerk. He moved out of state and did not wish to pursue prosecution. The case was dropped. Finally, an Anglo unemployed woman pointed a gun at her Anglo trucker live-in boyfriend. He did not want to press charges, and the case was dismissed.

These few cases of female violence resulted in minor or no sanctions. None of the offenders had prior criminal records, all of the cases were intraracial and intraclass, and only one victim wanted to pursue prosecution. The sentences given, especially in the one case of homicide, provide no support to the hypothesis that women who violate traditional female sex roles by committing violent crime against men are treated more harshly. They do, however, provide further support for the notion that violence between intimates is treated leniently, whether offenders are male or female.[3] We now turn to the bulk of cases, which involved neither sexual assault nor female offenders.

CASE DISPOSITION

The majority of cases were disposed of through a guilty plea (66.2 percent). When case dismissals are excluded, however, the proportion of cases pled rises to 98 percent. Only two cases resulted in a verdict of guilty by jury and one by judge. One case out of 204 resulted in a verdict of not guilty by jury trial. There was, however, a significant difference between the proportion of intimate and nonintimate cases disposed of through guilty pleas. Fifty-two percent of nonintimate cases and 79.8 percent of intimate cases resulted in guilty pleas. As would be expected, 82 percent of cases involving police officers as victims resulted in guilty pleas. There was also a significant difference in the proportion of cases dismissed. Overall, 32 percent of cases were dismissed by the court.

But a much larger proportion of nonintimate cases were dismissed than intimate (47 percent compared to 17.3 percent). The difference between the disposition of cases between intimates and those between strangers was significant (chi-square < .0002).

Case dismissal and disposition through guilty pleas may be one index of the readiness for trial of cases. That is, it would be expected that cases in which serious injury occurred, witnesses and evidence had been preserved, and offenders' prior criminal records were documented would be strong cases. Such cases would be less likely to result in dismissals, as the grounds for successful prosecution would be in place. They would also be more likely to result in pleas of guilt from offenders confronted with a "good case." It may be that intimate cases that reach the court involve a higher level of injury, evidence, and prior criminal offenses than those involving nonintimates. In terms of victim injury, 33 percent of intimate cases involved no injury, while 51 percent of stranger cases were not injured. This difference is not statistically significant but may have contributed to the more successful outcome of intimate cases. Comparison of case disposition with the presence of physical evidence suggests that this factor has relatively little influence, as 83 percent of cases dismissed had some physical evidence available. There was no statistical relationship between the disposition of cases and the presence of physical evidence.

The most commonly assumed reason for dropping cases of assault against intimates is the victim's failure to cooperate with prosecution. We did find that the participation of a victim as witness was significantly correlated with the disposition of cases (chi-square < .001). For cases resulting in guilty pleas, 60 percent of victims desired and followed through with prosecution, and only 2.3 percent were missing or unavailable. On the other hand, the case was dismissed when the victim was missing in 47.6 percent of cases and when the victim wanted charges dropped in 23.8 percent of cases. However, breaking the response of victims into intimate and nonintimate categories suggests that the stereotype of battered women's failure to cooperate is not entirely accurate nor relevant. Of all nonintimate victims, 27 percent were missing at the time of trial, 64 percent desired and participated in prosecution, and 6 percent requested charges be dropped. For intimates, only 7 percent of victims were missing, 16 percent said they wanted help not prison for their assailant, 33 percent desired prosecution, and 39 percent wanted charges dropped. The difference between intimate and nonintimate requests for dropping charges is significant, but it is important to recognize that 33 percent of intimate victims desired prosecution and an additional 16 percent were cooperative but stressed their desire that assailants receive help. This latter view of offenders was completely missing in the nonintimate group. In addition, the lack of victims' cooperation in prosecution was not always fatal to a case. In fact, of the cases where victims wanted charges dropped, 65 percent resulted in guilty pleas. However, in 16 percent where victims were cooperative and desired prosecution, cases were dropped. This suggests that battered women's participation as "good" witnesses is often unnecessary for successful prosecution. Of those victims requesting that charges be dropped, 70 percent had documented injuries that gave prosecutors leverage for obtaining pleas even without a willing witness. At the same time, cooperation of victims is no panacea for case dismissal, as 16 percent of cases were dropped against the wishes of victims.

SENTENCING

The punitive approach to battering is most inaccurate in the portrayal of sanctions imposed on successfully prosecuted cases. Sentencing decisions in our sample indicate that prison sentences are extremely rare even for felonious aggravated assaults. Only 11 percent of the sample received prison sentences. These were primarily cases of homicide, stranger rape, and severe battering. The modal category for years in prison was 1.5, with all but six offenders receiving 7.5 or fewer years. With good time and soft time, most of these offenders will spend less than four years in prison. Another 14 percent of offenders served between one and twelve months in jail, with all but nine spending three months or less. Jail was often combined with probation, restitution, and/ or fines. Probation was the most common sentence given, with 43 percent of offenders receiving between one and seventy months of probation. The most typical length of probation given was three years (22 percent). The vast majority of offenders paid neither restitution (82 percent) nor fines (88 percent).

The relationship between victim and offender was not significantly related to prison sentences for offenders ($t < .05$). The mean years in prison for nonintimates was .4, while for intimates it was 1.2. The average months in jail and restitution amounts were both greater for intimates, but fines were significantly greater for nonintimates (see Table 11.4).

CONCLUSION

What these data suggest is that people prosecuted for crimes of violence, whether against an intimate or a nonintimate, are treated relatively leniently. Although most cases are screened out through the funnel of the criminal justice system, at the point of going to court, 32 percent of cases are dismissed. For these offenses, serious enough to be filed as felonies, no punishment or penalty is imposed. If offenders are arrested for violent crimes in the future, their record will indicate no prior felony convictions, at least for these dismissed cases. For those cases actually resulting in a conviction, usually through a guilty plea, 43 percent will receive probation. Only 11 percent will spend time in a prison.

While some may view these data as an indication of the laxity of the modern criminal justice system, we do not take this position. The United States has one of the highest prison populations in the world, and Arizona is among the top five states in inmate populations. In 1989, there were approximately fourteen

Table 11.4
Mean Years in Prison or Jail, and Dollars in Restitution and Fines for Intimates and Nonintimates (means and standard deviations)

	PRISON	JAIL	RESTITUTION	FINES
INTIMATE	1.2	.93	651.00	10.00
	(4.2)*	(2.5)	(3951.00)	(41.00)
NONINTIMATE	.4	.18	223.00	35.00
	(2.1)	(.7)	(956.00)	(92.00)
2-TAILED T **	.078	.004	.285	.013

*Standard Deviation
**Separate Variance Estimate

thousand people in Arizona prisons. What is at issue is the response of the courts to interpersonal violence and its bearing on efforts to end battering.

Efforts to enhance the criminal justice response to battering have invested heavily in law enforcement. Laws and policies mandating the arrest of men who batter have been implemented in six states and at least forty-seven large cities (Crime Control Institute 1986). Civil suits have been brought against police departments for failure to arrest, with the largest resulting in a $1.6 million settlement and a made-for-television, prime-time movie (see *Thurman v. City of Torrington*). Though these efforts increase the chances that a violent man will be removed from the situation at the time of his attack, they are quite isolated from the rest of the criminal justice process. The most rigid mandatory arrest policy addresses only one aspect of the system. Requiring police to arrest when prosecutors do not file charges and courts do not impose sentences establishes a contradictory and frustrating mandate.

Hidden in the rhetoric about getting tough on domestic violence is the faulty assumption that nondomestic violence is treated as serious crime. These data indicate that it is not. Most violent crime in our sample was committed by people of the same social, economic, and racial categories as their victims. As Black (1976) pointed out and others have documented, horizontal crime is not viewed as seriously by the law as upward crime. Offenders closely related by blood or sexual ties to their victims were usually either given probation or had their cases dismissed. But so were offenders completely unrelated to their victims. Their links to victims were instead social, economic, and racial.

Efforts to control battering through criminal sanctions must be contextualized within a sociopolitical analysis of the nature of law. It has been argued that law functions to maintain patriarchal authority and male-dominated nuclear households (Dobash and Dobash 1979; Rifkin 1980; MacKinnon 1987). This may be true. However, the law also functions to maintain class and race boundaries. Among the vast numbers of legal violations that come before the courts, violent crimes perpetrated by people of the same social category as their victims are among the least threatening to these boundaries. They are regarded as a significant threat only when transgressing extreme moral boundaries, such as in patricide or brutal gang rape. Thus, a Chicana who stabs her Chicano husband to death is given one year in jail and five years' probation. A black woman who empties a revolver into her mother is committed civilly. An Anglo woman who smashes a bottle over her ex-boyfriend's nose and stabs him in the knee has charges against her dismissed. The overwhelming majority of offenders were male (85 percent), and their victims female (57 percent). Still, when women do commit violence against males, it is not automatically perceived as an upward crime and punished severely. Rather, the racial and economic characteristics of both victim and offender establish crimes of violence as nonthreatening to the dominant social order.

The only clear case of upward crime in our sample was the murder of a stepfather by his stepson. This case resulted in the most severe sanction in our sample, seventeen years. However, the rest of the cases occurred between people of similar economic and racial backgrounds. This, of course, mirrors the nature of violent crime in the United States, which is primarily intraracial and intraclass. However, the lack of interracial and interclass cases undermines comparisons and generalizations about the law's view of crimes of violence. A much larger and nationwide data base would be required to obtain this kind of information.

Intimate relationships tend to be established between people of the same social and racial backgrounds. Without denying the unquestionable sexual hierarchy that characterizes the United States, it appears that violent crime among intimates is treated leniently because of this social and racial homogeneity more than because of legal support for patriarchy. Otherwise, violent crime between non-intimates would be treated more punitively than that between intimates, and it is not. Instead, almost all crimes of violence in these data result in minor or no sanctions.

Given this information, it is not likely that calls to treat domestic violence as a crime will result in more and harsher punishment for men who beat their wives. Even the symbolic effects of public admission of wrongdoing discussed by Chaudhuri and Daly are unlikely to occur when almost all of the cases not dismissed are plea bargained out of court (Chaudhuri and Daly, this volume). They certainly will not be obtained in those 16 percent of cases that were dismissed in spite of the victims' requests for prosecution.

Perhaps it is relevant to reevaluate the strategy of relying on the criminal justice system to provide protection for battered women. Trying to make the system work for battered women as it works for other victims overlooks the difficulties of the system for everyone. To paraphrase MacKinnon (1983), law as such is not liberating for women. Neither is more law. Our data and analysis do not contradict MacKinnon's position on the maleness of law. The law does not address the fundamental sexual hierarchy that establishes the conditions under which women are routinely raped and beaten by men. The majority of our victims were women, and the majority of intimate victims were wives and lovers of their assailants. To characterize the law as "male" in this blindness, however, is to set up a difference that implies the potential for redress. However, these data suggest that the law does not address the fundamental conditions that establish the conditions under which neighbors, friends, brothers, and strangers are routinely violent toward each other.

If incarceration is used as a measure of disapproval, few of the violent acts in these data are strongly disapproved. A felony conviction does represent a sanction, even if the only penalty is probation. However, to victims who fear retribution, especially from intimates familiar with places of work, school, friends, and relatives, probation may represent meager protection. Examining the court's response to violence by men against men and by women against men suggests a high level of tolerance for such violence. Tolerance for wife beating in this context may simply be an extension of the more general lack of concern within the criminal justice system for violence that involves those of the same racial and economic group. The purpose of this system is to maintain the social order. Crime that does not threaten this order will be treated leniently if at all. The vast majority of crimes of interpersonal violence vent anger and frustration at those closest at hand, rather than at structural sources of unemployment, poverty, and pollution. Rather than threaten the status quo, they keep it safe.

NOTES

The authors would like to acknowledge the Arizona State University Women's Studies Summer Grant and College of Public Programs' Faculty Grant in Aid programs for funding this project. Thanks to Lynelle Blackwater, Andy Hall, Ria Hermann, Rob Schwartz, Rhonda Shapiro and Martin Silverstein for help in collecting and organizing these data. Thanks also to the Maricopa County Victim Witness Program.

1. Domestic violence is the term now in general use to refer to violence against a spouse. This term masks the fact that most spouse abuse is violence against women and is thus a politically loaded term. It is used in this chapter in referring to the rhetoric and bureaucratic categories of the criminal justice system.

2. Domestic violence is used in this section because it is the category used to generate information on case declinations. It is not synonymous with intimate violence as defined in the sample of cases filed because it excludes former spouses and lovers and current lovers who were not living together.

3. We are not suggesting that the majority of female homicide offenders are treated leniently. See Angela Browne, *When Battered Women Kill* (New York: Free Press, 1987) for a discussion of the sentences awarded women who killed their abusers. The majority received lengthy prison sentences. There was only one female homicide in our sample. The rest of the cases involved attempted homicide, assaults, or threats.

REFERENCES

Black, Donald. 1976. *The Behavior of Law*. New York: Academic Press.
Buzawa, Eve, and Carl C. Buzawa. 1985. Legislative Trends in the Criminal Justice

Response to Domestic Violence. In A. J. Lincoln and M. A. Straus, eds., *Crime and the Family*, pp. 134–47. Springfield, Ill.: Charles C. Thomas.

Crime Control Institute. 1986. Police Domestic Violence Policy Change. *Response* 9 (2): 16.

Dobash, R. Emerson, and Russell P. Dobash. 1979. *Violence Against Wives*. New York: Free Press.

————. 1992. *Women, Violence, and Social Change*. London: Routledge.

Estrich, Susan. 1987. *Real Rape*. Cambridge, Mass.: Harvard University Press.

Ferraro, Kathleen. 1988. The Legal Response to Woman Battering in the United States. In J. Hanmer, J. Radford, and E. Stanko, eds., *Women, Policing, and Male Violence*, pp. 154–84. London: Routledge.

————. 1989. Policing Woman Battering. *Social Problems* 36(1): 61–74.

Hanmer, Jalna, Jill Radford, and Elizabeth A. Stanko. 1988. *Women, Policing, and Male Violence*. London: Routledge.

LaFree, Gary. 1989. *The Prosecution of Sexual Assault*. Belmont, Calif.: Wadsworth.

Littrell, W. Boyd. 1979. *Bureaucratic Justice*. Beverly Hills, Calif.: Sage.

MacKinnon, Catharine. 1983. Feminism, Marxism, Method, and the State: Toward Feminist Jurisprudence. *Signs* 8(4): 635–58.

————. 1987. *Feminism Unmodified: Discourses on Life and Law*. Cambridge, Mass.: Harvard University Press.

Martin, Del. 1976. *Battered Wives*. San Francisco: Glide.

Pollock-Byrne, Joycelyn M. 1990. *Women, Prison, and Crime*. Pacific Grove, Calif.: Brooks/Cole.

Randall, Susan C., and Vicky McNickle Rose. 1981. Barriers to Becoming a Successful Rape Victim. In L. Bowker, ed., *Women and Crime in America*, pp. 336–54. New York: Macmillan.

Rifkin, Janet. 1980. Toward a Theory of Law and Patriarchy. *Harvard Women's Law Journal* 9: 83–95.

Schechter, Susan. 1982. *Women and Male Violence*. Boston: South End.

Searles, Patricia, and Pamela Berger. 1987. The Status of State Marital Rape Legislation. *Women's Rights Law Reporter* 10(1): 25–43.

Stanko, Elizabeth A., and Nicole Hahn-Rafter. 1982. *Judge, Lawyer, Victim, Thief*. London: Routledge.

Yllo, Kersti, and Michel Bograd. 1988. *Feminist Perspectives on Wife Abuse*. Newbury Park, Calif.: Sage.

LEGAL CASE

Thurman v. City of Torrington, 595 F. Supp. 1521 (D. Conn. 1984)

12

DO RESTRAINING ORDERS HELP? BATTERED WOMEN'S EXPERIENCE WITH MALE VIOLENCE AND LEGAL PROCESS

Molly Chaudhuri and Kathleen Daly

Although most facets of the criminal justice system are to a great extent severable from civil law, the response to domestic violence has included a considerable infusion of civil law concepts. The traditional criminal justice response that takes a crime from apprehension through prosecution to conviction and then imposes fines, imprisonment, and/or probation has been in practice ineffective because of limited victim-prosecutorial cooperation and the unwillingness of prosecutors and the judiciary to take crimes of abuse seriously. The typical result has been an inability of the system to maintain case prosecution through conviction. Even after conviction, the prospect of fines and/or jail may be inappropriate or even counterproductive, while probation, because of staff cutbacks, often lacks supervision.

One method now frequently used is the civil procedure of obtaining a restraining order to prevent further violence. A growing number of jurisdictions have made violation of these orders sufficient basis for an arrest. In addition, a few states, including Massachusetts effective in 1991, have made violation of a protective order subject to mandatory arrest.

In this chapter, Molly Chaudhuri and Kathleen Daly present a balanced view of the potential uses of such orders as well as their limitations. They describe the results of research based on the cases of women who received temporary restraining orders (TROs) from the New Haven Family Court. The researchers sought to determine the effect of TROs and found that they clearly had some deterrent value. Although offenders with prior convictions for violations of other statutes were found far more likely to violate TROs, the authors also reviewed the process by which TROs are granted.

Chaudhuri and Daly consider the mechanisms by which TROs may effect change in the conduct of the offender. They believe that the collateral effects of the TRO predominate to create an environment in which an offender will perceive that it is in his interest not to continue abuse. They found that police responsiveness was increased; that batterers were arrested; that the chance of women being battered again depended upon the prior criminal history, employment and substance abuse of the batterers; and that women were generally empowered to end the abusive relationship if they were economically and emotionally independent of the abuser. Other studies have shown that, in certain circumstances, TROs have not been effective, either because there is no mechanism by which police become aware of the orders or because they may be circumvented when used in isolation and without full commitment by the police, prosecutors, and courts. The challenge is to set conditions by which this potentially valuable tool becomes even more useful to the criminal justice system.

For the past fifteen years, feminist scholars and activists have documented the widespread nature of wife abuse.[1] A national survey of U.S. families in 1975 estimated that 1.8 million wives and 6 percent of married couples experienced severe forms of violence by their mates in that year alone (Straus, Gelles, and Steinmetz 1980). The authors and others knew these figures were conservative and told only part of the story: narratives of battered women revealed their horror, degradation, and pain (Dobash and Dobash 1979; Martin 1976; McNulty 1981; Pagelow 1981; Pizzey 1974; Walker 1979). Feminist demands for an appropriate legal response prompted changes in law, and to some extent, legal practice.

A common form of legal redress today is the civil protection or restraining order. This order offers a physically abused woman a temporary judicial injunction that directs an assailant to stop battering, threatening, or harming the woman and, where appropriate, other family members such as children. The order may have various names from state to state; here we term it a Temporary Restraining Order (TRO). Depending on the state, a TRO can be obtained in a civil or criminal court. If a batterer violates the TRO, he may be arrested (or a warrant issued for his arrest) and charged with civil contempt, criminal contempt, a misdemeanor of violating the order, or a combination of the three. In addition, the violator may be charged with any other criminal act carried out in the process of violating the TRO (such as trespass or assault).[2]

On a symbolic level, passage of TRO legislation reflects a significant shift from the traditional policy of state nonintervention in the reputedly "private" familial sphere; and in principle, it offers battered women state protection from violent men. But we know little about the TRO in practice. Which women invoke the TRO process? What are their experiences with the legal system? Does the TRO protect them from further abuse?

To address these questions, we analyze interviews with thirty women who sought a TRO from the New Haven, Connecticut, Family Court in 1986. We wanted to know whether batterers heeded or violated the TRO and whether police responsiveness to battered women changed after they received TROs. We also studied the women's evaluations of the legal process and legal actors such as police officers, attorneys, and the judge. Our research builds upon Grau, Fagan, and Wexler's (1984) survey of the impact of TROs, and draws from the larger literature on the police and court response to battered women. Summarizing the results, we find that about two-thirds of the men complied with the TRO during the two-month follow-up period, the police were far more responsive to the women's calls for help after they had TROs, and the women's experiences with the legal process were generally favorable. Compared with other jurisdictions studied in the 1970s and early 1980s, the TRO process in New Haven seems more routine, and the court more responsive. Yet, it is possible that police and court practices have improved in many other jurisdictions in recent years.

We shall first sketch legal developments in responding to wife abuse and describe the TRO. Then we trace Connecticut law and TRO process and give socioeconomic profiles of the women and their mates. The women's experiences—before and after obtaining a TRO and with the legal process—then take center stage. We conclude with a summary and discussion of the findings.

LEGAL DEVELOPMENTS IN RESPONDING TO BATTERED WOMEN

Under the guise of privacy rights and state noninterference in the "private" family sphere, U.S. common law permitted a husband to beat his wife unless it was "excessive."[3] In the 1870s, women's movement and temperance movement activists called for legislation to eradicate wife abuse (Dubois and Gordon 1984; Pleck 1979), and by the last quarter of the nineteenth century, a husband no longer had a "right" to beat his wife. Notwithstanding these legal changes, wife abuse continued to be justified or ignored by the police, courts, and general public (Pleck 1987).

By 1970 a coalition of feminist shelter workers, academics, and lawyers brought wife battering to public attention once again (Schechter 1982; Tierney 1982). As described by Tong (1984:141–44), several legal approaches were taken to protect battered women and control family violence: creating and enforcing criminal law and expanding civil remedies.

Criminal Law

Studies revealed that the police normally did not respond to battered women's calls (e.g., Bowker 1982; Berk and Loseke 1981; Walker 1979) and that battered women's experiences were trivialized as "noncrime" by prosecutors and judges (Stanko 1982, 1985; Vera Institute of Justice 1977). Such actions (or nonactions) were the focus of suits filed against prosecutors and police departments. Partly because of these suits[4] and the findings from the Minneapolis field experiment (Sherman and Berk 1984), a dramatic shift occurred in urban police department policies in responding to violence among family members. In 1984, 10 percent of the departments surveyed said arrest was their preferred policy; but by 1986, this rose to 43 percent of the police departments (Sherman and Cohn 1989: 125).

In addition to changes in police powers to arrest (see Victim Services Agency 1988, 1989),[5] states enacted legislation targeted at the criminal courts' handling of family violence (Quarm and Schwartz 1983, 1984).

Civil Law

Improving civil remedies such as the restraining order was the second major approach. Until the 1970s, battered women had to initiate divorce proceedings before requesting a TRO. This requirement and others (e.g., that a woman be married) were removed from state laws by the end of the decade. Before 1976, only two states had restraining order legislation specifically for battered women; but as Grau et al. (1984: 14) suggest, passage of the Pennsylvania Protection from Abuse Act in 1976 stimulated similar legislation in thirty-one states. By 1980, forty-five states and the District of Columbia had implemented special civil legal provisions for wife abuse (Studer 1983; Tierney 1982). By the end of 1989, almost all states had such provisions.[6] In addition to the TRO itself, states provide other related remedies such as temporary custody, alimony, and child support orders; temporary use and possession of property orders; and orders requiring violent men to participate in treatment or counseling programs.

A restraining order is an attractive option for battered women because the court is ordering a batterer to stop abusing the woman and the police may be more responsive to a woman who has a court order. TRO provisions vary from state to state, but in general, an order provides civil relief from physical abuse for battered women eighteen years of age or older. It is issued after a hearing on the petition and is of fixed duration, usually for no more than a year. If a batterer violates a TRO, he may be arrested for a crime, found in contempt of court, or both. The scope of a TRO can be restricted by how key concepts are defined in states' statutes. In many states, "abuse" means particular forms of physical abuse, and often excludes sexual abuse or psychological abuse; and a "couple" or "relationship" means a heterosexual couple, of a certain age or older, who have lived together.

CONNECTICUT LAW AND THE TRO PROCESS

Under Connecticut law, definitions of "abuse" and "couple" are more inclusive than in many states. "Abuse" includes forced sexual acts and threats to do harm, and "couple" may include lesbian or gay couples; the petitioner should be at least sixteen years old and does not necessarily have to have lived with the abuser.[7]

Restraining Orders and Protective Orders

Unlike most states, Connecticut has a dual system in which protective orders are issued in a criminal court and restraining orders are granted in a civil court.

Because states vary in how restraining and protective orders are defined,[8] we compare the two orders in Connecticut. A protective order can be issued, at a judge's discretion, to an offender who has been arrested in a family violence case in Connecticut. At arraignment in criminal court and as a condition of pretrial release, the offender may be ordered not to threaten, harass, assault, sexually assault, or attack the victim; the order may include a requirement that the offender stay away from where the victim lives or works. If the offender violates the protective order, he can be ordered back into court and the judge might raise his bond. Protective orders last only until the case ends (i.e., when the case is dismissed or nolled, if the defendant is acquitted at trial, or after the defendant is sentenced). Judges can, however, end the protective orders or modify them at any time before the case ends. Women are usually *not* notified of changes in protective orders or their termination. Although a woman may have a protective order, she may also want a restraining order because she needs an order that will last for a definite period of time and cover temporary custody and visitation of children.

In Connecticut, a restraining order is issued by a judge in civil court (family court) in a two-step process. In the first step, the woman (by herself or with the assistance of an attorney) files an "Application for Relief from Abuse."[9] She attaches an affidavit with the application, which describes violent incidents or threats of violence. The application is then presented to a judge, who may ask the woman some questions. A petitioner must show that she has been "subjected to continuous threat of present physical pain or physical injury by another family or household member" (Section 46b–15a). Because it is a temporary, emergency order, standard legal protocol in which both sides may present their stories is bypassed at this first step; thus it is termed an ex parte (or temporary) restraining order. The judge usually approves the application and, depending on the order, directs the abuser not to threaten, harass, assault, sexually assault, or attack the woman. The order typically directs a man to stay away from a woman's residence and, often, her place of employment. It may also order the man to move out of a residence that he has shared with a woman, and it can include orders for temporary custody and visitation of children.[10] Upon judicial approval, the clerk notifies the police that a TRO has been issued, and the batterer is served notice by a sheriff of the order and a court hearing date (the "show-cause" hearing). The sheriff's serving of the order is a crucial step: a TRO is not legally enforceable until it is served.[11]

The second step is the "show-cause" (or fourteen-day) hearing, which is scheduled two weeks later. At this hearing, both parties can present their version of events to the court. In giving her testimony, a woman may be confronting the abusive situation for the first time in public and, if the batterer is present, in front of him as well. She may also be subject to cross-examination by the abuser's attorney. In most cases, the man does not appear, and the TRO is continued for ninety days. (Technically, it is now a restraining order, not a temporary restraining order, but we will continue to call it a TRO.) At the judge's discretion, the period of time can be extended. If the TRO is violated, the woman would first call the police to report the incident. Then, she (or more likely, her attorney) documents what happened in preparing for a contempt hearing. If the family court judge finds the abuser in contempt for violating the order, then "the court may impose such sanctions as the court deems necessary" (Section 46b–15g). If the violation constitutes a criminal act such as trespass or assault (which it often does), then the batterer may also be subject to criminal proceedings.

Thus, in Connecticut there are some important differences between a restraining order and a protective order in terms of scope, time frame, and legal effect on abusers. But the practical effect of the orders on police practices is the same: whether protective or restraining, it is a court order. With its backing, the police are more likely to take a woman's call for help seriously.

Research Method

To assess whether restraining orders help battered women, we analyze interviews with a sample of women who obtained them. The women were selected by the first author, who observed courtroom proceedings in the New Haven Family Court in October and November of 1986. After a woman received a TRO (ex parte or at the show-cause hearing), she was asked whether she would be interviewed for a research project. Of thirty-three women asked for interviews, only three refused. We conducted a two- to three-hour interview with each woman the following week. Questions focused on the women's views of the police response, their evaluations of the judge and their attorneys, their assessment of the usefulness of the TRO, and demographic information about themselves and the batterers. The women also agreed to release their court affidavits, which helped to round out details about the violent episodes and demographic characteristics. Two follow-up phone interviews were carried out with each woman one month and two months after she was granted the TRO. The focus of these interviews was on whether the TRO had been violated and, if so, what happened.

Family Violence Law

At the beginning of the fieldwork, a legal change occurred. On October 1, 1986, Connecticut's Family Violence Prevention and Response Act went into effect. Among other things, the law says the police "shall arrest" persons who are suspected of committing a family violence crime. Family violence advocates in the state have interpreted "shall arrest" to mean mandatory probable cause arrest and have trained police officers accordingly. When the law first went into effect, some departments were prepared while others had not yet provided training for police officers. In New Haven, police officers were given training on family violence and its detection; at the time, a major concern was to avoid the mistakes made by the police in Torrington, Connecticut (see note 4). During the fall of 1986, we learned from several sources that some New Haven police officers were overreacting to the law by making inappropriate arrests of women, and, at times, bringing whole families to the station. Thus, one effect of the law on the sample of women we interviewed was that some of them were arrested.[12]

During our research follow-up period (December 1986; January and February 1987), the police may have been more responsive and conscientious in responding to women's calls for help, whether the women had TROs or not. We cannot know whether police responsiveness over the phone or at the scene was caused by women having TROs, the Family Violence Act, or both. Alternatively, because the Family Violence Act was new and focused on police powers of arrest (rather than on responsiveness to calls for help over the phone), there may have been no effect or an inconsistent effect of the law on police responsiveness to women's calls for help.

WHO OBTAINS A TRO?

The women obtaining TROs in our sample were 19 to 51 years old, the median age being 25 (Table 12.1). Compared with the New Haven population,[13] they were disproportionately black (53 percent) or Hispanic (30 percent); all but two women were involved with men of the same race or ethnicity, and four said they abused alcohol or drugs. Most women (80 percent) worked in fairly well-paying jobs such as executive secretary, bank manager, and department store manager. For the remainder, two were housewives and four worked in lower-paying jobs as clerical and sales workers. Annual incomes ranged from $10,000 to $42,000, with the median just under $20,000. Most women (77 percent) were married, but their average length of marriage was short: about a year and a half. The unmarried women had been cohabiting with their partners for periods ranging from eighteen months to three years. While 90 percent of the women had children, most had just one child. High proportions of the women had left their partners for short periods of time in the past. In describing the nature of abuse in their relationships, three women said they had been hospitalized from severe beatings (with a lead pipe, a piece of lumber, and a hammer), and four had been threatened with a weapon during violent episodes.

With the exception of race and ethnicity, men's and women's socioeconomic profiles differed. The men were somewhat older than the women, had fewer years of formal education, were more likely to have a prior criminal record, and were far more likely to abuse alcohol or drugs. The men were also more likely to be unemployed or to hold part-time jobs, but of those with paid jobs, their median annual income was just under $24,000.

Like Grau et al., we find that TRO-seeking women may differ from the larger group of battered women: they are younger, have completed more years of education, have paid jobs and earn more, and are in relationships of shorter duration with a history of separations. With a measure of financial and emotional independence from abusive partners, women who obtain TROs may be one step ahead of other abused women.

Table 12.1
Sociodemographic Profile

	Women (N=30)	Men (N=30)
Age (yrs)		
24 or less	37%	27%
25 to 30	57	36
31-39	3	17
40 or more	3	20
median	25	28
Race/Ethnicity		
black	53%	57%
Hispanic	30	33
white	17	10
Education (yrs completed)		
11 or less	40%	54%
12 or GED	33	33
more than 12	27	13
Employment		
full-time paid job	93%	60%
part-time paid job	0	17
unemployed	0	23
keeping house	7	0
median salary	$19,150	$23,500
Abuses alcohol or drugs?		
yes	13%	73%
Has been convicted of a misdemeanor or felony?		
yes, has prior record	0%	13%

	Couples (N=30)
Marital status	
married	77%
cohabiting	23
Median duration of the relationship (yrs)	1.5
Number of children	
none	10%
1	53
2	20
3 or more	17

BEFORE THE TRO: WOMEN'S EXPERIENCE WITH MALE VIOLENCE AND THE POLICE

The women were asked how many times they called the police for protection from an abusive partner before they sought a TRO. Their responses varied: 30 percent called the police once; 30 percent called five, six, nine, or ten times; and 40 percent called two, three, or four times. Their replies reveal that "battered woman" is hardly a homogenous concept: some women sought added legal means of protection more swiftly (or slowly) than others. What they shared in common was how the police responded to their calls. Officers would not come to the scene, or if they came, they were ineffective:

I tried to call the police so many times. But they didn't come a lot of the times, and when they did, they did nothing. . . . So I took out this order to stop him from beating me every night.

In describing what transpired over the phone, the women said they reported the nature of the beatings, their fear of being injured, and concern for their children's safety. Some simply wanted peace restored in their households, while others wanted the batterer arrested. One woman who had been so severely beaten that she had difficulty getting up from the floor to get to the phone, revealed some ambivalence about what role she wanted from the penal system:

I barely reached the phone. . . . I managed to get a hold of the police, and I told them exactly, blow by blow, what he had done to me. . . . I wasn't sure whether I wanted to see him go to jail, but I did tell them to get their asses over here right away before he got away or thought he could get away with beating me all night long.

Five women called the police wanting the batterer arrested, but the police would not come to the scene. The women were told that they were not "severely beaten" or that they lived in New Haven areas where violence was a "way of life," as this woman described what an officer said to her:

Listen lady, if we went to the home of every woman on Dixwell [a predominantly poor, black area] calling us to deal with a drunken husband, we wouldn't have any men on patrol to deal with real crimes. . . . Another arrest won't stop him from beating you up again.

Just as Ferraro (1989) finds in her research on police perceptions of battering, police officers regard violence as a "normal" and inevitable fate for certain segments of society.

There were other features of the violence that reduced the chances that the police would come to the scene: when the woman reported a verbal threat only, when a weapon or dangerous object was not present, and when only the battered woman, not others (like neighbors) called for assistance. This woman called the police after having been verbally threatened; she had been beaten by her spouse for years and knew the serious nature of his threats:

I could tell by the look in his eyes and that furious tone of his voice that he was going to beat the hell out of me. . . . I had seen that look and heard that voice so many times before, and I knew all too well what that meant. For once, I wanted to stop him before he got to me. I was so tired of always taking it, but the police didn't help. . . . "Has he hit you, ma'am? Has he actually done anything to you yet?" was all they asked.

Police response was expedited when neighbors also called. This may suggest, as one woman indicated, that the police respond to wife abuse calls primarily when the violence is disturbing the peace rather than when it is harming women:

The police only came when the people next door yelled at them about the noise. . . . Nobody seemed to care that I was on the floor bleeding everywhere.

But it may also be that, when neighbors call, the violence is especially serious, noisy, and has gone on for some time.

If the police came to the scene, the women said they were more likely to arrest a batterer when the officers witnessed him hitting the woman, when the woman had severe wounds and injuries, or when children were endangered. Some women criticized the police for seeming to be more concerned about the well-being of children than a woman's safety. As to the impact of serious injuries, one woman recalled:

I had called the police several times before, but it took the sight of my bloody face and legs for those damn pigs to do anything about him beating me.

When a batterer defied the police, either by verbal or physical retaliation, officers were likely to arrest him. But some women felt that in these cases, the officers were acting only to maintain their professional integrity and authority:

They had seen the house a wreck, the chairs overturned, the t.v. screen smashed, glass everywhere. Some had even gotten into my cuts. . . . I was crying like anything . . . but it was after he shoved the police out of his way that they finally took him away. They only worried that they might get hurt, but never mind me who had just gotten beat up and almost killed.

Arrest was not the typical police response. When the batterer was present, the police officers usually separated the couple, suggesting family and marriage counseling. If the batterer left before the police arrived, the police tried to calm the woman and told her to lock her door and to call the police if he came back to abuse her. Warrants were not issued for the men's arrests even when evidence was strong:

It was clear that he had beaten me up. He [the batterer] completely trashed the house. He had cut me all up and left me with blood stains on my clothes. I was disheveled. My kids were crying and frightened. My mother was there to witness the whole thing. . . . But the police just took my name down and said that I should call them if he came back. So they were basically telling me that I had to be beaten again if I wanted any kind of help from them.

Four women (and their assailants) were arrested when the police came to the scene. One woman "talked back" to the police officer, and in three incidents, the police saw the woman strike the batterer. Of her arrest for hitting the batterer one woman concluded, "The cops are all screwed up: they don't even know who the criminal is and who the victim is":

I couldn't believe he [the police officer] had the nerve to book me. Here I was all black and blue from his punches and with a broken ankle, and all I tried to do was defend myself. After I hit him [the batterer] once or twice, he didn't even have any scratches. I had plenty of marks all over me though.

For these four cases, charges were eventually dismissed against the men and women.

The women were clearly dissatisfied with how the police responded to them, both over the phone and at the scene. From a police perspective, the problems they face are threefold: they lack training, the law is unclear, and they are unsure if prosecutors or judges will follow through.[14] Yet, the women needed to be safe from abuse, and thus they sought other methods of protection from violent men.

AFTER THE TRO: ACCOUNTS OF SUCCESS
AND FAILURE

The events taking place in the two months after the women received TROs can be summarized as follows. Nineteen men (or 63 percent) adhered to the terms of the TRO; eleven (or 37 percent) did not. Two women said they allowed the man to enter their premises, and they believed they had voided the TRO by doing so. But, in fact, the men violated the TRO.[15] Of the eleven cases in which men violated the order, eight women called the police (one woman did not for fear of retaliation, and two did not because they thought the TRO was voided). Some women called more than once because the assailant violated the TRO several times. The police arrested two men at the scene; and later two men were arrested on other outstanding warrants. Warrants for the arrest of four men were outstanding, and no arrest was made.

During the two-month follow-up period, twenty women (or two-thirds of the sample) were not beaten or threatened by their partners. This rate of nonabuse for New Haven in 1986 is better than that reported in the four states analyzed by Grau et al. (1984) during 1980, although their study had a longer follow-up period (four months) than ours. Grau et al. find an overall nonabuse rate of 44 percent, but the rate was better for women who had suffered less-severe prior injury (56 percent). They conclude that the TRO is most effective for this latter group of women and more effective in curtailing verbal threats and harassment than physical violence. Our sample is too small to make such subgroup comparisons, but we can say something about the women's feelings of success with the TRO, their experiences with TRO-violators, and changes in police responsiveness.

Success

The women with success stories "managed to cope with the situation and go on with my life," as one woman said. She went on to describe these positive changes:

It is a wonderful feeling to be able to come home after work and not be afraid of being beaten up. . . . Just to kick back on the couch, have a beer, play with my child, to do what I want to do instead of having to cater to him. . . . No more making him dinner and always what he wanted to eat. . . . From time to time, I do miss him. . . . I did love him . . . but I do not miss the cuts, the bruises, the black eyes, the humiliation, and the constant fear. . . . The TRO has worked for me—he hasn't dared to visit me or beat me up again.

For the married women, there were new sources of tension because they were also involved in divorce proceedings. "But even with these worries," one woman said,

I am much better off now than when I had to be worrying if I'd be bleeding or even alive the next hour. You can never predict a man who beats his wife. You just have to live in fear every second of the day.

Failure

For the two women who believed they had violated the TRO by letting the man in, their reasons for doing so were economic and psychological. One woman said she needed cash to support her four children, and her abusive husband was her sole financial source: "The restraining order may stop the batterer from coming into the apartment, but the legal paper did nothing to help me pay for the rent, other bills, or food." Soon after this woman let the man in, he beat her. The other woman said she still loved her partner and needed to be with him:

I just wanted him to stop punching me whenever he damn well pleases . . . but I still care for him, miss him when he's not around. . . . We do have a lot of good times together. . . . I even love him after everything he's done to me.

This type of response, reported in several studies (Browne 1987; Ferraro and Johnson 1983; Loseke and Cahill 1984), reveals that some battered women remain emotionally tied to and in love with their assailants.

Of the eleven men who violated TROs, seven forcibly entered the women's premises: four smashed windows to get in (two also harassed the women at work), two broke down doors (one also harassed the woman at work), and one picked a lock. Two men entered by deceit: one used an old key, and the other was let in by a child. We shall elaborate a bit on these incidents. The most dramatic forcible entry was the man who climbed to the balcony on the second floor of the woman's apartment at two o'clock in the morning; he smashed the glass sliding door and entered her bedroom. Although this man yelled a lot at the woman, asking her how could she leave him, he did not assault her. (This man, the one let in by a child, and the one the woman let in because she desired to reunite did not beat their partners.) Two men who forced entry into women's residences by smashing windows did beat the women; and one came the next evening, beating and raping the woman.

As these examples suggest, there were multiple violations of the TRO by one man. For example, one man came to a woman's house four times, trying to convince her to take him back; he came with a dozen roses and chocolates in hand each time. At first she wanted to believe that he had changed, but he became violent during each visit. She threatened to call the police when he abused her, but she did not do so. The fourth time, when she was beaten "black and blue in the face," she called the police.

The man who picked the lock to get in a woman's residence had prior convictions for burglary, larceny, and drug violations. The woman painfully reported what happened next:

He said he just wanted to talk to me and hold me. He said if I took him back, he would never lay a hand on me again, and I wanted to believe him. . . . But I knew he hadn't changed. What made this time any different from the rest? . . . As soon as I tried to grab the phone to call the cops, he started slapping me and kicking me around.

For the two men who broke down doors to get into the women's premises, one was a former weightlifter and the other, a former athlete, "a star football player in his high school days," according to his wife. In both instances, the men sought revenge by beating their partners. Revenge against women for obtaining TROs fits these men's actions precisely: one woman said her assailant yelled about the TRO as he beat her; the other described the man as saying, "Nobody was going to tell him what to do in his own house." For the three men who harassed women at their jobs, their actions were not simply threats. One man "had the nerve," as a woman put it, to slap her and punch her in the work setting.

Although the numbers are small, it is useful to compare the men violating and adhering to the TRO (Table 12.2). Of the men who had a prior record of

Table 12.2
Comparison of Men Violating and Adhering to the TRO

	Violated TRO (N=11)*	Adhered to TRO (N=19)	Total (N=30)
Has prior record of misdemeanor or felony convictions (yes)	4	0	4
Abuses alcohol or drugs (yes)	10	12	22
Unemployed or part-time job (yes)	10	2	12
Race/Ethnicity			
Black	6	11	17
Hispanic	3	7	10
White	2	1	3
Number of times the woman called the police before getting a TRO			
once	0	9	9
2-4 times	6	6	12
5 times or more	5	4	9

*Of the 11 men violating the TRO, 8 beat the woman again.

convictions, all violated the TRO. (Note that none of the men with prior convictions had been convicted for family violence.) TRO violators were far more likely to be unemployed or working at part-time jobs, and they were more likely to abuse alcohol or drugs. There were no racial or ethnic differences. The women described the TRO-violating men as having a violent nature both in and outside the home and a general disregard for the law. For these men, a TRO has little impact. As one woman said, it is "just another piece of paper from the cops not to take seriously."

An intriguing finding shown in Table 12.2 is the relationship between the number of times the woman called the police and whether the man violated the TRO. For all nine women who called the police once, the man adhered to the TRO; but when women called two or more times, about half the men complied. We think this finding needs to be interpreted in the context of couple dynamics and the extent to which couples take the law seriously. If a woman calls the police once, is not satisfied, and then takes steps to obtain a TRO, she not only expects effective state intervention but also is ready to end the relationship. Perhaps the men in these relationships take both the law and their mates' actions seriously. We do not wish to overstate this finding, but we think it suggests the following: those women who take action quickly, that is, obtain a TRO soon after making one call to the police, stand a lower chance of being abused by their mates again.

Police Responsiveness

Eight of eleven women called the police when men violated the TRO. The one woman who feared retaliation said the assailant's constant threats "to kill me if I called the police" frightened her so much that she "couldn't get the guts up to call the cops." Police responsiveness to the women's calls for help changed dramatically after the women obtained a TRO. They always came when the women called; they arrived quickly and were supportive. It is likely that police officers regard TRO cases as more serious and women with TROs as more likely to follow through on a complaint; the new Family Violence Act may also have had an effect on police responsiveness.

Although restraining orders do help women in terms of the police coming to the scene, we would make two qualifications. First, police officers did not consider threats or other forms of verbal harassment to be "real" TRO violations. Although the police always came when called, once at the scene, the officers expressed frustration and anger at the women for having called them, according to two women. Second, just four of the eight batterers were arrested, two at the scene and two on arrest warrants. The four others fled before the police arrived, and although a warrant was issued for their arrest, they were not arrested during the two-month follow-up period. New Haven is like other jurisdictions: the police do not spend time tracking down offenders violating TROs or other crimes, except the most serious felonies. Instead, arrest warrants are served when men are arrested for other crimes (Martin 1976; Woods 1978). For the four arrested, none was sentenced to serve time in jail; all received probation terms and fines of $200 to $300.

WOMEN'S EXPERIENCE WITH LEGAL PROCESS

We highlight three features of the TRO process: the effect of counsel, women's experiences in the courtroom, and extralegal obstacles.

Legal Representation

Although we did not anticipate it, we found that the type of counsel affected the women's evaluations of the TRO process. Of the thirty women in this study, seventeen called the New Haven Shelter for Battered Women and were referred to the Yale Law School's TRO Project. Seven went to the Legal Assistance Association (or Legal Aid), and six sought advice from private attorneys.[16] The women were most satisfied with the student interns and attorneys at the Yale TRO Project and Legal Assistance, who seemed to take a personal and legal interest in the case. As well, the women evaluated the female attorneys (or interns) more favorably than their male counterparts, saying that the former better appreciated their dilemma, had a shared sense of identity, and gave the time to talk and listen to them.

The TRO Project. The Yale Law School's TRO Project brings together staff members of the New Haven Shelter for Battered Women, law students, and local attorneys (Legal Assistance and private), who supervise the law students. All but one woman praised TRO Project members. The woman who was critical felt that the student intern working on her case neither cared for nor understood her situation as a lower-class black battered woman:

Rich white folk, like this lawyer here, are always trying to help people like me out. But they don't know what it's like being beaten and the rest of the time being scared that you're going to be slapped or kicked around. They don't know why we've taken it for so long. How can they expect to understand and talk to the judge about our lives? All the law books in the world couldn't make them understand.

Her criticism echoes a more general concern by women of color in invoking a white male legal system: women of color may not want to call the police out of loyalty to men of color or "the community" (Rasche 1988; Richie 1985). The other women who were represented by TRO Project members gave the student interns high marks for putting forth "tremendous effort":

The student lawyer kept calling me every other day in the evening, asking me if I was OK, if I needed any help, if I felt safe, if he [the batterer] had tried to threaten me or the kids, if he had hurt me. . . . She reminded me of my court dates . . . helped me rehearse what I was going to say to the judge, my English not being that good and all. . . . Thank God she was there for me.

Because the attorneys supervising the law students had little contact with the women, the women's sole basis for judging them was how they acted in court. The women used such adjectives as "well-dressed," "sharp," and "cordial" in describing the attorneys.

Legal Assistance. With a staff of about a dozen attorneys, the New Haven Legal Assistance Association handles cases for indigent people on a fee-based sliding scale.[17] The women judged these attorneys positively, finding them "friendly," "organized," "hardworking and determined," and "sympathetic" to their situation. The women's main complaint was that some attorneys were "a little distant" and had too many other cases; thus they did not have enough time to talk with them, one woman saying:

I wished I had been able to tell my lawyer more of what happened . . . the details of the beatings. . . . Limiting our meetings to half an hour made it very difficult for me to open up to her.

Other Attorneys. New Haven area attorneys' fees to obtain a TRO ranged from $1,000 to $3,000 at the time of the interviews. Women who wanted private attorneys, who could afford them, or who believed they were ineligible for Legal Assistance paid for private counsel. Four of the seven women represented by these attorneys were generally satisfied, one saying, ''I had paid him a hell of a lot of money to do a good job, and he did it well.'' But the women also said they sensed little, if any, sympathy or desire by their advocates to understand their dilemmas. Perceived gender barriers partly explained women's dissatisfaction with these attorneys, as this woman describes her male lawyer's inability to comprehend her dilemma:

He kept on telling me that I should get a divorce and not let him [the batterer] see his son. . . . I don't want to separate a father and a son. . . . I also still love him, but the lawyer doesn't understand that. Maybe a woman lawyer would have.

In sum, the women judged legal representation according to these criteria: time spent giving personal attention and sensitivity to the women's situations. These qualities were more in evidence among the female advocates at the TRO Project and Legal Assistance than other legal counsel.

Experiences in Court

For most women, their experience with the legal process, both in and outside the courtroom, was positive and empowering. But for some, their experience was traumatic and difficult.

The Judge. In all the hearings observed, the family court judge, Frederick Freedman, granted the woman a TRO. The judge's role in the New Haven TRO process is routine, and unlike accounts of obstructionist judges in other jurisdictions (e.g., Crites 1987), Judge Freedman took the women's complaints seriously. As one woman said:

The judge seemed to understand my situation. He asked me a few questions and never doubted my statements. He wanted me to know how important it was that I hold up my end of the deal with the TRO to make it work. And once I assured him that this was such an important step in my life that I wouldn't blow it, he told me he admired my courage.

At the time of the research, the judge would sometimes meet with the woman, or with the attorneys and parties, in chambers before the ex-parte or show-cause hearings. Such meetings gave him ''a chance to put some faces behind the affidavits'' and made it possible for the parties ''to air out some of their dirty laundry in private.'' In recalling their conversations with the judge in chambers, several women said the judge expressed his admiration for their willingness to leave the violent relationship and to regain control over their lives. (Today the judge's schedule no longer permits him to speak with petitioners and defendants in chambers as he once did.)

In the Courtroom. At the ex-parte or show-cause hearings, a woman may have to answer questions about the most brutal battering incidents and describe details of her intimate life. During the time of our research, the women described in open court their experiences of being slapped, punched, kicked, raped, thrown down stairs when pregnant, knocked out by objects, sprayed with mace, partially blinded by bleach, scarred by burns, and threatened with knives and guns. Six women gave their stories with tears streaming down their faces, and three were even more emotionally distraught. When a woman could not continue with her testimony comfortably, the judge called a recess until she regained her composure. Plainly, there are emotional costs and trauma for some women in telling their stories.

Some women wished the judge would have used his power to exclude things from being said in the courtroom. One-fifth said they were embarrassed by a public hearing at which spectators could learn such intimate details of their lives. Women with histories of marital rape and brutal beatings especially felt invaded by the hearings, several saying it should have taken place in the judge's office.[18] These women's experiences are identical to those of rape victims who testify at trial: both groups suffer a second assault by the legal process (Smart 1989:26–40).

The burdens of seeking redress against violent men must be weighed against the potential benefits. In terms of the legal process itself, we have focussed so far on the judge's role and his routine granting of the TRO. Another ingredient is the possibility that a woman's attorney can deliver ''some justice'' when cross-examining the assailant. This woman recounted what happened in the show-cause hearing:

I couldn't believe my lawyer made him admit all the awful things he had done to me. . . . He had never admitted to knocking me out with a lead pipe before. He even admitted the time I had to go to my mother's since I didn't want any of the neighbors to see me with a black eye. . . . All this in front of a judge too. They went over the worst things he did, every bit, and nailed him on it. I finally felt there was some justice in this world.

For this woman, the measure of justice she received was when the man admitted his violence, ''the worst things . . . every bit,'' in a legal setting. This can be as important to a woman as police protection; and, in a speculative vein, it may be thought to signal a change in a man's behavior. The fact remains, however, that most men did not show up for the show-cause hearing and thus were not even placed in a position of being made accountable for their violence in court.

Extralegal Obstacles

The legal steps to obtain the TRO posed few problems for the women. Instead, their main difficulties were shame in telling employers they needed to go to court, losing time at work and, for the full-time homemakers, arranging for childcare. In the interview questions, we asked specifically about childcare as a constraint on getting to court, but many women spontaneously raised job-related problems. A frequent problem they mentioned was how to explain their time away from work: what "good story" would they give supervisors or co-workers? One woman told her supervisor she "had to have minor surgery" on the morning of her court appearance, and another said she "set up a special meeting with [her] son's elementary school teacher since he was doing poorly in school." Others said they had appointments with doctors and dentists. In addition to evidence suggesting that employers view battered women as high-risk employees,[19] the women had no reason to risk being stigmatized by co-workers and supervisors. Had we raised this issue explicitly, it seems certain that more women would have elaborated on these and other job-based problems.

SUMMARY AND DISCUSSION

Do restraining orders help? From the accounts of thirty women who obtained TROs in New Haven during 1986, we offer this answer: it depends on what predicate is supplied for the verb "help."

- If the predicate is *to increase police responsiveness*, the answer is, yes, we think so. After the women obtained TROs, the police responded more promptly. We cannot be sure, however, if the new Family Violence Act played a role in enhancing police responsiveness. We note that some officers believed that threats or verbal harassment did not constitute "real" violations and thus were annoyed when women called them for these reasons.

- If it is *to increase the likelihood of arresting batterers*, the answer is, probably not. TRO-violating men who are not arrested at the scene will likely not be arrested unless they are involved in other offenses.

- If it is *to reduce the chance that a man will batter again*, the answer is, it depends on the man's circumstances and motivation. If he has a prior criminal history, is unemployed or has only a part-time job, and abuses drugs or alcohol, he is more likely to abuse a woman again. We would note, however, that one in ten women in our study was beaten or threatened by men because the woman obtained a TRO.

- If it is *to empower women to end abusive relationships*, the answer is, in general, yes, but it depends on the degree to which women are economically and emotionally dependent on men. Two women in our study could not comply with the TRO: one could not pay the rent; the other wished to reunite. For some women, taking the steps to obtain a TRO already reflects their commitment to leave an abusive relationship, whereas other women are hopeful that the TRO might change the man's behavior.

We find that restraining orders can help women in ways other than increasing police responsiveness or deterring violent men. Paraphrasing Feeley (1979), the process is (or can be) the empowerment. This occurs when attorneys listen to battered women, giving them time and attention, and when judges understand their situations, giving them support and courage. As important, though unfortunately less frequent, women's empowerment can occur when men admit to what they have done in a public forum. Such conversations and admissions can transform the violence from a private familial matter, for which many women blame themselves, to a public setting where some men are made accountable for their acts. We note, however, the emotional costs for some women to speak in court: one in five was discomfited by having to describe brutal beatings and rapes in a public setting.

If the process of obtaining a TRO is partially its own reward, law students, attorneys, and judges must be sensitive to the particular dynamics involved in battering relations and render legal advice and decisions accordingly. Attorneys cannot be expected to be friends or emotional buffers for all their physically abused clients, but many women wanted such support from their advocates. What a judge and counsel say in court and in chambers has important consequences for how a woman can redefine herself and change her situation and for how a violent man can be brought to change his behavior.

Today increasing numbers of women are obtaining TROs in Connecticut courts without legal representation, a development we view with mixed feelings. On the one hand, it suggests that the legal process has become more accessible and that women are taking the initiative to use it themselves. On the other hand, the process can be complex, and a woman's success may be dependent on the goodwill of court clerks, judges, and sheriffs; if children and property are involved in the relationship, a lawyer may be necessary.

In New Haven the good news is that women obtained TROs without going through a legal obstacle course: they did not face scheduling delays or skeptical judges, which feature in studies of other jurisdictions (Crites 1987; Martin 1976; Stacey and Shupe 1983). The good news also is that most men did not violate the TRO during the two-month follow-up period; but when a man violated the TRO, the police arrived on the scene when a woman called. There is some bad news, however: one in three men violated the TRO; and of the eight cases in which women called the police to arrest these men, only half were arrested.

Plainly, the TRO is no panacea for woman battering. Like other strategies to reduce crime, police intervention (or its threat) may protect some victims from harm, but in a limited way. It would be naive to assume that TROs (and related police and court actions) could reduce or eliminate violence stemming from major structural relations of inequality (gender, class, and race) and the distorted ideals about love, sex, power, and violence associated with these relations. Men's violence toward women cannot be eradicated by legal reform, court edict, or police practices: the cultural and economic roots are too deep-seated (Breines and Gordon 1983; Klein 1982; MacKinnon 1983, 1987; Smart 1989).

It is important to see the irony of using state power to control violence and the mixed signals this gives to those arrested or jailed for crime: the state will use its legitimated forms of violence to counter violence. On one hand, advocacy groups argue that the state must take woman abuse seriously, at least as seriously as other crimes; otherwise, men's violence against women is condoned. On the other, as MacLeod (1987:88) asks, "If the court seems to flex its muscles to control his actions, could this not seem to the batterer to validate his use of power to control his partner?" We do not mean to diminish the strength and success of campaigns to eradicate violence against women. Rather, we want to underscore the problems of using penal law and practices to make violent men behave.

Despite the limitations of the police, courts, and penal system to control violent crime and of the TRO as a legal measure to aid battered women, we should not ignore the good news—the potential benefits of legal reforms like the TRO (Schneider 1986). Specifically, the steps women take to obtain a TRO can be salutary, for example, when they talk with supportive attorneys and an understanding judge and hear the batterer admit his behavior in court. If these steps help women to see their suffering in a different light and help men to see their behavior as wrong, there is some reason to be optimistic and to pursue avenues of legal redress.

NOTES

1. The language and theories used in analyzing violence between intimates are themselves significant, and we address two. First, we use the terms "wife abuse," "woman abuse," and "battered women" to describe women who were physically abused by men with whom they have (or had) an intimate relationship. Marriage is not a prerequisite for being a victim of battering: victims and perpetrators may be divorced, separated, or single. Second, as Kurz argues (1989), there are two major social science perspectives on wife abuse—"family violence" and "feminist"—each having its own vocabulary, methods, and interpretations. The latter perspective explicitly focuses on male domination and gender inequality as a major root of the problem, and that is the perspective we take here.

2. Restraining order legislation varies from state to state; although it can provide relief for various family or household members, we focus on relief for battered women. For reviews, see Brown (1988), Finn and Colson (1990), Grau et al. (1984), Lerman (1984), Lerman and Livingston (1983). Contact the Northeastern University Law School Domestic Violence Advocacy Project for a legislative compilation current through 1988. Although states use gender-neutral terms in TRO or related legislation, we use gender-marked terminology because it reflects by far the most prevalent and injurious victim-offender relation in intimate violence: men battering women.

3. But the court added in *State v. Black* (1864) that the state may be able to interfere with a husband's "domestic chastisement of his wife" where the husband's battering results in permanent physical injury. In *States v. Rhodes* (1868) the court stated that a husband was not liable for violence that "without question [would] have constituted . . . a battery if the subject had not been the defendant's wife." Historical reviews of law

and women's movement campaigns around wife abuse can be found in Dobash and Dobash (1977–78), Gordon (1988), Pleck (1987), and Woods (1978, 1981).

4. An early case was *Bruno v. Codd* (1977), in which New York City police and prosecutors agreed to treat wife abuse with the same degree of seriousness as assaults between strangers. A more recent case, *Thurman v. City of Torrington* (1984), had a greater sting when the plaintiff was awarded $2.3 million by a jury; on appeal Thurman received just under $2 million in compensatory damages in an out-of-court settlement with the City of Torrington, Connecticut, in 1985. At issue was the failure of the police to respond to Tracey Thurman's call for help. See Eppler (1986) for the constitutional questions raised in the case. The high monetary award put pressure on many U.S. police departments (via insurance companies) to implement training programs for police officers; the case was instrumental in the development of Connecticut's Family Violence Act.

5. Such shifts in police policy do not necessarily mean that police practices change: departmental priorities change over time (Berk et al. 1980, 1982), police officers vary in exercising their discretion (Sherman and Berk 1984), and a police chief's policy enunciations and intentions may have little effect on police practices (Ferraro 1989).

6. Commentators normally say that all but two (or three) states have protective or restraining orders for battered women, but they disagree on which states. Brown (1988, fn. 3, p. 261) says Idaho, New Mexico, and Virginia; while Finn and Colson (1990, fn. 1, p. 5) say Arkansas and Delaware.

7. Restraining-order provisions and definitions are part of the 1986 Family Violence Prevention and Response Act (amended in 1987, 1988, and 1989). They are codified in Connecticut General Statutes Sections 46b–15, 46b–38a through f, and 54–1g. See discussion in Brown (1988); there have been some changes in Connecticut law since this essay was published. Although petitioners should be at least sixteen years old, a TRO routinely covers a petitioner's children.

8. For example, in some states, whether an order is obtained in civil or criminal court, it is called a protective (or protection) order; while in other states, an order obtained in civil or criminal court is called a restraining order. The two terms can be used interchangeably to mean the same thing, and in many states, they do mean the same thing. In Connecticut, however, the two are legally distinctive (see Davies and Eppler-Epstein 1989; Legal Advocacy Project 1989).

9. Until 1988, petitioners had to pay a $90 filing fee; but this fee has been abolished.

10. Orders may also include such items as prohibiting a man from using his wife's car, giving a woman access to a car if it is in her husband's name, requiring a man to surrender his house keys, and keeping a man from the homes of particular friends and family members. Restraining orders raise potential claims about the violation of a batterer's constitutional rights, but because of the many ways in which abuse manifests itself in couple relations, such restraints may be necessary (Taub 1980).

11. In Connecticut, notice must be served at least five days before the show-cause hearing; otherwise, the TRO process must start again. It is up to the petitioner or her attorney to make arrangements with a sheriff to serve the order, which can pose problems. For example, we learned that some sheriffs do not like serving orders (and, in some instances, may not serve them) when they must go to dangerous parts of town to find batterers. Serving orders can be dangerous, and except for sheriffs who are employed by law firms, there is little money to be made serving orders ($25 to $50, though the fee can be waived for indigent clients).

12. The phenomenon is termed "dual arrest." Connecticut statistics for 1987 show

that of family violence incidents involving male and female partners, 14 percent involved the arrest of both. In some Connecticut cities, the rate was 20 percent (Menard and Davies 1989:9). Menard and Davies suggest that some arrests may not have been based on proper investigation or a determination of probable cause. Anecdotal information from victims and police reveals that some dual arrests result from a "genuine confusion [by police officers] over how acts of self-defense are to be viewed . . . in the context of a mandatory arrest policy" (p. 9).

13. The racial and ethnic composition of New Haven is 61 percent white, 32 percent black, 5 percent Hispanic, and 2 percent other group.

14. Evan Stark (personal communication); Stark has been involved in police training for domestic violence in Connecticut. Despite evidence to the contrary (Garner and Clemmer 1985), police officers may also believe that responding to family violence calls is more dangerous than other police work.

15. As a technical matter, only a judge can void a TRO. But at the time of the interviews, women at the New Haven Shelter for Battered Women were advised not to let the man into their residence because, if they did, the police may not respond to their calls for help. In addition, the judge may not find the man in contempt. A 1989 guide to family violence laws in Connecticut reveals how fuzzy this area is. With respect to protective orders, the authors say, "Some police officers may believe that the order should not be enforced if [the woman] . . . invites [the batterer] back, although legally he still can be arrested for being in violation of the order" (Davies and Eppler-Epstein 1989:14).

16. The referral process has since changed. Today women at the New Haven Shelter are channeled into the TRO Project via Legal Aid, and Legal Aid attorneys play a larger role in the TRO Project.

17. In New Haven, eligibility rules are flexible for battered women seeking legal redress. If a woman's weekly income exceeds a certain amount (depending on the size of her family), she may be referred to the Yale TRO Project or to a law firm which may take the case pro bono. We think it likely that some women in our sample retained private counsel without realizing they were eligible for low- or no-cost legal assistance.

18. It is possible, however, upon motion of counsel to the court, to have a closed-court hearing.

19. Employers may assume that a battered woman's assailant will disrupt the workplace or drain the woman to such a degree that she can no longer be an efficient employee (see Martin 1976).

REFERENCES

Berk, Richard A., Donileen R. Loseke, Sarah F. Berk, and David Rauma. 1980. Bringing the Cops Back In: A Study of Efforts to Make the Criminal Justice System More Responsive to Incidents of Family Violence. *Social Science Research* 9:193–215.

Berk, Richard A., David Rauma, Donileen R. Loseke, and Sarah F. Berk. 1982. Throwing the Cops Back Out: The Decline of a Local Program to Make the Criminal Justice System More Responsive to Incidents of Family Violence. *Social Science Research* 11:145–79.

Berk, Sarah F., and Donileen R. Loseke. 1981. Handling Family Violence: Situational Determinants of Police Arrest in Domestic Disturbances, *Law and Society Review* 15 (2):317–44.

Bowker, Lee H. 1982. Police Services to Battered Women—Bad or Not So Bad? *Criminal Justice and Behavior* 9:476–94.

Breines, Wini, and Linda Gordon. 1983. The New Scholarship on Family Violence. *Signs: Journal of Women in Culture and Society* 8(3):490–531.

Brown, Gary Richard. 1988. Battered Women and the Temporary Restraining Order. *Women's Rights Law Reporter* 10(4):261–67.

Browne, Angela. 1987. *When Battered Women Kill*. New York: Free Press.

Crites, Laura. 1987. Wife Abuse: The Judicial Record. In L. Crites and W. L. Hepperle, eds., *Women, the Courts, and Equality*. Newbury Park, Calif.: Sage.

Davies, Jill M., and Steven D. Eppler-Epstein. 1989. *A Guide to Connecticut's Family Violence Laws*. Hartford: Connecticut Coalition against Domestic Violence.

Dobash, R. Emerson, and Russell Dobash. 1977–78. Wives the ''Appropriate'' Victims of Marital Violence. *Victimology* 2(3–4):426–42.

———. 1979. *Violence against Wives: The Case against the Patriarchy*. New York: Free Press.

Dubois, Ellen Carol, and Linda Gordon. 1984. Seeking Ecstasy on the Battlefield: Danger and Pleasure in Nineteenth-century Feminist Sexual Thought. In C. S. Vance, ed., *Pleasure and Danger*. Boston: Routledge and Kegan Paul.

Eppler, Amy. 1986. Battered Women and the Equal Protection Clause: Will the Constitution Help Them When the Police Won't? *Yale Law Journal* 95:788–809.

Feeley, Malcolm. 1979. *The Process Is the Punishment*. New York: Russell Sage Foundation.

Ferraro, Kathleen J. 1989. Policing Woman Battering. *Social Problems* 36 (1):61–74.

Ferraro, Kathleen J., and John Johnson. 1983. How Women Experience Battering: The Process of Victimization. *Social Problems* 30 (3):325–39.

Finn, Peter, and Sarah Colson. 1990. *Civil Protection Orders: Legislation, Current Court Practice, and Enforcement*. Washington, D.C.: National Institute of Justice, U.S. Department of Justice.

Garner, Joel, and E. Clemmer. 1986. Danger to Police in Domestic Violence Disturbances: A New Look. In *National Institute of Justice: Research in Brief*. Washington, D.C.: U.S. Department of Justice.

Gordon, Linda. 1988. *Heroes of Their Own Lives: The Politics and History of Family Violence*. New York: Penguin Books.

Grau, Janice, Jeffrey Fagan, and Sandra Wexler. 1984. Restraining Orders for Battered Women: Issues of Access and Efficacy. *Women and Politics* 4 (3):13–28.

Klein, Dorie. 1982. The Dark Side of Marriage: Battered Wives and the Domination of Women. In N. H. Rafter and E. A. Stanko, eds., *Judge, Lawyer, Victim, Thief*. Boston: Northeastern University Press.

Kurz, Demie. 1989. Social Science Perspectives on Wife Abuse: Current Debates and Future Directions. *Gender and Society* 3 (4):489–505.

Legal Advocacy Project. 1989. Information about Protective Orders and Restraining Orders. Hartford: Connecticut Coalition against Domestic Violence and the Legal Aid Society of Hartford County.

Lerman, Lisa. 1984. Statute: A Model State Act: Remedies for Domestic Abuse. *Harvard Journal on Legislation* 21 (61):61–143.

Lerman, Lisa, and Franci Livingston. 1983. State Legislation on Domestic Violence. *Response* 6 (5):1–28.

Loseke, Donileen, and Spencer Cahill. 1984. The Social Construction of Deviance: Experts on Battered Women. *Social Problems* 31 (3):296–310.

MacKinnon, Catharine A. 1983. Feminism, Marxism, Method, and the State: Toward Feminist Jurisprudence. *Signs: Journal of Women in Culture and Society* 8 (4):635–38.

———. 1987. *Feminism Unmodified: Discourses on Life and Law.* Cambridge: Harvard University Press.

MacLeod, Linda D. 1987. *Battered But Not Beaten: Preventing Wife Battering in Canada.* Ottawa: Canadian Advisory Counsel on the Status of Women.

Martin, Del. 1976. *Battered Wives.* New York: Pocket Books.

McNulty, Faith. 1981. *The Burning Bed.* New York: Bantam Books.

Menard, Anne, and Jill Davies. 1989. Report to the Connecticut Task Force on Gender, Justice and the Courts on the Court's Response to Family Violence. Hartford: Connecticut Coalition against Domestic Violence.

Pagelow, Mildred. 1981. *Woman-Battering: Victims and Their Experiences.* Beverly Hills, Calif.: Sage.

Pizzey, E. 1974. Scream Quietly or the Neighbors Will Hear. London: Penguin Books.

Pleck, Elizabeth. 1979. Wife Beating in Nineteenth-Century America. *Victimology* 4 (1):60–74.

———. 1987. *Domestic Tyranny: The Making of American Social Policy against Family Violence from Colonial Times to the Present.* New York: Oxford University Press.

Quarm, Daisy, and Martin D. Schwartz. 1983. Legal Reform and the Criminal Court. *Northern Kentucky Law Review* 10 (2):199–225.

———. 1984. Domestic Violence in Criminal Court: An Examination of New Legislation in Ohio. *Women and Politics* 4 (3):29–46.

Rasche, Christine E. 1988. Minority Women and Domestic Violence: The Unique Dilemmas of Battered Women of Color. *Journal of Contemporary Criminal Justice* 4 (3):150–71.

Richie, B. 1985. Battered Black Women: A Challenge for the Black Community. *The Black Scholar* 16 (2):40–44.

Schechter, Susan. 1982. *Women and Male Violence: The Visions and the Struggles of the Battered Women's Movement.* Boston: South End Press.

Schneider, Elizabeth M. 1986. The Dialectics of Rights and Politics: Perspectives from the Women's Movement. *New York University Law Review* 61:589–652.

Sherman, Lawrence W., and Richard A. Berk. 1984. The Specific Deterrent Effects of Arrest for Domestic Assault. *American Sociological Review* 49 (2):261–72.

Sherman, Lawrence W., and Ellen G. Cohn. 1989. The Impact of Research on Legal Policy: The Minneapolis Domestic Violence Experiment. *Law and Society Review* 23 (1):117–44.

Smart, Carol. 1989. *Feminism and the Power of Law.* New York: Routledge.

Stacey, W., and A. Shupe. 1983. *The Family Secret: Domestic Violence in America.* Boston: Beacon Press.

Stanko, Elizabeth A. 1982. Would You Believe This Woman? Prosecutorial Screening for "Credible" Witnesses and a Problem of Justice. In N. H. Rafter and E. A. Stanko, eds., *Judge, Lawyer, Victim, Thief.* Boston: Northeastern University Press.

———. 1985. *Intimate Intrusions: Women's Experience of Male Violence.* Boston: Routledge and Kegan Paul.

Straus, Murray, Richard Gelles, and Suzanne Steinmetz. 1980. *Behind Closed Doors*. New York: Anchor Press.
Studer, Marlena. 1983. Wife Beating as a Social Problem: The Process of Definition. *International Journal of Women's Studies* 7 (5):412–22.
Taub, Nadine. 1989. *Ex Parte* Proceedings in Domestic Violence Situations: Alternative Frameworks for Constitutional Scrutiny. *Hofstra Law Review* 9 (99):95–128.
Tierney, Kathleen. 1982. The Battered Women's Movement and the Creation of the Wife Beating Problem. *Social Problems* 29 (3):207–17.
Tong, Rosemarie. 1984. *Women, Sex, and the Law*. Totowa, N.J.: Rowman and Allanheld.
Vera Institute of Justice. 1977. *Felony Arrests: Their Prosecution and Disposition in New York City Courts*. New York: Vera Institute of Justice.
Victim Services Agency of New York City. 1988. *The Law Enforcement Response to Family Violence: A State by State Guide to Legislation on the Law Enforcement Response to Family Violence Legislation*. New York: Enforcement Training Project, Victim Services Agency.
———. 1989. State Legislation Providing for Law Enforcement Response to Family Violence. *Response* 12 (3):6–9.
Walker, Lenore. 1979. *The Battered Woman*. New York: Harper and Row.
Woods, Laurie. 1978. Litigation on Behalf of Battered Women. *Women's Rights Law Reporter* 5 (1):7–31.
———. 1981. Litigation on Behalf of Battered Women—Update. *Women's Rights Law Reporter* 7 (1):39–44.

LEGAL CASES

Bruno v. Codd, 90 Misc. 2d 1047, 396 N.Y.S. 2d 974 (Sup.Ct. 1977) *rev'd in part, appeal dismissed in part*, 407 N.Y.S. 2nd 165 (App.Div. 1978), *aff'd* 47 N.Y.S. 2d 582, 393 N.E. 2nd 976, 419 N.Y.S. 2d 901 (1979)
State v. Black, 60 N.C. 162, 163, 86 Am. Dec., 436 (1864)
States v. Rhodes, 61 N.C. 445 (1868)
Thurman v. City of Torrington, 595 F.Supp. 1521 (D.Conn. 1984)

IV

CRIMINAL JUSTICE INTERVENTION AND VICTIMS

13

ROLE OF VICTIM PREFERENCE IN DETERMINING POLICE RESPONSE TO VICTIMS OF DOMESTIC VIOLENCE

Eve S. Buzawa, Thomas L. Austin, James Bannon, and James Jackson

This chapter focusses on the actual decision to arrest. Historically, attention has been given to the relationship between the victim's injury and the decision to arrest, tending to subject police to extensive criticism as an unresponsive organization.

This study explores an alternate hypothesis: that victim preferences may be critical to the officer's decision to arrest, rather than the seriousness of injury or whether there is a repeat offense. Data was collected as part of a study of practices of the Detroit Police Department, a department known to have an administration supportive of the needs of domestic violence victims.

The study reports that, with one key group in sharp disagreement, victims were found to be highly satisfied with the police response. The exception was male victims, who were three times as likely to be seriously injured, were less likely to call the police, and expressed dissatisfaction with the police response.

The article in turn raises an interesting policy question. Should objective criteria such as seriousness of the injury or the fact of a repeat call be the factor determining whether an arrest is made, or should victims be empowered with authority to decide the outcome regardless of what an outside "objective" advocacy group believes is best? This decision itself has major policy implications. If victim preference and not the satisfaction of "objective" criteria for arrests becomes the paramount goal, mandatory arrest policies should be abandoned and efforts should be adopted to increase the impact of the victim as an essential decisionmaker in the actions of the police. This inclusion could be accomplished both by preservice and inservice training of officers and by organizational policies that sensitize officers to the needs of victims. Although Detroit officers may have been responsive to victim preferences, in other jurisdictions officers were not even aware of what such preferences were (Buzawa and Buzawa 1990).

The whole area of victim empowerment itself merits study in the context of the criminal justice response to domestic violence. Other chapters, specifically Ford and Regoli's, suggest that in other contexts, such as the choice of prosecution alternatives, the empowerment of victims may lead to lower rates of recidivism. Further research is needed to see if this holds true in the earlier context of the decision to arrest.

It has been a truism among researchers that legal variables should predominate in the decision to arrest, for example, the strength of the evidence or the seriousness of the crime. An examination of the literature on the police response to domestic violence indicates an overwhelming bias against arrest (Berk and Loseke 1980–81; Black 1980; Brown 1984; Davis 1983; Parnas 1967). Empirical measurements of the rate of arrest have varied depending upon the legal and operational definition of the crime and according to officer, departmental, and community variations. However, regardless of measurement techniques, arrests have clearly been infrequent, with estimates of from 3 percent (Langley and Levy 1977) to 4 percent (Lawrenz, Lembo, and Schade 1988) to 7.5 percent (Holmes and Bibel 1988) to 10 percent (Roy 1977) to 13.9 percent (Bayley 1986).

Within the context of the bias against making an arrest, past empirical research on the decision to arrest focuses upon legal restrictions, departmental and individual characteristics of the police, the victim, the offender, and the behavioral interaction of the foregoing.

Departmental orientation and characteristics of the police department have been said to greatly affect the rate and quality of arrest. Research has shown that, independent of explicit policies mandating arrest, domestic violence arrest rates for certain police departments far exceed others. For such reasons, it has been noted that the orientation and policies of a particular department's administration, the degree and nature of training in domestic violence, and community characteristics all influence the rate of arrest (Bell 1984).

In addition to departmental characteristics, officer traits and characteristics appear to affect the orientation toward making arrests. Waaland and Keeley (1985) found that only approximately 58 percent of officers would make arrests when confronted with serious victim injury. Such a divergence in officer attitudes has been considered to be both idiosyncratic or correlated to sociodemographic characteristics of the officer. Although no consistent pattern has emerged, the preponderance of research suggests that female officers consider the crime of domestic violence differently than male officers do, although the extent to which this results in behavioral differences or in differential arrest rates is unclear (Homant and Kennedy 1984, 1985; Ferraro 1989; Stanko 1989).

Ascriptive characteristics of the victim and offender also have been reported to greatly affect arrest rates. It has been acknowledged that police make fewer arrests in cases where the victim is married and living with the offender (Worden and Pollitz 1984; Dobash and Dobash 1979; Martin 1976). Similarly, if the victim's life-style is perceived to include violence as a normal way of life, arrests are made far less frequently (Black 1980; Ferraro 1989). Perhaps because of racial stereotypes and/or a less service-oriented approach to the needs of minorities, white officers have tended to be less likely to arrest in cases of minority violence (Black 1980; Stanko 1989).

Finally, officers appear to make normative judgments about the conduct of the victim. If her conduct is not "appropriate" they appear far less willing to intervene aggressively (Skolnick 1975; Manning 1978). This is especially true if the victim is perceived as being quarrelsome or demanding in front of the officer as opposed to being rational and deferential (Ford 1983; Pepinsky 1976).

The demeanor of the offender also appears to be correlated with arrest rates. Arrests have been found to be very likely when the assailant remains violent in the officer's presence. This behavior may give the officer confirmation of past violence, hence provide a justifiable discriminator. Alternatively, it has been suggested that the officer may perceive such conduct as being an implied threat to his authority or as lack of respect independent of any indication of continuing violence (Dolon et al. 1986). Similarly, if the offender is belligerent or drunk, arrest is far more likely (Bayley 1986).

The foregoing findings implicitly concede that the decision to arrest is not based upon an overriding emphasis on the seriousness of the crime and the strength of the evidence against the offender. In fact, the clear orientation of the foregoing studies is that victim preferences do not greatly affect the decision to arrest. The collective impact emphasizes that the system denies empowerment to the victim. Her role is that of a passive rather than an active participant in the decision-making process.

In contrast, several studies have indicated certain circumstances in which victim preference does affect officer performance, specifically, in predicting arrest rates. Several studies in the early 1980s suggested that the policy of most jurisdictions actively discouraged arrest unless the victim pressed charges (Bell 1984; Berk and Loseke 1980–81; Worden and Pollitz 1984). These findings may no longer have much relevance in today's police organization. Recent years have seen a major shift in orientation to greater use of arrest sanctions. Hence, more recent research has reported that arrest decisions were far more influenced by organizational factors than by victim preference. In fact, Bayley (1986) reported that assailant arrest was not even correlated with victim wishes.

It is not surprising that victim preferences would be considered a valid discriminator for agency action. Given the known police desire to obtain "good" arrests, defined as those that result in felony convictions, the importance of this factor is obvious. Officers "know" that without victim cooperation any charge will either be dismissed by the prosecutor or result in an acquittal for failure of evidence. They may also believe that if the victim is unwilling to expend the effort to initiate a complaint, the seriousness of the attack or the victim's account may not warrant any police effort. Further, since domestic assault is usually charged as a misdemeanor assault, the arrest does not have the same meaning in the police subculture.

We believe that previous research accurately portrays the myriad factors intervening between the perpetration of a domestic assault and an arrest. However, it may also implicitly perpetuate the belief that the victim prefers arrest but finds that the system thwarts her efforts. The victim is either dissatisfied with the result or finds confirmation of the criminal justice system's failure to provide effective recourse.

RESEARCH DESIGN

The research reported in this chapter arose as a reaction to the results of one of the author's previous research efforts on behalf of the State of Massachusetts, a project conducted by the Massachusetts Anti-Crime Council which examined police officer reports from eight representative departments. One question requested the officers to report the victim's preferences for the police response.

The surprising result was that the officers in over 75 percent of the cases could not report the victim's preferences. This was one of the few items consistently lacking a response. Even when such information was requested on a report form, it seemingly was not considered worthy of inquiry nor necessary for administrative compliance. While suggestive of a lack of concern for victim desires, the former research clearly was of a preliminary nature, and no effort was then made to ascertain the reason for the failure to report victim preferences.

For purposes of the present research, the authors received the active cooperation of the Detroit Police Department. The city of Detroit was selected for a variety of reasons. First, the authors have done considerable past research with the Police Department and have extensive background knowledge of the city and of the department's administrators and officers. Further, the department has shown a commitment to handling domestic violence incident appropriately.

The current study was administered in cooperation with the commander of the Training Division. The stated goal of the project was to improve future officer training on domestic assault. Four precincts representative of the city's demographic characteristics were selected, two from the Eastern Division and two from the Western Division. The deputy chief in charge of each division was given Supplemental Arrest Reports, and officers in the selected precincts were instructed to complete these forms for all domestic assaults they responded to. Officers were assured that responses would be kept confidential and would not serve in any way as an evaluative criteria.

Approximately 165 reports were completed in a four-month period. The victims' addresses and telephone numbers were requested, as well as the number of a friend or relative who would know how to reach them should they relocate. Subsequently, 120 victims were then randomly selected for a follow-up visit. Extensive efforts were made to contact all selected victims, and repetitive contacts at varying times of day produced a sample of 90 victims. Because of the sensitivity of the information sought and the initial realization that much of the information could not be predetermined and specified on an interview form, one of the authors, Eve Buzawa, personally conducted all the interviews. After several preliminary visits, it became evident that there was a severe risk of losing valuable information by attempting to train other interviewers. Although the intent of the interview could be structured, specific questions frequently needed to be varied considerably depending upon the interaction with the respondent.

The interviewer travelled in an unmarked patrol car accompanied by a plain-clothes officer, usually a woman from the training section. In order to lessen respondent distrust, efforts were made to be as nonthreatening as possible. Victims were accurately told that a study was being conducted to determine their satisfaction with the police response to the incident and that all information would be confidential. Although ten of the original victims selected proved unreachable, not one interviewee actually contacted declined to participate. Some, in fact, were pleased by the interest in following up on their case.

Further, to minimize bias, the accompanying officer remained a good distance away during the interview, usually talking with children, neighbors, or the assailant. If the assailant was present, the officer would engage him or her in conversation out of the victim's hearing. Alternately, the victim was taken into an area where she could feel certain that the conversation wouldn't be overheard.

Victims generally appeared relaxed, and a few even thanked the interviewer for the visit. Some stated that they were surprised or that it was admirable to have the police department interested in following up with a personal visit. No hostility or anger was encountered from victims and only once from an intoxicated assailant.

There were two chief goals of the interview. First, an attempt was made to determine the accuracy of police reports, especially as to the officer's statements concerning the victim's preferred police action. A second objective was to obtain the victim's perspective about the dynamics of the domestic violence incident, the police-citizen encounter, and the recurrence of violence.

DATA ANALYSES

The Police Questionnaire

The results of the police questionnaire demonstrated a somewhat complex pattern of factors that were correlated with decisions to arrest or not to arrest offenders. The three primary determinants appeared to be the presence of others at the scene of the crime, whether the victim lived with the offender, and the victim's preference. In addition, the seriousness of the injury definitely affected the decision to arrest, but in a nonlinear manner.

The presence of bystanders during the abuse dramatically increases the chances that an arrest would be made (see Table 13.1). In approximately 50 percent of the forty-nine cases where witnesses were present, an arrest was made. However, in the far more typical case of an assault without witnesses, for example, at the victim and/or offender's abode, arrests were less than half as likely. It is in-

Table 13.1
Bystanders/Witnesses Present, by Arrest of Offender

Offender Arrested	Bystanders/Witnesses Present			
	Yes		No	
Yes	49%	(24)	22%	(21)
No	51%	(25)	79%	(83)

Chi-square = 11.2	Significance < .01	Phi = .29

Table 13.2
Were Children Present, by Arrest of Offender

Offender Arrested	Were Children Present			
	Yes		No	
Yes	42%	(28)	22%	(19)
No	58%	(39)	78%	(66)

Chi-square = 5.7	Significance = .02	Phi = .20

structive that very similar results occurred when children were present as witnesses during the assault. The only difference was that the presence of children apparently had somewhat less effect than that of other witnesses (see Table 13.2).

The reason for this finding is probably closely related to the concept of spousal abuse as a "hidden crime." It has long been a truism in the literature that a sizable body of criminal justice personnel view domestic violence as inappropriate for intervention by criminal law (Hartog 1976; Pleck 1979, 1989; Rothman 1980). The presence of witnesses, especially bystanders and those independent of the victim and offender, may convert the offense into a significant matter for many of these people. Alternately, witnesses may be of significance because such witnesses may corroborate the victim's account. From a purely evidentiary viewpoint, this perspective has merit, as the victim's account, if not independently substantiated, often is held suspect by the police. In this light, the presence of children who may not be reliable witnesses might not be as significant as the presence of truly independent outside witnesses. The legitimacy of this position from a policy perspective, is of course, subject to controversy.

As might be anticipated, the presence of weapons affected how the officer handled the incident. Table 13.3 indicates that, when guns or sharp objects such as knives were used, arrests occurred in 45 percent of the cases. This declined to slightly more than 25 percent when either blunt objects or bodily weapons such as hands or feet were used.

Table 13.4 demonstrated that, in this sample, the type of injury was significantly related to the probability of arrest. When a victim was seriously injured, over 50 percent of the offenders were arrested, which constituted the only sub-

Table 13.3
If Weapon Involved, Type, by Arrest of Offender

Offender Arrested	Type of Weapon Involved		
	Gun-Sharp Obj	*Blunt Obj-Other*	*Bodily Weapon*
Yes	45% (17)	26% (21)	27% (7)
No	55% (21)	74% (61)	73% (19)

Chi-square = 4.7   Significance = .09   Cramer's V = .19

Table 13.4
Seriousness of Injury to Victim, by Arrest of Offender

Offender Arrested	Seriousness of Injury to Victim			
	Serious	*Minor-Apparent*	*Minor-Claimed*	*None*
Yes	57% (16)	37% (17)	10% (5)	27% (9)
No	43% (12)	63% (29)	90% (46)	7% (22)

Chi-square = 20.8   Significance < .01   Cramer's V = .36

Table 13.5
Did Victim Live with Offender, by Arrest of Offender

Offender Arrested	Did Victim Live with Offender	
	Yes	No
Yes	39% (36)	17% (10)
No	61% (56)	83% (48)

Chi-square = 7.0   Significance < .01   Phi = .23

sample with an arrest rate in excess of 50 percent. The arrest rate, as expected, declined with the seriousness of injury, with 37 percent arrested in the case of minor but apparent injuries and 10 percent with minor injuries that were claimed but not observable. The only anomaly in the data is the rise for those who did not have any injury, where 29 percent of the offenders were arrested. We are not certain whether this figure is a statistical artifact or whether it might be related to officers' seeking to discourage "nuisance calls" by making arrests. Further focussed research into the motivation of officers in these cases would be needed to ascertain officer motivation.

The third factor that appears associated with rates of offender arrest is whether the victim lived with the offender. The association between arrest and living with the offender as demonstrated in Table 13.5 is both clear and expected. The literature, as cited earlier, has shown that officers are strongly influenced by the living accommodations of the victim. In this case, arrests were more than twice as likely where the offender and victim shared the same residence.

The sample did not show a statistically significant difference between treatment

Table 13.6
Victim Preference for Police Response, by Arrest of Offender

Offender Arrested	Victim Preference for Police Response	
	Prosecute	*Do Nothing/or Talk*
Yes	44% (15)	21% (14)
No	56% (19)	79% (53)

Chi-square = 7.1	Significance = .03	Cramer's V = .26

of assaults involving married couples and treatment of others. This was surprising in light of previous research and findings concerning arrests in cases of offenders and victims living together.

In fact, a markedly different picture emerges when we examine the relationship of the offender to the victim and arrest. We found that regardless of the marital/domestic status, that is, whether the offender was the victim's "spouse/ex-spouse," "boyfriend," "relative" such as in-law, or "other" (primarily acquaintances), the likelihood of the offender being arrested remained just about the same: 31 percent for assaults involving spouse/ex-spouse relationships compared to 29 percent for assaults involving acquaintances. This result is surprising in its failure to confirm previous literature that suggests that victim's marital status is a major predictor of police response (see especially Black 1980).

We are uncertain why this police action profile deviated markedly from expectations based on previous research. Perhaps when the overall domestic violence arrest rate climbs from the 5 to 10 percent level reported in most samples in the previous literature to over the 30 percent level characterized in this research, it characterizes a more activist police department. The effect in that type of department of marital differences in offenders and victims becomes (properly) submerged, while the impact of living together remains a key factor discriminating among probable police actions. Further research in high-arrest jurisdictions such as Detroit clearly is needed to measure the permanence and validity of this very tentative finding. If reinforced, it will demonstrate that victim's residence and not marital status may be the key to predicting police responses.

One other factor associated with the decision to arrest is the victim's preference. When the victim desired prosecution, which occurred 34 percent of the time (34 out of 101 cases), arrests were made in 44 percent (45) of the cases. However, as shown in Table 13.6, when the victim's preference was to do nothing or merely to talk or to advise the victims of their rights, in only 21 percent of cases (14 out of 67) were arrests made. This demonstrates that victim preference does in fact account for a significant portion of the decision to arrest.

The data were examined for significant differences in the profiles of incidents involving male victims of female (and occasionally male) violence compared to the more typical occurrence of male violence against females. Out of the 162 cases where the gender of victim was specified, 138 (85 percent) were female victims. Table 13.7 demonstrates that the profile of injuries to male victims

Table 13.7
Sex of Victim, by Seriousness of Injury to Victim

Seriousness	Sex of Victim			
of Injury	Male		Female	
Serious	38%	(9)	14%	(19)
Minor-Apparent	25%	(6)	30%	(42)
Minor-Claimed	21%	(5)	34%	(47)
None	17%	(4)	22%	(30)

Chi-square = 8.2   Significance = .04   Cramer's V = .23

shows that male victims reported almost three times the rate of serious injury as their female counterparts, 38 percent compared to 14 percent.

It is unclear why the male victims reported such high rates of serious injury. It is possible that, because of a reluctance of male victims to report domestic violence, only severe assault is ever brought to the attention of the police. As discussed later, male victims were the only identifiable subgroup of victims reporting negative police experiences, giving credibility to the possibility of a disproportionate underreporting by male victims, with only the most severe cases brought to the attention of the police. Differential severity of injury may also be related to a more frequent use of weapons by female offenders.

Despite differences in the rates of severe injury in male versus female victims and the differences in satisfaction reported by such victims, arrest rates of male and female offenders were very similar, 31 percent compared to 26 percent. Unfortunately, the relatively small number of female offenders (19) precluded a statistical analysis of such cases. However, the relatively similar rates of arrest may mask differential treatment of male and female defendants when the severity of the injury is controlled.

Several other relationships involving arrest of the offender with factors of age, race, and repeat offenses were also examined. No tables depicting these relationships are presented because neither the level of statistical significance nor the degree of association are as strong as those generated in Tables 13.1 through 13.7. Nonetheless, the trends uncovered suggest that they are noteworthy.

Except for victims fifty years old or older, a monotonic trend characterized the probability of arrest of the offender in the four victim age categories from "under 19" through "40–49." Only 27 percent of the offenders whose victims were under twenty were arrested. Arrests increased to 28 percent for victims aged twenty to twenty-nine, to 32 percent for victims aged thirty to thirty-nine, and to 42 percent for victims aged forty to forty-nine. For victims fifty or older, 36 percent of the offenders were arrested.

A somewhat similar trend characterized results when age of the offender was considered. In this case, however, the irregularity involved offenders aged forty to forty-nine. While only 11 percent of the under-twenty offenders were arrested, arrests increased to 29 percent for those aged twenty to twenty-nine and to 32 percent for the thirty to thirty-nine group. Arrests decreased to 20 percent for the forty to forty-nine group, only to increase to 41 percent for offenders fifty and older.

These results, while neither dramatic nor statistically significant, were somewhat surprising. There is nothing in previous literature indicating that age of victim or offender affects arrest rate. Therefore, this factor should be studied further. If results are repeated, it is possible that injuries or violence against older victims or assaults by older offenders are considered by police to be more serious than those involving younger participants. This in turn might be caused by officer expectations of violence among the young. Seeing uncontrolled violence among older people may create a perception of greater incongruity and hence more serious deviance that warrants official action. Alternatively, officers may be more receptive to the wishes of older victims.

With respect to race, black offenders were somewhat more likely to be arrested than their white counterparts, 33 percent as compared to 24 percent. Closely related to the foregoing statistic, when the victim was black the offender's arrest was more likely, 32 percent, compared to 26 percent for white victims.

If this difference is borne out in further research, the phenomenon is complex. The assumption that a largely white police force treats blacks more harshly than whites has little relevance in Detroit, where the police force is largely integrated, with about 70 percent of the patrol officers being minorities. Also, most responses to domestic violence calls are made by two-person teams with the vast majority of such teams containing at least one black officer. We believe that the higher arrest rates seen when black offenders and victims are involved are related to the previously observed phenomenon that black officers are less tolerant of black crimes and criminals than are whites (Black 1980).

Arrest of the offender is only slightly more likely when it involves a "repeated problem" at the address, 26 percent compared to 19 percent. If confirmed in subsequent research, this finding substantiates that there is only a very weak relationship between repeated problems at an address and officer conduct. This may be due to the fact that the officers responding to particular domestic violence calls are not aware of previous offenses, or alternately, do not care that such offenses have occurred in the past. The importance of this factor is that it contradicts existing practices concerning the impact of known recidivism on the likelihood and severity of subsequent responses by the criminal justice system.

The Victim Interview

Analysis of the victim interviews suggests a sample that is highly satisfied with the responses of the police department. Out of 110 interviewees, 93 (85 percent) stated that they were generally satisfied with the police response.

One aspect of the police response that most satisfied these victims was that the police responded in accordance with their preferences, that is, when the victim wanted an offender arrested, this was generally done even if no visible

Table 13.8
Satisfaction with Police Response, by Sex of Victim

Satisfied	Sex of Victim	
with Police	*Male*	*Female*
Yes	0% (0)	94% (93)
No	100% (12)	6% (5)

Chi-square = 37.4   Significance = < .01   Phi = .82

injury was present. It is noteworthy that in 37 percent of cases, an arrest was made without any visible injury. Although previous research indicates that such arrests are probably due to offender demeanor and officer/offender interaction (Skolnick 1975; Manning 1978), these data revealed the role of a second factor, victim preference.

Conversely, when the victim wanted the officers to simply want the violence to stop, leave the premises, or talk to the offender, they were largely satisfied when the police followed this course of action. Interviews revealed that, even in cases of serious injury, many did not wish to have the offender arrested and confirmed the officer's report that the victim's preference had been in fact non-arrest.

An analysis of the variance in the satisfaction of victims suggests several dichotomies. Of primary importance was the sex of the victim. The results of this analysis are depicted in Table 13.8. Clearly, the victim population divides along lines of gender. Although most female victims were satisfied, not one male victim was pleased with the police response. They stated that their preferences were not adhered to by the officers, nor was their victimization taken seriously. The lack of police responsiveness occurred regardless of the degree of injury. For example, one male reported requiring hospitalization for being stabbed in the back, with a wound that just missed puncturing his lungs. Despite his request to have the offending woman removed (not even arrested), the officers simply called an ambulance and refused formal sanctions against the woman, including her removal. Indeed, all the men interviewed consistently reported that the incident was trivialized and that they were belittled by the officers.

It is of course unclear whether the male victims are responding through the prism of perception. It is possible they feel somewhat more self-conscious about police intervention in this type of occurrence. Since the police data indicated that male victims, as opposed to female victims, were three times more likely to be seriously injured, police may be called in these cases only out of necessity. Interview data suggest that, in cases of male victims, the call was far less likely to be made by the victim. When males were less seriously injured than females, the police were more likely to have been called by neighbors or other parties and not by the victim. Therefore, there may be a defined subpopulation of victims, males, who are less likely to call police because of their perception or the reality of police indifference. Under such circumstances, police actions are likely to be more strongly criticized for any real or perceived slight, however minor. Male victims may also be embarrassed when female officers, present in high numbers in this sample, responded. Despite this, we believe there is some differential treatment by officers. Reported conversations between male victims and officers appeared to confirm that officers were substantively less sympathetic to the plight of a male victim.

Another obvious and interesting implication is that male victims may consequently be disproportionately underreported in victimization statistics, as suggested in other research (Steinmetz 1977–78, 1980). The fact that male victims were three times as likely to sustain serious injury if the police were contacted, indicates that men as victims are less likely to initiate the call themselves, unless serious injury forces such action, the fact that male victims were dissatisfied with the police response tends to confirm a general reluctance for male victims to involve the criminal justice system.

A study of the five female victims who were dissatisfied also strongly supports the proposition that dissatisfaction is related to the failure to follow victim preferences. The five women consistently indicated that they wanted a more aggressive police response, including on occasion arrest. When these preferences were ignored, they were dissatisfied.

At this point, other extralegal variables seemed relevant. In one instance, victim demeanor may have been a factor. During the interview, the victim described continually calling the police and, when they arrived, "yelling at officers for not doing their job." The officer accompanying the interviewer wryly observed that many officers would instantly dislike her and probably discount anything she said.

It is important to realize that not all cases of failure to follow victim preferences are unreasonable. One woman was not satisfied with the adequacy of an arrest. She recounted how she emphatically asked the police to beat the offender, as an arrest would have no affect. He apparently had been well used to arrest for other offenses. When the police refused and left with the arrested offender, she had her brother beat him up after his return home. She believed that only that action had deterred further violence.

Although there may be variance in victim response based on other sociodemographic characteristics such as race, ethnicity, age of victim and social class, the relatively homogeneous sample and the small number (17) of dissatisfied respondents precluded such an analysis.

The actions of the police officers were studied, however, to determine whether making an arrest appeared to influence significantly the level of victim satisfaction. This sample did not show any such correlation. Instead, satisfaction appeared to be wholly dependent upon whether the officers followed victim preference. Similarly, we found no difference based upon officer gender or race.

In this sample, the actions of black and white and male and female officers were consistently rated highly.

CONCLUSION

We recognize that use of the generic term "satisfied" may be somewhat simplistic. It is difficult to assert with accuracy the ways in which victims determine that they are satisfied. The term is, of course, largely dependent on victim expectations of "proper" police conduct and the impact their actions should have. For some victims, proper conduct means coming when called, especially in a poor inner-city setting, where many calls are never answered. At the opposite extreme, it is possible, though not likely in this sample, that others may deem themselves "satisfied" only when the police action can be directly tied in their own perceptions to an immediate arrest and a sustained cessation of violence by the offender.

For this reason, any study of victim satisfaction with police responses has only limited external validity. Subsequent studies therefore need to focus on variances in departmental response and victim expectations, including variations based upon victim sociodemographic characteristics and urban/urban/rural distinctions. In addition, although situational determinants such as the type of police response did not greatly affect the very high levels of victim satisfaction found in this sample, the finding that males were less satisfied and less likely to contact the police must be studied further to determine whether it relates to failed expectations of police conduct, that is, that the police refuse to take cues from the victim, or instead relates to the attitude and performance of the responding officer in the context of dealing with males as victims. It is possible that male victims have been neglected in efforts to provide more responsive police actions.

Major policy implications follow from this research. Specifically, there is a continued emphasis on the role of sanctions, that is, on making arrests, as exemplified by the growing number of local jurisdictions and states mandating arrests, thereby denegrating the traditional legitimacy of the exercise of officer discretion and the primacy of victim preference. The legislative intent is to remove police discretion to provide greater responsiveness to victim needs. However, a significant consequence is the simultaneous removal of victim discretion as well.

We tend to support an alternative approach, increasing the responsiveness of police to victim preference. However, such a policy does not automatically lead to higher rates of arrest and is, in fact, unlikely to be related to the seriousness of victim injury in any linear fashion. We recognize that some policy analysts reject the primacy of victim preference in determining the appropriate criminal justice responses. They believe that a victim who has frequently suffered repeated injuries, is often unable to escape the psychological constraints of tolerating violence without outside intervention. Also, such researchers believe that violence of itself should be punished as an offense against society for the long-term impact on the victim and other family members and because failure to punish indicates societal tolerance of further male domination.

We cannot answer such a normative position except to state that in responding to other aspects of interpersonal violence (with the obvious exception of murder and violence against legal incompetents such as children), victim preference has long been recognized as an appropriate factor in determining proper police action.

If we adopt the position that victim preference should be of primary importance, then the issue becomes how to ensure that outcome. We think that this could best be done by increasing police accountability. To some extent, this change is already happening throughout the country because of the impact of civil lawsuits against police for failure to honor victim preferences. However, lawsuits that may lead to multimillion-dollar judgments against nearly bankrupt municipalities cannot be regarded as the best way to ensure police accountability. Instead, such accountability could be accomplished by relatively modest modifications of police procedures at a minimal cost. For example, police reports could mandate requesting and reporting victim preferences. Regulations could also provide that victims sign the report and receive a copy. On the back of the victim's copy, referral agencies and sources of victim assistance could be listed, in English or any other appropriate language.

It appears critical to increase police officers' consciousness of the serious nature of domestic violence crimes and to provide clear, consistent direction to the officers to act in appropriate cases. When this is done, as in Detroit, a relatively high correlation is seen between the officer's perceptions of victim desires and the expressed victim concerns. If such knowledge is then acted upon and the victim's legitimate requests are followed, there may be no need for more drastic and costly remedies such as mandatory arrest policies.

REFERENCES

Bayley, D.H. 1986. The Tactical Choices of Police Patrol Officers. *Journal of Criminal Justice* 14:320–48.

Bell, D. 1984. The Police Responses to Domestic Violence: A Replication Study. *Police Studies* 7:136–43.

Berk, S.F., and D.R. Loseke. 1980–81. "Handling" Family Violence: Situational Determinants of Police Arrests in Domestic Disturbances. *Law and Society Review* 15(2): 317–46.

Black, D. 1980. *The Manners and Customs of the Police*. New York: Academic Press.

Brown, S. 1984. Police Responses to Wife Beating: Neglect of a Crime of Violence. *Journal of Criminal Justice* 12:277–88.

Buzawa, E., and C. Buzawa. 1990. *Domestic Violence: The Criminal Justice Response*. Newbury Park, Calif.: Sage.

Davis, P. 1983. Restoring the Semblance of Order: Police Strategies in the Domestic Dispute. *Symbolic Interaction* 6(2):261–78.

Dobash, R.E., and Dobash, R. 1979. *Violence against Wives: A Case against the Patriarchy*. New York: Free Press.

Dolon, R., J. Hendricks, and M.S. Meagher. 1986. Police Practices and Attitudes toward Domestic Violence. *Journal of Police Science and Administration* 14(3):187–92.

Ferraro, K. 1989. Policing Woman Battering. *Social Problems* 36(1):61–74.

Ford, D.A. 1983. Wife Battery and Criminal Justice: A Study of Victim Decision Making. *Family Relations* 32:463–75.

Hartog, H. 1976. The Public Law of a County Court: Judicial Government in Eighteenth Century Massachusetts. *American Journal of Legal History* 20:282–329.

Holmes, W., and D. Bibel. 1988. *Police Response to Domestic Violence: Final Report*. Prepared for U.S. Bureau of Justice Statistics, Washington, D.C.

Homant, J.R., and D.B. Kennedy. 1984. Content Analysis of Statements about Policewomen's Handling of Domestic Violence. *American Journal of Police* 3(2):265–83.

———. 1985. Police Perceptions of Spouse Abuse: A Comparison of Male and Female Officers. *Journal of Criminal Justice* 13(1):29–47.

Langley, R., and R. Levy. 1977. *Wife Beating: The Silent Crisis*. New York: Dutton.

Lawrenz, F., R. Lembo, and S. Schade. 1988. Time Series Analysis of the Effect of a Domestic Violence Directive on the Number of Arrests per Day. *Journal of Criminal Justice* 16:493–98.

Manning, P. 1978. The Police: Mandate, Strategies and Appearances. In P. Manning and J. Von Mannen, eds., *Policing: A View from the Street*. Santa Monica, Calif.: Goodyear Publications.

Martin, D. 1976. *Battered Wives*. San Francisco: Glide Publications.

Parnas, R.I. 1967. The Police Response to the Domestic Disturbance. *Wisconsin Law Review* 2:914–60.

Pepinsky, H.E. 1976. Police Patrolman's Offense-Reporting Behavior. *Journal of Research in Crime and Delinquency* 13(1):33–47.

Pleck, E. 1979. Wife Beating in Nineteenth Century America. *Victimology* 4(1):60–74.

———. 1989. Criminal Approaches to Family Violence, 1640–1980. In L. H. Ohlin and M. Tonry, eds., *Crime and Justice: A Review of Research, Vol. 11*, pp. 19–58. Chicago: University of Chicago Press.

Rothman, D. J. 1980. *Conscience and Convenience: The Asylum and Its Alternatives in Progressive America*. Boston: Little, Brown.

Roy, M., ed. 1977. *Battered Women: A Psychosociological Study of Domestic Violence*. New York: Van Nostrand Reinhold.

Skolnick, J.H. 1975. *Justice without Trial*. New York: John Wiley.

Stanko, E.A. 1989. Missing the Mark? Policing Battering. In J. Hanmer, J. Radford, and E. Stanko, eds., *Women, Policing and Male Violence*. London: Routledge and Kegan Paul.

Steinmetz, S. 1977–78. The Battered Husband Syndrome. *Victimology* 2:499–509.

———. 1980. Women and Violence. *American Journal of Psychotherapy* 34(3):334.

Waaland, P., and S. Keeley. 1985. Police Decision Making in Wife Abuse: The Impact of Legal and Extralegal Factors. *Law and Human Behavior* 9(4):355–66.

Worden, R.E., and A.A. Pollitz. 1984. Police Arrests in Domestic Disturbances: A Further Look. *Law and Society Review* 18:105–19.

14

FRAMING AND REFRAMING BATTERED WOMEN

Evan Stark

Evan Stark explores a markedly different aspect of the encounter between the criminal justice establishment and domestic violence, the system's treatment of those who respond to abuse violence by violent retaliation. He reports that prosecutors and courts have discounted or in many cases been unaware of the effects of domestic violence upon the victim's personality or behavior. This has been compounded by patriarchal views of the "proper behavior of battered women" that led to operational definitions of how a woman should respond. When a woman responds not by the permitted means of leaving or silent acquiescence, but instead by killing her tormentor, the criminal justice system is presented with a dilemma. On the one hand, the traditional concept of "mens rea," the intent to commit murder, logically appears inappropriate in the context of a tortured woman's desire to end abuse. Alternatively, traditional legal concepts of self-defense and temporary insanity contain restrictions rendering them clearly inadequate to contain this complex phenomenon. A violent act may appear premeditated to someone who doesn't realize the psychological, economic, and other constraints faced by women trapped in abusive relationships.

Currently, to the extent that the criminal justice system recognizes any problem, ad hoc remedies prevail. Prosecutors who vociferously demand conviction may recommend that sentencing be more lenient because of the events surrounding the ultimate act of violence. In addition, in acknowledging the inadequacy of the criminal justice system, several governors have recently used their gubernatorial prerogative to commute or pardon the sentences, en masse, of previously imprisoned women convicted of killing their husbands. As of the date of this publication, however, it is unclear whether and to what extent such ad hoc efforts to ameliorate rigidity in the criminal justice system will prove effective in a broader context.

As a result, a new, more coherent legal position has been developed, the battered woman syndrome (BWS) defense. Stark reviews the psychological basis, legal development, and use of the BWS defense in several criminal cases. He shows that the BWS defense has been successfully employed to explain the often seemingly irrational conduct of victims of domestic violence. However, he demonstrates that BWS, as a doctrine, has considerable limitations. It falls short as a legal defense, may affect the woman's perceived capacity to retain child custody, and in general grossly oversimplifies the complex pattern of entrapment characterizing victims of an abusive relationship.

In the last decade, "the battered woman defense" has become a widely used courtroom strategy and a rallying cry for freeing women convicted of killing their abusers—and justifiably so. Between 75 and 93 percent of the women in prison for homicide killed partners who physically assaulted them, most often in direct retaliation or to protect themselves and/or a child (Stark 1990; Browne and Williams, n.d.).

It has taken centuries for the courts to acknowledge the special status of battered women. Many in the legal establishment still believe that courts can (or should) do little to regulate violence in the home, that women provoke abuse, that expertise adds little to commonsense knowledge of wife-beating, and that how a man treats his wife is irrelevant to custody or visitation.

Still, the legal system has changed dramatically even since the first battered women shelters opened in the mid-1970s. Armed with several widely publicized court cases and research showing the extent of domestic violence, the Battered Women's Movement has successfully pressured states to consolidate and expand protections against abuse, make arrest standard police procedure, admit expert testimony on domestic violence, and give women ready access to orders of protection and restraint. Most recently, women imprisoned in Ohio and Maryland for killing or assaulting their batterers were pardoned and, in House Concurrent Resolution 172 (passed in 1990), the U.S. Congress expressed its "sense" that "for the purposes of determining child custody, credible evidence of physical abuse of one's spouse should create a statutory presumption that it is detrimental to the child to be placed in the custody of the abusive spouse."

Having won battered women's right to be heard in the courtroom, we must now ask what is being said in their name and with what effect.

The sheer rapidity of change has meant that images of battering presented to the court are often internally inconsistent and portray abused women in ways that can be as stereotypic in their emphasis on victimization as the old images were in their emphasis on women's culpability. Moreover, despite several highly publicized acquittals and the increasing willingness of prosecutors to plea bargain or to offer alternatives to incarceration in cases involving violence by battered women, each year large numbers of abused women lose custody to their batterers or are imprisoned for crimes of violence. For instance, a 1982 survey of new commitments to the New York State Department of Correctional Services revealed that of those women who reported having been abused by their spouses or partners—a third of all incarcerated women—95 percent were committed for violent offenses, usually involving their assailant.

Although expert testimony on battering remains eclectic, the prevailing view is that, as a result of violence, abused women suffer the "battered women's syndrome" (BWS), a form of diminished capacity that impairs their self-esteem and compromises their capacity to perceive or utilize alternatives to victimization, sometimes fatally. In criminal cases, this view can support strategies based on temporary insanity, diminished capacity, justifiable homicide and, very occasionally, self-defense. In civil cases, presence of the syndrome offers a basis for claiming liability in divorce, rights to custody, and even restitution for personal injury.

This chapter begins with a discussion of the legal dilemmas in access, understanding, and representation faced by battered women in the past. Next, the current use of the BWS is reviewed, asking whether its portrayal of the battered woman's response to violence and control overcomes or exacerbates these dilemmas. One problem, in my view, is that this clinical portrayal may accurately describe only a very particular subset of battered women, those who are white, middle-class, and relatively passive victims. Even in these cases, fundamental questions remain about whether the BWS frame helps overcome traditional obstacles to judicial recognition. In the final section, I suggest how battering can be "reframed" to more effectively represent abused women in criminal and civil proceedings.

DILEMMAS AND CONTRADICTIONS IN HISTORICAL CONTEXT

No more dramatic measure of women's limited recognition by the justice system exists than in a comparison of the legal status of battering and data on its extent and consequences.

When Dr. Anne Flitcraft and I examined women's medical records at Yale–New Haven Hospital between 1978 and 1983, we uncovered a startling fact: Assault by a male social partner accounts for more injury to women than auto accidents, mugging, and rape combined. Even more far-reaching than injury and death are the psychosocial consequences of abuse. We also found that woman abuse is a factor in almost half of all child abuse and in more than a third of all divorces and is a major cause of attempted suicide, alcoholism, and mental illness among women. Moreover, battered women suffer these problems disproportionately only after the onset of abuse, indicating that the violent relationship is the cause rather than the consequence of other problems. Homicide, almost always by an abusive partner, is the leading cause of death for black women under forty. Conversely, although women commit only 14 percent of all homicides, 51 percent of these involve a male partner (Stark and Flitcraft 1988, 1990; A Levinger 1966; O'Brien 1971; Stark 1990).

Despite its significance as a source of injury, death, family breakdown, and personal suffering, abuse has rarely been a major factor in criminal or civil proceedings involving battered women. Severe cases of battering were occasionally prosecuted in the past. But the typical situation, in which sporadic assault supports extensive control over a woman's life, has had virtually no legal standing. In homicide cases, fearing that prosecutors would use evidence of abuse to establish motive, female defendants often hid extensive histories of injury and suffering. The major exception involved defendants who pleaded insanity and appealed to the court's paternalism by insisting that their frail natures had "cracked" under persistent mistreatment.

Until quite recently, it would have been impossible to argue successfully that evidence of battering establishes a case for self-defense or justifiable homicide. An affirmative concept of female aggression was incompatible with the broad range of male prerogatives widely accepted until the mid–1960s or with popular views of female character. In most states, the so-called reasonable man standard applied in self-defense cases justifies killing only if an armed assault is underway, if opportunities to retreat or escape are closed, and if the force used is no more than needed to prevent attack. Although the standard usually allows for variation in how individuals perceive danger, it typically makes no provision for group differences such as those arising from gender inequality. Granting to the entrapment, paralyzing fear, and ongoing objectification typical of battering the same status given the danger created by a knife-wielding intruder means acknowledging that women's peculiar vulnerability is rooted in their social situation, not in nature—a view that directly contradicts popular prejudice.

To be sure, battering was a common target of nineteenth-century reformers. British feminists like Harriet Taylor, John Stuart Mill, and Francis Power Cobbe understood how male privilege in the economy translated into power in the home and demanded full economic and social justice for women to eliminate "wife-torture." Still, even so ardent a polemicist as Ms. Cobbe distinguished "the nagging harpy" or "virago" who got the worst of "mutual combat" from the "chaste, sober, honest and industrious" victim who suffered "wife-beating properly so-called" (Cobbe 1878). Cobbe recognized the severe violence used against working-class women in what she termed "the kicking districts" of London and Liverpool. But the implication of dividing worthy from unworthy victims was to deprive "rough women," the majority of whom were working class, of even the limited access to legal remedies afforded "respectable women," most of whom were middle class. Interestingly, this is the basic framework that dominates the work of Erin Pizzey, founder of Chiswick House, the first battered women's house in Britain. Relying on the work of Malcolm Carruthers at the Maudsley Hospital, London, she suggests there is a subset of battered women who are "violence prone" and "addicted to a hormone produced during violence, nonadrenaline" (Pizzey and Shapiro 1981).

In the United States, the legal history of domestic violence is inextricably linked to the evolution of a family-oriented social service system. As in Britain, the movement against wife beating began in the 1870s, when upper-class humane societies turned their attention from animals to children, then to women, striking a moral pose against the "cruelty" of "the depraved immigrant man" in "the dangerous classes." Assuming the same zeal as the home visitors who "policed" the immigrant poor, courts frequently fined and jailed batterers.

Unlike their British counterparts, however, the U.S. reformers were not feminists and generally opposed women's rights. They believed that wife abuse, women working, and women having the vote all threatened women's capacity to properly raise and protect their children, a view that has continued to shape how social work and family law approach abuse today. While the British campaigned for social and economic justice for women, U.S. reformers emphasized individual case finding and the use of services to maintain and restructure family life, what the French sociologist Jacques Donzelot terms "policing the family."

Because of these values, as working women and children challenged traditional domestic roles, family and children's agencies shifted the focus of their intervention from violent men to their wives and children. Courts were increasingly petitioned to stem the "maternal neglect" (often equivalent to women working) that produced "street children" (usually boys) and "sexual delinquents" (usually girls). By 1910, a complex process of case selection, disposition, and referral left family and children's agencies with broad jurisdiction over family problems; their authority to manage adoption, foster care, custody, and guardianship was often used punitively to sustain families in which mother and children were being assaulted (Stark 1989).

Despite this trend, as women emerged from the traditional farm economy and entered the wage market, their sense of personal entitlement continued to grow, even during the Depression. Historian Linda Gordon (1988) puts it well:

Economic dependence prevented women's formulation of a sense of entitlement to protection against marital violence, but it also gave them a sense of entitlement to support; by contrast, the growth of a wage labor economy bringing unemployment, transience, and dispersal of kinfolk, lessened women's sense of entitlement to support from their husbands, but allowed them to insist on their physical integrity. (p. 154)

While other industrial nations used transfer payments (such as a mother's wage or health insurance) to broaden the base of family support after World War II, family services in the United States remained narrowly focused, drawing on psychological theories of maternal bonding and attachment and emphasizing the pathological effects for mother and child of women's rejecting their identity as wives, parents, or sexual partners. The neglectful parent was now the "neurotic mother," "emotional abuse" (by mom) took center stage, and therapy for "damaged parents" replaced the material aid emphasized during the New Deal, a process Gordon terms the "pathologizing" of abuse.

The early social workers were well aware that, in a large proportion of child abuse cases, the same man abusing the child was beating the mother, thus depriving her of the capacity to parent. Nevertheless, behind beliefs in women's generic responsibility for homemaking and child rearing, the connection between wife battering and child abuse was inverted. Utilizing psychiatric and medical models of appropriate mothering, legal theorists redefined "child abuse" as a "gendered crime," which only women could commit. Meanwhile, violence against women faded from public view behind gender-neutral euphemisms like "marital discord." After the passage of child abuse laws in the late 1960s, state child protection agencies routinely used evidence of wife battering to charge mothers with "failure to protect" and to remove their children to foster care (Stark and Flitcraft, 1988, 1990).

Taking battering as an occasion to reinforce women's traditional roles created a number of dilemmas for battered women and their attorneys. Within the norm of domesticity, for example, the only recognized explanation when women responded violently to their abuse was that they were insane. In her ingenious study of women who killed their husbands or lovers, *Women Who Kill*, Ann Jones (1980) argues that it has been easier for courts to acquit on the grounds of insanity than to acknowledge that behavior widely viewed as part of the marriage contract could provoke a rational woman to violence. To the courts, the acceptable murderess was an innocent driven mad by moral corruption, social misadventures, or female sickness.

Jones recounts the case of Fanny Hyde, brought to trial in Brooklyn in 1872 for murdering her employer and lover, George Watson. Fanny's attorney, Samuel Morris, described how her seduction at age fifteen by Watson set off a chain of events which, in combination with her subsequent abuse at his hands and her "dysmenorrhea," led to "transitoria mania." Luckily, transitoria mania came and went in a flash. So did such variants as ephemeral mania, temporary insanity, and morbid impulse. Medical experts were commonly called in these cases to show how women's nature might easily become distorted, particularly during their menstrual periods, and, if they were unmarried or worked outside the home, drive them insane from "moral causes" such as extreme violence, incest, or rape.

Thus, one dilemma involved having to deny that the abused woman's response was rationally motivated, thereby rendering her experience unintelligible to herself and the wider female audience for such trials. The underlying message was paradoxical: the only way for women to survive life-threatening abuse was to step outside the bounds of civil discourse, in essence, to preserve their physical integrity by sacrificing their psychological selves. As noxious as it might be to set the murderess free, it would be far worse to permit a courtroom drama in which such common family practices as marital rape, child molestation, and physical abuse were shown to evoke violent outrage in their victims.

Consistent with the feminine stereotype, the insanity defense was premised on the belief that aggression and violence were unnatural in women. One side effect of this portrayal of normalcy was the automatic exclusion of working women, minority women, and any others who openly flaunted social convention.

As only "ladies" could be shocked into insanity, "rough women" were convicted and sent to jail.

An alternative to the insanity defense was to appeal to the court's paternalism by portraying the abused woman as frail and helpless, a stereotype that reinforced the belief that women were men's property, objects who might be acted upon but who could not act effectively on their own behalf. As is illustrated repeatedly by Gordon (1988), this sort of defense was effective primarily when women called on authorities to protect their children from violence, but not themselves, a strategy that often led to their losing their children and becoming even more isolated with the violent male. Because norms supporting women's subordinate status were an important source of battering in the first place, it could be argued that a defense based on women's submissiveness actually increased the vulnerability of women as a class to violence. In denying an affirmative role for female aggression in domestic life, the gender stereotypes upheld through court decisions implicitly disparaged women's aggressive behavior in the economic and political spheres as well, an outcome which the child-savers welcomed.

A third dilemma posed the dramatic act taken by the battered woman to resolve her specific problem against women's larger need for social justice. As Jones (1980) tells us, "women who blamed certain individuals rather than society for their grievances and who sought redress through personal revenge rather than political action did not threaten the social structure but, in effect, affirmed it."

Finally, implicit in the focus on "violence" (be it physical or sexual) as the catalyst that moved women to act decisively was the belief that they were supposed to remain passive when faced with "normal" (i.e., nonviolent) forms of control and domination. A corollary was that the justice of a woman's response could be measured by the severity of the physical injury she suffered. Threats, fear, minor assaults (no matter how frequent), and the most basic component of battering—control over money, food, sexuality, and other aspects of daily life—fell outside the range of court protection. By defining only the most severe injury as worthy of protection, the courts not only excluded the vast majority of battering situations, in which entrapment and fear motivate retaliation, but they effectively set a standard within which violence was permitted.

In sum, the legal system acknowledged abuse as long as the woman was framed as a passive, helpless, and ladylike victim driven mad by the violent excesses of a moral deviate. These terms were acceptable because they supported the oppression of women as a class, denying them an affirmative defense based on the capacity for aggression, rationality, and fear ascribed to men.

THE BATTERED WOMAN SYNDROME
AND SELF-DEFENSE

The defense of battered women who kill or assault their abusers continues to rely on the same basic strategies employed a century ago: insanity, self-defense, and something akin to a mixture of both, the "battered woman's defense" based on the existence of BWS.

One hundred years after Fanny Hyde was acquitted, a far more sophisticated insanity defense was used successfully in 1978 to win acquittal for a Michigan housewife, Francine Hughes, in the "burning bed" case. As with Ms. Hyde, the technical rationale for pleading temporary insanity was to make evidence of long-standing abuse admissible in court. One significant difference was that the defense attorney, Ayron Greydanus, argued that the battering itself caused Hughes's insanity, not a predisposing frailty inherited with female gender.

Greydanus resisted pressure from feminists to plead self-defense in the Hughes case, although the precedent for such a plea had been set the previous year when a Washington State Supreme Court granted Yvonne Wanrow a new trial. Despite pleading impaired mental state and self-defense, Wanrow, a Colville Indian woman, had been sentenced in 1974 to two twenty-year terms and one five-year term for wounding one attacker and killing another she believed to be a child-molester and rapist. In presenting what is known as the "Wanrow jury instruction," the appeals court held that a woman's reasonable perception of danger may differ from a man's. The Washington court was concerned primarily with the fear engendered by women's physical vulnerability in an assaultive situation that might not be life-threatening to a male.

The respondent was entitled to have the jury consider her actions in the light of her own perceptions of the situation, including those perceptions which were the product of our nation's long and unfortunate history of sex discrimination. . . . Until such time as the effects of that history are eradicated, care must be taken to assure that our self-defense instructions afford women the right to have their conduct judged in light of the individual physical handicaps which are the product of sex discrimination. (Cited in Jones [1980], p. 286)

The framework provided by the BWS goes beyond insanity and self-defense claims by offering a clinical picture of abuse in which a diminished capacity to perceive and select alternatives leads inexorably to the defensive use of violence, even when the threat of death may not appear immediate to an outsider. By describing abuse as a process with cumulative effects over time, it explains why a specific woman may become acutely sensitized to the danger of assault and feel particularly vulnerable to assaultive or threatening behavior from her partner. Most puzzling to a court is why women stay in abusive relationships or fail to escape when an attack seems imminent. In explanation, the BWS offers a psychological framework, the "learned helplessness" model of depression. Here again, cumulative exposure to violence leads victims to respond passively, even to what outsiders perceive as the most obvious avenues of safety. Breaking with traditional victim-blaming explanations, such as the theory of masochism, the BWS traces the profile of victimization, dependence, and relative helplessness commonly seen among abused women to the experience of violence, not to any intrinsic personality defects (Walker, 1979, 1984, 1989; Crocker 1985; Thyfault 1984).

The BWS framework was initially developed by psychologist Lenore Walker after she interviewed a number of formerly battered, primarily white middle-class women. Walker observed that violence in these cases followed a cyclical pattern, called "the cycle of violence," in which a period of tension buildup (minor abuse) was followed by an "explosion" (severe episodes), and then by "loving contrition," in which the woman was seduced into believing she would not be hurt again. Living through this cycle gives women false hope the relationship will improve, though, over time, as the cycle shortens or the period of contrition disappears, this hope may fade. Meanwhile, repeated violence evokes a depressive syndrome classified by the American Psychiatric Association (1987) as an example of post-traumatic stress disorder (PTSD). Supplementing classic symptoms of PTSD such as reexperiencing the trauma, hyperarousal (to detect reminders of the traumatic situation), and social withdrawal (to avoid similar situations), BWS may include low self-esteem, self-blame, fatalism, relative passivity, and an unwillingness to seek or accept help (learned helplessness). Possessed by an exaggerated sense of their assailant's control, battered women conclude that escape is impossible and concentrate instead on sheer survival, including everything from denial and numbing through proactive or retaliatory violence.

The BWS offers enormous insight into the battering experience, particularly where the defendant embraces traditional female roles; a clear pattern of post-traumatic disturbances exists, including a profile of low self-esteem and self-blame; retaliation is limited, possibly to the single act of assault or homicide; and a history of assault and/or injury has been carefully concealed. The case of Dila B. illustrates this pattern:

Dila B. had a prearranged marriage to "Mic," an ethnic Albanian, whom she had neither met nor talked to. They married shortly after she finished high school, and he got his "green card." Just two weeks after the wedding, Mic slapped Dila in the face for "laughing on the phone" and told her never to do so again. Concluding he was "the jealous type," she dismissed the incident, while vowing to obey his wishes. Shortly thereafter, he beat her again and then wanted to make love. When she refused, he tied her hands behind her back with a belt and "had his way" with her. Again her response was fear coupled with the determination not to refuse his demands for sex again. Beatings continued during her pregnancy and increased in frequency and intensity after Mic and Dila were forced to leave the apartment they shared with Mic's mother and sister because he had assaulted them. Over the next few years, Dila was assaulted several hundred times. She was regularly slapped, punched in the head, arms and legs, strangled and "kicked across the room." These assaults were accompanied by threats with a gun and by a pattern of control over sex, money, friendships, communication with family, Dila's physical appearance and over minute details of everyday life. Symbolic was a "log book" in which Dila was forced to keep a record of how she spent each day, including all expenditures and meal plans for the month. At night, Mic would call Dila downstairs, interrogate her about her entries in the log book, then beat her. "If I said something he didn't like, he would hit me. If I couldn't account for exactly where I was, he would hit me. If I forgot I saw someone, just a friend, no big deal, it would be like, "Why didn't you tell me you saw him? Despite the multiple assaults, Dila made only one visit to the hospital (for a "sprained finger") and never called the police or told her doctors or her lawyer about the abuse. A week before the fatal shooting, she packed the car and was ready to leave. But, instead, two nights later, fearing he would discover her plans, she unpacked the car and returned to the apartment. On the night of the shooting, she was kicked from room to room, until she felt she couldn't breathe. She considered, then rejected various means to escape as futile. Then he started again, knocking her flat. She thought something terrible would happen. They went to bed, but unlike previous occasions, he didn't "have his way." She awakened at 5:30 A.M., took his gun from above the dresser mirror and shot at him 5 times. Then she took their son downstairs, returned to get the gun (thinking he might follow her), and called the police.

Cases like Dila's are consistent with a popular stereotype that battered women stay with their abusers without protest. A recent episode of the TV series "L.A. Law" featured a woman who waited until her husband left her to sue for the damages she suffered over the twelve years during which he repeatedly assaulted and raped her. In the final sequence, she is rescued from "just having dinner" with her batterer, when her attorney reveals that she too was formerly abused and did nothing.

Situations in which abused women fail to seek help or protection are more common than we would like to think. But overall, they represent a relatively small proportion of abuse cases. Typically, the failure to escape has less to do with a woman's diminished capacity to perceive alternatives than with the actual level of control enforced through violence, cultural restraints, and institutional collusion with the batterer.

Following the shooting, Dila B. was so overwhelmed with guilt and self-loathing that she was briefly hospitalized as a caution against suicide, a pattern consistent with BWS. In fact, however, the structural dimensions of her entrapment explained her predicament at least as well as BWS. At the time of the shooting, Dila B. was a virtual hostage in her own home and lacked basic material and social supports. She had lost her job, had no access to money, and was cut off from her family and friends. Beatings often occurred in response to behaviors that could be interpreted as cognitive impairments, such as "forgetting" what Mic would tell her to buy, or as self-destructive, such as gaining weight or taking responsibility for problems she had not caused. But these behaviors can also be understood as efforts that symbolized Dila's dilemma of how to exercise control within her highly restricted setting, what I term "control in the context of no control." Her isolation was structural as well, not self-imposed. When she used the presence of a nephew to avoid a beating, Mic would beat her; when she met members of the Albanian community, he would question her about what she said or beat her for saying the wrong thing. The Albanian lore, which Dila B. respected, prescribes that a woman be ostracized for divorcing her husband

and that the husband retain custody of the child. Again, rational fear of these outcomes was as important in convincing Dila she could not escape from Mic as was low self-esteem. After several months in a battered woman's shelter, Dila B.'s confidence returned, and she has become an outspoken advocate for the rights of battered women. This outcome is consistent with the view that the major constraints on her capacities were external rather than self-imposed and that her depression after the shooting was reactive, not a symptom of chronic PTSD.

Dila B.'s situation is atypical. Most battered women employ a variety of strategies to secure their permanent escape and, from this standpoint, more closely resemble the "rough" than the "respectable" stereotype. That battered women are normally aggressive in pursuing their safety and defense is revealed by data showing that 65 percent of battered women eventually escape the abusive situation, even without outside intervention; that battered women seek medical care for their injuries even more promptly than auto accident victims; that battered women are typically forthright when asked about their situation; and that women hit men as frequently as they are hit (Cambell 1990; Teske and Parker 1983; Straus, Gelles and Steinmetz 1980).

Walker claims to have successfully employed the BWS defense in over 150 murder trials. However, researchers have questioned both the scientific and pragmatic basis for these claims (Schneider 1980; Schneider and Jordon 1981; Thyfault 1984). For example, forensic psychologist Charles Patrick Ewing offers a far less optimistic assessment of the effectiveness of the BWS defense. Reviewing twenty-six cases in which expert testimony on BWS was admitted, he finds that in seventeen, roughly two out of three, "the battered woman defendant was convicted of murder, manslaughter, or reckless homicide (Ewing 1987). To illustrate, Ewing cites the 1983 murder of Marshall Allison in his sleep, by his common-law wife Leslie Emick in response to a long-documented and brutal history of physical abuse. Emick's self-defense claim was bolstered by the testimony of a psychiatrist, who presented a faithful rendition of Walker's concept of the BWS:

The abused wife undergoes a personality change as the abuse increases. She becomes frightened and unable to project her thinking into the future. She lives her life from one beating to the next and her thoughts relate solely to her efforts to avoid the next beating. The wife is usually hopeful that, if she pleases the husband, the abuse will stop. For his part, the husband usually expresses remorse after a beating and attempts to reconcile with gifts and/or promises to refrain from abuse in the future. The wife then sees the husband in a different light and is filled with false hope. Another aspect of the syndrome is that the wife eventually feels that she cannot escape her tormentor and that she will be tracked down if she attempts to flee the situation. Her self-esteem vanishes and her confidence is shattered. She feels that no one would believe her if she told them about the abuse and, thus, she keeps it to herself. (p. 3)

New York's self-defense law excuses deadly force only if the defendant is "confronted by the appearance of danger . . . which aroused in her mind an honest and reasonable conviction that she was about to suffer death or serious physical injury . . . ." As is quite common in such cases, the prosecutor argued that abuse motivated Emick's violence and that "the very ongoing nature of the abuse prove(d) that Miss Emick was under no imminent danger, particularly from a sleeping man." Emick was convicted of first-degree manslaughter and sentenced to jail.

In Ewing's opinion, the problem here is the male-oriented criterion for self-defense, not the application of Walker's theory. Although this is an important issue, equally important is whether BWS captures the essence of battering; how testimony on BWS affects the court's perception of a client's capacity, particularly in custody or divorce proceedings; how targeting the microdynamics of a particular violent relationship rather than general issues of control and institutional discrimination affects public perception of women's rights; and whether, by highlighting responses that may typify middle-class rather than poor or non-white women primarily, the BWS frame provides a psychological rationale to sustain Victorian distinctions between "respectable women" who deserve a defense and "rough women" who do not. Finally, and perhaps most important, how does the BWS defense affect the victim of abuse?

Violence versus Entrapment

The BWS defense relies for its theory of "learned helplessness" on experiments with animals who became passive after exposure to repeated shock and/or physical deprivation. The link is by analogy to repeated physical violence. There are two problems with the emphasis on violence. First, although this is not Walker's fault, courts tend to use injury as a measure of violence, disparaging victims who have not been severely hurt. In fact, however, the vast majority of assaults in abusive relationships do not result in injuries requiring medical attention. Despite suffering between two and three hundred assaults in her five-year marriage, for instance, Dila B. reported injury only twice, when her finger was sprained and on the night of the shooting. Further, as doctors often fail to identify battering as the source of injury and victims are often prevented from explaining the source of injury to doctors, even reported injury can be difficult to document.

A second problem with the emphasis on violence is that it misses what is almost always the hallmark of the battering experience, "entrapment." In addition to violence, entrapment entails a pattern of control that extends structural inequalities in rights and opportunities to virtually every aspect of a woman's life, including money, food, sexuality, friendships, transportation, personal appearance, and access to supports including children, extended family members, and helping resources. To survive day to day, the victim may utilize defensive mechanisms such as minimization or numbing that compromise her ability to seek outside help. But the key elements in establishing her risk are almost always the actual level of isolation and the reality-based fear established by the peculiar combination of violence and control she is experiencing. Entrapment is typically aggravated as well by a range of helping responses that support the batterer's control either implicitly, as when doctors fail to ask about the source of injury, or directly, as when police fail to arrest, doctors offer pills or pseudopsychiatric labels, or child protective services remove a child rather than protect its mother. Frustrated help-seeking is so consequential for the battered woman because it converges with the batterer's pattern of denial, minimization, isolation, and blame. Focusing on entrapment emphasizes the strategic rather than the self-destructive aspects of a woman's behavior, the extent to which her psychological identity, put at risk by the hostage-like situation of control, forms around conflicts between self-protection, self-denial and destruction of the assailant.

Diminished Capacity to Parent

In custody, child protection, or divorce cases, the suggestion of diminished capacity carried by BWS can impugn a woman's perceived ability to parent. Most states define an abused child ''to include one whose parent knowingly allows another person to commit the abuse.'' Under this standard, termination of parental rights is usually upheld if the parent takes no action even though she knows about or is present at the abuse. In a recent case brought on appeal before the West Virginia Supreme Court, J.B.W. beat and tried to sexually abuse his daughter. On the first occasion, the mother, Mary W., reported the abuse to the appropriate agency, but she did so only after a delay of several days, because she could not get away from J.B.W. On another occasion, when she interceded, she was beaten and threatened with a knife. Nevertheless, the trial court found that Mary W. failed to protect her children by failing to keep J.B.W. away and by not separating from him. Her perceived inability to break from the pattern of abuse was described by the court specifically in terms of Walker's theory. Its decision read, in part,

Men who abuse their wives classically follow that pattern and the family follows that pattern. A man beats his wife, makes promises and they kiss and make up, and there is a period psychologists call ''the honeymoon.'' At some point following the honeymoon, there is a cycle of abuse and the cycle starts all over again.

Believing that Mary W. was suffering BWS, the court concluded she would continue to reconcile with her abusive husband, thereby further endangering her children, and placed the children in foster care (West Virginia Supreme Court of Appeals 1988).

A more insidious use of BWS involves strict application of the ''best interest of the child'' doctrine in custody decisions. Testifying against Concurrent Resolution 172 before the House Judiciary Subcommittee, a prominent psychologist and social worker argued that symptoms of BWS such as low self-esteem or depression impair a woman's capacity to parent. It follows, they insisted, that if the principle of awarding custody to the parent deemed psychologically more fit is applied consistently, custody should be denied to these mothers, even though their diminished capacity is the direct result of abuse by her husband (*Testimony* 1990).

More positive outcomes will undoubtedly follow as judges are sensitized and child protective services are forced to include protocols to protect battered women among their interventions. Still to be addressed, however, is the effect of the BWS frame on the victim of abuse, even where its reception is nonpunitive.

REFRAMING WIFE BATTERING

Not surprisingly, when a battered woman contacts an attorney, she is highly vulnerable to messages or strategies that reinforce her sense of entrapment. Even the best-intentioned legal strategy can lose the focus on battering that makes a victim a credible witness to her own experience. The case of Emily D. illustrates this process and how to correct it through reframing.

Shortly after her marriage to David D., Emily D. quit a Ph.D. program and the couple moved to upstate New York where he had been transferred. Emily describes David as completely uncommunicative and terrified by intimacy. Any attempts at communication were met with silence, withdrawal, then violence which, she claims, became "constant" soon after they moved to Maryland. In addition to threatening her repeatedly with guns, he choked her so badly she passed out on one occasion. His job kept him away from the house two weeks each month, but he gave her so little money that she could not afford gas for the car. After agreeing to a divorce, David changed his mind and Emily D. took her two daughters and fled to a shelter in San Francisco. Her husband charged her with kidnapping and she was found living under an assumed name, arrested by the FBI, the children were placed in foster care in California and Emily was returned to Maryland for trial. Her attorneys were able to have the criminal charges dismissed on a technicality, but they faced a complex custody battle in which an unemotional husband enlisted Emily's alcoholic parents to show that her aggressive and manipulative behavior jeopardized the children more than the violence which he minimized and blamed on her. Indeed, although Emily was tearful and frightened outside the court, in the courtroom she appeared defiant, even rude during preliminary hearings, seemingly confirming her husband's claims. In response, her lawyers called her in for what she experienced as a "grilling," urging her to act "less self-assured, less arrogant" in court, "more like the good mother." Emily tried to comply. But she felt even more isolated and confused. The result was that she became more aggressive, not less. In response to their dilemma, Emily and her attorneys decided to shift the emphasis in the case to the children. She charged that he had abused the children, "throwing the baby against the wall" on one occasion, threatening them with a gun, breaking their toys and terrifying them with threats. She said he showed no interest in parenting, played no role in the house, spending his time at home brooding and drinking. In a videotape prepared for the court by the childrens' attorneys, they recount being barricaded in a bedroom with their mother while their father pounded on the door. They also describe their fear of their father, and confirm the stories Emily tells about mistreatment in early childhood. A social service report prepared after the mother's arrest suggests the older girl is "exceptionally upset, very fragile and depressed." The younger daughter suffers a modest speech impediment which Emily traces to her being pushed during pregnancy. David denies having abused his wife or children. Although he admits he punched, slapped and choked his wife on several occasions and that she fell down the stairs when she was pregnant after he pushed her, he insists that in each case the results were either accidental (e.g., she fell because she "tightened" when he pushed her) or that he was provoked (punching her, e.g., after she made light of his mother's cancer). He denies any anger towards Emily, saying he feels sorry for her instead and expresses a willingness to place the girls in therapy or to go into counselling himself if it will help the girls. If he gets custody, he feels Emily should only be given visitation if she is in therapy and has "changed her ways." Although he claims to have done all the fatherly things with the girls, on cross-examination he admits he cannot remember the name of their daycare teacher, is unsure what grade his older girl is in and fails to recall any presents he ever gave the children. Psychiatric testimony suggests she may suffer an "agitated depression" (for which she is being medicated) and that he is "defensive to an extraordinary degree." An interview with his previous wife reveals no prior episodes of violence and neither his admissions of violence, nor her charges, are deemed relevant to the psychiatric report.

This case presented two central problems commonly confronted where battering is an issue. First, instead of the aggressive brute and passive victim portrayed by stereotypes of battering couples, the court saw an aggressive, demanding, even "rude" wife and an unemotional, religious, and apparently reasonable husband. The more Emily was told to correct her behavior, the more inappropriate she became. In response to this dilemma, the client and attorneys shifted the emphasis to child abuse. Here the issue was a lack of substantiation, the second problem. Indeed, although Emily talked about her abuse with neighbors, called the local and state police (to remove the gun), and discussed her situation at length in a women's crisis group whose leader urged her to "work things out," there were no reports of problems with the children. Even more important, the children could not have witnessed the incidents they reported on the videotape, supporting the conclusion that they had been coached.

By the time a case reaches this stage, it is extremely difficult to unravel behaviors that are adaptive to the battering, the client's "real" personality, and the images of battering conveyed to the client by key actors in adversarial settings. Emily pressured her attorneys to represent reality as she had lived it. But she was also confused about the extent of playacting needed to get what she wanted from the court. Sensing her ambivalence, her attorneys pressured her to present herself as compliant and submissive, behaviors the court would associate with the typical battered woman. When this failed, they agreed to shift the focus to the children's abuse.

To shape the court's understanding and to better prepare Emily for trial, the attorneys might have called advocates from a battered woman's shelter or psychologists expert in BWS, but this strategy can easily compound misconceptions of abuse. In studying shelter workers, Loseke (1987) found they accommodate the realities of their work situation by constructing a definition of "authentic abuse" that excludes women like Emily who disconfirm popular stereotypes. Thus, Hedda Nussbaum was denied a shelter space in New York City because she refused to identify herself as a "battered woman" until long after Joel Steinberg's arrest.

The images of battering conveyed by the expert on BWS are so powerful precisely because they capture significant dimensions of reality in many abusive situations: the propensity of the victims (or partners) to feel responsible for their problems; to believe that unless they move mountains, they have not done enough to end the violence; and to so overvalue their partners, that they view their own needs as less important. But framing these attitudes as cognitive deficits evoked by violence conceals an important part of the picture. When battering is understood as a means of enforcing structural inequalities in power, each of these attitudes can be reframed as strategic means of offering outward compliance while secretly maintaining a sense of control. Self-blame is a way of saying, "Last time, I did . . . it didn't work . . . next time, I will try . . . ." Even the woman's focus on the batterer's needs to the exclusion of her own gives her a secret sense that she can regulate his moods. As such attitudes are functional within the context of unequal power, they can be replaced by a more affirmative and holistic sense of self only as the power imbalance is redressed through a variety of legal maneuvers and social controls.

Many of the issues raised by shifting the focus in the custody hearing to child abuse go beyond the scope of this chapter (Sun and Thomas 1987; National Center for Women and Family Law 1988). Insofar as the factual problems are concerned, suffice it to say that, although battering is perhaps the most common context for child abuse, the reverse may not be true. Actual child abuse may not occur with sufficient frequency in battering relationships to justify a presumption of physical danger to the child unless previous incidents are documented. Meanwhile, although experts believe there are significant short-run as well as long-run consequences of wife battering for children, they are difficult to document, current opinion is divided on the seriousness of the problem, and attorneys must be prepared to argue that the father's violence is the issue, not the mother's provocations or failure to leave (Goodman and Rosenberg 1988; Giles-Sims 1985; Rosenbaum and O'Leary 1981). Caution must be exercised even where child abuse is documented, as the child protective agency may believe the mother is the negligent parent. Then, too, given the low expectations held in most jurisdictions about fathering, focusing on a father's neglect of his parental duties may simply highlight the mother's failure to provide compensatory parenting.

The Reframing Process

Reframing such cases proceeds from two premises, that a survivor's entitlement to justice derives first from her status as a woman, not as a mother, and that the children's best interest is served by ending the entrapment process typical of battering. The basis for this theory is that a woman's physical and psychological security is a minimal precondition for the nurturance and continuity of care children require, hence key to their emotional well-being. Joint custody and liberal visitation compromise the children's best interest by failing to establish the secure boundaries children require.

Emily's courtroom behavior was easy to unravel. In their relationship, where any sign of fear had been met with escalating violence, she had learned to cope by becoming outwardly aggressive, a pattern repeated when she confronted her husband in the courtroom. Realizing that this might jeopardize her custodial rights actually increased her panic and hence her defensive response, as did criticism from her attorneys, which she experienced as supporting her husband's claim that her aggressive and manipulative behavior were the main problems in the marriage.

By the time I was consulted, the main problem in the case was that the shift in emphasis to the children discounted the abuse of Emily herself and reinforced the message that her children's welfare was more important than her own safety. Emily had been placed in what psychologists call a "double-bind" and the result in court was that she displaced her suppressed rage at her own abuse by exaggerating the harm to her daughters. This put the girls in the untenable position of either recounting events they had not witnessed or questioning their mother's protective concern (why would she ask them to lie?), something they could not do in their vulnerable state. The net result was to make all parties more vulnerable and to support David's claims that his assaults on Emily were insignificant and that here, as in the marriage, she had turned the children against him.

Every aspect of this case indicated that David's major interest in custody was to extend the control he had supported through violence and withdrawal in the marriage into the postmarital period, to what may be termed "tangential spouse abuse." Tangential spouse abuse is often a successful strategy where an unemotional and hyperrational batterer confronts a victim who wants desperately to expose her husband's irrational and impulsive interior and will often act provocatively in court, as she may have in the marriage, simply to allay her anxiety. The keys to tangential spouse abuse may include a battering relationship where passive means of control are dominant (withdrawal, absence from home); little interest in parenting prior to the divorce; insistence on a protracted custody fight despite little chance of success; a highly defensive personal style; lack of empathy for mother or children; unwillingness to accept responsibility for the violence, the children's fear, or the breakdown of the marriage; and a pattern of denial, often extending to substance abuse, feelings of anger, and personal problems. Interestingly, men who present with this profile often test as psychiatrically normal. David agreed to seek counseling for his daughters but saw no need for it himself.

By focusing on tangential spouse abuse, I tried to shift the court's focus back to Emily's battering, encouraging it to reframe both Emily's and her husband's behavior as consistent with the objective danger. Emily felt confirmed, became less fearful in court—because others now also saw her husband as threatening—and provided the needed evidence. The reframing confirmed her sense that the children's danger was an extension of her own, allowed her to put their safety back in the perspective of her own and she accepted responsibility for the bind in which she had inadvertently placed them.

Due Process and Psychological Battering

In allowing women to use more force than men in similar situations, the Wanrow instruction acknowledges the gender specificity of violence and extends protection to women who fight or fight back against their assailants, the "rough women" denied access by the Victorian standard. This may explain why the women involved in the precedent-setting cases of self-defense—Joanne Little, Inez Garcia, Yvonne Wanrow, and Karen Straw—are all low-income or minority women. By contrast, the BWS has been used most successfully to defend "respectable women" such as Francine Hughes or Dila B.

Unfortunately, neither the Wanrow instruction nor the BWS defense are much use in cases where a "rough" defendant initiates the fatal violence.

Nathaline P. is a 35-year-old black substance abuser who lived with her two children in a second-floor apartment. During the course of her relationship with Larry W., she suffered assaults that included punches, kicks, an attempted drowning, an "ambush" with a club, rape, and multiple beatings. "Nat" had neither phone nor electricity and Larry W. had broken the window next to the back door and kicked in the front door so that it would not lock. On previous occasions, she had reported her injuries to the hospital, her social worker and the police. Larry W. had been in jail twice for his assaults and had just been released pretrial under a protective order. On the previous night Larry had threatened to cut her when she slept, a threat she took seriously because this had happened previously. Here is Nat's description of what happened next. "I heard Willie and Larry talking s——t under my front window. . . . Larry was talking about what he was going to do to me. Larry said he was going to f——k me up. I was leaning out the front window of the apartment and I yelled back . . . that he couldn't do anything more than what he did to me in the past. After that I decided to go outside. Larry is good for waiting and then coming to get me. I was afraid of what he was going to do to me. I was tired of his doing those things to me. I wanted to get him before he got me. I put my green long coat on and tucked the knife up my right sleeve. I walked out the back door. . . . I saw Larry coming out of the bar. Larry came up to me and I told him I was tired of his talking s——t to me and threatening me. I said "If you're going to do me, do me now." He told me he would come see me later, after dark. I slipped the knife down my sleeve into my right hand . . . and with the knife stabbed Larry once in the chest. I turned around and slid the knife back up my right sleeve and walked back to my apartment. . . . I thought of hurting myself but said no because he deserve everything.

Although Nat believed she would be assaulted that night, the standard preconditions for self-defense were lacking: there was no imminent or life-endangering threat (after all, she had survived his beatings before), she could have fled, or she could have called the police, as his presence near her house violated the protection order.

Was Nat suffering BWS? When we interviewed her in prison, she was being medicated for depression, had suicidal thoughts, was alternately flooded with rage and guilt, and reported nightmares about her own death, symptoms consistent with PTSD. Other psychological indicators of BWS included an ambiguous sexual identity, short-term memory loss, dull affect, and low self-esteem.

But BWS was contraindicated by a history of aggressive help-seeking, a clear understanding that Larry was responsible for the violence, and a self-consciously strategic attitude about her fate, having gone into the street to "get him before he got me." A history of prior arrests added to the problem of convincing a jury that Nat's cognitive deficits rendered her helpless. As important, Nat's major role conflict centered around her feelings that, although killing Larry made her a "bad mother," it had been necessary to protect herself. She was furious that her own mother could not see this. Emphasizing her diminished capacity would have undermined her sense that in refusing to remain a victim she had chosen the best path to "protect and provide."

Emphasizing entrapment as the modal experience in battering leads to two alternatives to the BWS defense. The first, the "psychological self-defense" (PSD) developed by Charles Ewing, is based on the subjective effects of entrapment. The second is based on assessing the means of entrapment employed, violence and control.

In conceptualizing the effects of battering, Ewing (1987) argues that we need to expand the concept of the self, normally equated with only physical life and bodily integrity, to include "those psychological functions, attributes, processes and dimensions of experience that give meaning and value to physical existence" (p. 62). With the escalation of abuse, "most battered women experience a turning point when the violence or abuse done to them comes to be felt as a basic threat, whether to their physical or social self or both" (p. 65). Suddenly realizing she is in grave danger, the woman is left in a state of "pervasive fear which consumes all of her thoughts and energies." It is out of this crisis—as the battered woman identifies with "the victimized self"—that she takes practical actions to see that the victimization stops or does not occur.

In the case of Dila B., the turning point occurred just a year before the fatal shooting when she realized, "I was living on the edge of a roof and any day he was just going to push me off." From that point on, the "pervasive fear" took over, and she focused only on what she could do each day to ward off her fate.

In the case of Nathaline P., the description of PSD helped reframe what might otherwise have seemed a cold and calculated decision to "do him before he does me" as a reasonable response to an accumulated assault on every aspect of her being. Suddenly, Larry's assaults on her apartment (e.g., the fact that she was denied a safe domicile), his violation of the protection order, and his threats could be joined with the ineffectiveness of outside helpers, the history of assault, and Nat's fear for her children in a picture of the paradox in which Nat had become trapped: she could negotiate the time and place of her next beating, but not whether it would occur. The other actors in the process—police, hospital staff, the court, even her friends—operated from this same premise, responding only after she had been hurt. Even in her decisive moment, the control she exercised over her fate was negative, challenging Larry to "do me now." Then, she stabbed him, preserving her psychological self by relieving what had become, for her, an unacceptable state of dread.

The emergent nature of battering can also be assessed along objective dimensions of violence and control, using factors found by Angela Browne and others to increase the probability that battering will culminate in homicide. With respect to violence, the issues are:

- serial assault (e.g., more than once a month)
- the presence and/or use of weapons
- threats to kill
- the occurrence of sexual assault
- physical and/or sexual assaults on the children
- substance abuse
- previous injury
- violence against others

With respect to control, the main issues are:

- control over money and food
- control over social relationships (primarily friends, family, children, and workmates)
- control over sexuality (where, when, how, how often, etc.)
- control over aspects of daily life

CONCLUSION

What creates a battered woman is neither violence per se nor the psychological status of either party, but the mix of social and psychological factors that make it seemingly impossible for the victim to escape or to effectively protect herself from abuse—what we have termed "entrapment." The entrapment process may extend to any and every facet of a victim's life and is as important an aspect of pretrial investigation as the violence. In reframing abuse in terms of entrapment, the defense of the battered woman becomes part of her empowerment, helping her to regain a voice that becomes increasingly clear and self-possessed as justice is done, inequalities in power are set aside, and she learns that the voice she hears is not hers alone.

REFERENCES

American Psychiatric Association. 1987. *Diagnostic and Statistical Manual of Mental Disorders.* 3rd ed., rev. Washington. D.C.

Bochnak, E. 1981. Case Presentation and Development. In E. Bochnak, ed., *Women's Self-Defense Cases: Theory and Practice.* Charlottesville, Va.: The Michie Co. Law Publishers.

Browne, Angela, and Kirk Williams. n.d. Resource Availability for Women at Risk and Partner Homicide. Unpublished paper. Family Research Laboratory, University of New Hampshire, Durham.

Cambell, Jacquelyn. 1990. Testimony before the Pennsylvania Select Committee on the Availability and Funding of Services on Domestic Violence, Harrisburg, Pa., February 20.

Cobbe, Francis Power. 1878. Wife Torture in England. *The Contemporary Review* 32: 55–87.

Crocker, Phyllis L. 1985. The Meaning of Equality for Battered Women Who Kill in Self-Defense. *Harvard Women's Law Review* 8: 121–53.

Ewing, Charles Patrick. 1987. *Battered Women Who Kill: Psychological Self-Defense as Legal Justification.* Lexington, Mass.: Lexington Books.

Giles-Sims, Jean. 1985. A Longitudinal Study of Battered Children of Battered Wives. *Family Relations* 34: 205–10.

Goodman, Gail S., and Mindy S. Rosenberg. 1988. The Child Witness to Family Violence: Clinical and Legal Considerations. In Daniel J. Sonkin, ed., *Domestic Violence on Trial*, pp. 97–118. New York: Springer.

Gordon, Linda. 1988. *Heroes of Their Own Lives: The Politics and History of Family Violence.* New York: Viking.

Jones, Ann. 1980. *Women Who Kill.* New York: Holt, Rinehart and Winston.

Levinger, G. 1966. Sources of Marital Dissatisfaction Among Applicants for Divorce. *American Journal of Orthopsychiatry* (October): 883–97.

Loseke, Donileen R. 1987. Lived Realities and the Construction of Social Problems: The Case of Wife Abuse. *Symbolic Interaction* 10, no. 2.

National Center for Women and Family Law. 1988. *Custody Litigation on Behalf of Battered Women.* Supplement. New York: National Center for Women and Family Law.

O'Brien, J. E. 1971. Violence in Divorce-Prone Families. *Journal of Marriage and the Family*, pp. 692–98.

Pizzey, E., and J. Shapiro. 1981. Choosing a Violent Relationship. *New Society* 23 (April): 37–39.

Rosenbaum, Alan, and Daniel O'Leary. 1981. Children: The Unintended Victims of Marital Violence. *American Journal of Orthopsychiatry* 51(4): 692–99.

Schneider, E. 1980. Equal Rights to Trial for Women: Sex Bias in the Law of Self-Defense. *Harvard Law Review*, pp. 623–34.

Schneider, E., and S. Jordon. 1981. Representation of Women Who Defend Themselves in Response to Physical or Sexual Assault. In E. Bochnak, ed., *Women's Self-Defense Cases: Theory and Practice.* Charlottesville, Va.: The Michie Co. Law Publishers.

Stark, Evan. 1989. Heroes and Victims: Constructing Family Violence. *Socialist Review* 19(1): 137–47.

————. 1990. Rethinking Homicide: Violence, Race and the Politics of Gender. *International Journal of Health Services* 20(1): 3–26.

Stark, Evan, and Anne Flitcraft. 1988. Violence Among Intimates: An Epidemiological Review. In V. B. Van Hasselt et al., eds., *Handbook of Family Violence*, pp. 293–317. New York: Plenum Press.

————. 1990. Women and Children at Risk: A Feminist Approach to Child Abuse. *International Journal of Health Services* 18(8): 97–119.

Straus, Murrary, Richard Gelles, and Suzanne Steinmetz. 1980. *Behind Closed Doors: A Survey of Family Violence in America*. New York: Doubleday.

Sun, Myra, and Elizabeth Thomas. 1987. *Custody Litigation on Behalf of Battered Women*. New York: National Center for Women and Family Law.

Teske, R.H.C., and M. L. Parker. 1983. Spouse Abuse in Texas: A Study of Women's Attitudes and Their Experiences. Criminal Justice Center, Sam Houston State University, Huntsville, Tex.

Testimony. May 15, 1990. Re: H. Con. Res. 172. Subcommittee on Administrative Law, Committee on the Judiciary, U.S. House of Representatives.

Thyfault, Roberta K. 1984. Self-Defense: Battered Woman Syndrome on Trial. *California Western Law Review* 20: 485–510.

Walker, Lenore. 1979. *The Battered Woman*. New York: Harper & Row.

————. 1984. *The Battered Woman Syndrome*. New York: Springer.

————. 1989. *Terrifying Love: Why Battered Women Kill and How Society Responds*. New York: Harper and Row.

West Virginia Supreme Court of Appeals. July 1, 1988. In the Interest of: Betty J. W., Dorothy NJ. W., James E. W., Sandra K. W. and Cassie A.W. #17482. Reversal opinion written by Justice Miller.

INDEX

ABOUT THE EDITORS
AND CONTRIBUTORS

THOMAS L. AUSTIN is a criminal justice professor at Shippensburg University, Shippensburg, Pa. He currently is working on an evaluation project for the Pennsylvania Department of Welfare.

JAMES BANNON has been with the Detroit Police Department since 1949 and has been Executive Deputy Chief of the Department since 1976. From 1978 to 1991 he served as chairman of the State of Michigan Domestic Violence Prevention and Treatment Board.

ARNOLD BINDER is a professor at the University of California, Irvine, and chair of criminology, law and society there. He has most recently completed research in the use of alternatives to the juvenile justice system and the control of deadly force in law enforcement, as well as in the empirical and constitutional bases of arrest as deterrent in cases of spousal abuse. He is currently writing a monograph that traces the development of arrest as a concept and process in English and American law.

TASCHA BOYCHUK is currently director of the Child Abuse Center at St. Joseph's Children's Hospital in Phoenix, Arizona. She serves as an expert witness and trainer on obtaining children's testimony on sexual abuse.

CARL G. BUZAWA is currently an attorney in private practice. He received his bachelor's degree from the University of Rochester, his master's degree from the University of Michigan in Political Science, and his J.D. from Harvard Law School.

EVE S. BUZAWA is a professor of criminal justice at the University of

Massachusetts-Lowell. She received her bachelor's degree from the University of Rochester and her master's and doctorate from Michigan State University. She has authored numerous articles and chapters in the areas of policing and domestic violence. Dr. Buzawa currently is editor of a five-volume series on *Gender and Crime* and the author of the forthcoming volume *Women as Victims*.

NAOMI R. CAHN is a visiting professor of law at Georgetown University Law Center and is the assistant director of the Georgetown University Law Center Sex Discrimination Clinic and co-director of the Emergency Domestic Relations Project. She has also served on the Board of the Washington, D.C. Coalition Against Domestic Violence.

MOLLY CHAUDHURI is Assistant Director to the Commission to Study Racial and Ethnic Bias in the Massachusetts judicial system. The Commission was appointed to examine and document any instances of racial or ethnic bias and develop meaningful remedial steps to eliminate them.

KATHLEEN DALY is an associate professor of sociology at Yale University. She has written on men and women prosecuted in criminal courts, prostitution, gender and white-collar crime, feminism and criminology, and feminist legal thought. She is currently writing on how gender and race construct court officials' justifications for punishment and of ways on representing "discrimination" with statistical and textual evidence.

DONALD G. DUTTON is a professor in the Department of Psychology at the University of British Columbia and a director of the Assaultive Husbands Project, a court-mandated treatment program in Vancouver, B.C., Canada. He is the author of *The Domestic Assault of Women: Psychological and Criminal Justice Perspectives*. His current research projects include the study of factors contributing to the emancipation of battered women, the co-presence of borderline personality disorder and childhood trauma in a subpopulation of assaultive males, and gender differences in affective responses to dyadic conflict.

KATHLEEN J. FERRARO is an associate professor of justice studies and women's studies at Arizona State University, in Tempe, Arizona. She has published on the experience of woman battering and the social and criminal justice responses to battering.

DAVID A. FORD is an associate professor of sociology at Indiana University in Indianapolis and president of University Research Associates. He is principal investigator for the Indianapolis Prosecution Experiment. He also directs the Training Project on Family Violence for the Indiana Law Enforcement Officers, a program of curriculum development and implementation for required continuing education of all officers in the state.

JAMES B. HALSTED is an associate professor of criminology at the University of South Florida. He has authored several scholarly articles on domestic violence in a number of academic journals and has lectured at major criminal justice conferences throughout the country.

STEPHEN D. HART is an assistant professor of psychology at Simon Fraser University. His primary research interests are in the area of clinical-forensic psychology and include criminal psychopathy, domestic violence, and mentally disordered offenders.

JAMES JACKSON is Commander of the Training Support Division of the Detroit Police Department.

LES W. KENNEDY is a professor of sociology at the University of Alberta. He is currently the coordinator of the Centre for Criminological Research. He has published papers on criminal victimization and community attitudes to crime and safety. In addition, he has been involved in research on Canadian and U.S. homicide trends, examining these data for clues concerning the social and familial roots of murder. He is the author of *On the Borders of Crime: Conflict Management and Criminology*.

DEMIE KURZ is co-director of women's studies at the University of Pennsylvania and a member of the sociology department. Her interests include gender and family issues. She has published articles on various topics related to domestic violence and divorce. She has been a member of the mayor's Commission Task Force on Domestic Violence in Philadelphia.

PETER K. MANNING is a professor of sociology and psychiatry at Michigan State University. He is the author of many articles and chapters in scientific publications, and has authored twelve books, including *Semiotics and Fieldwork* (1987), *Symbolic Communication* (1988), and the forthcoming *Organizational Communication*. His general research interests are in occupations and organizations, medical sociology and criminology, with special interest in fieldwork, semiotics, and qualitative methods. He is currently studying legal decision-making, nuclear safety regulation, and psychosocial aspects of AIDS.

JAMES MEEKER is an associate professor at the University of California, Irvine. He is in the criminology, law and society area of the program in social ecology. He has completed research in the area of alternative strategies in prosecuting white-collar and organized crime, as well as the use of arrest as a deterrent for misdemeanor spousal abuse. He is currently working on alternative delivery mechanisms for legal services to the poor and working poor.

GLENN L. PIERCE is the director of the Center for Applied Social Research

(CASR) at Northeastern University. During his tenure at CASR, he has directed studies on the character of demand for police services, the social and economic status of American families, the impact of legislative change on individual and organizational behavior, and the strategic role of information technology in public sector institutions. He has undertaken studies for a variety of municipal, state, and federal agencies and has also conducted research for private sector organizations and private foundations.

MARY JEAN REGOLI is research coordinator of the pediatric psychology laboratory at Indiana University in Bloomington. She also assists Bloomington's domestic violence and rape crisis center, Middle Way House, Inc., in an ongoing evaluation of the prosecution of family abuse cases in Monroe County, Indiana.

SUSAN SPAAR is the data archivist for the Social Science Quantitative lab at the University of Illinois–Urbana. Previously, she was a research associate at the Center for Applied Social Research at Northeastern University. She has conducted research on a variety of public policy-related topics including domestic violence, the police patrol function, and the social and economic status of American families.

EVAN STARK teaches in the Graduate Department of Public Administration, Rutgers–Newark, is co-director of the Domestic Violence Training Project, New Haven, Conn., has a private practice in Madison, Conn., where he emphasizes group work with men, and frequently serves as an expert consultant in legal cases involving domestic violence.

KIRK R. WILLIAMS is a professor in the Department of Sociology and a faculty affiliate in the Research Program on Problem Behavior, Institute of Behavioral Science, University of Colorado at Boulder. His most recent publications address issues concerning partner homicide, the control of wife assault, and sexual coercion in the university setting. He is currently involved in research on the risk of interpersonal violence, funded by the Harry Frank Guggenheim Foundation, and is writing a book on violent relationships.

MARVIN ZALMAN teaches criminal justice and political science at Wayne State University, Detroit, Michigan. His research interests are in constitutional law and criminal procedure, sentencing and penal policy, dispute resolution, and domestic violence policy.